Supernatural Selection

Supernatural Selection
HOW RELIGION EVOLVED

Matt J. Rossano

OXFORD
UNIVERSITY PRESS

2010

OXFORD

UNIVERSITY PRESS

Oxford University Press, Inc., publishes works that further
Oxford University's objective of excellence
in research, scholarship, and education.

Oxford   New York
Auckland   Cape Town   Dar es Salaam   Hong Kong   Karachi
Kuala Lumpur   Madrid   Melbourne   Mexico City   Nairobi
New Delhi   Shanghai   Taipei   Toronto

With offices in
Argentina   Austria   Brazil   Chile   Czech Republic   France   Greece
Guatemala   Hungary   Italy   Japan   Poland   Portugal   Singapore
South Korea   Switzerland   Thailand   Turkey   Ukraine   Vietnam

Published by Oxford University Press, Inc.
198 Madison Avenue, New York, NY 10016

www.oup.com

Oxford is a registered trademark of Oxford University Press

Library of Congress Cataloging-in-Publication Data
Rossano, Matthew J.
Supernatural selection : how religion evolved / Matt J. Rossano.
   p.   cm.
Includes bibliographical references and index.
ISBN 978-0-19-538581-6
1. Religion. 2. Human evolution—Religious aspects.
I. Title.
BL430.R67 2010
200.9—dc22   2009029518

9 8 7 6 5 4 3 2 1

Printed in the United States of America
on acid-free paper

Contents

Acknowledgments

As always I am indebted first and foremost to my family for their patience and support over the course of writing this book. Thanks also to my colleagues in the Thursday science and religion lunch group who were unfailingly skeptical, incisive, and insightful as they scoured my every idea for weakness and imprecision. Similarly, my editor at Oxford, Theo Calderara, pounced unmercifully upon my frequent lapses into dense jargon and impenetrable prose. If my writing is clear and my thinking forceful, then much of it is due to those mentioned above. Of course, the mistakes, misinterpretations, and inclinations toward simplemindedness and muddleheadedness are all mine.

Supernatural Selection

Introduction

The Origins of Religion

This book seeks to answer a very straightforward question: How did religion come to be? A common way of addressing such a question is to go back to a time prior to the existence of the phenomenon you wish to explain and show how various factors operated to bring the phenomenon into existence. To understand how the Roman Empire came to be, for example, one might show how the pre-empire conditions of the ancient Mediterranean world made Rome's emergence possible or even inevitable. This book treats religion the same way. But this immediately raises a question: Can we truly envision a world prior to religion? As far back as we can trace human history, there has always been religion. Indeed, some believers regard religion as a divine gift transcending human history. Treating it as a consequence of the same haphazard stew of historical forces that drive human affairs seems to border on sacrilege.

But God moves in mysterious ways, and while there may or may not have been a time before God, there most certainly was a time before the idea of God (or gods). This time cannot be found in documented human history, however, but only in human evolutionary history (or prehistory). Thus, religion came to be because religion evolved. Though not intending sacrilege, this book does aim to provide a clearly specified, step-by-step model of religion's evolutionary history. Using evidence from a wide range of disciplines, including archaeology, anthropology, primatology, psychology, and neuroscience, I sketch a model of religion's origins beginning about a half million years ago through the Upper Paleolithic (about 35,000 years ago). I believe that there is enough evidence to make the model plausible and that it is articulated with enough precision to allow for testing. Like anyone else, I have my biases, prejudices, and point of view, but I try hard to be neither an apologist for religion nor a religion-basher. The story itself is interesting enough and needs no agenda-pushing on my part. The model I present, however, does have important implications for how we view religion in the modern world and for addressing many of the controversies surrounding it. I do my best to present all of this in a clear, objective, and hopefully engaging way.

The evidence I present and the evolutionary scenario I outline lead to an important conclusion about the nature of religion: Religion is about relationships. In other words, religion is a way that humans relate to each other and to the world around them. Our ancestors half-devised and half-stumbled-upon this way of relating about 70,000 years ago because it offered significant survival and reproductive advantages. Thus, contrary to what most researchers believe, I strongly contend that religion is (or maybe was) an adaptation. It emerged as our ancestors' first health care system, and a critical part of that health care system was social support. This had important ramifications for group solidarity and cooperation. As we shall see, religiously bonded groups tend to be far more cohesive and competitive than "secular" ones.

I'm well aware that, for some folks, calling religion an adaptation amounts to nothing less than heresy. But I think the evidence warrants even stronger conclusions. For example, religion is vitally important to morality. No, religion is not the origin of morality, but religion does make us more moral (of course, here it is critically important to define "morality"). I will also make the case that religious ritual was critical in the evolution of our uniquely human cognitive endowment. To put it (too) simply, but (intentionally) provocatively: Religion made us human.

Models of Religion: Where Mine Fits In

The model I present is unique in that it does not really "fit in" to the current framework of theories on religion. To understand this, however, we must first look at what types of theories are out there and how mine relates to them.

A theory is supposed to explain something. Germ theory explains why we get sick, and gravity explains why apples fall from trees. Why do we have religion? That's a far more complicated question because religion itself is multifaceted. Thus, theoretical approaches to religion have typically carved off some aspect of religion—such as ritual behavior, supernatural beliefs, or the role of gods in addressing human concerns—and tailored the approach to specifically address that aspect. What we are left with then are models that primarily explain (or purport to explain), for example, why people engage in ritual, but do little to explain why people believe in miracles. These theoretical approaches can be categorized into five different types: (1) commitment theories, (2) cognitive theories, (3) ecological theories, (4) performance theories, and (5) experiential theories.[1]

Commitment theories are based on the idea that cooperation within human groups is individually beneficial (in that it provides access to resources that would be unavailable to a single person) but hard to establish (because cheating can always provide greater short-term gains). Religion helps to solve the cheating problem by virtue of its capacity to identify trustworthy people. The means by which religion identifies these people is "costly" signaling—where people signal their good intentions to others by using a sign that is hard to fake. The sign used must be "hard to fake" in order to be reliable. Otherwise, cheaters too will flash the sign frequently in order to try to deceive others and advance their own nefarious goals. In the animal world, for example, a male frog's deep-throated croak is a costly signal of robust health and good genes. This is so because making a loud resonating croak is difficult for such a tiny-bodied creature. Weak, sickly, immature, or otherwise compromised frogs simply can't croak with the same authority as healthy ones. Picky females listen carefully and only select "the real thing" for mates.

Likewise, religion forces people to demonstrate allegiance to irrational beliefs to show that they're fully committed to group norms of reliability, honesty, and reciprocity. Somewhat ironically, then, commitment to irrational beliefs serves a very rational and adaptive goal—securing individual benefits through enhanced group cooperation. In ancestral settings, only those who truly believed the gods were watching and keen to punish the unworthy would willingly subject themselves to painful rites of initiation. Those witnessing the rites could be fairly certain that the initiates were fully committed to the tribe's values and therefore would make good warriors, mates, and comrades. The analogous situation in modern settings might be found in instances where those who attend church regularly are believed to make better friends, business partners, and spouses.[2] Often this belief proves correct.

Not surprisingly, commitment theories primarily address the public expression of religion and the behaviors that mark religious group membership: rituals, initiation rites, moral directives, and behavioral proscriptions. Important as these elements might be, commitment theories have nonetheless been criticized for leaving out the important mental aspects of religion. For example, anthropologist Scott Atran asks why it is that secular groups or ideologies can have behavioral obligations as demanding as religious ones, yet still fail to have as enduring an effect on individuals and cultures.[3] The answer to this, he argues, requires understanding the mind, and understanding why belief in supernatural beings and religious mythologies is so easily transmitted from mind to mind, generation to generation.

Cognitive theories are based on the idea that religious belief and behavior arise from the complex integration of a number of separate mental modules that evolved for nonreligious but often adaptive purposes. For example, an "agency detection module" is an evolved mental mechanism for identifying agents in the natural world. An agent is an organism whose behavior is driven by intentions, goals, and desires. Thus, if I watch a hawk swoop down suddenly toward the ground, my gut inclination is to assume that the bird did so because it was "hungry" and "wanted" to snatch a small rodent on the ground. Seeing agency where it doesn't exist seems to be a common feature of the natural world—think of a cat attacking a wind-blown paper bag as if it were a mouse, or a human hearing haunting voices in the wind. In both cases the hyperactive agency detection system provides advantages by making sure the organism seizes every potential opportunity to obtain prey (in the case of the cat) or to avoid becoming one (as in the case of the human). Given the adaptiveness of overextension, our agency detection system leaves us prone to assuming that unexplainable natural events such as storms, floods, or drought are the result of the actions of supernatural agents.

Similarly, the "attachment system" promotes fitness by compelling infants to maintain close proximity to caregivers. When activated in conjunction with the hypervigilant agency detection system, it could compel us to form emotional attachments to perceived supernatural agents and to seek close proximity to them through prayer, ritual, or simply presence at a holy place (church, grave site, etc.), especially when in distress. Thus, in the cognitive view, religion is typically seen not as an adaptation in and of itself, but instead as a consequence of our cognitive/emotional attributes and the manner in which they interact.

As with commitment theories, cognitive theories explain important aspects of religion, but fail to provide a complete explanation. The major element they leave unaddressed is the motivational pull of religious belief and behavior. That religion calls upon a variety of mental systems hardly makes it unique; language, mathematical skills, and musical abilities can make the same claim. But it would be absurd to think of someone dying for their math. Furthermore, while emotional attachments can be formed to a variety of imaginary agents (children with Santa Claus, or adults with soap opera characters), the enduring nature and level of commitment that characterizes peoples' attachment to God and other religious figures is unique. Cognitive approaches alone are unlikely to find an adequate explanation for this.[4]

Ecological theories explain religion as a method that helps humans manage the natural world. Although religious ritual seems to operate on an otherworldly plane, it often serves a very practical function. Anthropologist Roy Rappaport was one of the leading exponents of the ecological regulation approach to religion. His detailed analysis of the *kaiko* pig-feast ritual among the Tsembaga people of New Guinea showed that while the ostensible purpose of the Tsembaga's intermittent slaughtering of pigs was to offer sacrifice to their ancestors, the feast cycles also kept the pig population from outstripping the carrying capacity of the local environment. Additionally, the festival effectively distributed surplus wealth and facilitated trade. Similar examples have been noted in the Bali water temple system and the salmon fishing rituals of the Native Americans of the Upper Klamath River valley in Northern California.[5]

While ecological regulation theories have been important in certain anthropological circles, they have played only a limited role in most evolutionary approaches to religion. In part this is because these models rely heavily on group selection processes, which until very recently were out of favor among evolutionists. However, a form of group selection, called cultural group selection, has gained increasing legitimacy among many anthropologists, evolutionary biologists, and psychologists.[6] Cultural group selection argues that under certain conditions, groups with more effective norms for generating cooperation, motivating self-sacrifice, accessing and dispersing resources, and maintaining stability and cohesion out-competed groups with less effective norms. Thus, the ecologically effective rituals that we currently see would be the result of groups with more adaptive rituals having out-competed other groups with less adaptive ones over the course of evolutionary history.

Ecological theories address one aspect of religion—ritual. Even ecological theorists, however, would not claim that this represents the totality of religion's functions. Such things as counterintuitive beliefs or the role of supernatural agents in addressing existential concerns are not central features of an ecological approach. Thus, as with the commitment and cognitive approaches, the ecological approach fails to provide a complete explanation for religion.

Performance theories focus on rituals, ceremonies, and other community-based religious activities. These activities are thought to perform important sociological functions, such as reaffirming a tribe's social structure, providing divine authority to its norms and traditions, and reviewing and transmitting its history. The fact that these functions typically reinforce a group's cultural infrastructure led renowned sociologist Emile Durkheim to conclude that religious practices often provided a means for society to deify itself by making its mores divinely sanctioned rather than just humanly constructed.[7]

Recent work on the role and function of religious ritual has demonstrated that these rituals are generally structured in a way that is similar to more mundane activities.[8] In other words, religious rituals follow the basic format of any action sequence where an agent performs an action (often using some instrument) on a patient. So, for example, a minister baptizing an infant is, in terms of the action being performed, not really different from a man washing a baby. An agent (man) performs an action (washing) using an instrument (water, washcloth) on a patient (baby). Why, then, is the baptism recognized as a special "religious" action (a ritual), while the other is seen as a run-of-the-mill event? Ritual theorists argue that the fundamental difference is simply that the religious action is presumed to involve a supernatural agent, while the ordinary action is not. This divine involvement marks it as extra-ordinary.

These extra-ordinary rituals can take two forms: agent-special, where a supernatural agent is acting upon ordinary patients; and patient-special, where ordinary agents are acting upon supernatural patients. Baptism is agent-special because it is assumed that God or some supernatural agent (acting through the minister or priest) is affecting the baby (babies being ordinary in everyone's eyes except, of course, the parents'!). Rituals where ordinary agents (you and I) offer sacrifice or worship to a supernatural being are patient-special since it is believed that these offerings will affect the supernatural being in positive ways. Agent-special ceremonies are relatively infrequent, often highly emotional, and commonly associated with life-transforming events (baptisms, rites of initiation, funerals, etc.). Patient-special rituals are more frequent (weekly worship service) and more sedate.

There is something else interesting about these rituals and their effects—especially the more emotionally engaging, less frequent, agent-special ones. To the extent that these ceremonies have powerful, transformational effects on people, it is the presence of the supernatural that is usually given credited ("the Spirit was present"). Even nonbelievers may feel the effects of these rituals and experience some relatively lasting impact from them. In their case, however, the credit is attributed not to anything supernatural, but instead to some amorphous but perfectly natural "mental energy," "the spirit of the community," or "the power and beauty of tradition."[9] In many cases the difference between believers and nonbelievers here is probably not that great: Both might make reference to some "spirit" present in the ritual; they may only differ on the nature of the spirit.

Atran argues that in their emphasis on the sociological aspects of ritual and ceremony, performance theories neglect the individual mental aspects of religion. In other words, the decision-making/reasoning processes, motivations, and cognitive inferences that underlie an individual's involvement in ritual play only a small role in most performance theories.[10]

Experiential theories concentrate on the religious experience itself. The classic example of this approach is found in psychologist William James's groundbreaking work *The Varieties of Religious Experience*. For James, the foundational core of religion was the religious or mystical experience. Surveys suggest that somewhere between 35% to 47% of the population have had some form of intense spiritual experience or a closeness to a powerful spiritual force.[11] James identified a number of qualities common to the religious experience, including:

1. Ineffability—the fact that the mystical experience cannot be adequately described in words.
2. Noetic quality or enlightenment—the fact that while mystical experiences are profoundly emotional, they also provide deep insights and authoritative truths to the individual involved. Often these insights involve an awakening to the unity of all things and a deep sense of oneness with the divine.
3. Transience—the experiences are fleeting and temporary; they rarely last longer than a few moments.
4. Passivity—though mystical experiences can be facilitated through meditative practices, rituals, and other techniques, their actual occurrence is spontaneous and unpredictable. The person accepts the experience and cannot will it to occur.[12]

Since James's work, other qualities such as realness and unusual percepts have been proposed as additional qualities.

In recent years, neuroscience has taken up the quest to understand the religious experience. Imaging techniques have been used to identify the specific brain areas involved in the religious experience. The studies have been diverse, often involving different meditative or prayerful practices across a range of religious traditions.[13] The brain areas involved have also varied, but a few commonalities appear to be present, especially in the frontal lobes and superior temporal sulcus/inferior parietal lobule. Neuroscientist Andrew Newberg's results are particularly relevant to understanding mystical states. Using experienced Buddhist meditators, he found that while areas of the frontal cortex increased in activation during the peak of the experience, areas of the parietal cortex reduced their activity below baseline levels. This reduction in parietal lobe activity may help to explain the sense of cosmic unity or loss of the subjective self that meditators often claim accompany intense mystical states: The parietal cortex is important for processing one's sense of bodily boundaries and orientation in three-dimensional space.

While neurotheology (as it is sometimes called) holds great promise in deepening our understanding of the role of the brain in religious states, it is still very much in its infancy, and interpreting its findings are difficult.[14] Moreover, it is still unclear how these findings can or will be integrated with those of the other approaches.

The Proposal at Hand

Nearly half a century ago anthropologist Anthony Wallace argued that religion should be thought of not as a specific "thing" but rather as a collection of activities. Included among these activities were (1) addressing the supernatural, (2) offering/sacrificing, (3) exhorting (as in motivating conformity to divine codes), (4) avoiding (as in taboo), (5) manipulating psychological states, (6) reciting myths and moral codes, (7) becoming inspired, (8) dancing and singing, (9) imitating and simulating, (10) touching, (11) eating and drinking (of sacred or special food and drink), (12) congregating, and (13) placing symbolic objects.[15]

In many respects the current approach is consistent with this spirit. However, the model I propose contends that underlying all the actions that Wallace identifies is a common thread: relating. In varying degrees, all of Wallace's actions involve how members of a religious community relate to each other, to the physical world around them, and to the supernatural world they envision. Religion is a way of relating where supernatural agents are active players. Supernatural relationships act as mediating influences on people's other relationships. To better understand this, consider the following scenario:

A woman has one child—a daughter. Obviously, the two of them have a direct personal relationship. Sometime later, the woman adopts another girl. As might be expected, bringing a new, unrelated sibling into what had formerly been an exclusive mother-daughter relationship creates tensions. Intermittently, these tensions surface openly in arguments and conflicts between the "sisters." But to some degree, the sisters temper their anger toward each other because of their mutual love of their mother. On some occasions they clash, but on others they hold their tongues, find ways to compromise, and even work constructively together—"for mom's sake." Even after their mother's death, they continue to relate to each other with an eye toward what mother would have wanted. Their direct relationship is always mediated by a third party.

In this example, the mediating influence was generally positive. This is not always the case. The important point, however, is that the mediating influence has an effect. Now, replace "mother" with "God," or "the ancestors," or "the Virgin Mary." Once humans could envision supernatural relationships, these relationships exerted a similar mediating effect on all their other relationships. Furthermore, it affected how they viewed the world around them and their relationship to it. The natural world was no longer simply inert matter, but a living gift of the creator, with its own spiritual and social reality.

So where does this religion-as-relationship approach fit in with the various models described earlier? The model proposed in this book is not intended as a competitor to or replacement for any of these approaches. Nor, however, does it fit neatly within any of them. Instead, the current model provides an overarching framework that incorporates cognitive, commitment, performance, experiential, and even ecological dimensions.

For example, commitment theories address the signs that religious groups use to identify members that can be trusted. Many species use hard-to-fake signs to indicate commitment to such things as territorial or offspring defense. Only humans, however, appear to be capable of signaling commitment to abstractions such as moral principles or cultural norms and obligations.[16] An individual's relationship with other group members may depend on whether or not he or she is willing to display the necessary signs of commitment. For religious believers these signs are even more powerful since supernatural agents serve as witnesses to and potential enforcers of these commitments.

Cognitive approaches describe the evolved mental faculties that make envisioning supernatural relationships possible. For example, the hyperactive agency-detection model very likely provides one of the cognitive foundations on which ideas about supernatural agents are built. This system, in combination with the attachment system, provides the mental and emotional basis for forming close personal relationships with supernatural agents. Although often neglected in many cognitive approaches, another important component of the human cognitive system, episodic memory, very likely plays an important role in these emotional attachments as well. Episodic memory is our (possibly unique) ability to mentally travel back in time when recalling past personal events or project forward in time to envision future scenarios. It is this system that very likely provides the basis for our existential anxieties—our concern over the inevitability of suffering and death. This concern can serve as a strong motivator for forming and maintaining supernatural attachments that may help to allay existential anxieties.

Performance theories explain the rituals and activities that individuals and communities use to interact with their gods. Ritual behaviors have a deep evolutionary history as a mechanism for regulating relationships. Rituals are especially useful when careful communication is required so that social interactions don't break down or degenerating into violence. For example, unless reassured with ritualized sounds or gestures, subordinate monkeys will flee from approaching dominants. The bowing and genuflecting common in many religious worship services are only a small step removed from the conciliatory gestures chimpanzees used to signal appeasement, subordination, or the desire for reconciliation.[17] Since they are built upon a deep evolutionary history of primate social rituals, it is unsurprising that religious rituals follow the same basic pattern as other, secular social activities or that they serve important social functions such as reinforcing group solidarity and transmitting cultural traditions. In the same way that subordinates ritualize their encounters with dominants in order to minimize the potential for dangerous miscommunication, humans ritualize their encounters with the gods to avoid offense.

Experiential theories examine the subjective experience of religious relationships. Encountering the divine during ritual, prayer, or contemplation is often described in relational terms—an engagement with the incomprehensible other. Theologian Rudolf Otto described this using the Latin phrase *mysterium tremendum et fascinans*—incomprehensible, fearsome, yet irresistibly attractive mystery. William James's work as well was dedicated to understanding this experience and the effect it had on people. Though religious experiences are described differently by individuals from different cultural backgrounds, one commonality appears to be that such experiences are relational.[18]

Ecological theories address how religion and ritual regulate a community's interaction with the natural world. At first blush it may seem that this approach falls outside of the relational realm. However, in animistic traditions, the natural world itself is understood as a social partner. For example, in many traditional societies, hunting is not just a subsistence activity but a sacred exchange between man and nature. The prey must be persuaded to give up its body to the hunter, and the hunter must perform proper rituals so the animal's spirit can be returned to the earth.[19]

Bringing nature into the human social sphere can serve as an effective mechanism for more sustainable, less destructive use of natural resources.[20] Thus, an assumption typically underlying the ecological approach is that one's community is in a relationship with and owes a "social" debt to a spirituality-imbued natural world.

The Diversity of Gods and Religion

Viewing religion as relationship helps make sense of the wide array of gods, spirits, and other supernatural agents that populate most religions, as well as the wide diversity of practices that can be considered "religious." A popular notion about the origin of religion is that it emerged as a means of ameliorating our anxieties over death and suffering. A serious problem with this view is that throughout our history the gods have been an awfully varied lot—and not always comforting. However, if religion is a supernatural extension of social life, then this diversity is to be expected. The supernatural social world, like the human social world, will run the gamut of characters—some attractive and alluring, some boorish and tedious, and others nothing short of repulsive. While some gods provide solace, others—especially those who deal in death—may be anything but comforting.

Anubis—one of the Egyptian gods of the dead—was portrayed as a jackal-headed man the color of rotting flesh. Anubis's counterpart among the Mayans of Mesoamerica was Ah Puch, god of the underworld. Ah Puch had sockets but no eyes and a decomposing, skeletal body that smelled as bad as it looked. It's hard to imagine how anyone could look forward to meeting these characters. As if the gods of death weren't disheartening enough, the ancient view of the afterlife was often equally depressing. In book 11 of the *Odyssey*, for example, Homer has the dead Achilles lamenting to Odysseus: "Say not a word in death's favor; I would rather be a paid servant in a poor man's house . . . than king of kings among the dead."

Even gods with no connection to death could be nasty characters. The Sumerian goddess Inanna (called Ishtar in Babylon) was an assertively sexual goddess whose violent, unpredictable emotions were thought to produce floods, windstorms, and other natural disasters. Her volatility was also associated with the mayhem of battle. The witches and spirits that continually harangue the Fang, a traditional people living in Cameroon, are known to inhabit bodies, induce sickness, cause accidents, and just generally sow confusion and misery. As if the natural world alone was not sufficiently demoralizing, our ancestors seemed compelled to augment it with supernatural forces designed to intensify its gloom. If religion's primary purpose was comfort against the vagaries of life, we could have wished for much better than the gods and myths we inherited.

What about religious practices? It might seem that religion-as-relationship would only apply to those aspects of religion that are communal—public worship services, rites of passage, and shared myths and doctrines. This, however, would be a mistake. A fundamental premise of this book is that religion represents a "supernaturalization" of human social life. At a certain point in our evolutionary, humans added a supernatural layer to their social world. Relations with the supernatural have both public and private aspects, just as human relationships do. Many religious activities that on the surface seem non- or even antisocial can be understood as vehicles by which devotees deepen their relationship with supernatural agents or forces. For example, meditation, monastic isolation, fasting, or other forms of self-inflicted suffering may all be ways of enhancing an individual's perceived closeness to a deity or cosmic force. Similarly, moral prescriptions and proscriptions can help to both define and solidify an earthly community and fortify that community's relationship to its deity, as well as the relationships of individual community members to that deity.

Finally, just as human relationships are characterized by certain symbols (a wedding ring, a cherished heirloom, a love letter) and "sacred" places (a shared home, the location of a first date, a grave site), so are supernatural relationships. A contemplative garden, a statue, and prayer beads (to name just a few things) may all serve to help people draw nearer to a supernatural agent. While religion is primarily relational, that does not mean it is restricted to what is commonly seen as "social." To the religious person, isolation from others may still be "social" in that it enhances one's connection with a god or spirit. Just as lovers often sneak away from a party for time alone, the religious person often sneaks away from society for private rituals with his or her spiritual mate.

Relationships and Reason

Understanding religion as a way of relating also casts the question of the "reasonableness" of religion into a different light. For most scientists and philosophers, religion is inherently unreasonable because it espouses the supernatural. Since there is no evidence for the supernatural, only by abandoning reason can one be religious. Cornell biologist William Provine expressed this attitude succinctly by claiming that to be religious one had to "check one's brain at the church house door."[21] But in the realm of relationships, this logic gets turned on its head. For humans, relationships are essential, yet there is something inherently "unreasonable" about them. Moreover, trying to impose rationality upon them only serves to make their existence nearly impossible. In his essay "The Will to Believe," William James attempted to unravel this paradox and defend the reasonableness of religious faith. To do this, James placed religious belief within the broader context of human relationships and the necessity of *relational trust*:

> Turn now from these wide questions of good to a certain class of questions of fact, questions concerning personal relations, states of mind

between one man and another. *Do you like me or not?*—for example. Whether you do or not depends, in countless instances, on whether I meet you half-way, am willing to assume that you must like me, and show you trust and expectation. The previous faith on my part in your liking's existence is in such cases what makes your liking come. But if I stand aloof, and refuse to budge an inch until I have objective evidence, until you shall have done something apt, as the absolutists say, *ad extorquendum assensum meum*, ten to one your liking never comes.[22]

James's rather flowery turn-of-the-century language can be difficult for modern readers to follow, but his point is a simple one—if we want friends, we have to be willing to trust them. To demand up-front evidence of someone's trustworthiness is to risk insulting the very person we wish to call "friend." So we have to take our chances, put ourselves at risk, or forever be a lonely island unto ourselves. Thus, for James, it is rational to take this risk since the rewards of personal relationships far outweigh the intellectual compromise required to set things in motion. James then extends this logic to religion:

To take a trivial illustration: just as a man who in a company of gentlemen made no advances, asked a warrant for every concession, and believed no one's word without proof, would cut himself off by such churlishness from all the social rewards that a more trusting spirit would earn,—so here, one who should shut himself up in snarling logicality and try to make the gods extort his recognition willy-nilly, or not get it at all, might cut himself off forever from his only opportunity of making the gods' acquaintance.[23]

Just as we are quite reasonable in trusting (i.e., putting faith in) the goodwill of others whom we wish to call "friends," the gods await our befriending as well—if only we would extend to them the same trusting spirit. What separates the religious person from the skeptic is this "relational risk-taking." The religious person has extended the hand of trusting friendship to the gods. The skeptic withholds the hand until satisfactory evidence is forthcoming that such a relationship is even possible. The critical difference is relational—the religious person establishes the "spiritual" relationship, the skeptic does not, and this makes all the difference.

James is not alone in claiming that at its core, religion is relational. The famous Jewish philosopher Martin Buber argued similarly—that the essence of biblical faith was the trusting I-thou (as opposed to I-it) encounter between humans and God. In other words, God-human interaction has a natural intersubjective character, not an alien or mechanized one. Contemporary Catholic theologian John Haught goes so far as to argue that trust—trusting in God, in the intelligibility of the universe, in the inherent meaningfulness of existence, in our capacity to find truth—is simply another term that the Bible uses for faith. Some may find these arguments convincing, and others may not.[24] What is clear from them, however, is that when thoughtful people seek to understand whatever logic there might be behind religious faith, they inevitably turn to the relational realm.

Relationships and Evidence

Why relationships? The answer, I believe, is that when it comes to religion, the relational realm provides something that science cannot: evidence for religion's "reality." Take, for example, the very notion of God. It has been argued that one quality that God must surely possess is that of being greater than humans. God must be greater than I am. Thus, God must *at least* be a personal subjective consciousness, otherwise, God is less than I am and therefore not worthy of being called "God."[25]

But what evidence can verify the existence of another's subjective consciousness? There can be no conclusive empirical test for consciousness, because consciousness by definition eludes the objective, third-person methodology of science. This, in fact, is a long-standing philosophical conundrum called "the problem of other minds." How can I truly know that you are another conscious agent? There is no conclusive test to verify that you are a self-aware, experiencing agent and not a zombie designed to behave in exactly the same way as a real human, but with no actual inner life.[26]

Yet I take something of a minor leap of faith and assume you to be at least as conscious and self-aware as I am. This leap is noteworthy both for the fact that I do it so effortlessly and for the fact that when I do it my life is infinitely enriched by the intellectual, emotional, and social benefits that accrue from relationships with other (presumably) conscious beings. But if scientific evidence cannot convincingly verify the presence of consciousness, then what can? The best we can do is to relate to another being and see if its relational behavior reminds us of ourselves. If the actions, reactions, and expressions I observe in you are the same ones that arise in me because of my conscious mental states, then I must assume that you experience those states as well. Relationships, not science, provide the relevant evidence (such as it is) for the existence of other minds.

Thus, just as none of us can *know* as a scientific fact that others are conscious beings, we cannot know that there is a suprahuman consciousness out there. This inconclusiveness breeds doubt in the skeptic. But for the believer, the mind of God is found in their relationships with others, with life, and with a world that they see as bathed in divine mystery. It's simply another of those unscientific leaps of faith that litter the ground on which relationships, religion, and human life itself are built.

If relationships provide the evidence for religion's validity, then we are indeed in a quandary over the issue of God's existence. Whether God exists or not falls outside of the objective realm. It is subjective—based on people's relational experience. As such, it is an unsolvable problem. Chapter 1 takes up this unsolvable problem and explores its implications in more detail.

1

Natural Relationships and Supernatural Relationships

Honoring the Dead

In April 2008, the phone rang at the home of Howard Enoch III. It was the U.S. Army. Howard's father would finally be coming home. Sixty-three years earlier, in the waning days of World War II, Second Lieutenant Howard "Cliff" Enoch Jr. climbed into his P-51D Mustang fighter for a mission over Halle, Germany. He never returned. When the Iron Curtain enveloped the site where Enoch's plane went down, the army declared his remains "unrecoverable." But dedicated members of the U.S. Army's Joint POW/MIA Accounting Command refused to give up on Cliff Enoch. In 2004, their review of crash sites in the former East Germany revealed suspicious plane fragments near the village of Doberschutz. Two years later, an onsite excavation team found what appeared to be human remains. The remains were flown to a laboratory in Hawaii for DNA analysis while the army continued to study the crash-site evidence. In the end it led to the phone call—and a burial with full honors at Arlington National Cemetery.

"Remarkable" is how Howard Enoch described the events of that spring. "I will now have a place . . . to know where he is . . . to be close to him," he said. "Before this, I always thought of my father as a young man, sitting in a beautiful pasture in Germany, waiting for someone to bring him home—and that is what happened." Commenting on the extraordinary effort the military expended in retrieving and identifying the remains, army spokesman Johnnie Webb explained that it was important for people to know that the "creed and tradition" in the military is to "leave no one behind." The military, he said, would always do their utmost to "honor that promise."[1]

A bittersweet story. But most would agree that it ends as it should. It is right and good that the brave young soldier be returned to his home, his country, his family. The human desire to keep loved ones near, even in death, hardly needs an explanation or justification. Yet very little of this story can be defended as *reasonable*. Cold logic would correctly conclude that it is of no consequence where Cliff Enoch's remains are buried, or even whether they are ever conclusively identified. After 60 years there's no doubt that he is dead. His loved ones have gone on with their lives, and the skeletal remnants care nothing about the ground under which they lie. From a practical standpoint, a backyard cross is as good a remembrance place for the downed pilot as a cemetery plot. And wouldn't the army's limited resources be better spent on increased health and education benefits for veterans or better housing for military families, rather than on the retrieval of a few old bones?

Howard Enoch was welcoming back a man whom he had never known. Now 63 years old, he was born after his father Cliff was shot down. The fallen hero was but a picture on the wall, a story only rarely broached, more a myth and a spirit than a man. But is it fair to say that Howard and this spirit were strangers to each other? Was there no relationship here at all? The fact that it just *feels* wrong—cruel, even—to simply let Cliff Enoch's bones lie anonymously in some far-off foreign land suggests that the answer is no. And if it is no, then this might offer some justification for the military's extraordinary efforts to retrieve those bones. After all, if you're going to convince people to risk their lives for their country, then sometimes that country must go to excessive lengths to not "leave them behind." None of this is likely to pass a rigorous rational examination. But doing right in life sometimes means that reason cannot be the sole light by which your moral compass is set.

Human life is not a science. The good life isn't a theory to be operationalized, tested, and replicated before it is deemed useful. For better or worse, life must be lived, here and now; and what is valuable about it we often must discern, on the fly, as best we can. The hard-nosed rationality so valued in scientific circles seems oddly incompetent when facing the human complications of real life.

This observation is by no means novel. Decades ago, the economist Robert Frank recognized that our passions often thwarted our best attempts at being perfectly rational economic agents.[2] Oddly, this was often a good thing. Dispassionate logic could easily prevent us from making the personal commitments necessary to take advantage of some of life's greatest opportunities. Success in life often entails some seemingly irrational risks. We make promises, form deep emotional attachments, and put faith in family, friends, and neighbors based on partial and ambiguous data—data that would never pass muster in a scientific journal. But the rigors demanded by good science—empirical testing, adequate controls, reliable measures, falsifiable conditions, replication—come off as nothing short of insulting when imposed upon a potential friend, date, or marriage partner. We aren't interested in someone who can't trust us, so we have to risk trusting others.

This unscientific risk-taking, or what Frank called "the commitment problem," is the very thing that makes life human. At some point we just have to dive in, follow our guts, and experience what life and human relationships have to offer. Religion is a lot like that. In this book, I shall argue that religion is all about how we experience life and, most especially, how we experience relationships. Just as we don't use science when choosing our friends or spouse, very few of us allow science to determine whether or not we are religious. While that bit of news may be reassuring to some, it is downright maddening to others.

The Story I Shall Tell

This book is about religion—what it is, where it came from, and, most critically, how and why it evolved. I attempt (with some success, I hope) to offer a coherent narrative about the evolution of religion. In outline form, the narrative goes as follows: By at least 500,000 years ago, our hominin[3] ancestors had the conscious motor control to engage in coordinated group rituals of social bonding—in other words, they could sing and dance together. Around 100,000 years ago, our ancestors (*Homo sapiens sapiens*, who shall also go by the title "anatomically modern humans," or AMH) made their first foray out of their home continent of Africa into the Levant region of the Middle East—what is now Lebanon, Israel, and parts of Sinai. Cold conditions and advancing Neanderthals, however, quickly chased them back to Africa.

Then, quite possibly, a calamity of unimaginable proportions struck: About 70,000 years ago, a massive volcanic eruption in a far-off land brought on a global ecological crisis. This crisis only accentuated the rapid climate changes and accompanying resource shortages that were common during this period. All this took its toll—humans nearly went extinct. The few who endured were forced to create new strategies for survival, which included establishing unprecedented levels of intergroup cooperation. Religious rituals were central to these new strategies. As social life became increasingly complex, human imagination expanded. From out of this enhanced imaginative capacity, especially childhood imaginative capacity, the idea of the supernatural was born. The supernatural added a new spiritual dimension to social life.

The supernatural "layer" that our ancestors added to their social world was filled with ever-vigilant gods, spirits, and ancestors, who monitored their people for strict adherence to tradition and scrupulous avoidance of taboo. But these spirits could be inspiring and comforting as well as menacing—our ancestors often formed close emotional attachments to them just as modern religious people do with God, Jesus, patron saints, local deities, and other supernatural agents. By adding the supernatural to their social world (i.e., by "supernaturalizing" their social lives), our ancestors created strongly cohesive and formidably competitive social groups. Starting about 60,000 years ago, they broke out of Africa once again and began a worldwide expansion to the far corners of the globe. In the process, they displaced all other hominins and eventually became the earth's sole hominin species. Wherever they went, they took their religion—their supernatural attachments—with them.

What Is Religion—Really?

Over the years, anthropologists and sociologists have struggled mightily to define exactly what religion is. My contention is that at its heart, religion is a certain type of relationship that people (and only people) have—a relationship with God, gods, spirits, supernatural beings, deceased ancestors, and the like. This is what I mean when I say religion represents a supernaturalizing of social life.

Somewhere in our evolutionary past, our ancestors' cognitive faculties became such that they were capable of envisioning their social world as including more than just family, friends, and fellow-group mates who happened to be immediately, physically present. This envisioning began with just a vague sense of a healing power that they could contact and direct using ritual. Over time this sense broadened and elaborated. They envisioned an entire social world that extended both "upward," to include dead ancestors, spirits, gods, and other supernatural beings, and "downward," to include nonhuman wild and domesticated animals, ultimately including pets. If we think of the immediate, human social world as horizontal, then we can think of this extension of the social world as vertical, reaching up to the sky for spirits and gods, as well as down to the ground for four-legged friends and other creepy-crawly things. This supernaturalizing was not just a quantitative "add-on" to social life; it changed the very nature of people's human relationships. Friends, family, fellow-group mates, and the natural world itself had a spiritual nature as well as an earthly nature that had to be considered in our relationships with them.

Once religion is understood as an extension of the social world, a number of other issues fall into place. For example, the all too easily misunderstood and often misrepresented role of religion in morality becomes clear (or at least clearer). Religion is not the origin of morality—social life is—but it is hardly irrelevant to morality since religion extends social life in important ways. Furthermore, religion and ritual are intricately intertwined because ritual is essential to social life, and if religion extends social life, then logically it must extend ritual as well. The anthropomorphic (humanlike) yet superhumanly powerful nature of gods and spirits makes perfect sense within this framework. We need spiritual beings to whom we can relate (thus anthropomorphism), but we also need some reason to desire such a relationship (thus power, accessible through ritual). The fact that religion seems to involve both reason and emotion is easily understood within this framework as well since social life requires both.

Finally, understanding religion as relational helps to explain why religious beliefs can be so tenacious even in the face of what seems to be contradictory evidence. Objective evidence and meticulous logic have only limited impact on religious beliefs because a significant part of the evidence for the belief is the subjective experience of the relationship itself. When it comes to religion, *experience is the evidence*. Understanding this may provide a more constructive perspective from which to approach the recent God wars that have broken out. Seeing religion as relationship is certainly not an antidote to the venom that has been spewed of late over religion and its role in society, Still, recognizing this can serve to diffuse some of the bitterness driving the recent God wars, and may lead to more productive exchanges between the devout and secular.

The God Wars

Religion is a hot topic. In recent years an onslaught of books exploring the origins of religion has hit the market. The issue has been addressed from nearly every possible angle, including archaeological, anthropological, primatological, cognitive, and neuroscientific.[4] The upsurge in scientific interest in religion coincides with (or possibly results from) religion's increasing salience in global politics. For millions worldwide, religion provides strength, solace, and a powerful sense of community; but for others, religion's prominence in many of the world's most vexing and divisive issues is deeply troubling.

In America especially, the appropriate role of religion in education, jurisprudence, and social policy has been a source of ongoing and sometimes acrimonious debate. It is hardly surprising, then, that a few have found this an opportune time to foment the next chapter of history's God wars. For some scholars, the only effective response to the threat of creationism and militant fundamentalism is a more aggressive atheism. This atheism finds no virtue in peaceful coexistence with moderate religion. Instead, it seeks to stamp out all religion. This atheism has itself been harshly critiqued.[5]

This state of affairs is rich in irony. While the bickering over God has grown ever more acrid, science has made astounding progress on religion. The good news is that we know more about religion today then ever before. The bad news is that this knowledge has done little to help us deal with it reasonably. One book is unlikely to dramatically shift this state of affairs. However, if my conclusion that at its core religion represents a "super-naturalizing" of social life is more or less correct, then this may give us a better perspective from which to approach public conflicts over religion. Relationships, after all, are transformational. The world often looks very different from "inside" a relationship than from "outside" it.

Since religion is fundamentally relational, you can't simply talk people out of it using objective, third-person evidence. Relationships are experienced subjectively, in the first person, and it is this subjective, first-person experience that actually constitutes the evidence for the relationship. Furthermore, it is from within the context of the relationship that people define key terms such as "God," "religion," and "evidence." Often the bottom line is that you can't prove to somebody that they don't have a relationship. If their experience is of having a relationship, then it is that experience itself that is the evidence for the existence of the relationship (and therefore the relationship partner). Likewise, you can't impose a relationship on someone who is perfectly content as is. Thus, we are often left with opposing camps that have a hard time talking to each other.

Relationship as Transformation

As we get to know someone more intimately, we empathize with them more deeply. Increasingly we understand the world from their point of view and appreciate how their motivations and values play into their actions. Sometimes this experience can be life-changing, offering us insights from another that expand and enrich the way we see ourselves and approach the world. A beloved teacher, a demanding coach, an unremitting rival, an unlikely friend, a long-sought lover—whose life at some point has not been transformed by one of these? Relationships, in fact, are the primary means by which we grow and our lives take new directions. When this happens, it can often be difficult to communicate with those who have not had a comparable experience. They just don't seem to get it. To highlight this, allow me to spin a bit of a fictional but not implausible tale:

Eddie and Cruiser have been friends since childhood. The two of them and their circle of buddies have been hanging around together for as long as anyone can remember. But lately things have changed. Cruiser ("the Cruise," as he is known) has been spending far more time with his new girlfriend, Betty-Lou, than with his old chums. Cruiser has had many girlfriends before (as have all the other boys), but there's something about Betty-Lou that's different. She's a classy lady—a far step up in quality compared to Cruiser's past romantic partners. The Cruise may very well have found his first real love.

Though he has been trying hard to keep up appearances, recently Cruiser has been entertaining thoughts about how juvenile Eddie and the rest of them seem: Do they really think they can spend the rest of their lives just hanging around, playing cards and shooting pool? Is there anything really satisfying or truly fun about that stuff? And then there was that incident last Thursday night at Benny's weekly Texas Hold'em party. The boys have bummed money off Cruiser before, but $50 seemed a bit excessive. Cruiser was planning on a special night out with Betty-Lou, and that cash was essential. Why couldn't anyone understand that? Don't any of them really care about what makes Cruiser happy? Have all of them been hanging around low-class women so long that they can't see the real thing when it comes along?

Finally, at the behest of his buddies, Eddie confronts Cruiser about his sorry disposition of late. Not surprisingly, the whole encounter goes badly—the two had to be separated to avoid fisticuffs. They couldn't even talk to each other anymore. Now this is hardly the first case of longtime buddies breaking up because of someone's girlfriend (the Beatles, anyone?). But why does it happen? I would suggest that a key factor here is that *relationships radically change perspectives.*

As well-intentioned as Eddie might have been, he was probably ill-advised to confront Cruiser. A meeting of minds between the two was bound to be a challenge, given that each is coming from a very different relational perspective. Cruiser is "within" a relationship that has transformed his entire view of life. Meanwhile, Eddie, standing outside of the relationship, sees Cruiser as having changed only for the worse. Stepping back and analyzing the situation reveals exactly what it is that Eddie and Cruiser now see so differently and how that sabotages their communication.

The first problem is definitional. Constructive communication requires that the parties understand terms in approximately the same way. One of the crucial issues facing Eddie and Cruiser is that of happiness or "having fun." Since Cruiser has been with Betty-Lou, Eddie has seen him as painfully unhappy—how can he possibly be having any fun when he's not with the boys anymore? Isn't that what fun has always been for the two of them? For Cruiser, however, fun has become something very different. Eddie doesn't know what real fun means to Cruiser anymore primarily because of the paucity of decent women in his life. They have different definitions of fun that are determined by the types of relationships they have with women. Fun with their usual cadre of female companions means one thing (Eddie understands this). Fun with a high-quality woman means something else entirely—something that Eddie is clueless about and that Cruiser himself only came to understand since his Betty-Lou revelation. Maybe things would have gone differently between Eddie and Cruiser if someone had stopped them right there and forced them to come up with a common definition of fun. Likewise, if someone backed the God warriors up a step or two we might find that much of their enmity stems from vastly different definitions for key terms, which themselves might be based in widely different subjective experiences of life and relationships.

Because Eddie and Cruiser define key terms differently, they have widely varying interpretations of common experiences. For example, both can agree that Cruiser has changed. But Eddie experiences Cruiser's change as a plunge into an emotional malaise, while Cruiser sees it as maturation. For Eddie, Cruiser's unprecedented conflict over money at the weekly card game stands as evidence of Cruiser's despondent state. Cruiser's experience of that same event was quite different—it provides evidence of a new-found concern over the real value of money. At bottom, Eddie and Cruiser have diametrically opposing views about Cruiser's relationship with Betty-Lou. From Eddie's third-person perspective the relationship has been a disaster for Cruiser. But from Cruiser's first-person perspective it has been the best thing that ever happened to him. Neither can convince the other of his position, because for each, it is the experience itself that constitutes the evidence for the conclusions he has drawn.

Consider another relational example: people and their pets. If someone could show you beyond any scientific doubt that your pet does not understand a word you say, has no real notion of what you're thinking, and is entirely incapable of offering you the same kind of love, concern, and compassion that you bestow upon it, would it make any difference in the way you relate to your pet? If you knew intellectually that your pet simply could not have the kind of relationship with you that you are convinced you have with it, would it matter? Would you go home and suddenly stop talking to or playing with your beloved pet because some pipe-toting PhD somewhere told you it's a deceptively lopsided affair? The answer, of course, is no. We academics have been trying to convince people of the big "pet lie" for decades now, and it has had absolutely no impact. People (myself included) continue to enjoy their pets just as much as before the big "pet lie" was revealed.

Why do we so readily fall for it? Once again, it is because of the experience we have in the relationship. The bodily reactions and facial expressions of most pets match what would be expected from a creature that experiences the mental states and emotions with which humans are familiar. Or, to put it more simply, it sure seems as if Fido likes me, understands me, and enjoys my company. Furthermore, most people like the experiential consequences of their pet relationships (i.e., they enjoy caring for their pets, they have fun with them, their pets bring them companionship and happiness, etc.). The argument that pet owners are weak-minded, delusional imbeciles can easily be countered by empirical studies showing that pet ownership can have positive health benefits.[6] If science cannot break people of false notions about pets, a topic on which it can make reasonably definitive statements, then what chance does it have when making pronouncements about the supernatural, a topic on which it cannot?

The View from Outside

The God wars are plagued by both definitional quagmires and subjectivity. From the outside, the scientifically minded regard God as an odd if not outright infuriating concept. Science reveals a matter-based world operating by physical laws, devoid of any evidence of supernatural intervention. Where in this picture is there room or need for an omniscient supernatural being?

To his credit, atheist champion Richard Dawkins is clear on how he defines God—he is a personal God and a "designing" God.[7] As a personal God, he is bound to answer prayers, forgive and punish sins, intervene occasionally with miracles, and regularly fret about the good and bad behavior of his people. As a designing God, he is responsible for every minute detail of the natural world. For Dawkins this is precisely the kind of God that science cannot tolerate. Einstein's metaphorical God of the cosmos, Jefferson's deist God, Spinoza's pantheist God—superfluous, yes, but far more palatable for those who simply can't be weaned off the infantile diet.

From outside, events in the natural world so obviously contradict the possibility of this personal-designer God that the need to even point it out is tiresome. Miracles, answered prayers, divine justice—all require violating the laws of physics, and that just doesn't happen. And as for divine design, one need only consider the excessive predation and extinction that characterize the evolutionary process to know how ludicrous that idea is. The evidence is clear: Some 99% of all species that ever existed are now extinct. What a waste! For Dawkins, this easily refutes the presence of a benevolent or even intelligent God. Any God who intended to create humans certainly could have done it without all the suffering, bloodshed, and death inherent in the evolutionary process.[8] To read the world any differently is to allow the whale of ignorance to swallow you whole.

The View from Inside

For those for whom God exists as friend, wise counselor, or loving spirit, Dawkins's critique is foreign to the point of being almost inscrutable. The existence of a personal, benevolent God—so obscured from Dawkins's view—is plainly obvious to them. The answered prayer is in the chance meeting with the long-lost friend, or in the promotion that was *not* granted but that forced a needed change of career. The divine design is in the hopeful sunrise after the storm; or in how the fire's fury destroys yet cleanses and, in its aftermath, how the fragile shoots of renewing green bravely poke up from the still-smoldering earth.

These differences are more than just mere interpretive gloss. Religion affects the most basic processes guiding our visual perception. A recent study showed that Dutch Calvinists respond significantly more slowly than Dutch atheists do to visual patterns that are diffusely spread across a scene.[9] This has been linked to the Calvinist doctrine of "sphere sovereignty," where each sector of society is believed to have its own equal standing in terms of responsibility and authority. Being raised in an environment where this doctrine is prevalent appears to affect early perceptual processing such that local details take on greater significance. This difference in visual processing was found despite the fact that the Calvinists and atheists shared a common culture and were matched on variables such as educational background, age, IQ, and socioeconomic status. The authors summarized the findings in stark terms:

> It seems possible that religious beliefs may indeed lead to different and . . . sometimes incompatible interpretations of the same incident. That this can happen is a well-known empirical fact, but that it can originate in basic automatic visual operations that precede conscious representation is surprising and in some sense worrying—as it seems to work against the scientific ideal that careful observation is sufficient to reach agreements about basic facts and what we consider reality.[10]

From the initial processing of visual inputs to the ultimate interpretation of experience, believers and nonbelievers really do see the world differently.

To the believer, perfectly natural events reveal the unmistakable breath of the supernatural. For theologian Paul Tillich, it is in this profound experience of life's "depth" that God is to be found:

> For if you know that God means depth, you know much about Him. You cannot then call yourself an atheist or unbeliever. For you cannot think or say: Life has no depth! Life itself is shallow. Being itself is surface only. If you could say this in complete seriousness, you would be an atheist; but otherwise you are not. He who knows about depth, knows about God.[11]

This experience of "depth" has led many to view God not so much as a "designer" who obsessively controls all the minutiae of the natural world, but instead as a "parental" figure, far more intent on persuading and inspiring his creation than dictating to it. Theologian John Haught expresses it this way:

> From Augustine and Aquinas to recent religious thinkers such as William Temple and Pierre Teilhard de Chardin, God is seen not so much as directly engineering this life-endowed world as arousing the world to self-creativity.[12]

From a specifically Christian perspective, this inspiration is toward increasing self-sacrifice. The Christian God is a God who willingly renounces the power to impose his will on the universe and instead models (through the image of Jesus) humility and service as the highest ethic. From the Jewish perspective, the entire notion of a personal-designer God is a rather tangential one. One's relationship with God is far more a matter of practical behavior than of any theological commitment to God's nature. In other words, first and foremost, a good Jew follows God's laws; whether he or she actually believes in Dawkins's personal-designer God is quite secondary.[13]

Even the massive suffering and death of the evolutionary process take on a new meaning within the religious relationship. Suffering is the school by which souls are built, argues Haught.[14] As any parent knows, simply giving a child whatever he or she wants produces an ungrateful, spoiled child. One appreciates the true value of something only by earning it through sweat and sacrifice. The human soul (however one wishes to define it) is not free, and it is only in understanding its profound cost that one can be truly grateful for its presence.

My point here is not to convince you of the rightness or wrongness of any particular worldview, only to impress upon you how different the same thing can look depending upon one's (relational) perspective.

For his part, Dawkins dismisses all this pontificating as little more than intellectual flabbiness.[15] Maybe so, but within the religious relationship, the world takes on a much different cast. Deeply moved by what they see, religious thinkers over the years have constructed a long-standing theological tradition addressing the very issues that Dawkins finds so devastating to their faith. Unfortunately, this tradition and today's aggressive atheism seem only to talk past each other for want of a common language with which to describe the very different worlds they encounter.

So, then, what are we left with? Are we simply to resign ourselves to the fact that these opposing forces have no hope of constructive dialogue? Not necessarily. For those of goodwill, a path toward communication is possible, but one must first recognize the proper questions to ask. Preaching to one's own choir about God's existence or nonexistence, his greatness or depravity, his necessity or necessary termination is only a sure recipe for deepening animosities behind increasingly fortified boundaries. You can't tell someone they don't have a relationship that they are convinced they have. Likewise, you can't force someone into a relationship they are not interested in.

A modest proposal, then: Let us agree that the issue of God's existence is irresolvable and that it is irrational to debate irresolvable issues. Instead, let us focus our energies on the consequences of a relationship with God (or, more generally, the supernatural). If that relationship compels individuals to live lives of greater compassion, service, and healthy self-restraint, then the relationship is probably worthwhile. If that relationship produces only self-righteous arrogance, ignorance, and intolerance, then a divorce is preferable. The critical question guiding the God discussion should not be "Is there something supernatural to relate to?" Instead, it should be "Are we better off with or without these supernatural relationships?"[16]

Defining Religion

While numerous and various definitions of religion have been proposed, most of them include some relational theme. I am not the first to propose that religion represents an expansion of the human social realm. Nearly half a century ago, anthropologist Robin Horton offered a definition of religion that focused squarely on this very element: "Religion," he wrote, "[could] be looked upon as an extension of the field of people's social relationships beyond the confines of purely human society."[17] In what follows, I will review and critique a number of definitions; however, it is Horton's that best captures the model of religion that I am proposing.

In his book *Primitive Culture* (1871) anthropologist Edward B. Tylor claimed that, at minimum, religion required belief in supernatural beings.

Tylor's colleague James George Frazer concurred with this sentiment but added the additional notion that the supernatural beings must have some power over man's destiny: "By religion, then, I understand a propitiation or conciliation of powers superior to man which are believed to direct and control the course of Nature and human life."[18] The classic definition of religion found in the *Oxford English Dictionary* (1971) echoes that of Frazer: "recognition on the part of man of some higher unseen power as having control of his destiny, and as being entitled to obedience and worship." More recent definitions follow this basic theme—that fundamentally religion entails the belief in supernatural entities that have the power to direct human destiny. For example, according to sociologist Steve Bruce religion involves "beliefs, actions, and institutions predicated on the existence of entities with powers of agency (that is, gods) or impersonal powers or processes possessed of moral purpose (the Hindu notion of Karma, for example) which can set the conditions of, or intervene in, human affairs."[19]

Psychologists of religion Michael Argyle and Benjamin Beit-Hallahmi are more concise: "A system of beliefs in a divine or superhuman power, and practices of worship and other rituals directed toward such power." Another sociologist, Rodney Stark, writes, "Religion consists of very general explanations that justify and specify the terms of exchange with a god or gods." Stark's definition explicitly brings in the notion of reciprocity between powerful gods and the relatively weak humans who wish to influence them through worship and sacrifice.[20]

The relational elements in these definitions are not difficult to see. The essential feature of religion is the recognition of a spiritual realm populated with powerful agents. Humans must interact with these agents in order to direct or influence the dispensation of their power. Thus, humans relate to gods or spirits in a prescribed manner—through ritual, sacrifice, and prayer. Using these specific relational tools, humans engage the gods and secure their goodwill. Humble prayer brings a favorable divine response; Agamemnon sacrifices his daughter Iphigeneia to the goddess Artemis in return for calm seas, a mystic fasts in order to unite with God, and so forth.

Recently, definitions emphasizing belief in gods and human interaction with them have been eclipsed by definitions emphasizing the human search for the sacred or the transcendent. Definitions in this category include "a covenant faith community with teachings and narratives that enhance the search for the sacred"; "a personal or group search for the sacred that unfolds within a traditional sacred context"; "a set of symbolic forms and acts that relate man to the ultimate conditions of his existence"; and "the inner experience of the individual when he experiences the Beyond, especially . . . when he actively attempts to harmonize his life with the Beyond." William James's definition of religion falls into this category: "Religion, in the broadest and most general terms possible[,] . . . consists of the belief that there is an unseen order, and our supreme good lies in harmoniously adjusting ourselves thereto."[21] Alfred North Whitehead offers a somewhat more poetic (and far wordier) definition:

> Religion is the vision of something which stands beyond, behind, and within, the passing flux of immediate things; something which is real, and yet waiting to be realized; something which is a remote possibility, and yet the greatest of present facts; something that gives meaning to all that passes, and yet eludes apprehension; something whose possession is the final good, and yet is beyond all reach; something which is the ultimate ideal and the hopeless quest.[22]

Though less obvious, the relational element is still present in these definitions. Many theologians and religious scholars have argued that the search for the sacred is essentially a relational one—that is, either searching for a particular kind of relationship to the sacred, or searching for sacredness within the context of one's human relationships.[23] The "search for the sacred" or the "[harmonizing of one's] life with the Beyond" or the "adjusting [of ourselves to] an unseen order" all require actions directed toward others in our community. The community itself becomes endowed with a divine character such that human relationships and human activities are themselves seen in a supernatural context. Thus in this model, one's relationship with the supernatural is often mediated through one's relationships with others and with the world at large. Rituals of worship serve to remind believers of the divine nature of all existence.

Religion as Relationship

> In our ordinary human experience it is other personal subjects that matter most to us, and no amount of scientific expertise can tell us who they really are. Would it be otherwise with God . . . ?
> . . . Just as the story of anyone's life is the story of relationships— so each person's religious story is the story of relationships.[24]

Some may find it odd to say that people have "supernatural" relationships just as they have "natural" ones. But for most religious people this is, in fact, what religion is all about. When people are asked which of the following most closely reflects their view of religious faith—(1) a set of beliefs, (2) membership in a church or synagogue, (3) finding meaning in life, or (4) a relationship with God—51% of them pick (4), compared to 20% or less for all the others. In his surveys of both the general public and college students (both largely Christian, but not necessarily evangelical), psychologist of religion Lee Kirkpatrick finds that over two-thirds respond affirmatively to the statement "Do you feel you have a personal relationship with Jesus Christ and/or God?" Decades of studies on religion as attachment indicate that there is considerable overlap between human relationships and relationships with supernatural agents.[25]

The quality of one's interpersonal attachments has important psychological ramifications. Securely attached children find comfort, safety, and anxiety reduction when in close proximity to their caregivers. Furthermore, adults who have strong social attachments are typically healthier, happier, and more confident than those with no attachments or lower-quality ones. Similar outcomes have been documented for relationships with God. Increasing degrees of religious commitment correspond to increases in one's sense of personal competence and control as well as decreases in trait anxiety. These positive outcomes appear to be attributable to the relational aspects of religion. A number of studies show that such measures as "the experience of God in prayer" or the "proximity and depth of a divine relationship" correlate more strongly with measures of well-being than do other religious variables. Furthermore, those who view God as warm, responsive, and caring (i.e., those with a secure attachment to God) score significantly higher on measures of well-being and life satisfaction and lower on measures of depression, loneliness, and the presence of psychosomatic symptoms than those who view God as impersonal, uncaring, and distant (i.e., those with an avoidant attachment).[26]

The type of personal relationship that one has with significant others (especially parents) turns out to be a good predictor of one's relationship with God. Among Catholic teenagers, the perception of parents as loving and nurturing was positively correlated with an image of God as loving, comforting, and nurturing. A similar result was found with fourth graders. Among adolescent boys, images of God are often closely aligned with their perception of their father. An alcoholic, "bad" father was more often associated with a negative image of God. These associations tend to remain intact through adulthood. Those with unusually secure attachments to parents are often among the most religiously committed. Female seminarians and nuns, for example, have been found to have exceptionally secure attachments to their mothers and typically perceive their mothers as highly supportive and helpful.[27]

In a survey of over 200 adults, Kirkpatrick and Shaver found that those classified as being in secure relationships were more likely to view God as loving, accessible, and noncontrolling compared to those in avoidant relationships. People with a history of avoidant attachments are, in general, less religiously committed and more likely to profess agnosticism.

Furthermore, religious conversion is significantly more likely for those adults who, as children, had insecure attachments to parents. One argument is that they might be attracted to a supernatural relationship as compensation for an inadequate human one. Anthropologist Roger Lohmann provides some support for this view by showing that religious conversion is primarily the establishment of a new relationship with a supernatural agent and only secondarily the adoption of a new set of doctrines.[28]

Many of these same patterns have been observed cross-culturally and in non-Christian religious traditions. For instance, a close correspondence has been found between a culture's prevailing parenting style and the prevalence of benevolent or malevolent deities in that culture's religious system. Rejecting parenting styles were associated with a prevalence of malevolent deities, whereas accepting parenting styles were associated with benevolent deities. Hinduism provides another example of attachment dynamics at work. In Hinduism, striving for enlightenment is a central concern. Two of the paths for achieving this are largely nontheistic: *Karma-marga* is the way of works and action; *jnana-marga* is the way of wisdom and philosophy. However, 90% of Hindus follow the way of devotion (*bhakti-marga*), where adherents seek salvation through the mercy of God. This devotion often involves prayers, sacrifices, and other ritual activities designed to draw one nearer to the divine. Most faithful Hindus appear to experience a relation to the divine similar to that of Christians with Jesus or God. This also seems to be true for Buddhists, the vast majority of whom follow the polytheistic Mahayana tradition rather than the nontheistic Theravada tradition.[29]

Lee Kirkpatrick, one of the leading researchers on attachment theory and its application to religion, concludes his review of the religion and attachment literature thusly:

> I am suggesting that attachment is not merely a metaphor for people's perceived relationships with God, but "really" is an attachment relationship in every important sense. Attachments differ from other kinds of relationships not by strength, but by function, and I have tried to show here that relationships with God function in the same manner as relationships with parents during childhood.[30]

Developing Relationships

A relational framework describes not only peoples' experience of religion, but also the process of acquiring a particular faith or a particular orientation toward faith. In the past few decades, researchers have debated whether adopting a religious faith is better understood through a *compensation* model or a *correspondence* model. Compensation refers to the fact that for some individuals, supernatural agents provide the protection, nurturance, and security often lacking in their human relationships—especially parental relationships. These individuals often have a history of insecure attachments to parental and romantic figures, and supernatural attachments appear to compensate for these deficiencies. Correspondence applies more to individuals with a history of secure attachments to parents and romantic partners. They tend to gradually acquire the same religious attitudes and traditions their parents held, part of which involves the view of God or other supernatural agents as creator, wise counselor, or trusted friend. This dual path to religion corresponds roughly to William James's earlier distinction between the "once-born" and "twice-born" religious believers.[31]

Empirical evidence for both these processes has been found, prompting some to argue that religion comes to people from both "within" and "without."[32] By "within" they mean by virtue of people's internal need for emotional security and regulation (insecurely attached individuals). By "without" they refer to those who readily adopt the religious tradition of their parents and community (securely attached individuals). Relation-ships—whether positive or negative—are thus the catalysts for religiosity.

Finally, Kirkpatrick provides evidence that religion's historical endurance may be attributable to the fact that it provides its members with such an extraordinary breadth of relational resources. His conclusion builds on the work of Robert Weiss, who identified six types of relational bonds in humans: (1) *attachment bonds* provide comfort and a secure base, (2) *affiliation bonds* provide social integration and a sense of community, (3) *persistent alliance bonds* provide long-term commitments to each other's well-being, (4) *nurturance bonds* provide support when in distress, (5) *collaboration bonds* provide cooperation in the pursuit of shared goals, and (6) *help-obtaining bonds* provide guidance and counsel. While most personal relationships fall into one or just a few of these types, religion may be unique in that it has the potential to cover most if not all of these needs. This is partly because religion draws on not only a vast network of human resources, but perceived supernatural ones as well.[33]

In Good Times and Bad

The evidence that people form attachments to God and other supernatural agents underscores the usefulness of a relationship model in understanding religion. If a primary element of religion is relational, then we would expect the full range of relational emotions to be present in people's interactions with supernatural agents. Just as in human relationships, when relational trust in the supernatural agent is questioned or broken, anger, confusion, and a sense of betrayal may ensue. Thus, we would expect that along with the joy and comfort often associated with religious faith, the more negative relational emotions would emerge periodically as well. Evidence confirms this.

The 1988 General Social Survey found that 63% of Americans reported being angry at God at one time or another. This anger was typically triggered in response to some negative life event that caused personal suffering, loss, or trauma. God was often seen as either actively or passively responsible for the event, even when a human perpetrator was behind it. In some cases the feeling of abandonment and betrayal was so strong that it caused the person to question God's existence. Twenty-one percent of college students who had suffered a major negative life event reported a decreased confidence in God's existence, while 9% had become atheists.[34]

Interestingly, the same factors that predict forgiveness in human relationships are relevant in determining whether individuals forgive God for suffering that they believe is God's fault. Forgiveness is more forthcoming to the extent that (1) God is not seen as having intentionally caused suffering, (2) the person involved has a greater sense of humility and tolerance, (3) the person's prior relationships with God and others were close and secure, and (4) the person's general level of stress is low. As with human relationships, interventions to repair the human-God relationship are designed to resolve negative emotions and rebuild trust. This may be done by encouraging the individual to approach prayer as a conversation with God where one expresses emotions and "listens" for God's reply (through imagery or reading sacred texts). In Judaism the practice of *hitbodedut*—speaking to God as one speaks to one's closest friend—is often encouraged as a means of repairing one's relationship with God.[35]

The range of emotions present in relations with supernatural agents is certainly not confined to Western monotheistic traditions. Among many traditional Asian and African societies, the ancestors are the primary supernatural relational figures. Indeed, these societies typically do not make a distinction between the earthly tribe and the generations of ancestors who have gone before them. They all constitute one interconnected, interactive society. Thus, relationships with deceased ancestors may be as convoluted and complicated as those with parents and relatives.

The Lohorung Rai are a traditional horticultural people living in the Arun Valley of eastern Nepal. For the Lohorung, the ancestors are as present and relevant in everyday life as living members of their family and tribe.[36] Though the ancestors deserve respect because of their age and experience, the Lohorung also see them as almost childlike in their need for constant reassurance, attention, and placation. The ancestors are easily upset and lacking in discipline. Small, daily acts of ritual and sacrifice are required to keep them contented and their egos unbruised. Even more elaborate rituals are required for major life events—such as the birth of child, who must be introduced to the ancestors with proper ritual in order to avoid misfortune and ostracism.

As wise guardians of tradition, the ancestors serve as steadfast reminders of Lohorung values and history. For this reason they are honored and even feared because of the ease at which they take offense. But they are also understood to have fading mental and physical powers owing to their advanced age and at times must be cajoled or commanded not to overstep their proper place. In the midst of all this, the Lohorung firmly believe that maintaining a good relationship with the ancestors is essential to their personal and tribal well-being. Like human relationships, these supernatural relationships must be constantly monitored, nurtured, and, when necessary, repaired.

Religion and the Brain

Evidence for religion as fundamentally relational can also be seen in the brain. Recent advances in neuroscience allow researchers to monitor brain activity while subjects are engaged in various mental activities, including religious or mystical ones. For example, one study used positron emission tomography (PET scan) to monitor brain activity as believers achieved a religious mental state by reciting the 23rd Psalm. The PET scan detects cerebral blood flow, allowing researchers to see which parts of the brain are demanding more resources and therefore (presumably) working harder.[37]

Other studies have used similar testing procedures. For example, Canadian neuroscientist Mario Beauregard had nuns recall their most intense mystical experience; meanwhile, he monitored their brain activity using functional magnetic resonance imaging (fMRI). Though the technology is somewhat different from PET, the bottom line is basically the same: fMRI allows researchers to make inferences about which parts of the brain are demanding more resources when certain cognitive activities are taking place. PET and fMRI have also been used to study specific meditative practices and their effects on the brain. Finally, University of Pennsylvania neuroscientist Andrew Newberg and colleagues have pioneered the use of SPECT (single photon emission computed tomography) in studying the effects of meditation in both Catholic nuns and experienced Buddhists meditators. Though less precise in localizing brain activity, SPECT is also less intrusive than other measures and allows subjects greater freedom in achieving "peak" meditative experiences.[38]

Though these studies have used different subjects, brain scan technologies, and methods of achieving religious or mystical states, a consistent finding is activation in two brain regions: the prefrontal cortex and the superior temporal/inferior parietal cortex. Importantly, other brain imaging studies have found these same two regions to be critical to social functioning. The prefrontal cortex is important in understanding other's motivations and goals in social situations. Furthermore, the frontmost part of the prefrontal cortex (the orbital prefrontal cortex) is important in reading facial cues and emotions. The superior temporal sulcus is important in detecting biological movement, processing dynamic facial cues, and attributing agency or goal-directedness to actions and actors.[39]

A very recent study has found that at the brain level, talking with God is the same as talking to a friend.[40] Researchers had 20 devout Christians carry out both religious (reciting the Lord's Prayer, improvising a prayer to God) and secular (reciting a nursery rhyme, improvising a prayer to Santa Claus) activities. As with earlier studies, when subjects improvised a prayer to God, there was activation in the prefrontal and superior temporal/ inferior parietal cortices (among other areas). Importantly, the prefrontal cortex was not active when subjects made improvised prayers to Santa Claus. Even though the outward actions were the same, the brain made an important distinction between a partner who was believed to be capable of reciprocating (God) and one who was considered purely fictional (Santa).

A recent review of the neuroimaging literature on religious experience has concluded that "relational cognition" lies at the core of brain's response to the divine. Neuroscientist and theologian Nina Azari points out how the broad areas of the frontal cortex active in religious experiences are also critical for such social cognitive functions as understanding others' intentions, social decision making, and empathizing. This, she contends, provides compelling evidence that the religious experience is deeply intertwined with what she calls "relational cognitivity." Reinforcing Azari's conclusion is a recent study showing that areas of the frontal lobe, well established as being part of the brain's Theory of Mind system, are integral to people's religious beliefs. Theory of Mind refers to our capacity to infer desires, emotions, intentions, and other mental states in others.[41] Thus, the parts of the brain governing interpersonal relationships govern religious beliefs and experiences as well.

Summary

However we define religion, it is defined in relational terms, either with regard to an exchange relationship with powerful supernatural agents or as a response to a perceived sacred cosmic order that calls us to relate to other humans and to the world in a different, more meaningful way. When we examine the physical and psychological properties of people's relationships with supernatural agents, they appear in nearly all important respects to mirror those present in human relationships. Secure attachments to people predict secure attachments to gods and spirits. Secure attachments to gods and spirits provide the same safety, comfort, and anxiety-reducing benefits associated with secure human attachments. Additionally, the physical health benefits associated with secure human attachments are present in supernatural relationships as well. Those whose human (especially parental) relationships have been unsatisfactory are significantly more likely to undergo a religious conversion, suggesting the need for supernatural compensation for inadequate human attachments. Finally, important parts of the social brain are activated when someone has a religious experience, suggesting that in many respects the brain treats a religious experience as a social encounter. Religion is many things, but the relational element is at its core. Nonrelational religion, if it is religion at all, is hollow.

2

Making a Good Impression

A Joyful Noise

I am sitting in a small lounge at the Catholic Life Center on the South Acadian Thruway in Baton Rouge, Louisiana. Adjacent to me is a small chapel. It's dark, so I can't actually see what's in there, but I'm familiar enough with Catholic places of worship to guess: a small receptacle in the doorway with holy water; rows of pews facing a small altar with statuettes of Mary and Joseph on either side and a crucifix above it. In another part of the lounge a few young people are strumming guitars and practicing songs about Jesus—"Yes Lord, yes Lord, I've traded my sorrows for joy." Teenagers, most still in their school uniforms, jostle about, appear and disappear—lots of laughing, hugging, everyone talking at once.

Tapping away on my laptop is a bit more challenging amid all the noise, but the commotion actually reinforces my central theme: that religion is about relationships. In one sense, the Catholic Life Center could easily be confused with any other teen gathering place. Get a bunch of teenagers together in a building, and they act pretty much the same whether or not there are crosses on the walls. But in another sense this is not like most other places. To begin with, there are the aforementioned crosses, which only slightly outnumber the portraits of popes and bishops—all brightly clothed and smiling warmly. Equally frequent are the various iconic renderings of the Virgin Mary and crucified Christ. Once within its confines it's hard to escape the fact that this setting concerns itself with more than just the ordinary—the supernatural is of concern as well. I'd be surprised if these reminders of the supernatural didn't have some effect on the way the young people relate to one another. For one thing, taking the Lord's name in vain is probably a rarity here. It's probably also a safe bet that the kids are a tad more respectful and just generally nicer here than out on the streets. Don't get me wrong—I'm not accusing them of hypocrisy. I'm simply making the mundane point that most people adjust their behavior to fit their surroundings.

With that in mind, imagine for a moment being constantly surrounded by reminders of the supernatural. Imagine a group of our ancestors on the African savanna or in a jungle clearing on Java Island. No statues or crucifixes, of course. But they aren't necessary. Everything is supernatural. The trees, the clouds, the wind, the rising and setting sun, the baby's breath upon your naked skin—to our ancestors they were all reminders of the supernatural. Once the hominin mind was capable of envisioning the supernatural, everything in nature was subsumed within it.

Still, a question remains: Why? Why would our ancestors have cultivated such an imagination? It seems to make no sense. If evolution is about surviving long enough to out-reproduce your competitors, then isn't it painfully obvious that those of our ancestors who kept their minds focused on the practical business of survival would have easily out-competed those who wasted precious energy on useless imaginings about spirits and gods? Maybe not, for evolution can move in mysterious ways. Religious imagination, it turns out, was not a frivolous adornment, but an indispensable piece in the practical business of survival. It was as central to life as fire, the spear, and mother's breast. Those who supernaturalized their social lives out-competed the no-nonsense secularists of our past, and their legacy is the youthful, joyful noise all about me.

Humans and Neanderthals in the Levant

Despite protestations from various quarters, there is simply no question concerning the origins of humanity: We evolved from African apes. If you could travel back in time about 7 million years to East/Central Africa, you would find a smallish hairy ape running about the forests. It was from this hairy ape that two evolutionary branches emerged: One eventually produced modern-day chimpanzees, and the other produced us. The hairy ape from which these two evolutionary branches arose is referred to as the human/chimpanzee common ancestor.

As east Africa became increasingly dry, what was once dense, unbroken jungle gave way to a patchwork of forested areas interspersed among open savannah. The forerunners of today's chimpanzees (and bonobos) remained steadfastly committed to the remaining forests, while our ancestors cast their lot in the open territory. These "open-territory apes" were the genesis of the hominin evolutionary branch—our branch. Over the course of the 7 million years or so since that fateful split, numerous hominin species emerged, including the various Australopiths and members of the genus *Homo*. Genetic and fossil evidence point to the emergence of anatomically modern humans (*Homo sapiens sapiens*) somewhere between 200,000 and 150,000 years before present (ybp).[1] In other words, humans with bodies and brains pretty much like yours and mine were running around Africa as early as 200,000 years ago.

About 100,000 years ago, we have the first evidence of anatomically modern humans (AMH) venturing beyond the borders of Africa. An interesting drama played itself out in the Levant region of the eastern Mediterranean, an area that includes parts of the modern states of Lebanon, Syria, Jordan, Israel, and the Sinai Peninsula. Around 130,000 ybp, evidence from Tabun Cave in Israel indicates habitation by Neanderthal (or Neanderthal-like) hominins. Around 100,000 ybp, other sites in the region (Skhul and Qafzeh Caves) show evidence of habitation by anatomically modern or near-modern humans. Their presence, however, was only transient. About 30,000 years later the humans were gone and Neanderthals once again occupied the Levant. There were probably brief episodes where Neanderthals and modern humans shared and directly competed for space and resources in the Levant. More often, however, climate stacked the deck in favor of one or the other such that direct confrontation was negligible. Warmer conditions gave the advantage to modern humans, colder conditions to the Neanderthals.[2] As conditions changed, either one or the other probably sensed it was time to move on.

So here begins a critical part of our story. Sometime shortly after 100,000 ybp, our *Homo sapiens sapiens* ancestors in the Levant could sense that their sojourn in this new land was rapidly coming to an end. The cold seemed interminable, and those squat, tough-looking immigrants from the north were drawing ever closer in increasing numbers. Game was getter harder and harder to find. It was best to follow the others southward to warmer, more hospitable territory.

The history of Middle Paleolithic Levantine habitation gives us the first possible hint of group competition at work in hominin evolution. This was not to be the last time that humans and Neanderthals would occupy the same space—a space that was never big enough for both of them. But the slow march of *Homo sapiens sapiens* southward out of the Levant proved anomalous. Like General MacArthur on the Philippine shore, they would return, and the next time it would be for good. From the Levant to the four corners of the globe, modern humans would venture forth unhindered by climate, Neanderthals, or any other obstacles. What changed? Were our ancestors just too nice the first time around and needed the experience of failure to harden them up a bit? Actually, no. Strange as it may seem, their initial failure was not because they were too nice, but because they weren't nice enough. To be more competitive at the group level, our ancestors first had to increase their ability to cooperate with each other. Cooperative groups are highly competitive groups—and cooperation requires increased, not decreased, niceness.

An Overabundance of Niceness

At first blush, the idea that humans would turn out to be the most success-ful species on earth seems a bit crazy. We appear to have few attributes that would lead to evolutionary success. We are not very fast or strong. We can't fly or climb trees very well. Our digestive system can't handle leaves or grass. We have no fur to protect our skin or horns to ward off enemies. Our canine teeth are paltry, and no one would mistake our pathetic little nails for claws. Sharks can out-swim us, kangaroos can out-jump us, rabbits can out-procreate us, and to top it all off, koalas are cuter. Unimpressive indeed are we to the casual observer—vastly ill-equipped to face a hostile world. Oddly, the one thing we do have in abundance is niceness. By evolutionary standards we are far nicer than we should be. Not that niceness is entirely useless in the evolutionary game. Being nice can actually work as a strategy for survival and reproduction. But as we shall see shortly, our niceness seems to be gratuitous. It goes far beyond the limited form of niceness that actually has self-interested genetic benefits. It is our gratuitous niceness that has been source of much controversy and discussion among evolution-minded researchers. And it is our gratuitous niceness that holds the key to understanding both our immense success and our propensity for religion.

The Evolution of Altruism

What humans lack in *personal* survival traits (e.g., horns, fangs, body armor, blinding speed) we more than make up for in our ability to act collectively. We work together better than any other species, and this is the key to our success. This was what changed between our first venture into the Levant and all subsequent ones. Getting individuals to work together often means setting aside personal interests for group-level ones. All organisms, including humans, are inherently short-sighted, and short-sighted self-interest can undermine collective interest even when everyone in the collective would benefit more, in the long run, from cooperation. How, then, can evolution get selfish, short-sighted humans to set aside selfishness long enough to cooperate with others in order to achieve an even more beneficial long-term goal? The answer is to fight fire with fire—in other words, make it in an organism's interests to be unselfish (at least under some circumstances). This rather creative use of self-interest is the first step toward a limited form of altruism and morality. This "first step" does not come easily, however; it is built upon a multitude of smaller steps—going right down to the first principles of natural selection.

Evolution Basics

Most people think evolution it is complicated. In fact, it is quite simple. Natural selection—the primary mechanism responsible for evolutionary change—is based on four very straightforward principles. So intuitive are these principles that when Darwin and Wallace first laid them out, Darwin's friend and fellow naturalist, Thomas Huxley, openly chastised himself not for thinking of them first.

PRINCIPLE 1: VARIABILITY This one hardly needs much explaining. Get a group of teenagers together and it's easy to see that they are not clones; in a litter of puppies, some are bigger, furrier, friskier than others; rabbits come in different colors and temperaments, and so on and so forth—stuff varies.

PRINCIPLE 2: HERITABILITY To one degree or another, the variability observed in organisms is due to the genes they inherited from their parents. Of course, genes interact with environments to produce the organism on which selection operates. Genetic differences do, however, represent a key source of variance passed on from one generation to the next.

PRINCIPLE 3: COMPETITION Because resources are limited, organisms must compete to secure what they need for growth, survival, and, ultimately, reproduction; and as a result of that competition . . .

PRINCIPLE 4: EVOLUTION Inherited traits that offer an organism an advantage in the competition for resources will tend to get passed along at a higher rate than neutral or disadvantageous traits will. It is the transmission and spread of advantageous inherited traits that produces the change over time in descendant generations that we call "evolution."

So by way of a very simplistic example: Suppose you could travel to the cold frozen north as it was tens of thousands of years ago. Principle 1 says that organisms vary, so quite possibly you might observe rabbits with many different coat colors. Principle 2 says that this variability in coat color is due to the genetic material each rabbit inherited (per chance) from its parents. Principle 3 says that the resources needed to sustain rabbits are limited. Rabbits need to eat grass and other vegetation, and those resources are limited (very much so) in the cold, frozen north. Furthermore, wolves need to eat rabbits—so at the same time that the rabbits are competing with each other to get enough grass, they are also, in a very real sense, competing not to get eaten by wolves. (One is reminded of the old joke about the two hunters who happened upon a hungry bear. "I'm not worried," one hunter said to the other. "I don't have to outrun the bear, I only have to outrun you.") Principle 4 says that those inherited traits that provide some advantage in the competition for limited resources will tend to spread. Not surprisingly, those rabbits who were lucky enough to inherit the white-fur genes tended to get eaten less often by wolves because they were better camouflaged against the snowy landscape. Since they were more likely to survive, the white-coat trait was passed along at a higher rate than other coat-color traits. Hence, in the Arctic today we find almost exclusively white-coated rabbits.

Cooperating to Compete

It is principle 3 that transfixes most of us—competition, the "Nature, red in tooth and claw" struggle for survival. The dramatic chase of predator and prey, the lock-horns battle of stags over territory, the heartless abandonment of the sickly cub—all emblematic of nature's pitiless principle of survival-of-the-fittest. This has its purpose: Future generations are most likely better off without the genes of the slower prey, weaker stag, or sickly cub. But direct conflict is not the only way that competition can unfold. Cooperation as a competitive strategy has just as deep an evolutionary history as the more familiar "butting heads" variety. Consider, for example, the lowly slime mold. The separate cells that make up the slime mold can and often do exist separately from one another. However, when conditions are not conducive to individualism, they unite to form a unit that can sometimes exceed 100,000 cells. This mold forms a stalk from which spores are launched, often by hitching a ride on the back of an unsuspecting bug. The stalk cells eventually die, but their death is not in vain. Since the slime mold cells are clones, they live on through the spores they helped to spread. Their sacrifice has the honorable effect of serving the greater good of slime.[3] The important point, however, is that by forming a cooperative community where some (the stalk cells) act as a support for others (the spores), all are able to reap a reproductive reward that none could accomplish singly.

A little over 40 years after Darwin published *Origin*, Russian naturalist and political anarchist Petr Kropotkin published *Mutual Aid*, which examined the cooperative tendencies of many species. Kropotkin intended his book as an alternative to what he perceived as the overemphasis on competition in Darwin's work. But Darwin had already struggled with the issue, acknowledging that the social insects were one of the major challenges to his theory. If evolution is all about getting genes into the next generation, how could generation after generation of sterile ants, bees, and other insects have evolved, all of whom seem perfectly content to forgo their own reproductive opportunities for that of a reproductively hyperactive queen? Social insects are only the tip of the altruistic iceberg. Other equally perplexing examples abound: Rather than starting their own families, some Florida scrub jays work as "helpers in the nest" assisting in the care and feeding of another pair's nestlings. Similar helpers have been found among African wild dogs, jackals, and hyenas. Among ground squirrels, a vigilant sentry willingly places her own survival in jeopardy by alerting others of an approaching predator with a loud alarm call. Finally, lionesses are known to generously suckle other's offspring.[4] All these "nice" acts seem to run contrary to the idea that everyone is in it for themselves (or, more accurately, for their genes). Why help someone else's genes?

Kin Selection, Reciprocity, and Indirect Reciprocity

A satisfactory answer to this question remained elusive until 1964, when William Hamilton proposed the idea of inclusive fitness. His solution was a straightforward one: Nice creatures actually weren't helping another's genes. They were helping their own. Hamilton called attention to the fact that direct descendants are not the only way of propagating one's genetic material. Relatives and their offspring "count" as well. So, for example, since I share 50% of my genes with my brother, helping him successfully raise two children is as good as raising one of my own. Helping him raise three is even better. Thus, a full appreciation of any organism's reproductive success must include the descendants of relatives as well as direct offspring. Social insects slavishly give themselves to the hive or colony in order to propagate the queen's offspring, with whom they are more closely related than their own. The helper birds, dogs, and lionesses are not helping indiscriminately. They are helping kin—a form of behavior known as kin selection or kin altruism. The "helpers-in-the-nest" birds, for example, are typically "older brothers" who are not yet ready to establish their own territories. In the meantime, helping mom and dad with younger siblings is an evolutionarily smart way to bide your time. Even the ground squirrels are not true altruists. They raise the alarm when family members are in the vicinity, but not when unrelated squirrels are nearby. Unsurprisingly, the tendency to be biased toward kin—extending a certain niceness or cooperativeness exclusively to relatives—is found in humans as well.[5]

As groups grow larger, however, encompassing not just immediate kin but also nonrelatives, natural selection must find ways to forge cooperation among organisms that share little or no familial connection. One mechanism for doing this is called reciprocal altruism: simple tit-for-tat arrangements where a current favor is traded for one in the future. One intriguing example of this is found among vampire bats. These bats cannot go long without a blood meal, and the chance of success for any individual bat on a given night is highly variable. To help spread the risk, bats regurgitate blood to one another in the cave. If you've come up dry for the night, it's nice to have a friend who scored the mother lode. This sharing, however, is not indiscriminate. A bat is most likely to share with another who had a history of reciprocation.[6]

Reciprocal arrangements appear to be present among nonhuman primates as well. Primatologist Frans de Waal found that chimpanzees who recently groomed one another were more likely to share food later. Similar behavior has been documented in capuchin monkeys. When one monkey helped another to obtain food, the one getting the food was likely to share some of the spoils. After a hunt, chimpanzees often share the meat. But as we have seen in other cases, this sharing is not random: It occurs more often among members of the hunting party, between the dominant male and his allies, and between the dominant male and females with whom he has consorted in the past. While these examples suggest that reciprocal arrangements among nonhuman animals are reasonably widespread, one recent review suggests otherwise. Psychologist Marc Hauser has submitted many of the purported instances of animal reciprocity to an intensive critique. While falling short of concluding that animal reciprocity is nonexistent, he argues strongly that it is far more restricted than previously thought.[7]

One reason why reciprocity might be rare among nonhuman animals is that in the evolutionary game, cheating on reciprocal relationships can be so much more lucrative than playing fair. So while a smart chimpanzee shares food only with those who groomed him in the past, a really smart chimpanzee finds a way to get groomed while keeping all the food for himself. One way to mitigate the cheating problem is to restrict reciprocal relationships to those who are likely to repay. If chimpanzee A notices that chimpanzee B has cheated chimpanzee C, A would be smart to avoid reciprocal arrangements with B. Biologist Richard Alexander terms this "indirect reciprocity"—where reputation becomes a critical factor in determining with whom reciprocal arrangements are made.[8] The rule is a simple one: "Make reciprocal agreements only with those of good reputation."

There is evidence that animals take reputation into account in their interactions with others. For example, guppies often take turns "inspecting" for predators—a potentially lethal activity. Those who do their fair share of inspecting tend to remember those who don't and often prefer not to associate with them. Additionally, when chimpanzees are confronted with a task that requires collaboration, they tend to choose a partner with a record of past success. Chimpanzees also appear to remember an alpha male who was tyrannical in his authority and resist his reemergence to power. Again, it is not surprising to find plenty of evidence that humans too are exquisitely sensitive to reputation.[9]

Summing Up: Why Be Nice?

This body of research has provided us with a clear set of evolutionarily sound reasons why organisms would be nice: (1) They are nice because they helping kin, which from a genetic point of view is actually tantamount to helping oneself. (2) They are nice because they are expecting something in return later for their niceness. (3) They are nice because they are trying to establish a reputation for fair play, which would enhance the chances that they will be chosen as partners in future reciprocal relationships. Notice that in each of these instances a self-interested motivation lies behind the outwardly nice behavior.

It may seem odd that the origins of generosity, fair play, and, ultimately, morality lie in genetic self-interest. Doesn't that tarnish good behavior? Not necessarily. That the origins for these ostensibly moral behaviors are found in enlightened (genetic) self-interest does not mean that every human act has a cynical motive behind it. In the natural world, the moral sense had to start somewhere; but whether it stays at that level in any individual human is certainly a different matter. Even so, a dispassionate examination of our own behavior might reveal how few indeed are the instances where we are *truly* selfless. Aren't we just about always looking for something in return, even if it is just an acknowledgment that we did "some good"? (And don't we feel slighted if that acknowledgment is not immediately forthcoming?) By nature, all creatures (including humans) are designed to guard their individual (genetic) interests. The cold, hard truth is that if we weren't designed that way, we wouldn't be here. Our plunge into the evolutionary origins of niceness only reinforces something that we all pretty much knew was true but we don't like to admit—true altruism is a rarity; real sacrifice is a precious gem; genuine selflessness is not instinctual, but the product of hard-won effort. All the more reason to admire it when it does happen.

The Evolution of Human Niceness: Are the Usual Explanations Enough?

Are kin selection, reciprocal altruism, and indirect reciprocity adequate to explain human levels of cooperation? It has often been pointed out that humans engage in a variety of activities where the payoff seems hard to identify: anonymous donations to charity, generous tipping while on vacation, habitual blood donations, volunteering at soup kitchens. Even something as simple as queuing up calmly for movie tickets and casting dirty looks at "cutters" can get complicated when examined closely. In none of these instances is someone directing efforts specifically toward kin, nor is any reciprocity anticipated, and the possible effects on reputation are remote at best.

A number of recent studies suggest that the usual theoretical suspects may not fully explain human cooperation. What these studies demonstrate is that under some circumstances people's cooperative tendencies appear to arise from an internalized need to follow group norms. A full account of human niceness therefore requires an understanding of the evolutionary origin of group norms and how they affect our thoughts and actions.

A paradigm called the Prisoner's Dilemma (PD) has been used extensively to study human cooperation. The PD is a game where cooperation between two "players" can produce greater rewards than selfishness. However, cooperation entails the risk of being exploited.

Here's an example. The police arrest two people, A and B. The case against them is weak. If both A and B remain silent, they will only get two years in prison. Two years is not much, but suspect A wants to avoid prison altogether. He makes a deal with the police: If he provides incriminating evidence on B and B remains silent, then B will get 10 years and he (A) will go free. In other words, B takes the rap for everything. The police let him know, however, that B has made the very same deal. Additionally, the police tell him that if they both incriminate the other, they will both get five years.

So what should A do? If he remains silent, he runs the risk of incurring the most severe punishment—the ten-year sentence. Betraying his partner is the only way to avoid this. However, the same is true for B. If A and B trust each other they could each end up with a relatively light sentence—only two years. But if either has any reservations about the other's loyalty, then they both must talk, and that way they end up with at least five years. In this way, the PD effectively pits our defensive and trusting instincts against one another.

The interesting finding is that our trusting instincts win out far more often than any theory predicts. In one-off encounters—where opportunities for reciprocity or reputational enhancement are nil—anywhere from 20 to 50% of players will cooperate with their partners (i.e., they will keep silent). To put it another way, even when A stands no chance of getting a later pay-back from B, or any benefits from an enhanced reputation, he is still much more likely to trust B, and risk incurring the stiffest penalty, than we would expect him to be. This suggests that humans are naturally set at a higher "default value" of trusting than the usual evolutionary theories of altruism would predict.[10]

This finding has been replicated using another game scenario called the Ultimatum game. In this game, one player, called the proposer, is given a sum of money (say, $10). The proposer is then allowed to split the money in any proportion he or she desires with a second player, called the responder. So, for example, the proposer could keep all the money and give the responder none, or the proposer could split the money equally ($5 for pro-poser, $5 responder). The responder has the option of either accepting the proposer's offer or rejecting it. If the responder accepts the offer, both get to keep their money. If the responder rejects the offer, then neither player gets to keep any money. In terms of pure self-interest, the proposer should offer a split that maximizes his or her gain (such as $9 for proposer, $1 for responder). Likewise, the responder should be willing to accept any nonzero amount since acceptance will always lead to greater monetary gain than rejection (even just $1 is still $1 more than what the responder had prior to the offer).

As with the PD game, however, even in anonymous one-shot interac-tions where the effects of both reciprocity and reputation are eliminated, both proposers and responders show unexpectedly high levels of coopera-tion. Proposers tend to offer 30–45% of the money, and responders tend to reject offers lower than this. This suggests that both parties are operating by a norm of fairness and are willing to forgo selfish gains in order to adhere to this norm. If this is so, then we would expect the average splits offered by proposers and the acceptance/rejection thresholds of responders to show cultural variation depending on the norm of fairness present in that culture—and this is exactly what has been found.[11]

Finally, "public goods" games have provided another venue for dem-onstrating that people will often follow social norms even when it is costly and contrary to their own self-interest. In public goods games, people are provided with an initial sum of money and are given the option to allocate a certain proportion of it to a communal pot. The experimenter then aug-ments the pot by some proportion (often doubling it) and redistributes the money equally to all participants. So, for example, suppose that four play-ers are each given $10. If all four put half of their money into the communal pot (bringing that total to $20), and the experimenter doubles and redistributes the money, then each player ends up with \$15—\$5 more than they started with. Thus, with equal levels of cooperation all players come out ahead. However, suppose that only three players contribute half and one player contributes nothing (thus, \$15 in the pot). Now with doubling and redistribution each player gets \$7.50, so the three cooperators end up with \$12.50, while the noncooperator gets \$17.50. Thus, freeloading can lead to a greater payoff than cooperating, provided enough cooperators are still left in the group.

Repeated rounds of public goods games usually lead to a breakdown of cooperation, as players realize that freeloading results in greater gains and each player increasingly protects himself or herself from exploitation. However, if players are allowed to punish freeloaders, a high level of cooperation can be maintained. A number of studies have shown that even in anonymous one-shot scenarios where reciprocity and reputational effects are eliminated, players will engage in the costly punishment of freeloaders.[12] That is, they will allow substantial sums to be deducted from their own purse in order to extract a price from the freeloader. This demonstrates that people will aggressively enforce group norms even when it is contrary to their own self-interest.

Lab studies showing the costly enforcement of group norms have been complemented by real-world observations. Anthropologists Natalie and Joseph Henrich have recently shown how the same adherence to and enforcement of group norms are demonstrable in the daily lives of members of the Chaldean community in Detroit, Michigan (USA).[13]

The Origin of Group Norms: Is Group-Level Selection Needed?

If the concept of group norms is necessary to provide a complete explanation of human cooperation, then from where did group norms originate? In one sense the answer to this is easy and uncontroversial: Group norms are simply rules or conventions of behavior that naturally emerge within groups to help organize them—such as people lining up for movie tickets or keeping to the right on sidewalks. At another level, however, the origin of group norms becomes far more contentious. If different norms emerge among different groups (which is highly likely) and these groups compete with each other (more contentious), the result would be that those groups with more adaptive norms would proliferate, while the groups with less adaptive norms would slowly die out (taking their norms with them). Thus, group-level competition (or group selection) could account for the commonly occurring norms present today. However, until very recently the notion of group selection was anathema to most evolutionists.

The perceived strength of theoretical concepts such as kin selection, reciprocity, and indirect reciprocity was that they seemed to provide an adequate explanation for prosocial behaviors without any recourse to group selection. Group selection, or the notion that some things evolve for "the good of the group" or "the good of the species," had fallen badly out of favor in the mid-1960s after George Williams published a critical and highly influential review of the theory.[14] The problem with group selection was fairly simple: How could a trait that offered group-level benefits, such as indiscriminate helping, possibly spread in descendant populations if it constituted a disadvantage to the one possessing the trait?

For example, reconsider the "helper at the nest" bird. Suppose there is some gene that predisposes a bird to help others raise their nestlings (a vast oversimplification but useful for present purposes). If this bird goes around helping other birds in his flock raise their young, that is certainly "good for the flock." However, this helper bird is helping to raise young who are not his own and thus do not share his "helper" gene. His efforts are having the ironic effect of benefiting the reproductive success of those without a genetic disposition toward helpfulness while detracting from his ability to propagate his own genes. Helping others actually raises the likelihood that the next generation will be disproportionately populated not by helpers, but by lazy birds who sit around waiting to be helped. Nice guys (or nice guy's genes) lose again. An example such as this highlights the dead-end logic of any explanation that relies on group selection or "good of species" arguments.

Any evolutionary explanation for the spread of helping behaviors must somehow specify how the helping behavior did not simultaneously handicap the helper's chances of reproductive success. Kin selection, reciprocal altruism, and indirect reciprocity all pass this critical test. Individuals are helping others, but they are not helping in such a way that they jeopardize their own genetic self-interests. There is always some payback for their helpfulness, whether it be through kin descendancy, favors repaid later, or benefits accrued through the enhanced status of a good reputation.

In recent years, though, a limited form of group selection has made a comeback. A number of researchers have made a compelling case that the mechanisms used to explain cooperation in nonhuman species are inadequate for understanding the full spectrum of human cooperation. They contend that a form of group-level selection called "cultural group selection" is required in order to fully explain human niceness.[15] Cultural group selection is the idea that human groups with varying cultural norms compete with one another—and some groups win, while others lose. This competition could take the form of direct conflict, or it could involve the movement of people from less successful to more successful groups, with immigrants adopting the culture of their new group, or some combination of the two. In any case, the end result would leave certain groups and their cultural norms standing, and others disappearing.

Evidence for Group-Level Competition

One of the most commonly cited examples of cultural group selection in action was the conflict between the Nuer and Dinka tribes of southern Sudan. In the early 1800s the Nuer began a steady expansion and conquest of Dinka territories. Anthropologist Raymond Kelly studied this process and concluded that had British colonialism not halted the conflict in the early 1900s, the Dinka would most likely have been wiped out.[16] The Nuer and Dinka, who were descended from common stock, had much in common in terms of lifestyle, subsistence practices, and technology. However, a key cultural difference lay at the heart of the Nuers' success. In Nuer culture, bride-price payments were made exclusively to paternal relatives, while among the Dinka, bride-price payments were diffusely spread across both paternal and maternal relatives. The Nuers' more restrictive policy had the effect of cultivating strong patriarchal alliances among Nuer clans. These alliances were critical in times of conflict with other groups. Dinka alliances were more fragile and less kin-based. In all their years of conflict there was not a single instance of a Dinka defeat of a Nuer army. The Nuer/Dinka conflict does not appear to be an isolated event. Evidence from traditional societies in both North America and New Guinea indicates that intergroup conflicts similar to that observed between the Nuer and Dinka were not uncommon. In New Guinea, over a 25-year period, extinction rates for tribes in different regions ranged from 8% to 31%. A worldwide sampling of hunter-gatherers shows that 64% engage in warfare at least once every two years, and only 10–12% could be considered "peaceful."[17]

These historical/ethnographic data are complemented by recent laboratory findings. One study recently pitted two societal norms against each other in a public goods game.[18] They allowed participants to play under either a sanctioning ethic, where free riders could be punished, or a nonsanctioning ethic, where they could not.

Initially, most of the players chose the nonsanctioning ethic. But over time, the vast majority (nearly 93%) switched to the sanctioning group, where they contributed generously to a public fund and actively punished free riders. They did this even if they had been stingy and practiced free riding when in the sanction-free context. The sanctioning ethic, with its inherent threat of punishment, simultaneously encouraged generosity and discouraged free riding, resulting in greater overall rewards for all players. This experiment provides an empirical demonstration that group norms matter.

A group with a cultural norm of cooperation coupled with active punishment of noncooperators can win out in direct competition with a group possessing a more individualistic norm when people are allowed free migration between the groups.

Evidence for group-level competition can also be gleaned from genetic and archaeological sources, suggesting that this form of competition may extend deep into our evolutionary history. Converging studies examining mutation patterns in mitochondrial DNA point to a rapid population expansion in certain anatomically modern human populations in Africa beginning at around 70,000 ybp. Archaeologist Paul Mellars argues that a socially and technologically advanced group of modern humans expanded precipitously at this time, absorbing or replacing both adjacent African hominin populations and, in relatively short order, far-flung archaic hominins worldwide. Evidence of intentionally procured and transported red ochre and other mineral pigments goes back more than 200,000 years. One purpose of these pigments may have been as body markings used for social or group-level identity. By 130,000 ybp there is evidence of perforated shell beads, which may have served a similar purpose. Thus, by about 200,000 years ago, hominins were consciously marking themselves along tribal lines—lines along which competition for mates and resources very likely took place.[19]

Collectively these data suggest that group competition was not a trivial force in our ancestral past and that groups with social norms that offered a competitive advantage (such as the Nuer) were likely to proliferate. This finding should not necessarily be surprising. Darwin himself looked to group-level competition as a mechanism behind the emergence of moral behaviors among humans.

> It must not be forgotten that although a high standard of morality gives but a slight or no advantage to each individual man and his children over the other men of the same tribe, yet that an advancement in the standard of morality and an increase in the number of well-endowed men will certainly give an immense advantage to one tribe over another. There can be no doubt that a tribe including many members who, from possessing in a high degree the spirit of patriotism, fidelity, obedience, courage, and sympathy, were always ready to give aid to each other and to sacrifice themselves for the common good, would be victorious over other tribes; and this would be natural selection.[20]

Getting Cultural Group Selection to Work

If groups with different norms competed with each other in our evolutionary past, and the groups with "better" norms won out, then this seems to provide a tidy explanation for why humans today seem compelled to follow certain norms (such as fairness) even when it goes counter to their individual self-interest. But another question arises: What prompted individuals to start following norms in the first place, especially when those norms put them at a fitness disadvantage? Aren't we just back to the old group selection problem again?

While cultural group selection sounds good in theory, getting it to work in practice requires surmounting a formidable obstacle. The personal benefit of being part of a good group has to exceed the benefit gained by being selfish. Suppose I do Fred a favor that costs me three hypothetical units of evolutionary fitness. If, on the whole, my group is a cohesive, altruistic, "good" group, then I might reap some of this cost back by virtue of my enhanced reputation for niceness within the group, and I might get even more of it back when Fred repays my favor (since in a good group most people follow a norm of fairness that compels them to repay favors). Thus, when all the chips are counted my altruism may have cost me very little, or I may even have come out slightly ahead. This is what researchers call "cheap altruism."

Altruism can be kept cheap in groups where members routinely follow and enforce a norm of cooperation (or, as I like to say, a "norm of niceness."). But suppose my group is not so good; suppose that it has no norm of niceness but instead follows a different norm—a norm of individualism. My favor might be looked upon by other group members as evidence that I am a "sucker," and thus I reap few or no reputation points. Moreover, if Fred never pays me back (as happens more often in a "bad" group), then indeed my altruism has been quite costly. In this instance selfishness (like Fred's) is far more beneficial.

Let's extend the scenario even further. What about acts like those mentioned earlier: anonymous donations to charity, tipping in an out-of-town restaurant, queuing up calmly for concert tickets, and so on? Suppose one had been raised in a "good" group where generous acts were almost always either "cheap" or even personally beneficial. Over time one might become habitually nice since one's experience has suggested that, on average, niceness is likely to lead to personally beneficial or at least no-worse-than-neutral results. Or, possibly, one might be inclined to be nice in order to ensure that the group remains a "good" group, where the niceness norm is respected and altruistic behaviors are encouraged. This may be the origin of the gratuitous niceness often present among humans. I give blood or tip generously in a strange restaurant in the hopes that my actions and example will raise the general level of altruism around me, which may in turn come back to benefit me directly—if, say, I someday need a transfusion—or indirectly, as when the cashier at the grocery store pops two cents in the register so that I don't have to break a dollar.

The bottom line is that gratuitous niceness works evolutionarily only if we can keep it "cheap." Keeping it cheap means that it must occur within the context of a "good" group, one that is likely to appreciate and reward altruistic acts. For this to happen, two conditions must be met: (1) noncooperative selfishness must be punished by cohesive, stable, and broad-based coalitions where the cost to individual coalition members is low and the deterrent effect is high, and (2) the number of cheaters within a group must be kept low so that the need to punish is infrequent.[21]

We are then led to a critical evolutionary question: How did our ancestors establish and maintain these conditions such that "human" levels of cooperation could emerge? It is here that religion very likely played an important role. To ensure good groups where gratuitous niceness can flourish, we must accomplish two things: (1) get people to follow the rules (i.e., the norms of niceness) and (2) motivate people to punish those who don't follow the rules. With this in mind, images of commandments being handed down from mountaintops or Puritans putting people on display in stocks in the village square fall powerfully into place. But divine laws and inquisitors' racks were not the first or even the most effective tools in religion's arsenal for getting people to behave. In its earliest evolutionary stages, religion simply took advantage of a very natural and very potent mechanism for behavioral control. When is it that people are most likely to behave? When they are being watched.

Social Scrutiny and the Reduction of Selfishness

Cheating—taking benefits without repayment—undermines reciprocal altruism. Cheating, however, can be drastically reduced when people know they are being watched. Considerable social science research has demonstrated that when people know their actions are under public scrutiny they adhere more scrupulously to group norms and behave more reasonably, courteously, generously, honestly, and (for males) bravely. Furthermore, publicly observed behaviors also have a stronger impact on one's self-perception than private behaviors do.[22]

A number of recent studies have demonstrated the power of perceived public scrutiny in generating prosocial behavior. For example, one study used the aforementioned public goods paradigm to test the effect of perceived public observation on generosity.[23] Subjects played the game on computers in a common room, but separated by opaque dividers in order to retain anonymity. However, in one condition an image of a cute-looking robot face (Kizmet) appeared on the screen as the game was played. When subjects were under Kizmet's "gaze," donations to the communal pot increased nearly 30% compared to when donations were done "privately." An important message from this study is that even when our "rational" mind knows we are not being watched (subjects, after all, were confronted by an *image* of an inanimate robotic face), the mere suggestion of public scrutiny affects us at a more primal, unconscious level. The same automatically triggered anxiety-provoking nervous system mechanisms that warn us of physical threat are very likely kick into action at the faintest hint of public observation.

A second study demonstrated that these same automatic responses can be found outside the lab. For years a staff room at the University of Newcastle in England operated using the "honesty box" system, where employees paid for drinks by simply putting the appropriate amount of money in a small container; no cashier monitored the process to ensure that the correct amount or, for that matter, any amount was put into the box. Over a number of weeks, Melissa Bateson and her colleagues Daniel Nettle and Gilbert Roberts alternated the poster just above the box such that it depicted either flowers or a set of eyes staring right at the would-be drink purchaser. They found that during the weeks when the eyes were present, average contributions to the honesty box increased nearly threefold. "Our brains are programmed to respond to eyes and faces whether we are consciously aware of it or not," Bateson commented afterward.[24]

Maybe even the eyes and faces are superfluous. Another recent study showed that mere unconscious verbal hints of public or supernatural observation can produce increases in prosocial behavior.[25] Subjects played the dictator game, where one subject (the giver) is given a sum of money that she is allowed to share in any way she chooses with a second subject (the receiver). Both giver and receiver are allowed to keep the amounts allotted to them. So if the giver is provided $10, she can keep all $10 or split it in any fashion with the receiver.

Prior to playing the game, givers were required to unscramble words to create sentences. For some subjects the sentences contained religious words such as "God," "spirit," "sacred," and so on. For others, the sentences contained either no consistent conceptual references, neutral references, or secular moral references such as "court," "jury," "police," and so forth. Subjects who received the religious primes were found to be significantly more generous compared to subjects in either the "no reference" or "neutral reference" conditions. For example, while givers in the "no reference" and "neutral reference" conditions allocated, on average, only $1.84 and $2.56 respectively to receivers, givers who saw religious references allocated $4.22 (study 1) and $4.56 (study 2). Interestingly, givers who saw secular references were as generous (averaging $4.44) as religiously primed subjects. These increases in generosity occurred despite the fact that nearly all the subjects reported that they were unaware of the conceptual references in the sentences. The authors specifically cite unconscious mechanisms sensitive to the potential for public evaluation as a highly likely explanation for the results: "In sum, we are suggesting that the activation of God concepts, even outside of reflective awareness, matches the input conditions of an agency detector and, as a result, triggers this hyperactive tendency to infer the presence of an intentional watcher."[26] The fact that the secular terms present in this study made reference to punishment and surveillance (e.g., court, jury, police) seems to offer confirmation for this interpretation.

Finally, another study has found that our "hyperactive tendency" to be on the lookout for judgmental observers is so sensitive that it can even be triggered by ghost stories. Subjects playing a competitive computer game were less likely to cheat if they had been told beforehand that a ghost had recently been spotted in the lab. Not even animals appear immune to the powerful effects of public scrutiny. When it is being watched by other fish, the cleaning wrasse fish grooms its customers in the friendliest possible way, but without an audience it enjoys a nibble or two of the customer's skin.[27]

These studies provide a strong empirical basis for a commonsense intuition: Everyone acts better when under the public eye. The fear of public condemnation is a powerful motivating force for getting people to internalize and follow group norms of altruism. It is in following these norms that humans display levels of cooperation not found in other species. The power of public scrutiny stems from two basic evolutionary mechanism: (1) reputation building, and (2) fear of punishment. Thus, while perceived public scrutiny compels people to internalize group norms, leading to higher forms of cooperation than would be expected based on traditional evolutionary mechanisms, public scrutiny's power is, nevertheless, still rooted within these same traditional mechanisms. Religion, then, simply extends these basic mechanisms into a supernatural realm. The reputation we build is not only with fellow group-mates with but with gods and spirits as well. The punishment we fear is not only human in origin, but supernatural as well.

Reputation

As discussed earlier, the risks of reciprocal altruism can be reduced by cooperating only with those who have a history of repaying debts—indirect reciprocity. Indirect reciprocity implies that reputations can be an important currency in establishing cooperative relationships, and there is evidence that humans are extremely sensitive to reputation. Among many hunter-gatherers, a man's reputation as a successful hunter serves as a "quality display" affecting both his social status and reproductive success. In "honor" cultures such as the Saga of Iceland or the American South, social order was based on an individual's reputation for upholding social expectations.[28]

In the laboratory, public goods games have provided an avenue for investigating the process of reputation-building as it relates to reciprocity and prosocial behavior.[29] Findings indicate that when subjects know a person has behaved selfishly in an earlier round of the game, they are significantly less helpful to that person in subsequent rounds. Furthermore, helping is itself affected by whether or not one's reputation is being affected by the act of helping. One study found that those in a position to be generous were half as likely to do so if their generosity was irrelevant to their reputation-building. These studies suggest that we are naturally inclined to keenly observe others and adjust our behavior toward them accordingly, while doing our best to ensure that our public actions have the highest possible reputation payoff.

These effects have been replicated broadly across varied cultural settings. Research with public goods games has been carried out in numerous industrialized societies (the United States, Western Europe, Yugoslavia, Japan, and Israel) and 15 hunter-gatherer or small-scale societies in 12 countries across five continents.[30] While important cross-cultural variability is present, some general patterns have emerged. In nearly all cases, people evidenced a profound concern for establishing and guarding a public reputation for fairness (as defined by their culture), and they were willing to engage in costly punishment of those who violated social norms.

Human reputation effects are also magnified by language. An action need only be observed by a single other person (even surreptitiously) to have enormous consequences for the actor's public image. This fact is not lost on hunter-gatherers, who vigilantly and vigorously enforce their egalitarian ethic using gossip, cautionary tales, threats to reputation, and occasional physical aggression.[31] That reputations can suffer based on covertly observed actions may well have made the notion of supernatural observation a relatively effortless stretch for the evolving human mind.

Punishment

Public scrutiny has an impact not only on reputation, but also on physical well-being. When public shame or mere threats to reputation are inadequate to enforce cooperation, our ancestors may very well have resorted to physical punishment. Physical punishment, however, is personally costly. For example, suppose chimpanzee X grooms Y, only to have Y later refuse to share food with him. Punishing Y might be a good thing both for X personally and for the entire group. But how is Y to be punished? X could directly confront Y—but a fight could leave X with more bruises than the lost food was really worth. X could attack Y's relatives (a strategy not uncommon among nonhuman primates—and human primates, for that matter), but there is no guarantee that it would be effective or result in fewer bruises. X could get a bunch of friends together and they could collectively attack Y. That should reduce X's "bruising" cost, but the cost of lining up the allies could prove prohibitive.

Biologist Paul Bingham argues that it is exactly this "cost of punishment" problem that places constraints on the within-group altruism seen in nonhuman primate groups. Among monkeys and apes, cheating is just too easy to get away with. To evolve levels of altruism approaching those seen among modern humans, our ancestors had to somehow get over the "cost of punishment" hurdle. How did they do it? Bingham argues that it was by developing effective strategies for "punishment at a distance." Unlike other primates, humans are especially accurate and lethal throwers. We have become so familiar with the talents of baseball pitchers and football quarterbacks that we may fail to appreciate how truly unique their skills are in the animal kingdom. Furthermore, ethnographic evidence shows that these abilities are not necessarily restricted to just a few. In traditional societies where hunting with projectiles is common, the throwing accuracy of hunters can be astounding. Experienced hunters among the Khoikhoi of southern Africa are said to be able to hit a target the size of coin at a hundred paces. Using only thrown stones, Australian aboriginals can bring down wallabies and birds, both in flight and from high nests.[32]

This leads Bingham to propose that our ancestors may have used projectiles (i.e., stoning) to threaten or injure noncooperators. He points to several lines of evidence in support of this model, including (1) the fact that changes to the hand and leg bones that enable effective throwing arose at the same time as increasingly sophisticated social structures, (2) the fact that throwing implements appear to be overrepresented in the archaeological record compared to the evidence for hunting and intergroup conflict, suggesting that a substantial portion of these implements were used for intragroup "law enforcement," and (3) the fact that throughout human history within-group violence has often been more lethal than between-group violence. In the twentieth century, for example, it is estimated that between 170 and 360 million people were killed by their own governments, compared to around 42 million in the century's notorious wars.[33]

Contemporary research has demonstrated the zeal with which humans engage in moralistic punishment even when it is personally costly. To achieve humanlike levels of cooperation in relatively large groups (roughly

10–50 individuals), punishment of cheaters (and possibly even punishment of those who fail to punish cheaters) may be required. If "punishment at distance" using thrown implements lowered the cost of punishment for our ancestors, thus making it more likely that group members would willing follow altruistic group norms, then "punishment at a supernatural distance" would have lowered those costs even further.[34]

Summing Up: Getting People in Line So They Can Be Nice

Earlier I argued that organisms are nice for three reasons: (1) They are helping kin, (2) they are looking forward to later reciprocation or are themselves reciprocating an earlier favor, and/or (3) they are looking to reap the rewards of a good reputation. None of these are uniquely human. To the degree that humans engage in nice behavior that appears to fall outside these boundaries, it very likely due to the fact that more cooperative groups had a fitness advantage over less cooperative ones in our ancestral past. I argued that there are two ways for groups to establish and maintain intragroup cooperativeness that extends beyond the boundaries of kin selection, reciprocity, and indirect reciprocity: (1) by motivating people to follow group-based social norms, and (2) and by motivating them to punish those who don't follow social norms. One of the chief sources of this motivation is social scrutiny—the idea that we are being watched and judged by others. Given the close-knit nature of the hunter-gatherer groups from which we evolved, the notion of being constantly watched and evaluated was a familiar one. Experimental work shows that we are hypersensitive to the cues that suggest public observation of our behavior. Furthermore, this same work shows that we are naturally hypervigilant against freeloaders and cheaters who threaten group cohesion and that we have effective means of bringing them into line.

Back to the Levant

Shortly after 100,000 ybp, Neanderthals displaced humans in the Levant, pushing them back to their African homeland. But life in Africa was tough as well. Rapid climate changes producing cycles of drought and resource deprivation were not uncommon. As if to put an exclamation point on these brutal cycles, around 70,000 ybp Mount Toba on Sumatra Island erupted, degrading the global climate even further. Our species was nearly wiped out. However, a bold few managed to survive. Not only did they survive, but over time their numbers expanded. Recent genetic evidence indicates that around 70,000 ybp a select subset of the modern human population in Africa began a dramatic expansion. Coincident with this expansion is evidence of new tool technologies and some of the first signs of symbolic thinking—the most famous of which are the incised ochre plaques and perforated shell beads dated to around 75,000 ybp from Blombos Cave in South Africa. From out of Africa, a new species emerged that could no longer be turned back. "New" not in the sense of body structure, for in that way the new creatures differed only modestly, if at all, from their predecessors of 100,000 earlier; but new in the sense of cultural organization.[35]

These new humans had found ways to work together that were unprecedented in evolutionary history. They were more cooperative, more socially complex, and better-organized than any species that had come before. And a key to how they achieved this unprecedented level of social organization lay deep in a cave of the Tsodilo Hills of Botswana. It was here in 2006 that University of Oslo archaeologist Sheila Coulson discovered a ritually modified "snake rock," dated to around 70,000 ybp.[36] The boulder, 6 meters long by 2 meters high, had a natural snakelike appearance that had been intentionally modified so that incoming natural light gave the impression of scales on its surface, while firelight gave the impression of undulating movement. For Coulson, these modifications strongly suggested that the site had been used for consciousness-altering rituals. The python plays an especially prominent role in San creation myths, and the Tsodilo Hills are thought to be sacred. Thus, it is around this same time that we have the first evidence of religion. Our ancestors had enlisted the supernatural as a player in their social world, and this, I believe, made all the difference in their social transformation.

3

"Every Move You Make"

First Signs of the Supernatural Eye

We humans are hypersensitive to the barest hints of public observation and quickly "make nice" whenever we think we are being watched. Social scrutiny, however, has its limitations—as any parent knows, you just can't watch everyone all the time. But the gods can. When religion first emerged among our hominin ancestors, one of its chief functions was to increase social scrutiny, which increased conformity to social norms. In our evolutionary past, more cohesive, cooperative groups had an advantage over more individualistic ones. This advantage was very likely decisive during times of resource stress, when group competition intensified.

Sometime between the disappearance of *Homo sapiens* from the Levant (about 100,000 ybp) and the Upper Paleolithic in Europe (about 35,000 ybp), some of our ancestors thought up the idea of a supernatural world. The world they envisioned was inhabited by spirits, ancestors, and gods who were keenly interested in the behavior of their earthly charges and kept a close eye on them, ready to pounce on the first signs of deviance. The idea was an evolutionary winner. Groups who had it fanned out across the globe and quickly overwhelmed those who didn't. In this chapter, I argue that in its earliest manifestation, religion represented a supernaturalizing of social life.

The Social Transformation of the Upper Paleolithic

Why are we (*Homo sapiens sapiens*) the only hominin species left on earth? Two hundred thousand years ago, when anatomically modern humans first emerged, there were at least four other hominin species around. Additionally, for the first 100,000 years or so of our ancestors' existence, the archaeological record reveals nothing to distinguish them from other hominins, and certainly nothing to predict their eventual dominance.

For many decades, most archaeologists and anthropologists believed that the advanced cognition that gave *Homo sapiens* a decisive advantage over other hominins emerged suddenly in what was called an "Upper Paleolithic Revolution." Around 40,000 ybp, the European archaeological record erupts with a trove of remains indicating a quantum leap in thought and behavior: sophisticated tools, stunning cave art, ceremonial weapons, abstract figurines, evidence of food storage, and elaborate burial sites with symbolic grave offerings.[1]

Increased social complexity was a key component of this revolution. Cro-Magnon (our forerunners in Europe) settlement sites from the Upper Paleolithic (UP) are generally larger and more spatially structured than those of Neanderthals. The larger sites could indicate either more people at a particular site or greater seasonal aggregation of otherwise dispersed groups or both. In any case, it is an important social change from earlier periods. Cro-Magnons also participated in far more long-distance trading networks than Neanderthals. One recent study found that Cro-Magnons and Neanderthals differed only marginally in their hunting tactics and success rates. Instead, what gave modern humans an advantage was not technological or strategic but social. Modern humans were able to coordinate their foraging activity over larger ranges, and they took advantage of extensive, far-flung trading networks.[2]

The UP also offers the first evidence of elaborate burial sites with abundant grave goods. These burials show that UP societies were becoming increasingly stratified. Obviously, not everyone was buried with such ceremony. We can surmise that those offered such an elaborate send-off were the elites of what was no longer a purely egalitarian hunter-gatherer world. Relatedly, it is at this time that prestige objects become regular features of the archaeological record. Such objects typically denote status in traditional societies. By the time of the Upper Paleolithic, *Homo sapiens sapiens* had become the most socially sophisticated species on earth. Other hominins simply couldn't compete.[3]

The idea of an Upper Paleolithic revolution implies that it took about 100,000 years for the human mind to catch up with the human body, and that it did so only after migrating from Africa to Europe. Recently, however, this idea has been challenged by those who believe that modern thought and behavior emerged gradually and that the process began in Africa. These researchers point out that some forms of sophisticated tools and behavior such as blade production, seasonal mobility, and the use of grindstones and barbed points can be found in the African archaeological record as far back as 100,000 ybp, possibly even earlier. Even more compelling are symbolic artifacts such as the intentionally inscribed red ochre plaques from Blombos Cave in South Africa (believed to be over 75,000 years old) and the perforated shell beads apparently used as personal ornamentation (between 130,000 and 70,000 years old). The aforementioned long-distance trading networks probably first began in Africa as well. The shell beads and certain tools (such as those of the Howiesons Poort industry) are made of raw materials that are not indigenous to the locations where they have been found.[4]

Genetic studies complement these archaeological findings. They show a dramatic population bottleneck followed by a relative population explosion among particular human groups in Africa sometime between 80,000 and 60,000 ybp. It was this subpopulation of *Homo sapiens* that eventually trekked out of Africa and conquered the world. A probable scenario is that cycles of drought (possibly accentuated by the Mt. Toba eruption) brought African *Homo sapiens* to near extinction. From a remnant of only about 2,000 breeding individuals, a small group of technologically and socially sophisticated humans began a precipitous expansion that eventually engulfed all of Africa and then the world. Central to their social sophistication was religion. At the same time of the worldwide spread of modern humans we see the first compelling evidence for the religious practices of shamanism, animism, and ancestor worship. Echoing the famous anthropologist Roy Rappaport, my view is that this is more than mere accident. Religion played a nontrivial role in the achievement of distinctively human society.[5]

Religion's "Primitive" Traits

It is impossible to know exactly what religion was like when it first emerged. However, we can identify what are likely to be religion's most ancient traits. Here's how the process works: If we observe similar traits across related species, we can infer that those traits were most likely inherited from their common ancestor. For example, about 7 million years ago humans and chimpanzees shared a common ancestor. Humans and chimpanzees also share a number of traits in common, such as five-fingered hands, full-spectrum color vision, and toolmaking abilities. Because these traits are shared across the two species, we can infer that they were probably present in the ancestor of both species. They are "primitive traits" passed on to both descendant species by the ancestral species, not traits that evolved independently in each species after their split from the common ancestor.

There are also several traits chimpanzees and humans don't share. For example, unlike chimpanzees (and all other African apes), humans have high paternal investment in offspring, hairless bodies, and a habitual upright stance. These traits were probably not present in the common ancestor and evolved uniquely along the hominin branch after its divergence from the chimpanzee branch. These are "derived" traits.

Thus, where we observe greater ubiquity we can infer greater antiquity: An increasingly widespread trait is likely to be a more ancient one that possibly traces back to the origin of the species. Using this same logic, we can attempt to identify religion's "primitive" traits. The traits of religion that are universal or near-universal across traditional hunter-gatherer, horticultural, or pastoral societies are likely to be religion's primitive traits—ones with a deep history that might trace back to the very origins of religion. Furthermore, we can gain even greater confidence in the antiquity of these traits if we can find evidence for them in the archaeological record. Even with all this evidence, we cannot, of course, be certain that these traits are religion's *original* traits. But the combination of ubiquity and antiquity provides the best markers of religion's primitive traits.

Using this approach, three traits emerge: ancestor worship, shamanism, and the animistic belief in natural and animal spirits.[6] Each of these traits represents a "supernaturalizing" of social life—a way in which our ancestors expanded the social world to include a supernatural layer filled with ever-vigilant spiritual monitors.

Ancestor Worship

> You, son of [so and so], why do you kill us your children? Why do you turn your back on us? Here is your beast. Take it. Look after us for we are looking after you. Why do you send illness on this child? You are greedy, you are always ready to find fault.

The quotation is from Hilda Kuper's account of the Swazi of Southern Africa.[7] The Swazi often address an ancestor as if scolding an indignant child or grumpy elder. This attitude toward the ancestors is not uncommon. Among the Lohorung Rai of eastern Nepal, ancestors are treated as equal parts unruly children needing discipline and direction, and grand-elders deserving respect and patience.[8] The emotional complexity with which the living relate to their deceased relatives mirrors, in many respects, that found among typical family members. And why shouldn't it? The ancestors are as much a part of the community as the living. The community is the living and the dead—the present and the departed; or (in a distinction particular to modern Westerners) the natural and the supernatural.

Ancestor worship is widespread across traditional [9] religions in Africa, Asia, the Pacific Islands, and the South American tropics. In his survey of traditional African religions, missionary and religious scholar Geoffrey Parrinder states flatly, "All Africans believe in the ancestors, as ever-living and watchful." Half a world away, on the Solomon Islands, the same attitude persists among the Kwaio people, for whom daily interaction with ancestors is as routine as eating, drinking, and sleeping. Interacting with the ancestors, however, does not always happen within the context of recognizable rituals. Efe Pygmies regularly interact with ancestors in the forest and in dreams, but they engage in hardly anything that would look to us like worship. The role of the ancestors is more ambiguous among native populations of North America. Among tribes in the East and on the plains, ancestor cults are infrequent, and, as is the case with many native Australians, the recently departed are often regarded fearfully. Interestingly, it is among the more socioeconomically stratified populations of America's northwestern coast that ancestor worship is more prevalent.[10]

ARCHAEOLOGICAL EVIDENCE: UPPER PALEOLITHIC BURIALS
Along with its (near) universality among traditional societies, ancestor worship also has deep evolutionary roots. Evidence of these roots can be found in elaborate Stone Age burials tens of thousands of years old. In many respects these burials reflect the rituals found among present-day traditional people, such as the Torajan highlanders of Sulawesi, Indonesia: [11]

Wrapped in a special cloth, the body would be preserved for months as the family (already a wealthy one by island standards) amassed the even greater resources necessary for an appropriately lavish funeral. Over the next few weeks, a series of minor rituals would continue to mark the passing—pigs would be sacrificed, chickens and the occasional water buffalo slaughtered—in honor of the dead man and his family. Finally, when all was ready, the funeral itself would commence. Dignitaries from neighboring villages would arrive, greeted by bejeweled and colorfully dressed junior members of the deceased's family. In all, hundreds—maybe thousands—would gather to participate in the ceremony, with elites housed in temporary shelters, and commoners left to fend for themselves. Before the assembled throngs, more buffalo would be sacrificed, and a giant stone would be toted in a procession and erected at the burial site. Before the funeral was done there would be feasting, an important exchange of gifts, and other rituals offered in respect for the dead and gratitude for the living.

In modern societies, funerals are for the living, not the dead. The elaborate Torajan burial is for the living *and* the dead. For the living, the ceremony marks the passing, allows time for mourning, and reinforces old friendships and alliances shaken by a leader's demise. The ceremony is equally important for the dead, however, for the deceased is not really gone; he has simply changed his residence and assumed new responsibilities. His earthly power and influence are merely transferred to the cosmic realm. The pantheon of ancestors who have gone before him must be made aware of his standing. He is to be received in the next world as a powerful spirit-chief, consonant with his status on earth. The extravagant funeral makes that clear. The funeral is also a sacrifice to him—a gift of respect that will earn his earthly people reciprocation in times to come. Centuries hence, should someone come across the great stone marking his burial site and the many offerings interred with the body, they will know that this was a powerful man and an honored ancestor.

Indeed, we *have* come across ancient burials reminiscent of the Torajan, some of which date as far back as nearly 30,000 ybp. Though interpretations of these sites differ, a substantive case can be made that Upper Paleolithic and Neolithic burials provide some of the first credible evidence of ancestor worship. Evidence of intentional burial with possible grave goods is present prior to this time, but in the Upper Paleolithic intentional burial becomes associated with two other factors that strengthen the case for ancestor worship: social complexity and elaborateness.

The Upper Paleolithic provides the first evidence of socioeconomically stratified societies. Abundant natural resources (migrating herds, rivers rich with fish) and technological advances allowed Upper Paleolithic peoples to move from being egalitarian hunter-gatherers to transegalitarian or complex hunter-gatherers.[12] Egalitarian hunter-gatherers move constantly in search of resources. This highly mobile lifestyle is simply not compatible with the accumulation of possessions. Instead, they subsist on what they can carry along with them: a few hunting weapons, digging sticks, slings for carrying infants, a few items to help construct temporary shelters, and their immense knowledge of their environments. By contrast, complex hunter-gatherers typically use more sophisticated technologies for harvesting and storing seasonally abundant resources (e.g., nets or traps to catch large quantities of fish during spawning season).

It is in the Upper Paleolithic that we see the first signs of hunting technologies such as traps, snares, and weirs for harvesting large quantities of game. It is also in this period that evidence of food storage pits is present, indicating that humans were storing surplus resources for later use. Furthermore, the richest Upper Paleolithic settlement sites in France, Italy, Spain, and Ukraine are situated in steep valleys and river fjord zones that would have been prime territories for the hunting of seasonally migrating animals. All of this supports the notion that Upper Paleolithic peoples were leading more sedentary lives with greater private ownership of resources and more pronounced social inequalities.[13]

In contrast to egalitarian hunter-gatherers, ancestors play an increasingly prominent role in complex hunter-gatherer societies. Resource-rich territories (e.g., streams abundant with fish, certain migration routes) critical to an entire community's well-being are typically claimed by elite families within the tribe by virtue of their ancestral lineage. For example, among the Tlingit of North America's northwestern coast, the nobles are typically from clans who claim ownership to the fishing weirs (traps) in the most prized territories. Social elites typically justify their privileged status through their filial link to powerful ancestors in the supernatural realm, whose benevolent proprietorship over resources generously provides for the entire tribe.[14]

In the Upper Paleolithic we also see unambiguously elaborate burials. Burial sites such as Sungir, Dolní Věstonice, and Saint-Germain-la-Rivière attest to the presence of an elite class whose members were laid to rest with great ceremony and lavish grave offerings. Among more recent complex hunter-gatherers, burials like this usually occur with the expectation that the deceased is soon to take his or her place as a powerful ancestor in the supernatural realm. Arguably the most impressive Upper Paleolithic burial site is Sungir, about an hour from Moscow. Here three bodies were uncovered— an adult male and two adolescents. Each was elaborately adorned with thousands of fine ivory beads, necklaces, and bracelets. Additionally, ivory spears and other artifacts were interred with the bodies. Archaeologist Randall White has estimated that the labor-hours necessary to produce the beads alone would have run into the thousands—per body. Though less elaborate than Sungir, the triple burial at Dolní Věstonice in the Czech Republic features bodies lavished with necklaces of ivory and pierced canine teeth, while at Saint-Germain-la-Rivière a young adult female was interred with "imported" and carefully perforated deer-tooth ornaments.[15]

The Neolithic (8000–3000 ybp) site of Lepinski Vir provides evidence of burials within domestic structures. Located on a bank above the Danube in the Carpathian Mountains, Lepinski Vir is composed of about 50 permanent structures, many of which contain unusually large hearths decorated with carved boulders, human bones, and other artifacts. In many structures, a burial vault is located below the hearth. The small size of the structures and the scarcity of domestic refuse suggest that Lipinski Vir was not a permanent residence, but an intermittent religious site for feasts, rituals, and veneration of the dead. Similar Neolithic grave sites have been found at Sannai Maruyama, Japan, and in Skateholm and Bredasten in Scandinavia. These sites may be analogous to sacred sites honoring the dead found among Native Americans of the northwestern coast, Maya Indians of Central America, and Melanesian Islanders. The monuments, ornaments, and grave offerings associated with Upper Paleolithic and Neolithic grave sites are consistent with the practices of ancestor cults of today's complex hunter-gatherers.[16]

THE ANCESTORS AS SOCIAL PLAYERS While archaeological evidence suggests that ancestral cults may reach deep into human prehistory, anthropological evidence indicates that ancestors are social players in the ongoing activities of *living* communities.[17] From his years of living and working with Malawi tribesmen, missionary and anthropologist T. Cullen Young concluded:

> To . . . African men and women in the backland villages, life from day to day, and we might legitimately say, from moment to moment, has no meaning at all apart from ancestral presence and ancestral power. . . . the African community is a single, continuing unit, conscious of no distinction, in quality, between its members still here on earth, and its members now there, wherever it may be that the ancestors are living.[18]

Wherever ancestor worship or veneration is found, the ancestors themselves are seen as "interested parties" in the current affairs of the community. For example, among the Kwaio people of the Solomon Islands, the ancestors are believed to be ever-present bearers of both good and bad fortune.[19] They play an active role in the community's health, prosperity, fertility, and general success (or lack thereof) and are especially attentive to rules of taboo. Violations of taboo can anger an ancestor and bring about misfortune unless proper sacrifices are made.

Among the Lohorung Rai of Nepal, a newborn baby is not considered a community member or even a "person" until it is ritually "introduced" to the ancestors. This is believed to be essential to the future health and success of the infant, so much so that until it is completed (usually five or six days after birth), all other ancestral rites *by all* households within the community are prohibited. In this way, the ritual demands of the ancestors force the entire community to be involved in the future prospects of every newborn. Though important cultural variations exist, the notion of ancestors as "interested parties" who must be appeased and who punish transgressions is a common theme worldwide.[20]

Why are the ancestors interested? The reasons vary, but common themes are present. Often, the land and the ancestors are intimately connected. Among many African tribes, ancestors are the ultimate owners of the land, responsible for its productivity. Among Australian aboriginals, ancestors are thought to be a part of the land itself. After creating the land, the ancestors' spirits returned to it, inhabiting the mountains, streams, and other landforms. In other instances, ancestors are thought to return to the community in the form of animals who provide information or resources to the living.[21]

In other societies, such as the Maori or many traditional African tribes, the ancestors' very existence depends on the fertility and fidelity of the earthly community. By remembering the ancestors through cultural traditions, and by procreating—which provides a means for the ancestors' rebirth into the community—the existence of the ancestors is sustained. Thus, ancestors are thought to be especially concerned with upholding social order through right behavior, observance of tradition, and avoidance of taboo, so as to ensure the community's continued fecundity and the security and legitimacy of its offspring. Finally, the ancestors may simply be regarded as powerful spirits who can provide protection, fertility, and prosperity in return for honor and sacrifice.[22]

However it is envisioned, the ancestor's role is unambiguously *social*. They are ever-watchful, active players in the social world, with interests, concerns, and goals that must be considered by the living. This is emphasized by the fact that the living often regard the ancestors with the same emotional cross-currents that typically characterize relations with a parent or other familial elder—respect, fear, affection, and occasionally resentment.[23] Even after their physical departure, the ancestors remain active, attentive "elders" of the earthly family.

Shamanism

> Night descends, the meat is eaten and candles are lit. One of the men appears older than the others and wears a necklace of pierced fox teeth around his neck. Throughout the evening he has been lowering his face close to the smoldering herbs and inhaling deeply. He now takes a flat slab of slate and draws upon the surface, cutting into it with a flint point. As he does so the other people gently chant. Within a few minutes he is finished, and the engraved slate is passed around the circle. He has drawn a horse; it has been carefully depicted and pro-portioned quite correctly. This slate is placed to one side. The old man—a shaman—starts again: a deep intake of the intoxicating smoke, a few minutes of intense concentration amid more chanting, another slate to pass around the circle. That too has the figure of a horse. And so this continues . . .

This is archaeologist Steven Mithen's imagining of a late Upper Paleolithic shamanistic ritual.[24] As we shall see shortly, the possibility that shamanism might stretch back tens of thousands of years is based in much more than just imagination. Before reviewing the archaeological evidence, however, we must first get a handle on what is meant by "shamanism." Strictly speaking, shamanism is associated with traditional societies across Siberia, Central Asia, and the Saami regions of Scandinavia. Shamanistic practices of one form or another, however, have been observed worldwide. It is no exaggeration to say that nearly every traditional society engages in some form of shamanistic practice.[25]

The term "shaman" comes from the Tungus root *saman*, meaning "one who is excited or raised" or simply "to know." This reflects the fact that the shaman's function is to enter an altered state of consciousness wherein he or she connects with spiritual forces in order to gain knowledge or cure illness. The shaman, then, is a spiritual practitioner—a specialist whose job is to interact with the spiritual world. The main tool of the shaman is ritually induced trance. Through years of training, often starting in childhood, the shaman perfects the art of altering his or her consciousness so as to unite with powerful supernatural forces. Through these forces the shaman gains important knowledge about how to use his or her spiritual powers to benefit the community, although it should be noted that using spiritual powers for malevolent purposes is not unheard of. Shamanism is one of the world's oldest forms of religious activity.[26] Two lines of archaeological evidence trace it back to at least the Upper Paleolithic: (1) the ritual use of deep cave sites and (2) images and artifacts depicting human/animal amalgamations.

ARCHAEOLOGICAL EVIDENCE: DEEP CAVE SITES About every two weeks or so the !Kung San gather for healing dances. The events are extraordinary spectacles. As the night descends and the fires burn, shamans dance themselves into ecstatic trance states where n/um, spiritual healing energy, boils up from within them. Once the healing power of n/um is activated, shamans lay hands on all those present, directing healing energy into them. It is not uncommon for the chanting, dancing, and healing to go on all night, as the n/um-animated shamans seem impervious to fatigue. Though diminished in frequency, the trance-dances of the !Kung continue to this day. The history of the !Kung healing ceremony is a deep one, preserved not only in oral traditions, but also by ancient rock-art depictions. Southern African rock art contains images of shamans, dressed in their familiar animal disguises, dancing furiously, sometimes bleeding from the mouth or nose as a result of their intense physical exertion and ecstatic mental state. Though dates for the art are unclear, many are thought to be thousands of years old.[27]

Rock art is not the only archaeological evidence of prehistoric southern African shamanism. As discussed previously, the 70,000-year-old ritually modified snake rock in a deep cave site of the Tsodilo Hills of Botswana may be the oldest evidence of shamanistic rituals. If so, it suggests that shamanism emerged among anatomically modern humans prior to their exodus from Africa. As they spread from Africa to Europe, they took their religion with them. The deep cave sites of Europe provide some of the most compelling evidence of shamanism among Cro-Magnons.

A number of researchers have argued that Upper Paleolithic cave art depicts shamanistic themes and rituals. Archaeologist David Lewis-Williams notes that the idea of a three-tiered cosmos is a common theme in shamanistic traditions. In this view, the world of daily experience sits between spiritual worlds both above (in the sky) and below (underground, underwater). He interprets much of the Upper Paleolithic cave art as reflecting this theme. For example, the very fact that cave artists often used deep, isolated, difficult-to-access recesses of the cave as venues for their work suggests to him that they were attempting to draw nearer to the lower spiritual realm. Furthermore, intentionally painted handprint impressions are not uncommon in many deep cave sites. Lewis-Williams argues that these handprints represent a symbolic "pushing through" the earthly membrane of the cave wall in order to access a spiritual world "just beyond."[28]

Archaeologist Bryan Hayden has summarized a number of converging lines of evidence consistent with the hypothesis that Upper Paleolithic deep cave sites were venues for shamanistic rituals. First, ethnographically, caves are frequently understood as a gateway to the underworld. Second, remains that would suggest regular use, such as torches, fires, tools, or food, are rare at these sites, suggesting that they were occupied only sporadically—as would be expected of ritual venues. Third, the spaces where paintings and other ritualistic artifacts are found are often small and isolated, heightening the sensory effects that would induce ecstatic states. Fourth, many of the animals depicted at these sites are not ones commonly used for food; instead, they appear to have symbolic importance as representations of power or ferocity. Furthermore, some of the animal images are purely mythic, such as the long-horned horselike creature of Lascaux, possibly the result of shamanistic hallucinations. Fifth, along with the strange animals, many cave sites also have bizarre symbols and graphics that closely resemble the visual experiences that commonly occur when one falls into an altered state of consciousness. Finally, at many of these sites, one finds children's hand and footprints. Among complex hunter-gatherers, children are commonly involved in rituals of initiation where highly emotive, consciousness-altering rituals are used to call upon guardian spirits. Taken together, this evidence supports the idea that these deep cave sites were used for shamanistic rituals where altered states of consciousness and union with the spiritual world were achieved.[29]

ARCHAEOLOGICAL EVIDENCE: IMAGES AND ARTIFACTS A consistent theme in shamanism is that of "soul flight," where in the midst of an ecstatic mental state, the shaman's spirit inhabits that of an animal or unites with the animal's spirit. Shamanistic "soul flight" may very well lie behind many of the over 50 part-human/part-animal images found among Upper Paleolithic cave art. Along with these images, researchers have also found similar figurines and sculptures such as the half-man/half-lion face from El Juyo, Spain, or the lion-headed human statuette from Hohlenstein, Germany.[30]

Two particular cave-art images are especially compelling to many archaeologists as reflective of shamanistic themes. The "sorcerer" image from the sanctuary at Les Trois-Frères shows a partially upright horselike creature with reindeer antler, owlish eyes, bear paws, and a human beard. It has been interpreted by some as a shaman uniting with his animal spirit-helper. Even more stunning is an image located in the shaft at Lascaux. Just below a drawing depicting a wounded bison, a man with a birdlike head appears to be suspended in midair or possibly falling. The man's body is rigid, and he appears to have an erection. Adjacent to him is a bird perched upon a staff. The fact that the man is sexually aroused suggests that he is not dead, but more likely in some highly emotional mental state. The birds, the staff, and a possible depiction of hunting or conflict (the wounded bison) are all motifs associated with shamanism that add credence to the notion that this is a shaman in the midst of an ecstatic spiritual transformation.[31]

The Fumane Cave of northern Italy provides perhaps the oldest image of a shaman. Dated to around 35,000 ybp, it depicts a person dressed in the familiar ritualistic garb of a shaman, complete with the distinctive antlered headgear. This image is similar to more recent rock-art images from Siberia that also depict recognizable shamanistic paraphernalia, including antlered headgear, elaborate animal costumes, and wood frame drums.[32] The Fumane image provides evidence of shamanism at the very beginning of the Upper Paleolithic. In combination with the earlier mentioned find from Tsodilo Hills, this evidence strongly suggests that the roots of shamanism predate the Upper Paleolithic.

SHAMANISM THEN AND NOW Just because shamanism extends deep into our evolutionary history does not necessarily mean that the current practice of shamanism is comparable to what our Paleolithic ancestors were doing. Whenever we use the practices of existing traditional societies as a model for our ancestral past we must be cautious since current practices are influenced by current ecological and social conditions—conditions that may be vastly different from those of the ancient past. However, there are reasons to suspect that current shamanistic practices may mirror those of the deep past. First, while shamanism today varies greatly across the globe, a core commonality exists—that is, the altered state of consciousness used to connect with the spiritual world. From the tropics to the Arctic, the shaman is defined by the ecstatic mental state that he or she achieves. Since this mental state is a human characteristic, not specifically dependent on particular social or ecological conditions, once the human mind evolved the capacity for it, there was potential for shamanism.

Second, shamans were (and are) typically chosen from among the mentally eccentric members of a community. Those who, as children, showed signs of "having visions" or falling spontaneously into trances, or those whose imaginative or mental powers seemed to miraculously contribute to their recovery from illness, were often seen as good candidates for shamanistic training.[33] Today, these traits might be actively discouraged, hidden, dismissed as simply childhood imagination, or seen as signs of mental illness. In the ancestral past, however, they would have been signs of a supernatural calling. People with shamanistic traits are always present within a community. What changes over time is how the community reacts to those traits.

Finally, while we can never be certain that Paleolithic images do in fact depict shamanistic rituals, there are similar but more recent images for which continuity with contemporary shamanism has been more reliably established. For example, in southern Africa centuries-old San rock art depicts traditional healing dances still practiced by the San today. The same appears to be true of some Native American rock art, which reflects initiation ceremonies and shamanistic vision quests.[34] Thus, we have a verifiable history of shamanistic rituals and ceremonies being depicted in traditional art. That Paleolithic artists may have done the same is no surprise.

THE SOCIAL ROLE OF THE SHAMAN The shaman's popular image as a bizarre mystic often obscures his or her more important social function. This function, however, has not been lost on those who study shamanism. Swedish anthropologist Ake Hultkrantz argues that it is the very core of shamanism: "[The shaman is] a social functionary who, with the help of guardian spirits, attains ecstasy in order to create a rapport with the supernatural world on behalf of his group members."[35] This rapport can take many forms. For example, a shaman may be called upon before the community embarks on an important endeavor, such as a hunt. The shaman may enter the spirit of the hunted animals and try to convince them not to resist the hunters, or he may simply gather and report important information about the animals' movements and attitudes.

In the wake of a natural disaster, poor harvest, social discord, famine, or epidemic, the shaman may be called upon to help relieve community suffering. Individuals may seek out the shaman when they suffer sickness or misfortune. In either situation, the shaman's function is to communicate with the ancestors or spirits who may be responsible for these perils. Often, the shaman finds that violations of taboo have aroused supernatural anger. By attributing supernatural authority to the observance of taboos, the shaman reinforces group norms and discourages divisive individualism. Whatever the specific task, a good shaman serves as an emissary to the supernatural world, intent on repairing or enhancing the community's relationship with the supernatural as well as its own internal bonds. As Cambridge anthropologist Piers Vitebsky puts it, "The mystic is also a social worker."[36]

Two examples highlight this. A famine-threatened Iglulik Inuit village in northern Canada enlisted a local shaman to go on a spiritual journey to the sea spirit Takanakapsaluk to find out why the community's recent hunts had been unsuccessful:

> The community gathers in a house and the shaman sits behind a curtain. . . . he calls to his helpers saying again and again "The way is made ready for me, the way opens before me!," while the audience repl[ies] "Let it be so." Finally, from behind the curtain the shaman can be heard crying "Halala—he—he—he, halala—he—he!" . . . his voice can be heard receding even further into the distance: "Halala—he!," until it is lost altogether. During the shaman's absence, the audience sits in the darkened house and hears the sighing and groaning of people who lived long ago.[37]

The journey to the lair of Takanakapsaluk is a harrowing one, and when the shaman arrives, the goddess vents her anger at him. He manages to mollify her, and she informs him that the sea's bounty has been withheld from the village because of their frequent violations of taboo. His return is no easier, and he emits a huge gasp upon reentering the house. He calls upon the assembly to confess their sins; members of the community arise, one after another, openly admitting their various transgressions. This mass catharsis is highly therapeutic. The session ends with a palpable spirit of goodwill, and optimism now pervades the community. The sins of individuals, until now successfully hidden from the human community, were brought to public light through the shaman's intercession. Similar examples of this sort have been noted among shamanistic rituals in Nepal, Korea, and Japan.[38]

Among the Sora of eastern India, the shaman's role is somewhat different. Although she (most shaman tend to be women) may intervene during a crisis, more often the shaman acts as an intermediary in the community's ongoing dialogue with the dead.[39] Shortly after death, a person's spirit is thought to be volatile, causing mischief and mayhem among the living. Any illness or misfortune may be blamed on the spirit of a recently departed friend or relative. Mourners gather around a shaman who calls upon the spirit so that it can be questioned about its actions, motivations, and state of mind. These dialogues may persist for weeks, or even years, as the living and the dead sort out their relationships. Often a negotiated settlement is achieved: The spirit agrees to become a guardian to a child who is to bear her name. Though the shaman's role here is less dramatic, her social significance is no less crucial. Since the social world involves the dead as much as the living, the shaman is a vital thread linking the two—maintaining, repairing, and transforming social bonds.

Animal and Natural Spirits

The belief in a spiritual force pervading all of nature is common among hunter-gatherers. Powerful animal spirits play a prominent role in the art, myths, and religious beliefs of traditional people as culturally and geographically diverse as the Aborigines of Australia, the Inuits of the Arctic, the Ainu of northern Japan, the Bushmen of South Africa, the Jahai of Malaysia, and numerous native North and South American tribes. Animal spirits were also prominent among the great chiefdoms of pre-Columbian America (e.g., Aztecs, Toltecs, Incas) and the early great civilizations of the Old World (Egypt, Mesopotamia). There are some exceptions and variations. For example, while Aka Pygmies believe in animal spirits, neither Mbuti nor Baka Pygmies do. Instead, Baka Pygmies believe in anthropomorphized "game spirits," while the Mbuti see the entire forest as a living spirit.[40]

Evidence for possible animal cults among our hominin ancestors takes a number of forms. First, Upper Paleolithic cave art contains thousands of animal depictions. In some instances the arrangement of animals suggests a segregation into masculine and feminine motifs. Second, at both Les Trois-Frères and Chauvet Caves there are chambers that appear to be dedicated to specific animals (or animal spirits). The "Lion Chapel" at Les Trois-Frères contains a large feline mural along with the remains of a fire surrounded by apparently deliberately placed bones. In the "bear chamber" at Chauvet Cave, there is a bear skull carefully placed atop a large limestone block. Below the block are the remains of a fire and more than 30 other bear skulls that seem to be intentionally placed.[41]

Third, at the Dolní Věstonice site in the Czech Republic, fragments of clay-baked animal forms dating to around 23,000 ybp were uncovered. They seem designed to explode when heated. Archaeologist Brian Hayden argues that these were probably used in some ritual associated with the celebration of animal spirits. Taken together, this evidence has compelled many investigators to argue that animal and other natural spirits played a prominent role in Upper Paleolithic religious practices.[42]

THE SPIRITS AS SOCIAL PLAYERS As with the ancestors, natural and animal spirits are an extension of the human social world. The spirits are social players whose interests and concerns must be considered by the living, especially in activities involving the utilization of natural resources. Individual exploitation of natural resources can be reduced by cultural prohibitions. These prohibitions can be made even more effective if buttressed by supernatural authority.

For example, in many hunting-gathering societies, hunting is not just a subsistence activity, but a sacred reciprocal exchange between social actors. The prey must be persuaded to give up its body to the hunter for food, and the hunter must perform proper rituals so that that animal's spirit can be returned to the earth. Related to this is the widespread concept of a "master of animals"—an animal spirit that guards nature against human exploitation and ensures the continual supply of animals through reincarnation. Ake Hultkrantz maintains that this notion is "extensive" among native peoples in South America and "extremely common" in North America. Similar concepts are found among Efe Pygmies in central Africa, the Chenchu and Paliyan of southern India, and the Batak of the Philippines. Additionally, reference to a "master (or mistress) of animals" can be found in Minoan and Myceanaean mythologies. Waste and sacrilege angers this master spirit, who may withhold resources from offending humans.[43]

Bringing nature into the human social sphere helps constrain how humans utilize natural resources. For example, the Itza' Maya of the Guatemalan lowlands regard the forest as alive with protective spirits. This plays a key role in their utilization of forest resources. They are, by and large, less likely than others to ravage the natural world. Similar findings have been documented among the Rock Crees of northern Manitoba and Saskatchewan.[44]

While there has been much debate over the role the spirits play in resource management, there are compelling examples where a shared religious orientation toward the land has been effective in getting competing communities to share collective resources.[45] For example, competing groups of Native Americans of the Upper Klamath River Valley of northwestern California managed a critical resource (salmon) using ritual.

Sacred ritual marked the start and duration of the harvesting season so that no single group could dominate the resource at another's expense. No fishing was permitted until all the proper rituals were completed, and violations aroused the anger of both those conducting the rituals and the supervising spirits. Violators suffered the spirits' wrath, thought to include "bad luck" and a poor catch. These beliefs were taken so seriously that as the rituals were conducted, people fled the riverbank for the surrounding mountain slopes so as to avoid the sacrilege of even gazing upon the fires built to cook the first salmon.[46]

Recent analyses indicate that the Northwest Indians had the skill, technical capacity, and appetite to decimate the Klamath Valley fish stocks but were inhibited from doing by their culture.[47] Today, 30 species of salmon (including those of the Klamath) are on the endangered species list. Ironically, current laws governing fishing are similar to the proscriptions practiced by the Northwest Indians, but the sacred orientation to the land is absent.

Across the globe, on the island of Bali, we find another example of a ritual solution to a resource management problem. For centuries the native Balinese have grown rice on steep terraced hilltops, sharing the water that flowed down the mountainside by diverting it from the main stream to the fields of different communities. But how can one prevent those upstream from diverting all the water, leaving none for those downstream? This challenge is further complicated by the need to seasonally rotate fallow and active fields among the competing groups.

This organizational nightmare was managed effectively for centuries by the water temple system.[48] A temple honoring a local deity was located at each branch in the downstream flow. The temples operated hierarchically, so that as one moved upstream the number of communities served by that temple increased, as did the generality of the deity (i.e., the number of people worshipping that deity increased). At the summit was the massive temple of Dewi Danu, the goddess of all the waters. Each temple was a meeting place for the groups served by the diverted waters originating at that point. Disputes at one level could be taken to the next level up for resolution, with the high priest of Dewi Danu serving as the ultimate authority. The steep climb from temple to temple acted as a natural disincentive to "frivolous appeals." But this alone does not explain the long tradition of success enjoyed by the water temple system. Of even greater significance is the fact that the temple priests who mediated disputes possessed a uniquely effective combination of vast technical knowledge of rice cultivation and metaphysical authority granted only to clerics.

In an attempt to increase productivity, in the 1980s the Indonesian government replaced the water temple system with more modern practices and bureaucratic oversight. The results were disastrous.[49] Eliminating the intricately coordinated rituals associated with rice cultivation disrupted the synchronized planting patterns required to control pests. When fertilizers and pesticides failed, crop production plummeted. The critical lesson was that coordinated planting patterns were key to successful rice production, and religious ritual was key to this coordination.

In many ways, the experience in Bali was reminiscent of a similar situation in ancient Rome, where secular authority was equally impotent in producing equitable resource management. According to the ancient historian Frontinus, public water flows from the Roman aqueduct were often brought to a standstill because of landowners illegally diverting resources to "water their gardens."[50] Modern technology and secular law often fail in providing the most critical element needed for effective resource management: the motivation to cooperate.

Summary

Religion often implies the mystical, the magical—the superstitious. The practical world of daily living is juxtaposed to the world of the supernatural. But this misses the mundane fact that religious ritual often has utilitarian aims. Over 40 years ago, Roy Rappaport described how the religious rituals of the Maring-speaking peoples of central New Guinea constructively regulated intercommunity conflict as well as other social, economic, and ecological issues.[51] The Klamath River and Bali examples amplify his original observations. In our evolutionary (and not so distant) past, human cooperation often benefited from viewing nature as an intentional social player. If the attitude of traditional people today is indicative of our ancestors', then it is very likely that (unlike contemporary Westerners) our ancestors didn't see the supernatural as a distant, disconnected, or even distinct realm. Familiar ancestors and guardian spirits were ever-present, readily interacting in everyday human affairs. Shamans had special access to this spiritual world, relaying its messages, and directing its energies in productive ways. The "natural" social world included the "supernatural," and religion (as we call it today) was simply the means by which that part of the social world was made accessible.

That religion's primitive traits represent a supernaturalizing of social life is not meant to suggest that more recent traits (such as monotheism or articulated theologies) do not also serve this function—quite often they do. That this characteristic is "conserved" even as religion has evolved and changed lends further support to the notion that at its core religion is relational. The significance of these particular ancient traits, however, is that (a) they coincide with evidence of a substantial advance in human social complexity, suggesting that religion played a role in the achievement of that complexity, and (b) they indicate that as far back as we can trace religion in the archaeological record, it represented an augmentation of social life.

By the Upper Paleolithic, then, religion was present. The supernatural world was already well-ensconced in human social life. The spirits were watching. The ancestors were vigilant against violations of taboo. The shaman was on call to intercede with, query, and mollify the spirits. The evidence from Fumane Cave and Tsodilo Hills, however, suggests that religion may very well have preceded the Upper Paleolithic. The next chapter will delve more deeply into the details of religion's origins. What happened during that period of time preceding our ancestors' final, decisive march out of Africa? What circumstances transformed them into religious creatures, and how did this "religious conversion" play out?

4

The African Interregnum, Part I

Good Rituals Make Good Friends

We now have the outlines of our story. Sometime after 100,000 ybp, anatomically modern humans (AMH) retreated from the Levant back to their African homeland. By 60,000 ybp they were back, expanding inexorably across Europe and Asia and leaving evidence of an unprecedented level of cognitive and social sophistication. Part of this unprecedented sophistication was religion, in the form of ancestor worship, shamanism, and animism. We will now take a closer look at that period from about 100,000 to 60,000 ybp—a time that I call "the African Interregnum." It was during this time that our ancestors were transformed from just another hominin species, to *the* hominin species. A critical part of this transformation was religious. How did this happen?

The story begins with a colossal ecological disaster that nearly brought an end to the hominin enterprise. People often find religion after grave personal suffering or tragedy. It was no different with our ancestors. The few humans who managed to survive this disaster did so by finding unprecedented ways to expand social cooperation. Religious ritual was essential to establishing and maintaining never-before-seen levels of social complexity. Furthermore, ritual behavior was the very mechanism by which we acquired our uniquely human capacity for symbolic thought. Thus, religious ritual made us human.

The Toba Eruption and Its Aftermath

Our ancestors' first excursion out of Africa ended badly. Increasingly cold conditions and encroaching Neanderthals proved too much for them. By about 90,000 ybp, they disappeared from the Levant and were back in the familiar confines of Africa. But life in Africa wasn't easy either. Periods of drought and resource deprivation were not uncommon, and the African Interregnum itself was marked by rapid climate changes and ecological stresses. If University of Illinois archaeologist Stanley Ambrose is correct, ecological conditions went from tough to horrendous sometime between 75,000 and 70,000 ybp. At around this time, Mount Toba on Sumatra island erupted, creating a global catastrophe. To appreciate Toba's impact, compare it to the largest volcanic event in recorded history—the Mount Tambora eruption of 1815. Tambora displaced some 20 cubic kilometers of ash and released high levels of sulfur into the stratosphere, resulting in a "year without summer." Toba is estimated to have displaced *800 cubic kilometers* of ash, leading to at least six consecutive years of volcanic winter.[1]

Ambrose contends that much of Southeast Asia suffered massive deforestation. The decade or so of volcanic winter that followed had global effects, lowering temperatures, shortening or eliminating growing seasons, stressing ecosystems, and producing widespread extinctions. A thousand-year ice age followed on Toba's heels; global temperatures remained abnormally low for the next millennium. Researchers debate Toba's effects on hominins. It is possible that only scattered populations of hominins survived in a few tropic refuges such as equatorial Africa. However, other evidence suggests that many hominins did survive in Europe and Asia.[2] Even apart from Toba, the period beginning about 100,000 ybp was one of rapid and sometimes calamitous climate change. Toba may have only accentuated the shifting cycles of climate change already burdening our African ancestors.

Whether directly attributable to Toba or not, genetic evidence confirms that AMH suffered a major population bottleneck around 70,000 years ago, prior to their final, decisive emergence from Africa.[3] Their numbers may have plunged to as low as a mere 2,000 breeding individuals—as close to extinction as humans have ever come. The surviving humans were of a select subpopulation that expanded precipitously thereafter, replacing other adjacent human groups and eventually replacing all other hominins worldwide. These lucky few were the ones who derived a "social solution" to changing climates and traumatic circumstances.

Archaeological Evidence of the Social Solution

The !Kung San of southern Africa are traditional hunter-gatherers who live in the harsh habitat of the Kalahari desert. Critical to their success is a system of intergroup gift exchange called *hxaro*. Exchanging gifts builds trust and cooperation among different *bands* (tribal subgroups), producing further exchanges of other material goods as well as vital bits of information such as where to find game or water. Body ornaments, such as shell beads worn as necklaces, are commonly exchanged gifts in *hxaro*.[4]

The first appearance of shell beads in the archaeological record dates to around 100,000 ybp and is associated with AMH from the Levant. Beads have also been found at Blombos Cave, South Africa, and Oued Djebbana, Algeria, both dating to around 75,000 ybp, and at Enkapune Ya Muto, Kenya, dating to about 40,000 ybp.[5] Thus, from about 100,000 to 40,000 ybp, AMH were making shell beads suitable for purposes similar to the *hxaro* practice of the !Kung. The fact that each find is composed of beads of a single type suggests that a particular value was associated with them, supporting the notion that they were used as gifts. Furthermore, the Skhul and Oued Djebbana shells were found at sites remote from their seashore origin, suggesting that they were transported there, possibly by trade networks.

Beads are not the only evidence of expanded trade networks in Africa at this time. Stone tool kits from this period have been unearthed in both southern and eastern Africa. The tools—called the Howieson's Poort, Still Bay, and Mumba tool industries—are puzzling because in many ways they appear "precious," far more modern in their construction than what would be expected for the time. Furthermore, these kits include fine-grained tools made from nonlocal, "exotic" raw materials. Stanley Ambrose concludes that these tools reflect a social response to ecological stress. As resources dwindled, local populations of AMH expanded their ranges and engaged in greater intergroup resource exchange networks, including the exchange of raw materials and artifacts. This process began what Ambrose calls the "troop to tribe" transition in human evolution.[6] Increasingly, survival meant interacting with groups on the perimeter of one's range—groups often composed of more distantly related kin and outright strangers. While these expanding alliances provided access to more widely dispersed resources, they also put pressure on social/cognitive and communicative capacities.

The Upper Paleolithic (about 35,000 ybp) record also provides indirect evidence consistent with this hypothesis. There is considerable evidence that Upper Paleolithic AMH (i.e., Cro-Magnons) were more socially sophisticated than their Neanderthal counterparts. First, Cro-Magnon campsites are larger, more frequent, more intensely used and occupied, and more spatially structured compared to those of Neanderthals. Second, many of these sites show evidence of seasonal aggregation, larger group size, and other signs of social complexity and stratification. Third, while there is evidence of wide-ranging trading networks among Cro-Magnons, similar evidence is lacking in Neanderthals. Archaeologist Clive Gamble's comparison of the relative "social landscapes" of Neanderthals and Cro-Magnons reinforces this point by demonstrating that Cro-Magnon raw material exchanges occurred across significantly longer distances.[7]

While isolating social factors apart from technological or ecological ones is always problematic, this body of evidence suggests that whatever advantage Cro-Magnons may have had over Neanderthals, the social aspect of it was very likely the most important. The social solution initiated by AMH in Africa remained in place as they spread geographically. To put it simply, they took their trading culture with them.

Thus, we have a considerable body of archaeological evidence indicating that AMH were more socially sophisticated than other hominins and that an important aspect of this sophistication was unprecedented intergroup trading networks. This increased social complexity appears to have had its origins in Africa sometime during the Interregnum period and was very likely impelled by the ecological stress resulting from rapid climate changes, possible accentuated by the Toba eruption. The next question we must address is: How did AMH manage to create and sustain this complicated social world? The answer is one with a deep history in animal social life: ritual.

Why Focus on Ritual?

Ritual is a rule-governed and generally rigidly sequenced pattern of behavior that is attention-getting and formalized. For example, consider "scrotum-grasping," a common ritual used for social bonding among male baboons.[8] Two males wishing to signal friendship will take turns briefly holding each other's testicles. Grabbing and ripping at the genitals is common when primates fight; thus, the scrotum-grasp can be understood as a ritualized version of this fighting action. However, it is a formalized or more restricted form of the fighting action—a momentary grasp rather than aggressive grabbing and ripping. The act itself is undoubtedly attention-getting, and it follows a rule-governed, relatively invariant sequence: One baboon strides up to another using a rapid, straight-legged gait. As he approaches, he looks directly at the other baboon, making affiliative gestures such as smacking his lips, flattening his ears back, and narrowing his eyes. The other responds in like fashion, and then after a quick hug they present their hindquarters and the fondling begins.

Building increasingly complex social arrangements, especially where it involves establishing relationships with wary out-group members, undoubtedly put pressure on many aspects of late Pleistocene hominin social life. There are good reasons to believe that our ancestors confronted this challenge using ritual. First, ritual behavior is widespread across the animal kingdom, especially where cautious communication is required.[9] For example, among many mammals aggressive males can be a threat to females. How can a male get close enough to a female for mating purposes without scaring her off? Among deer, elk, and moose, an approach ritual— the low stretch—signals benign intent. In the low stretch, the male emulates a calf approaching to nurse. By approaching this way, the male signals his nonaggressive intent and is able to get close to the female.

Second, because of its attention-grabbing quality, ritual creates the conditions for extended social interactions. It does so by directing attention at the ritual signal and away from threatening cues and defensive responses. For example, when approaching subordinates, dominant female monkeys use particular grunting vocalizations to signal their nonthreatening intentions, forestalling the subordinate's natural tendency to flee. A successful approach can lead to another common social ritual among primates: grooming. Grooming causes the release of endogenous brain opiates, which help bring about a mental state conducive to social interactions. In this sequence, then, one can see how successfully executed ritual can focus attention on a relevant signal (the approach grunt), inhibit defensive emotions (fright in the subordinate), and allow time for social bonding emotions (associated with grooming) to operate.[10]

Third, social rituals designed to build trust, promote group harmony, and reinforce social relations are common among primates. The baboons' scrotum-grasp falls into this category, but other examples abound. When chimpanzee, bonobo, and spider monkey foraging parties reunite, they engage in ritualized acts of welcoming and social reaffirmation that include mutual embracing, kissing, group pant-hooting, and grooming. Gelada baboons use rhythmic back-and-forth vocalizations to signal benign intent during close-quarter feeding sessions. These vocalizations allow two baboons to peacefully feed near one another. Chimpanzees also have a discrete set of behaviors used to signal the desire for reconciliation. If a loser between two combatants wishes to make peace, he will often approach the victor with submissive bows and vocalizations, holding out his hand in a begging gesture. By embracing and kissing the supplicant, the victor signals his acceptance of the loser's peace offering. This reconciliation ritual signals something of a quid pro quo on the part of the former combatants:

The subordinate acknowledges the dominant's higher status (with bows and vocalizations), and the dominant assures the subordinate that hostilities will cease (with hugs and kisses). The wealth of social rituals present among our primate cousins indicates that our hominin ancestors were preadapted for using ritual as a means of social bonding and could call upon a rich repertoire of them in their everyday lives.[11]

Fourth, specific rituals appear necessary for certain categories of social interaction. For example, the scrotum-grasp ritual is typically restricted to older male baboons, who often need to form strategic alliances against younger, stronger males in order to secure mating opportunities. It is noteworthy that younger males usually fail to complete this greeting ritual and are less likely to form social alliances than older males.[12] Thus, no scrotum-grasping, no social alliances.

Fifth, the ability to utilize ritual effectively is affected by upbringing and observation. For example, rhesus macaque monkeys generally do not reconcile after conflicts, while stumptail macaques do, using what is called the "hold-bottom" ritual, where one stumptail puts both hands on the other's hips. Stumptails have a less combative social world than rhesus macaques do, and the higher frequency of postconflict reconciliation is one reason why. Primatologist Frans de Waal showed that juvenile rhesus monkeys who were housed for several weeks with stumptails would gradually adopt the habit of frequent postconflict reconciliation and would maintain this behavior for several months after returning to their own social groups.[13] Thus, socialization can train individuals to use ritual signals to manage within-group conflict.

Finally, ritual behavior is fundamental to the development of many other social/cognitive skills. Thus, when natural selection targets ritual, it targets a key mechanism by which other social/cognitive skills develop. Faced with the challenge of communicating carefully and effectively to suspicious out-group members, our ancestors would naturally have turned to a mechanism with a deep history of facilitating social bonding: ritual. In doing so, they also would have been tinkering with the foundation upon which other social/cognitive capacities are built. This tinkering did nothing less than create the conditions necessary for the emergence of uniquely human, "modern" cognition. To understand how this happened, we must first try to nail down what is meant by modern cognition. Tiger Woods provides us with the first clue.

Ritual Behavior and the Origins of Modern Cognition

[Tiger] Woods has become the exemplar of mental discipline. After watching Woods walk stone-faced through a roaring crowd, the science writer Steven Johnson, in a typical comment, wrote: "I have never in my life seen a wider chasm between the look in someone's eye and the surrounding environment."[14]

Tiger Woods's trademark is mental focus—the ability to concentrate on the task at hand without being distracted. Often the distractions arouse reflexive or what are called prepotent responses. For example, a pain signal in the leg would reflexively cause most of us to alter our stance or adjust our weight so as to reduce the pain. This, however, could have detrimental effects on our golf swing. Very few of us can match Woods's ability to filter out pain so as to maintain proper form and thus place the ball where we want it. Woods may be an extreme example, yet this ability to willfully focus attention on a selected signal in the face of powerful competing signals may be the key to uniquely human cognition. How so?

Though researchers joust over exactly what mental characteristics separate us from other animals, most would include the capacity for symbolic thought among the contenders. Archaeologists Christopher Henshilwood and Curtis Marean, for example, argue that modern cognition is best defined by the use of symbolism to organize behavior. Examples would include using body ornaments as social markers, using external informational storage devices (such as hash marks on bone) to tally days or star movements, and using artwork to expresses religious sentiments or record history. Symbolically organized social life not only leaves traces in the archaeological record, but also provides a mechanism whereby cultural achievements are not just transmitted but are made available for continual refinement and improvement. While other species show evidence of culture, the ratcheting effect of cultural accumulation appears to be uniquely human.[15]

But what does it take to think symbolically? Consider a common symbol—the dollar sign, $. The $ is truly symbolic in the sense that it is an utterly arbitrary convention. It looks nothing like the actual currency for which it stands, and it rarely occurs in the same temporal or spatial context as actual money. Thus, as a sensory image, there is nothing about the $ to indicate that it "stands for" or represents money. You simply have to know it—or, more importantly, you have to have the mental capacity to *be able to* know it.

Consider another example: Some of humanity's oldest artwork is found in Australia. Much of it consists of highly stylized animal depictions as well as geometric forms such as concentric circles, spirals, linear designs, and arrays of dots.[16] While researchers have clues as to the meaning of these remains, a complete understanding would undoubtedly require one to be embedded within the culture that produced them. In other words, they are very likely symbols in the same sense that the $ is a symbol. They probably have purely arbitrary aspects that are culturally determined.

Furthermore, to appreciate them as symbols one has to have the mental capacity to focus on what they represent while simultaneously ignoring their irrelevant aspects. A symbol is not what it seems. Indeed, often what it looks like is inconsistent with its meaning as a symbol (the $ looks more like an S than like money). Its meaning is not in its appearance or in the spatial/temporal context in which it frequently appears. Instead, a symbol is simply what we all agree that it is.[17] To a certain degree, all humans must do what Tiger Woods does so effectively on the golf course: keep our minds focused on the task or symbol-relevant information while filtering out more immediate, but distracting, competing signals.

Modern Cognition and Enhanced Working Memory

Working memory capacity may be the key to modern cognition. In a series of articles, psychologist Fred Coolidge and archaeologist Tom Wynn have built a compelling case that the emergence of uniquely human cognition resulted from a slight but significant increase in working memory capacity.[18] Working memory capacity refers to the ability to hold goal-relevant information in mind while engaged in cognitive or behavioral tasks. Suppose my task, for instance, is making a spear. As I'm doing this I must hold in mind a number of relevant bits of information, such as whether the size and shape of the stone is right for the wooden shaft to which it will be affixed, whether the stone has been sharpened enough to kill the prey, whether the wood is sturdy enough to be effective but light enough to throw, and so forth. At any point in the process, I might get distracted by how pretty the stone looks or how I'd like to use the wooden shaft to thump my noisy neighbor in the next cave or any number of other irrelevant signals. Greater working memory capacity equals a greater ability to "stay on task" and ultimately complete the toolmaking process.

This increase made AMH better able to hold information in mind, especially information about behavioral procedures and intended goals, in the face of competing signals or response competition.[19] Thus, when confronting cognitive challenges, AMH were better equipped to resist distractions and avoid unproductive habits of thought and behavior. This ability, Wynn and Coolidge argue, was essential for exploring novel relationships, engaging in cognitive innovation, and ultimately creating and using symbols.

Similarly, increased working memory capacity is very likely necessary (though maybe not sufficient) for what psychologist Michael Tomasello calls "shared intentionality."[20] Shared intentionality is the uniquely human capacity for sharing emotional, cognitive, and attentional states and coordinating actions relevant to those states. As an example, ponder what is necessary for Max and me to successfully work together to repair his truck. First, we must share a number of mental states; for example, we must agree that the starter motor needs replacing (a shared goal). We must both *want* to do the task (a shared desire or emotion). Second, we must successfully coordinate actions relevant to that state/goal. I must recognize that Max will have to lie on his back and use both hands to loosen the bolt (his role), while I hand him the tools and keep the light on the work area (my role). Holding in mind the shared goal while coordinating the separate roles each partner plays in achieving that goal can be demanding, especially under adverse conditions.

Despite these challenges, humans are masters of shared intentionality, engaging in coordinated acts ranging from relatively simple ones, such as holding a conversation, to highly complex ones, such as performing a symphony. Shared intentionality, Tomasello argues, is the foundation upon which all uniquely human cognition arises. Shared mental states provide the basis for constructing shared meanings (symbolism), creating shared communicative symbols (language), and identifying mental states as the forces behind behavior (theory of mind).

Shared intentionality lies at the heart of the human capacity for culture. A recent analysis found evidence for increasing behavioral and technological complexity and innovation in Neanderthals from 160,000 to 40,000 ybp. This led the authors to argue that cultural differences were likely more responsible, than cognitive ones for whatever advantage AMH may have had over Neanderthals. But culture and cognition need not be mutually exclusive. It may be that a modest cognitive difference—such as a slight but significant enhancement of working memory, which in turn created a greater capacity for shared intentionality—accounts for a huge cultural difference. Furthermore, a difference in culture can provide greater support for more complex forms of cognition.[21]

A more complex social environment is directly connected to cognitive performance, including working memory. A recent study found that those who had greater levels of social engagement scored higher on measures of cognitive function. Furthermore, ten minutes of social interaction (discussion of a controversial social issue) was as effective as engaging in nonrelational intellectual activity (reading for comprehension, mental rotation tasks, crossword puzzle solving) in boosting performance on both speed of processing and working memory tasks. This finding is consistent with recent neuroimaging studies showing that social reasoning involves broad areas of the frontal lobe that are used in working memory and executive control. Interestingly, neuroimaging studies of brain activity during stone tool construction have failed to find activity in these same areas of the frontal lobe. This suggests that social factors were likely more responsible than technological ones for the working memory enhancement that ultimately produced uniquely human cognition.[22]

Ritual Behavior and Working Memory

A number of studies show that the demands of ritual behavior tax working memory capacity, especially when the ritual requires inhibiting reflexive responses. For example, suppose an initiation ritual requires one to endure pain or isolation. In this case, one must focus attention on the ritual acts while suppressing the natural tendency to escape the pain or threat (such suppression is also referred to as "inhibiting prepotent responses").

Working memory and the direction of attention are controlled by specific parts of the frontal lobe. These same areas of the frontal lobe are essential to inhibitory control, supporting the contention that the frontal lobe, especially on the right side, is central to the ability to filter competing signals, inhibit immediate emotional reactions, engage in willful actions, and exercise self-control.[23]

A number of studies have demonstrated the frontal lobe's role in the inhibition of prepotent responses. For example, Canadian neuroscientist Mario Beauregard monitored brain activity while subjects viewed erotic films.[24] Not unexpectedly, they found that the films increased activity in areas of the brain known to be associated with sexual arousal. However, when the subjects were given specific instructions to inhibit any sexual response, areas of the brain associated with sexual arousal showed no increase in activity, but the activation of areas of the frontal lobe associated with impulse control did increase.

A second example is found in studies looking at brain responses to interracial stimuli. Faces of racial out-group members can induce an automatic fear response in people similar to images of snakes and spiders. Indeed, studies of both African Americans and Caucasian Americans show automatic activation of the brain's fear center (the amygdala) when the faces of other races are shown. However, this response is reduced when subjects are given extended time to think. During this time, increased activity occurs in frontal lobe areas associated with self-control.[25]

Recently it has been shown that an increase in working memory capacity allows greater resources to be dedicated to inhibitory processes.[26] This, in turn, increases the likelihood that subjects will be capable of maintaining focus on their current task. As one practices a task, more and more aspects of the task become automatic in nature, freeing up working memory capacity for inhibition.

Ritual behavior requires the willful direction of action and the suppression of prepotent responses. As mentioned earlier, ritual's attention-getting quality involves directing attention to a particular signal, while at the same time directing attention away from defensive reactions (recall the approach grunts of dominant monkeys). Furthermore, the repetitive elements of ritual provide opportunities for practice, freeing up working memory capacity for greater inhibitory control. In our ancestral past, this ability to exert inhibitory control would very likely have been stressed to unprecedented levels. Evidence from traditional societies indicates that social rituals designed to build group solidarity and establish intergroup alliances are extremely demanding in terms of self-control, focused attention, and inhibition of prepotent responses. Furthermore, those who successfully complete these demanding rituals tend to gain fitness advantages in the form of greater access to resources (via reciprocal arrangements), enhanced status, and better psychophysical health.

Social Rituals among Traditional Societies

We have seen that the social world of our late Pleistocene ancestors was growing increasingly complex and very likely included unprecedented intergroup trade alliances. The construction and management of this social world would have required more demanding social rituals. Looking across a range of traditional societies, three types of social rituals are common when it comes to enhancing within-group social cohesion and building between-group alliances: rituals of trust-building and reconciliation, rituals of initiation, and shamanistic rituals of community and individual healing. Of course, the degree to which these ritual practices can be projected into our ancestral past is unclear. However, they provide the best starting point for understanding past rituals, and a consistent feature of them is physical and psychological rigor.

Rituals of Trust-Building and Reconciliation

As intergroup interactions became more frequent, rituals for establishing trust between different groups and for maintaining cohesion within groups very likely rose in importance. Examples of these rituals from traditional societies show that they frequently "ritualize" the expression of explosive emotions that must be contained if trust and reconciliation are to be achieved. By exhibiting these dangerous emotions in ritual form while controlling their effects, participants signal their willingness and ability to let longer-term group-level interests direct their actions.

Disputes among the Ammassalik of Greenland are often addressed using a traditional "drum match," where the aggrieved parties drum and sing about how the other has injured them. These matches represent a highly stylized extension of the wider practice of singing and drumming for pleasure. Tradition governs nearly every element of the match, including the tone, expression, and movement of the participants. This, however, does not eliminate the tension inherent in the ritual.[27] As the singer and listener face each other, the singer uses mocking tones to detail the listener's personal and familial faults. Even as the confrontation escalates—the singer occasionally butts heads with the listener—the listener remains frustratingly indifferent to the singer's taunts and accusations. When the singer is done, the roles reverse. Matches are rarely settled in one round; in fact, they may be continued for months or years.

An even "edgier" example is the peacemaking ritual of the Yanomamo, a traditional people of Amazonian jungle.[28] The party requesting a truce invites its enemies to a ceremonial feast. As their adversaries arrive, the host warriors recline unarmed in hammocks. With weapons drawn, the "guests" taunt their hosts with insults and intimidating gestures. But the hosts remain calm and unaffected by the threats. In time, hosts and guests trade places, and the threats and insults begin anew. Only when each is satisfied as to the other's peaceful intentions does the feast begin, with the groups exchanging gifts, forging new alliances, and arranging marriages. Of course, the situation could easily turn back into violent conflict if either side senses treachery or mistakes simulated hostility for the real thing. But as long as the ritual is respected, explosive emotions are constrained and trust emerges.

Finally, among the Maring-speaking people of New Guinea, a traditional pig feast, the *kaiko* festival, serves as the forum for establishing or reinforcing martial bonds among warriors of different camps. When the visitors enter the host's grounds they do so aggressively, singing, dancing, and charging onto the feast venue with axes brandished.[29] But the "attack" is only apparent. An invitation to "help dance" at *kaiko* is understood to involve a pledge to support the hosts in battle. The aggressive dancing demonstrates the guests' ability and willingness to fight alongside their hosts. Though the dancing signals solidarity, it has an undeniably competitive edge. It is not hard to imagine the festival degenerating into a riotous frenzy where intergroup alliances are spoiled rather than strengthened. But as long as the ritual is allowed to regulate the emotions, the alliance is safe.

Our late Paleolithic ancestors' rituals of trust-building and reconciliation may not have been as elaborate as these. However, even the most mundane ritual of this type requires some level of self-control. A handshake is not far removed from a swinging fist. Those of our ancestors unable to inhibit their aggressive or defensive inclinations long enough to allow for ritual-based trust and reconciliation to take hold very likely found themselves social outcasts, separated from the reciprocal benefits of within- and between-group alliances.

Rituals of Initiation

Adolescent rites of passage occur in over 70% of traditional societies. The severity of these initiations varies and tends to increase where ecological or external threats are greater. Among aboriginal societies in Australia, for example, the severest initiation rites are found among tribes living in the driest, harshest conditions. This is consistent with "costly signaling theory," which argues that rituals serve as indicators of group commitment. Greater commitment would be required in more demanding conditions, where survival depends on the effort and cooperation of others.[30]

The rapid climate changes and resource stresses of the African Interregnum period would have put intense social pressure on our ancestors. Maintaining social stability while establishing intergroup relations would undoubtedly have led to heightened social tensions. Though neighboring groups would have been essential for material trade and information exchange, the xenophobic nature of humans in general, and of tight-knit traditional societies in particular, would have made these interactions a constant source of tension and unease. Group interactions almost always entail an elevated degree of group competition. Thus, it is not unreasonable to conclude that initiation ceremonies may have either arisen or intensified in the late Pleistocene as the social world became more complex. There is some archaeological evidence consistent with this speculation.

Hand- and footprints of children and adolescents are not uncommon at many Upper Paleolithic deep cave sites, suggesting that they may have been involved in rituals there. Indeed, there is considerable evidence that many deep cave sites were ritual venues. Among traditional societies, children and adolescents are often involved in initiation ceremonies where isolation, altered states of consciousness, and encounters with sacred spirits occur. "Vision quest" initiations among Native American tribes, where a young person is isolated at a sacred site in order to receive spiritual guidance, is a prototypical example of this. Thus, the hand- and footprints found at Upper Paleolithic deep cave sites could indicate the presence of adolescent initiation rites extending as far back as about 30,000 ybp. Furthermore, the Tsodilo Hills "snake rock" mentioned in chapter 2 may indicate the presence of initiation rituals tens of thousands of years earlier. While it is impossible to know exactly what type of rituals might have been associated with this find, the setting is consistent with those involving altered states of consciousness, a common aspect of vision quests.[31]

Adolescent rites of passage can be trying events. Severe rites require the young person to endure isolation, deprivation, physical pain, and psychological stress. For example, female initiation ceremonies among many traditional societies in southern Africa involve forced seclusion, bloodletting, genital cutting, and rigorous training in ceremonial dances. Deprivation, beatings, exhaustive physical exertion, exposure to harsh elements, genital mutilation, ritual scarring, tooth removal, and forced dancing and chanting are among the torturous trials included in many male initiation ceremonies among Australian aborigines, Native Americans, New Guinea tribes, Pacific Islanders, and many African tribes. Possibly the most dramatic of these initiations was the famous Mandan Indian Sun Dance ceremony, in which new warriors were suspended from the top beam of a large ceremonial enclosure with ropes attached to skewers embedded in their chests. They might remain there for hours or days as dancing and chanting went on below them.[32]

With regard to modern cognition, the important point is that the capacity to endure such rituals required a degree of mental control over reflexive responses that only humans have mastered. It is hard to know how severe our Pleistocene ancestors' earliest initiation rituals may have been. But current ethnographic models indicate that to some degree they would have required initiates to inhibit natural prepotent responses in order to signal their commitment to the tribe. The ability to do this would have been an exercise in conscious mental control over automatic, defensive behaviors. This ability is a critical hallmark of the enhanced working memory capacity necessary for symbolic thinking. Furthermore, those initiates best equipped to pass these tests very likely achieved higher status, and hence greater reproductive success, within the tribe.

Shamanistic Healing Rituals

As we have already seen, shamanism represents a third type of ritual with roots dating deep into our evolutionary history. By tying supernatural authority to social norms, shamanism strengthened *within*-group cohesion. Archaeologist Brian Hayden, however, has pointed out that shamanistic rituals would have been a critical *between*-group bonding mechanism as well:

> Given the sparse population densities of most hunter-gatherers, . . . an alliance between even a few bands would represent territories of many

thousands of square kilometers. . . . Groups that had the potential for such religious emotions and used them by holding rituals in which participants entered into ecstatic states, communicating with common deities or totemic ancestors, would be more likely to survive because of mutual help in times of need.[33]

Neighboring groups bonded by emotionally powerful rituals would have been more likely to share resources during times of scarcity, thus providing insurance against starvation, giving them a fitness advantage over purely "secular" groups.

Shamanistic rituals typically involve sensory deprivation, the ingestion of psychoactive substances, rhythmic drumming, dancing, and chanting, often by hypnotic firelight, all designed to produce altered states of consciousness. These conditions typically evoke powerful emotions that have strong social bonding effects—a crucial component of Hayden's hypothesis that religious ritual emerged as a means of creating intergroup resource-sharing alliances. Indeed, ritualized behaviors where groups engage in coordinated rhythmic actions can result in the release of brain opiates that facilitate social bonding. Furthermore, synchronized activities have been found to significantly increase cooperative behavior among participants.[34]

Along with its role in strengthening social cohesion, sociologist James McClenon argues that in our evolutionary past, shamanism would have been our ancestors' primary means of healing. Research confirms that ritual healing practices involving altered states of consciousness can be effective for maladies where one's mental state is a significant factor. About every two weeks the Kalahari !Kung conduct "healing dances," where shaman healers dance about frenetically, laying on hands and transmitting healing power to all present. These dances are considered essential to the health and vitality of the !Kung, both individually and as a community.[35]

It is not hard to imagine our late Pleistocene ancestors engaging in similar rituals around a blazing campfire. At times these rituals may only have involved group chanting, dancing, or hypnotic silence before the flames (the benefits of which should not be casually dismissed). At other times they may have involved intensely dramatic shamanistic ceremonies where soul flight, supernatural encounters, and "miraculous" healings took place. Shamanistic healing rituals such as those of the !Kung always involve techniques designed to bring about a health-enhancing altered state of consciousness. In our ancestral past those most able to achieve this state would have had a selective advantage over others by virtue of its positive physical and psychological effects.

McClenon has marshaled considerable evidence indicating that those of our ancestors who were most susceptible to the beneficial physical and psychological effects of shamanistic rituals had a selective advantage over others in surviving illness or injury, overcoming debilitating emotional states, and enduring the rigors of childbirth.[36] This "ritual healing" theory is based on a number of converging lines of evidence, including:

1. The universality (or near universality) of ritual healing practices across traditional societies.[37]
2. The fact that ritual healing always involves hypnotic processes and altered states of consciousness.[38]
3. Evidence showing that hypnotizability or the ability to achieve a mental state highly prone to suggestion is measurable and variable and has heritable components.[39]
4. The finding that ritual healing is often highly effective for a range of maladies where psychological factors are involved, such as chronic pain, burns, bleeding, headaches, skin disorders, gastrointestinal disorders, and the discomforts and complications of childbirth; and, relatedly, the fact that meditative practices affect levels of beta endorphins, serotonin, and melatonin, all of which are implicated in immune system function, pain reduction, and subjective well-being.[40]
5. The evidence from comparative and archaeological studies indicating the existence of ritual, altered states of consciousness, and care of the sick among our primate cousins and hominin ancestors.[41]
6. The fact that the earliest medical texts (from Mesopotamian and Egyptian civilizations) closely connect healing with religious ritual.[42]
7. The finding that anomalous events associated with ritual, such as "miraculous" healing, are effective in inducing supernatural beliefs.[43] Thus, healing rituals would have reinforced supernatural beliefs among our ancestors and encouraged their expansion.

What this evidence indicates is that ritual healing can be effective health care. Thus, shamanistic healing rituals would have disproportionately enhanced the health of those whose brains permitted the deepest immersion in the rituals. What type of brain would this have been? It very likely would have been a brain with increased working memory capacity.

Shamanism, Neuroscience, and Working Memory

Shamanistic healing rituals may have been important in selecting for the enhanced working memory capacity necessary for modern cognition. Techniques for altering consciousness activate the same areas of the frontal lobe critical to working memory, focused attention and inhibitory control. Furthermore, studies have shown that meditative practices can produce long-term changes in both brain structure and attentional capacities and that they increase levels of a brain chemical (arginine vasopressin, or AVP) critical to learning and memory.[44]

The shamanistic practices of our ancestors may not have been as formal or rigorous as current meditative techniques, but even relatively mundane tasks requiring focused attention are known to activate areas of the prefrontal cortex involved in working memory.[45] Thus, when our ancestors were engaging in rituals around a campfire, focusing their attention on the flames or chanting a repeated phrase to the rhythm of a pounding drum, they were very likely taxing the specific areas of the brain involved in attention and working memory. Those whose brains were most "ritually capable"—by virtue of increased working memory and attentional control capacity—would also have been the ones to reap the greatest fitness benefits.

The Fortuitous Mutation

To construct and sustain an increasingly complex social world, our ancestors needed ever more demanding social rituals. These rituals would have taxed working memory, providing a fitness advantage to those with greater working memory capacity and attentional control. As discussed in chapter 2, for evolutionary change to occur, advantageous traits must be passed along genetically from parent to offspring. Thus, the trait of greater working memory capacity must have involved a heritable genetic change. Stanford archaeologist Richard Klein has argued that ultimately the difference between us and other hominins was a fortuitous genetic mutation that reorganized brain structure and function, resulting in a critical cognitive advantage.[46]

As an explanatory mechanism, a fortuitous mutation would seem to require no deeper causal force. Mutations, it has generally been thought, are more or less inevitable and largely random. However, recent work in evolutionary developmental biology has provided a clearer framework for understanding how "random" genetic mutations are translated into nonrandom traits expressed in the physical body.[47] Mutations may be far less random than originally thought, because the process of development places constraints on how genetic mutations get expressed physically in the organism.

A Baldwinian Process

In 1896 three researchers—James Mark Baldwin, Conway Lloyd Morgan, and Henry Fairfield Osborn—independently proposed a model of selection meant to augment natural selection. Their model became known as the Baldwin effect. The effect provided a mechanism for allowing environmentally induced changes (resulting from either learning or physiological adaptation) to become genetically heritable ones.[48] According to this principle, acquired traits do not directly affect genes, but they could create or contribute to the conditions that would, in time, genetically establish them in the population.

The classic example of this was provided by British biologist Conrad Waddington, who exposed pupal fruit flies (*Drosophila melanogaster*) to heat shock.[49] Some of the heat-shocked pupae later developed into flies without the typical cross-vein pattern on their wings. Waddington bred the no-cross-vein flies and once again exposed their pupal offspring to heat shock. After successive breedings, Waddington found that the no-cross-vein trait would emerge in nearly 100% of the offspring even in the absence of heat shock. In other words, what was initially an environmentally induced trait (the no-cross-veins trait) eventually became encoded and transmitted genetically.

Human-raised (called "encultured") apes provide a second example with clear implications for human evolution. Encultured apes are raised in constant contact with humans and human culture, sometimes to the point of being treated like human children. These apes acquire a number of cognitive skills not found in wild apes, including deferred imitation (the ability to imitate an act hours or days after the act has been demonstrated), tool use, imitative learning, and, most famously, language. This could provide a model for how hominins acquired increasingly complex cognitive skills. These skills may first have appeared as novel acquired traits brought on by environmental demands. Then, as those demands persisted, a Baldwinian process could have led to the traits becoming genetically heritable and stabilized. Interestingly, over the course of hominin evolution, the environmental demands were increasingly caused by hominins themselves in that they were creating social conditions that favored certain traits. For example, traits such as greater inhibitory control of reflexive responses and increased working memory capacity would both have been favored by increasingly demanding social rituals.[50]

How can a trait brought on by an environmental change become genetically heritable? One way is for the environmental demand to "unmask" hidden genetic variation already present in the organism.[51] For example, occasionally a human infant is born with webbed feet or the beginnings of a tail. These anomalies (called "atavisms") indicate that the information for these structures is still present in the human genome. Evolution did not eliminate this information; it simply hid it, or turned it off, so that it has no effect on the normal course of human development. But environmental stress can sometimes turn this information back on. Russian biologist Dmitri Belyaev's work on the domestication of silver foxes provides a demonstration of this process.

Belyaev found that as he selected foxes for the behavioral trait of tameness, a wide variety of other physical changes emerged, including the length of the reproductive season, the levels of sex and stress hormones, the droopiness of the ears, the lengths of tails and legs, the spotting on the fur, and even the shape of the skull. Belayaev argued that this cluster of variability emerged too quickly to be solely the result of genetic mutations. Instead, he argued that they resulted from epigenetic changes brought on by environmental stress. By epigenetic changes, he was referring to changes in gene regulation—how the effects of genes are switched on and off during the course of development. To put it crudely, genes that had previously been turned off in the foxes were being turned on, and vice versa. Thus, one effect that novel environmental pressures can have is to push development off its typical (called "canalized") pathway, revealing previously masked genetic variation. Natural selection can then begin to sift through these newly emergent traits, keeping the helpful and discarding the harmful. It is highly likely that short-term evolutionary changes do not depend on random mutations at all, but on epigenetic changes that over time become genetically stabilized.[52]

About 70,000 years ago, human development was knocked off its normal path by increasingly demanding rituals. This environmental change was created by hominins themselves in response to the need to form larger, more complex social arrangements. As development carved out new trajectories, differences in working memory capacity emerged. Social selection favored greater working memory capacity, and modern cognition was born.

Baby Rituals

Earlier I claimed that ritual was the mechanism by which other critical social/cognitive capacities developed. By tinkering with ritual, our ancestors were tinkering with the very foundation on which other social/cognitive capacities are built. So what's the evidence for this?

All the elements of ritual—attention-getting, formalization, rule governance, invariant sequencing—are found in the earliest social interactions between infants and their caregivers. Furthermore, these interactions are pivotal in the development of social/cognitive skills. Let's begin with ritual's attention-getting quality. Within the first few hours after birth, human infants are designed to attract and hold the attention of their adult caregivers using imitation. Human infants less than an hour old imitate facial expressions such as tongue protrusion, mouth opening, and eye blinking. The creative and effortful nature of these imitative behaviors indicate that they are more than just reflexive; they are provocative, specifically intended to attract and engage adults in early social interactions.[53]

Evidence for neonatal imitation is present in other primates as well. By two or three months of age, however, human infants demonstrate a range of social competencies that surpass those of their primate cousins. Chief among these is the ability to engage in extended back-and-forth social exchanges with adult caregivers, such as when Mom smiles at baby, prompting baby to smile back, prompting Mom to "reply" further with a "hi," leading baby to giggle, and so on. Developmental psychologist Colwyn Trevarthen describes these early, extended interactions as an intricate mother-infant "dance."[54] It is in this social dance that the next two elements of ritual are present: invariant sequencing and rule governance.

Reciprocal social exchanges between mothers and infants follow a strict sequence.[55]

1. Initiation—where either participant engages the attention of the other.
2. Mutual orientation—where the infant's initial excitement calms and mother's vocalizations become soothing.
3. Greeting—characterized by the infant smiling and moving his or her limbs and the mother becoming more animated.
4. Play dialogue—where mother and infant take turns exchanging sounds and gestures. This turn-taking has been called "protoconversation" because it follows the same social conventions as conversation.[56]

It is in these protoconversations that the third aspect of ritual, rule governance, is apparent. Infants seem to innately understand the rules of taking turns in social interaction and become distressed when they are violated. Experiments with the "still face" provide evidence of this.[57] In these experiments, after some protoconversation with their infants, mothers unexpectedly become unresponsive, offering an emotionally neutral face. The effect is dramatic. The infant will often look away, then attempt to reengage mother with a wary smile. For a time the infant alternates looking away with glances back at the mother to see if she "snaps out of it." Eventually the infant gives up, disengaging entirely. The still face is distressing to the infant both because of Mom's unexpected unresponsiveness and because it violates conversational rules.

The fourth element of ritual, formalization, is easily seen when protoconversations expand into social games, the best-known of which is peek-a-boo. The peek-a-boo gestures are restricted forms of the actions they represent. One does not actually hide the face in peek-a-boo; one represents it by just placing the hands over the eyes. Thus, well before a child's second birthday, he or she has had considerable experience with ritualized social interactions. In fact, these are the primary means by which the infant enters into the human social world, and it is from within that world that social/cognitive development proceeds.

Ritual and Social/Cognitive Development

Ritual's role in infancy matches, in two important respects, the role it plays in adulthood. First, early social rituals provide a framework for interpreting the intentions behind actions. For example, psychologist Jerome Bruner has demonstrated that social games such as peek-a-boo have well-defined roles and rules that allow players to understand and predict the actions of others.[58] The game thus allows interactions to proceed without threat. Under most circumstances, suddenly pushing one's face into an infant's and saying "boo" is likely to send the infant into a screaming fit. Within the context of peek-a-boo, however, it is a thrillingly anticipated behavior, understood as playfully arousing, not threatening. The predictability of the game constructively regulates defensive emotions, allowing the social interaction to proceed without spinning out of control.

Second, early social rituals train children in emotional self-regulation. Mother-infant turn-taking involves eye-to-eye gazing, bringing their emotional states into harmony by virtue of the infant using mom as an emotional reference point. If Mom smiles, the infant responds with joyful expressions. If Mom is sullen, the infant reduces its activity and becomes more subdued. It is through this social/emotional referencing that infants learn to regulate their emotional states so that they can participate in increasingly extended and attentionally demanding social interactions. Furthermore, this emotional regulation is critical to dealing with novelty, allowing them to explore new environments and situations without becoming unnecessarily defensive and fearful.[59]

It is this ritual regulation of emotion that has allowed early social interactions between human infants and caregivers to reach unprecedented levels. Though interactions between ape mothers and infants often involve mutual gazing and social smiling, nothing approaching protoconversation has ever been observed. Furthermore, while autistic children often imitate, their ability to engage in protoconversation and other extended social interactions is typically impaired. Michael Tomasello and colleagues argue that the unique human capacity for shared intentionality is critically dependent upon these early mother-infant social exchanges and protoconversations.[60] From these, infants learn a number of critical skills, such as (1) how to regulate emotion and use social interactions as learning experiences, (2) how to use their social partner as an information source for evaluating experience, and (3) how to use the ritual context as a framework for interpreting events and emotions.

A critical lesson emerging from these mother-child social rituals is that the mother's mental state tells you something essential about the events at hand. This creates the foundation for understanding others as intentional agents and related social/cognitive skills, such as social learning, theory of mind, and language. The tragic cases of severe child neglect and the intellectual impairments associated with it provide evidence that biology alone cannot produce uniquely human social cognition. The social/cognitive intelligence that makes humans unique has its roots in the way that infants and their caregivers interact with one another over the first two years of life.[61] Autism specialist Peter Hobson puts in succinctly:

> If a child fails to experience interpersonal engagement, the elaborate circuitry of the brain proves to be about as useful as computer hardware working with inadequate software. The computer can still do fancy things of a rather humdrum kind, but it cannot support creative symbolic thinking.[62]

Critically, there is also evidence that adult caregivers vary in their skill for engaging in these early social rituals with their infants. Mothers with a history of greater sensitivity to their infant's emotional state and to the rules that govern social interaction reengaged their infants more smoothly and effectively after the still-face disruption. These more "ritually capable" mothers engaged their infants in longer, more productive, and more satisfying social exchanges. Caregivers who were too directing or controlling impaired the social/cognitive development of their infants.[63] Just as it does today, variance in mother's ritual competence would have had important implications for the social/cognitive development of infants in our ancestral past.

Raising Children During the African Interregnum

Beginning about 70,000 ybp, AMH began to engage in increasingly demanding intergroup and intragroup social rituals. More "ritually competent" adults became parents who engaged in increasingly extended, cognitively enriching social exchanges with their infants. Their infants grew to be more socially competent adults generally, and more ritually skilled ones in particular. By virtue of their greater social/ritual skill, these adults had greater reproductive success. As fathers, they were better able to coordinate resource-acquiring actions with other males. As mothers, they were better able to engage in protoconversations and other extended social exchanges with their infants. Thus, a cycle was in place for the emergence of increasingly more sophisticated social/cognitive abilities, ultimately leading to the enhancement of working memory capacity necessary for modern cognition.

Unique Culture Produces Unique Cognition

If the cognitive difference that separated AMH from other archaic hominin forms came down to a fortuitous genetic mutation that enhanced working memory capacity, then why did that mutation arise only in *Homo sapiens sapiens*? Or to put it another way, what selection pressure was unique to *Homo sapiens sapiens* that made this mutation fitness-enhancing?

This question is an especially vexing one because there is so much about *Homo sapiens sapiens* and Neanderthals that is the same. In terms of toolmaking, there is very little, prior to the Upper Paleolithic, that distinguishes one group from the other. Both groups also collected natural pigments, built fires, and engaged in large mammal hunting. In fact, recent studies have shown that Neanderthals were highly skilled hunters and foragers; their abilities compared favorably with those of Cro-Magnons.[64] Thus, it is hard to argue that the cognitive demands of hunting, toolmaking, or survival in harsh climates differentiated *Homo sapiens* from Neanderthals. If these activities created selection pressures for enhanced working memory capacity and symbolism, then these traits would have arisen in Neanderthals as well.

But what if there was something different about human culture? And what if this something different specifically targeted focused attention and working memory? Currently there is no evidence of wide-ranging trading networks in any hominin species other than AMH.[65] This suggests that only AHM had reason to be regularly engaging in demanding social rituals. Furthermore, evidence of supernatural beliefs is also restricted to AMH, again implying that only humans were regularly engaging in shamanistic healing rituals.

If our ancestors' culture possessed unique ritual selection pressures, then it stands to reason that a genetic mutation affecting working memory capacity was far more likely to arise and spread in them and not others. Furthermore, if these ritual pressures selected for parents and infants capable of engaging in extended social exchanges, then Baldwinian forces may have made the emergence and spread of this mutation almost inevitable. Many, many species engage in ritualized behaviors. But only our hominin ancestors had highly demanding social rituals laced with supernatural themes—and these were the rituals that gave us uniquely human minds.

Summary

This chapter has covered a considerable amount of ground, but its major points can be summarized fairly succinctly.

1. Hominin social life became increasingly complex in the late Pleistocene. Hominins expanded their home ranges and created intergroup trade alliances with neighboring bands. This complexity very likely arose in response to ecological pressures and cycles of resources scarcity.

2. Social rituals, including rituals of reconciliation, trust-building, initiation, and shamanistic healing, would have been critical to the creation and maintenance of this more complicated social world.

3. The increasingly demanding ritual requirements of adult life gave a fitness advantage to more "ritually capable" individuals. This advantage was gained through the health benefits, status enhancements, and resources acquisition advantages associated with ritual competence.

4. Ritual activities used to create intergroup trust and intragroup cohesion would have required focused attention and response inhibition, activating brain areas associated with working memory. Thus, increased working memory capacity was very likely one of the cognitive qualities associated with "ritual competence."

5. In mothers, this increased "ritual competence" manifested itself in their ability to engage their infants in ever longer, more socially and cognitively enriching bouts of social interaction.

6. These extended bouts of mother-infant social interaction threw infant development off its normal pathway, revealing new variance in cognitive capacities, including working memory capacity. As these children matured, this new variance was then available for further filtering by ritual selection pressure until increased working memory capacity was stabilized genetically in the population.

5

The African Interregnum, Part II

The Evolution of Supernatural Imagination

In the previous chapter we saw that the necessity of creating increasingly complex social arrangements, especially intergroup trading networks, led to the creation of new rituals. Among the new rituals were shamanistic rituals of individual and community healing. While rituals of reconciliation, trust-building, and initiation very likely involved supernatural elements, shamanistic rituals were the first to explicitly invoke the supernatural. Initially, the supernatural was probably envisioned as simply a healing force. By the Upper Paleolithic, however, our ancestors' supernatural world was richly endowed with gods, natural spirits, and watchful ancestors. How did they emerge?

Religion and Imagination

That religion requires imagination seems indisputable. Supernatural agents (gods, demons, spirits, etc.), magical forces (miracles, karmic/divine justice, intercessory prayer, etc.), otherworldly places (heaven, hell, etc.), and a "purposeful" universe are common religious beliefs even though none have a solid empirical basis. Instead, they are abstractions that people are compelled or inclined to envision. But from where did these visions arise? In this chapter I will argue that the origins of supernatural imagination are found in the close connection between imagination and social cognition. Imagination is a key mechanism by which social intelligence develops. As their social world became increasingly complex, hominins—especially children—were selected for greater imaginative abilities. These more imaginative humans envisioned a more elaborate supernatural world.

It has been argued that what lies behind humans' supernatural inclinations is either our tendency to overattribute agency (interpreting a shadow as a threatening stranger) or our pervasive anthropomorphism (seeing faces in the clouds).[1] While these may indeed explain some of our supernatural tendencies, this account leaves too many things unexplained. First, overattributing agency is not unique to humans, but supernatural thinking is (as best as we can tell). Second, there is no obvious reason why the agents we imagine should possess other peculiar characteristics, such as omniscience, the ability to invoke magical forces, or the desire to enact retributive justice. Finally, there is no reason why agency overattribution should lead one to posit such things as immortal souls or an inherently purposeful universe, both of which humans seem naturally inclined to do.

A more complete explanation may be found in the curious observation that all of the aforementioned unexplained characteristics are found in childhood imagination. The core theme of this chapter is that this "curiosity" is not a mere coincidence. Childhood imagination coevolved with the adult social world, serving as a preparatory mechanism for that world. The supernatural features of childhood imagination, such as magical forces or immortal beings, actually facilitate a child's developing social skills. Thus, imaginative children are more likely to become socially skilled adults, and in our ancestral past this increasingly translated into greater reproductive success.

What Is Imagination?

In the current context, imagination is defined as the ability to create situational models unconstrained by the realities of the immediate present.[2] A situational model is a mental representation of how an object or system operates, or how an event is organized. If this model is unconstrained by the immediate present, then it is free to vary beyond what sensory inputs imply. For example, consider what goes on in the mind of someone reading a story. The immediate reality of reading is momentarily set aside as the person envisions the story's events based on the author's description (e.g., "It was a dark and stormy night"). Having developed this capacity, humans are able to mentally represent not just immediate sensory inputs (what *is* happening), but also *models* based on interpretations of those inputs (what *could have* happened, or what *might* happen in the future).

A child demonstrates this capacity in a number of ways. By age two or three, most children are able to engage in pretend play, where they understand how objects are redefined to fit with imagined events and scenarios. For example, if children are told that yellow bricks are bananas and red bricks are hay, they will feed yellow bricks to the monkeys and red bricks to the horses. Furthermore, if additional animals must be fed, children will not reuse the already "eaten" bricks. Counterfactual thinking provides a second example. Even though 3- and 4-year-olds rarely construct or express counterfactual statements, they nonetheless can imagine alternative scenarios and can distinguish between factors that would and would not have changed an outcome. For example, they realize that little Cindy might not have hurt herself so badly when biking if she had put her helmet on first, but that putting her apron on first would have made no difference.[3]

There is only scant evidence that nonhuman primates might have a similar (albeit more primitive) capacity. Two recent studies have shown that chimpanzees and bonobos will select tools in anticipation of using them hours later in order to obtain food, suggesting that they can plan for the future. Primatologists Dorothy Cheney and Robert Seyfarth propose that living in fission-fusion communities, where group members are often separated from each other for hours or days, may have selected these apes for a (limited) capacity to envision future encounters with other group members.[4] Since most other primates, including nearly all monkeys, live in more static communities, it is not surprising that evidence of future planning in them is largely lacking. All of this suggests that our hominin ancestors very likely possessed a primitive capacity for future planning and possibly building situational models. However, it was the ecological stresses of the late Pleistocene that created the conditions for the full flowering of this capacity.

The Origins of Imagination: Primate Agency Detection

The first step in constructing a situational model is very likely agency detection—the ability to impute internal mental states, such as goals and desires, to others. In doing so, one builds a mental model assigning an unseen force (a goal or desire) as the cause of a particular behavior. Understanding agency is a necessary step in developing a full-blown theory of mind, where others are understood to have not only have goals and desires, but also beliefs, theories, and inferences.[5]

There is evidence that our primate cousins have a limited capacity for agency attribution in that they appear to distinguish accidental from intentional actions. However, there is no evidence that they understand the beliefs and rational inferences that motivate actions.[6] So a nonhuman ape may recognize that a human "wants" an apple and is therefore vigorously shaking a tree limb. The ape may not, however, understand that the young man shaking the limb is trying to impress the pretty girl who just happens to be walking by because he believes that she might like him and that if he offers her a gift she might agree to a date. The ape's model simply doesn't get that elaborate.

The Origins of Imagination: Infant Imagination

In just the first few months of life, infants are able to distinguish self-propelled movement (a bird flying) from induced movement (a thrown ball). Furthermore, they expect self-propelled movements to be rational. So if a 12-month-old infant watches a display where a (self-propelled) ball moves up and over a barrier and comes to rest next to another ball on the other side, the infant will be surprised if the ball continues this same path of motion when the barrier is removed.[7] Why? Since the ball's motion is self-generated, the infant endows the ball with a goal—to join its mate on the other side of the barrier. The "up and over" motion makes sense when the barrier is present, but it makes no sense when the barrier is absent, since the goal can be more readily achieved using a direct path.

Studies such as this have shown that from a very early age infants interpret self-propelled, flexibly moving visual displays as representing rational, goal-directed entities. Furthermore, if an object's actions are contingent with an infant's actions, such as an object "lighting up" when-ever the infant moves or "babbling" in reply to the infant's vocalizations, then the object is understood as a social partner.[8] These working assumptions are impressive for their early emergence, but they probably do not represent something uniquely human.

Infant vervet monkeys emit alarm calls at seemingly self-propelled objects, such as falling leaves, suggesting that they interpret the movement as emanating from a living, goal-directed source. Infant chimpanzees interpret self-propelled, flexibly moving visual displays (such as the ball-and-barrier display described earlier) as rational, goal-directed entities, just as human babies do. Furthermore, baboons expect a certain rational order to their social world: They show evidence of confusion when a dominate appears to make submissive vocalizations to a subordinate. Finally, Harry Harlow's classic work with infant rhesus monkeys showed that nonhuman primates readily develop social attachments to inanimate objects that display a key set of perceptual features. This evidence, along with that demonstrating a limited capacity for future planning in some great apes, reinforces the conclusion that our hominin ancestors had a modest capacity for constructing situational models.[9]

Childhood Imagination and Social/Cognitive Intelligence

Harvard psychologist Paul Harris has summarized a wealth of research demonstrating that childhood imagination provides the basis for the development of social/cognitive intellect. This evidence takes a number of forms. First, being absorbed in an imaginary world does not harm the child's ability to distinguish fantasy from reality; indeed, some studies suggest that highly imaginative children may be more capable of making this distinction. Second, children's pretend play retains the causal properties of the natural world and forces children to operate within those bounds. For example, when pretending to bathe a teddy bear, children recognize that imaginary water flows downward from the faucet, so teddy is appropriately held below it. Additionally, children recognize that the water causes teddy to become wet, not dirty or sticky, and that a towel is needed to dry teddy, and so forth. So even though the envisioned scenario is imaginary, it still follows the basic causal properties of the natural world.

Even children's magical thinking retains the basic constraints of the physical world. Children are far more likely to believe that a wish was granted if the wish conformed to two basic principles of physical causality—priority and exclusivity. Priority means that the causal force occurred prior to the effect, while exclusivity means that other obvious causes were not available to explain the effect. Thus, when children enter into a make-believe world, the basic fabric of reality is retained.[10]

Third, joint pretend play can be cognitively demanding. Children must both coordinate actions with their play partners and respond to their own and their partner's pretend stipulations. For example, consider a situation described by Dunn and Dale where a 2-year-old boy and his older sister were playing "trains." At one point the sister claimed that the train was stuck and told her brother to fill it with gas. The boy responded by pretending to pour gas into the train (making the appropriate sound effect). The sister, however, noticed that the gas was spilling and told the boy to pour it into another location on the train. In this example the boy easily and appropriately responded to his sister's stipulation that the train was stuck and needed fuel; though his sister had suddenly changed the course of events, the boy accommodated smoothly. Furthermore, once having accepted that the train needed gas, the boy easily adapted to the next play stipulation: that he was spilling the pretend gas and needed to pour it in a different location. Keeping up with the transforming imaginary landscape as players introduce new elements, redefine play objects, and freely alter the flow of events requires that children constantly update their mental model of the play scenario.[11]

Fourth, the cognitive demands of pretend play produce enhanced social reasoning skills.[12] As they engage in pretend play, children interact with the imagined world from the perspective of the characters they envision. They express the emotions, moods, attitudes, and behaviors appropriate to the role. This role playing sharpens children's skill in understanding the world from another's point of view. Children who more frequently engage in role playing score significantly higher on tests measuring their understanding of others' mental states and how others' thoughts, emotions, desires, and beliefs vary based on situational factors. Preschoolers who engage in more pretend-play role playing are seen as more likable and receive higher sociability ratings from peers and teachers. Finally, increased engagement in simple make-believe activities, either alone or with others, has been positively linked to understanding others' mental states. Enhancements of social intelligence have also been linked to another category of pretend play: imaginary companions.

Cross-culturally, as many as 65% of 7-year-olds have or have had imaginary friends or pretend-play partners (e.g., stuffed animals or toys endowed with personality). Children with imaginary companions are often precocious on a number of measures of social awareness and empathy. For example, these children are typically less shy, more sociable, and more emotionally expressive, and tend to score higher on theory-of-mind measures than children without imaginary companions. Additionally, children with imaginary companions are able to produce more complex sentence structures and are more capable at referential communication than children without imaginary companions. Referential communication refers to the ability to recognize what verbal information another needs in order to understand something and to effectively express that information. These positive effects may not be confined solely to children. Teenagers who make reference to imaginary friends in their diaries tend to be more socially competent and have better coping skills.[13]

While social/cognitive enhancements are associated with imaginary companions, their absence has been associated with deficits. The lack of imaginary friends has been associated with poorer performance on measures of emotional understanding. Furthermore, children lacking in pretend play, role playing, and imaginary companions are at higher risk for a serious social/cognitive deficiency: autism.[14]

Mechanisms by Which Imagination Facilitates Social Cognition

How does pretense facilitate social intellect? Imagination serves to bridge the cognitive gap between the minds of self and other.[15] In a typical "false belief" task, a child and an adult look into a box labeled "cookies" and see that the box actually contains crackers. The box is then closed, and a second adult enters the room. The child is then asked, "What does the (second) adult think is in the box?" Even though the outside label says "cookies," most 2- and 3-year-olds will claim that the adult thinks there are crackers in the box. Thus, they fail to recognize that the second adult's thoughts (informed by the label) can be different from reality. It is not until a child is somewhat older (4 to 5 years old) that he or she appreciates that what a person thinks is not necessarily true.

In an alternative version of the false belief task, after the child has looked into the box (seeing crackers), an adult enters the room and says either "I see the label says cookies, so I think there are cookies in this box," or "I'm going to imagine that there are cookies in this box." In either case, the child is then asked what the adult thinks is in the box. Three-year-olds performed significantly better on trials where a person suffered under a false *imagination* about the contents of the box, compared to a false *belief*.

Thus, it appears that the recognition that imagination can vary from reality precedes the recognition that belief can. The critical difference, according to psychologist Jacqueline Woolley, is that belief is an epistemic state, while imagination is a fictional one.[16] In other words, a belief is *supposed* to accurately represent reality (even though sometimes it doesn't), while imagination is not. So if Mom "believes" that bananas are good for you, then they are. But if Mom "pretends" that a banana is phone—well, of course, she knows it's not really true. Because imagining does not imply empirical accuracy, it easier for children to appreciate its potential divergence from reality, and that appreciation facilitates a child's growing awareness of other minds and how they work. The fact that children perform better on false belief tasks after having done false imagination tasks offers support for this interpretation.

Harris and his colleagues have found evidence of a similar effect of imagination on deductive reasoning.[17] They gave children ages 4 to 6 years unfamiliar syllogistic reasoning problems, such as "All fish live in trees," "Max is a fish," and then tested them on their ability to derive valid conclusions. When the problems were presented in a straightforward declarative manner, the children performed rather poorly (younger children more so than older ones). However, when presented as "make-believe" problems, both age groups improved significantly. To achieve the "make-believe" stance, the experimenter simply adopted a more dramatic tone of voice (as if telling an exciting story) and prefaced the syllogism with something like "Imagine you are on a strange planet where . . . all fish live in trees." Follow-up studies showed that this effect was exhibited cross-culturally and had long-term impacts on children's reasoning performance.

In explaining this effect, Harris discusses how imagination encourages children to set aside the constraints of current reality so that alternatives can be considered. Imagination focuses a child's attention on novelty in a way that simple declaration or description does not.[18] So even though an idea or premise may seem strange or far removed from the child's experience, imagination encourages her to accept its possibility and consider its implications. This, Harris argues, is the same process that occurs during pretend play when play partners invoke stipulations to which the child must adjust ("Stop, you're spilling the gas!"). Moreover, it is the precursor to the way adults construct situational models for understanding narrative. Imagination is a convincing way of getting children to set aside immediate reality and consider the implications of unfamiliar or unusual ideas. As the child matures, the social world becomes one of the primary venues for deploying this skill ("Maybe Jane is late because she's angry about what Julie said to Tom").

There is even evidence that imagination facilitates social skills in adults. As adults read fiction, they typically become absorbed in the author's narrative world, vicariously experiencing events from the protagonist's perspective. Frequent fiction-readers score higher on measures of empathy, reading emotions from facial expressions, and other measures of social acumen.[19] Interestingly, reading copious amounts of nonfiction was a negative predictor of social skill (reinforcing the stereotype of the socially inept professor).

Supernatural Imagination

Imagination prepares children for the complexities of the adult social world, and those complexities were deepening during the African Interregnum. During this period the first archaeological evidence of possible supernatural beliefs emerged, in the form of the Tsodilo Hills snake rock. By the Upper Paleolithic (35,000 ybp), evidence of supernatural beliefs is found in the cave art, abstract artifacts, and elaborate grave offerings common at many sites. This suggests that for tens of thousands of years, supernaturalism of one form or another was a widespread feature of hominin social life.

This opens up the possibility that childhood imagination provided the "source material" for much of what eventually became adult supernatural belief. If this were so, then we would expect childhood imagination to possess a range of supernatural elements reflective of adult religious belief. These elements may be "unrefined" or immature compared to adult theology, but they provide the raw materials from which supernatural concepts are fashioned. Recent research has identified at least four features of childhood imagination that may have served this purpose: omniscient supernatural agents, magical causation, imminent justice, and pervasive (called "promiscuous") teleology.

Omniscient Supernatural Agents (God)

Traditional theories of children's concept of God typically argued that God was simply an extension of a parental figure.[20] Recent evidence, however, demonstrates that children's idea of God departs in important ways from their ideas about parents, and thus represents a unique category unto itself.

Children clearly differentiate God's mind from their own and their parents'. To demonstrate this, one study showed children a series of ambiguous visual displays that required explanation before they could be fully understood.[21] Both before and after the displays were explained to then, the children were asked if either their mother or God would understand the displays. Even before they understood the displays themselves, most 3- and 4-year-olds claimed that God could understand them but that their mothers could not. Furthermore, after the displays were explained to them, most children claimed that their mother now understood them as well. In other words, they confused their mother's knowledge with their own. Most of the children, however, did not change their estimation of what God would know. Note that neither what Mom was presumed to know, nor what the child knew, served as a basis for deciding what God knows. This evidence provides no support for the hypothesis that children use either their parents or themselves as models for constructing their understanding of supernatural agents. Instead, God is the one who knows and perceives everything and who retains this ability even as the child learns more and more about the limitations of other (human) agents.

False belief tasks further confirm this human/divine distinction in children's understanding of other minds. Using the typical false belief paradigm, where children of different ages are asked what another will think is in a box that is labeled as containing one thing (e.g., crackers) but contains something else (e.g., pebbles), researchers have found the typical developmental pattern. That is, younger children (about 3 years old) claimed that human and nonhuman agents (a monkey, a girl named Maggie) would think pebbles were in the box, while older children (5 to 8 years old) claimed that they would think that crackers were in the box. Children at all ages, however, claimed that God would accurately know what was in the box. This finding has been replicated cross-culturally, suggesting that it is a general developmental pattern. A similar pattern has been observed with perceptual stimuli: As children get older, they increasingly appreciate the limitations of human perception, while at the same time claiming that God has no limitations. These results suggest that while an understanding of the limitations of human minds takes time to develop, an understanding of God's mind comes earlier and easier. Children appear to be especially "prepared" to accept and understand supernatural agent concepts.[22]

It is also important to note that while supernatural agents routinely know more than mere mortals, they are not always regarded as omniscient. Yukatek children (rural Mayan villagers from Yucatan Mexico) group lesser spirits (Chiichi) with humans on false belief tasks and distinguish what they know from both more significant Mayan deities (Sun and Forest Master) and from the Catholic God (who is viewed as omniscient).[23] This work indicates that while all-knowing supernatural agents are common in childhood thinking, omniscience is not simply blindly applied to all supernatural agents. Culture often serves to differentiate these agents in terms of how extensive their knowledge actually is.

Magical Causation

Just as supernatural agents exist as a distinct "agent" category in children's minds, magic exists as a distinct causal category. One study presented 4-, 6-, and 8-year-olds with what appeared to be magical transformations—objects seemed to either change shape or disappear. In general, the tendency for children to explain these transformations by invoking magic declined both with age and with their ability to find alternative physical causes. The response pattern also revealed another interesting finding: For children, physical causes and magical causes were mutually exclusive. Magic was invoked only when (1) the event was a clear violation of ordinary rules of causality and (2) no other physical explanation was available to account for the event.[24]

As an explanatory category, magic is the cause of unexplainable things. As kids get older and learn more about physical causality, unexplainable events grow ever fewer, and magic is less frequently invoked. However, this does not mean that magic withers as a meaningful category. As children increasingly understand what is possible (through the operation of physical forces), their ability to imagine the impossible grows in concert.[25] For example, it is not until a child understands death that he can envision immortality.

Psychologist Jesse Bering investigated how children interpret the actions of invisible agents. He and his colleagues had 3-, 5-, and 7-year-olds guess which of two boxes contained a ball. The children were told that an invisible person, Princess Alice, would somehow warn them if they were about to pick the wrong box. After this, the child selected a box by placing her hand on it, while clever experimenters (surreptitiously) either flickered a light on and off or caused a picture to fall.[26]

How children interpreted these events showed an interesting developmental trend. The 3-year-olds made no connection between the events and Princess Alice. They were pure materialists, claiming that the light flickered because it wasn't working right or the picture fell because it wasn't stuck to the wall very well. The 5-year-olds understood that Princess Alice was responsible for the events, but they did not attribute any special meaning to them. Only the 7-year-olds claimed that Princess Alice was both responsible for the events and was trying to warn them that they had picked the wrong box. This study suggests that a certain level of cognitive maturation is necessary to connect unlikely world events with supernatural intentions. It may be that it is only when one understands a physical law (thoughts and desires cannot affect physical objects) that one is in a position to imagine the significance of that law's potential violation (a message from supernatural agent).

A similar trend was found in another study where children were presented with an incredible machine capable of shrinking rooms.[27] Children under five generally accepted that a machine could shrink a room. Older children, however, recognized that this was impossible and searched for alternative explanations for the functioning of the machine (explanations that might have included magic).

Developmental trends in magical thinking show that it emerges around age three or four, then shows a rapid decline in the early school years. For example, while 71% of 3- and 4-year-olds claim that wishing is causally effective, only 31% of 5- and 6-year-olds do. Importantly, however, the opposite trend has been reported regarding the efficacy of prayer. Furthermore, there is evidence that even well-educated adults behave as if a magical form of contagion is possible. People will avoid wearing laundered clothing known to have been previously worn by a mass murderer or will recoil from an artifact once owned by Hitler, as if some evil, transmittable "essence" has been imparted on the objects through past association. By the same token, people will often revere objects or articles known to have been associated with holy people. Often this is accompanied by a strong desire to touch these items or, if possible, the people themselves.[28]

This suggests that various forms of magical thinking, often ones that are culturally supported, will be retained into adulthood. For example, recent studies have shown that in highly secular Britain, traditional Christian beliefs have declined over the past half-century, but belief in ghosts has more than doubled (from 15% to 31%), while belief in such things as reincarnation and future-foretelling have remained steady at around 25% and 50%, respectively. Similar, culturally appropriate forms of adult magical thinking have been reported among the Yoruba of southwestern Nigeria, indicating that these tendencies occur cross-culturally.[29]

Imminent Justice

Renowned developmentalist Jean Piaget noted that young children (roughly six to nine years of age) find "quite natural the connection between the fault that has been committed and the physical phenomenon that serves as punishment."[30] Furthermore, these punishments are assumed to be "automatic" and emanating "from the things themselves." For example, when children were asked why a bridge collapsed, causing the child on it to fall into a river, they responded that it was because the child had earlier stolen some apples. This notion—that the world is organized such that good behaviors are rewarded and bad behaviors punished—is often referred to as "imminent justice." Since Piaget, other studies have cast more light on the tendency of children to engage in this type of thinking.

As with magical thinking, imminent justice thinking appears to fill a certain conceptual niche. First-, third-, and fifth-graders were more likely to invoke imminent justice when motives and outcomes matched (i.e., a person with a bad motive was "punished" or a person with a good motive "rewarded") and when the cause of the outcome was ambiguous. Thus, if a clear alternative physical explanation for the outcome was not forthcoming, children often built a moral connection between the outcome and the earlier behavior.[31]

Similarly, other research has found that simply knowing what outcome a person had incurred affected how that person was judged. Six- to nine-year-old girls watched a vignette of a girl either finding money on the street or getting hit by a falling bookshelf. The children then rated how good or bad the girl in the vignette was. The "fortunate" girl was rated as being just as "good" as another girl whom they had seen actively helping another. Additionally, the "unfortunate" girl was rated as being worse than the good girl. Thus, simply seeing an outcome affected how the children interpreted the character of the person involved.[32]

Imminent justice thinking appears to be a natural outgrowth of children's understanding of prescriptive rules combined with their growing imaginative capacities. Paul Harris's work has shown that from a very young age (by two or three) children are highly sensitive to prescriptive rules—rules that obligate one to behave in certain ways under certain conditions (e.g., when riding your bike you must wear a helmet).[33] Furthermore, they treat these rules as obligatory even when they are novel and seemingly illogical (e.g., when Sara rides her bike, she must wear an apron). This, Harris and his colleagues argue, makes adaptive sense, given that many social and safety-related directives that children must follow must strike them as highly arbitrary ("If you say please, you can have a cracker," "If you take a nap, we'll go to the park later," etc.).

The obligatory nature of prescription, combined with the child's growing ability to envision counterfactuals, often leads her to conclude that if an outcome was bad, a prescriptive rule was probably broken.[34] In other words, children can readily imagine that an agent who engaged in behavior X, resulting in a "bad" outcome, not only *could have* engaged in behavior Y, but probably *should have* done so. This is especially likely to occur in situations where alternative explanations for an outcome are not immediately obvious to the child.

As children learn more about physical causes (such as germs that cause disease), their tendency to invoke imminent justice declines, often to levels below that of adults. However, consistent with findings on magical thinking, children are more likely to invoke imminent justice when confronting outcomes that are unfamiliar or hard to explain. Imminent justice thinking coexists with more scientific explanations for events and outcomes through adolescence and adulthood.[35]

Pervasive (Promiscuous) Teleology

Imminent justice thinking can be seen as part of a much broader tendency in children to envision the world as inherently purposeful. Psychologist Deborah Kelemen calls this "promiscuous teleology" and argues that its origins lie in human social intelligence. The social world acts as the child's reference point for understanding the natural world. Given that the human social world is pervasively intentional—both human actions and human-created objects (forks, hammers) are usually purposeful—the natural world is assumed to be as well. In fact, this assumption is not uncommon among adults. Hunter-gatherers typically use an anthropomorphizing strategy—that is, they assume that animals have intentions, goals, and desires similar to those of humans—to predict the actions of animals, often to great success. Furthermore, despite pervasive secularism, Fate and Destiny remain popular explanations for low-probability life-changing events in Western Europe. Childhood teleological thinking manifests itself in a variety of ways.[36]

Jean Piaget described animistic and anthropomorphic thinking as typical characteristics of "preoperational" children (children ages two to six). Children this age often endow inanimate and natural objects with the qualities of living organisms (animism), and more specifically with human wants and desires (anthropomorphism). For example, when asked why the sun shines or the wind blows, children often respond, "To keep me warm" or "To help me fly my kite." Later research found evidence for this type of thinking across a wide range of different cultures.[37]

It is important to note how seamlessly teleological thinking weaves into the child's overly generous animistic and anthropomorphic tendencies. The wind is for "flying my kite." The sun's purpose is to "keep me warm." Kelemen found that 4- and 5-year-olds apply teleological thinking as readily to the natural world (lions are for going in the zoo, or clouds are for raining) as they do to human-made artifacts (spoons are for eating soup) and body parts (eyes are for seeing). Even when 7- and 8-year-olds are specifically told that adults prefer physical explanations for the properties of natural objects (rocks are pointy because of erosion), the children insist on teleological ones (rocks are pointy so that animals won't sit on them and squash them). Additionally, 5- to 10-year-old children from both fundamentalist and nonfundamentalist households preferred God as the reason for the emergence of different animal species. Similar results were found for preschoolers in both American and Britain.[38]

Piaget was probably wrong in his assumption that this manner of thinking represented an inability to understand the physical aspects of causation. However, these studies and others suggest that Piaget was probably right to assert that children are inherently biased toward thinking of the natural world as purposely designed in the same way that human-made artifacts are. In fact, so pervasive is this tendency that Kelemen claims that children are "intuitive theists."[39] As with magical and imminent justice thinking, various forms of teleological thinking persist into adulthood.

Who "Invented" the Supernatural?

The connection between childhood imagination and social competence produces something of a chicken-and-egg problem with regard to the emergence of the supernatural. Who first "invented" it—children or adults?[40] If it was adults, then it would seem that the supernatural elements of childhood imagination arose because they helped prepare children for the already present supernatural aspects of the adult social world. If it was children, then the supernatural aspects of childhood imagination arose simply as a by-product of the greater imaginative capacity in general, and over time adults co-opted certain elements of it into the adult world. I don't believe the evidence clearly favors one explanation over the other. However, here's my best guess.

Increasing social complexity selects for generally more imaginative children because these children tend to grow into more socially skilled adults. Supernatural imagination is simply one aspect of children's general increase in imaginative capacity. When these more imaginative children mature, their expanded imaginations manifest themselves in many ways. One way that proves to have a fitness advantage is in postulating a healing force that is controllable through rituals. Thus, shamanistic healing rituals are born and the supernatural becomes incorporated into the adult social world. Incrementally, more and more adult-modified aspects of childhood supernatural imagination are incorporated into the adult world because they prove functional. For example, postulating ever-watchful spirits offers individual benefits by way of increased group cohesion and cooperation. As the adult supernatural world grows increasingly defined and differentiated, that in turn sets parameters for the kinds of childhood supernatural imaginings that are most useful as preparatory mechanisms. Thus, a dynamic is set in place whereby childhood imagination provides raw materials that become incorporated into adult social life, and adult social life continually shapes the broad framework within which childhood imagination develops. In other words, they co-evolve.

To fill out a more complete evolutionary history of supernatural imagination, two more questions must be addressed: (1) What was hominin imagination like prior to the African Interregnum? and (2) What prompted adults to incorporate childhood imaginings into their social world?

Imagination Prior to the Interregnum

There is no reason to think that hominin imagination was entirely absent prior to the Interregnum. Some archaeologists have argued that the symmetry and aesthetic quality of some tools shows that toolmakers mentally envisioned the final product and used this image to guide them. This claim, however, is not without critics. Hominin imagination might also have been necessary for the creation of multicomponent or composite tools, which emerged about 300,000 ybp.[41] Creating a composite tool can take hours or days, because the toolmaker has to fashion individual pieces separately before combining them. This requires that the toolmaker keep an image of the final product in mind while at the same time consciously monitoring the ongoing construction process, making adjustments along the way.

Given that nonhuman primates possess some imaginative capacity, it would not be surprising that hominins of roughly half a million years ago were capable of envisioning a tool and using that image to guide its construction. Brain imaging research confirms that areas of the visual system are activated during stone tool construction.[42] It is telling, however, that this evidence of imagination remains relatively isolated for hundreds of thousands of years: There are no artworks, abstract figures, or other signs of humanlike creativity. The next evidence that one might point to, the beads and body ornaments associated with expanded trade networks, are notable in that they emerge much later (not until about 100,000 ybp) and are related to social factors. Prior to the Interregnum, hominin imaginative capacities were probably sufficient for tool making. If there was any ability to envision spirits or other supernatural concepts, it was not preserved in the archaeological record.

We have already seen that childhood imagination facilitates adult social intelligence. However, it is not enough to simply say that as our ancestors' social world became more complex, people became more imaginative and supernaturalism exploded. How did children's supernatural imaginings become incorporated into adult social life? I think there are two natural entry points from which the supernatural imagination of children could make its way into the adult social world: ritual and the soul.

The Supernatural and the Enhancement of Ritual

> As long as you are alive you must do your rituals. The only people who don't do rituals are the dead. . . . So if you are alive and you don't do the rituals, you are . . . [drifts off] [You are what?] You are the same as dead.[43]

The first entry point for supernaturalism into adult world would have been already-present social rituals. Including the supernatural had the immediate effect of intensifying these rituals. It made them more effective, more dramatic, and just more fun. This provided an incentive for taking childhood supernatural imaginings and creatively including them in adult ritual behavior and then more broadly in adult social life.

In the previous chapter, I briefly mentioned the healing dances of the !Kung San of southern Africa. That earlier reference focused on these dances as an example of a shamanistic ritual, one that may give us a model for understanding similar rituals of our ancestral past. What may have been lost in that earlier reference is just how much fun these dances are for the participants. Healing dances are held about every two weeks and are eagerly anticipated. They have about them the air of a community festival. The shamans who instigate healing claim that when they enter *kia*, the altered state of consciousness that produces healing power, it is an emotionally intense experience—an experience of utter transcendence. They claim that they are more fully alive, more fully themselves when they are in *kia* than when they are in their normal state of consciousness.[44] Furthermore, this feeling of transcendent joy is not reserved for just the rare few—among the !Kung, half the men and 10% or more of the women are shamans/healers. And don't forget that while shamans are achieving *kia*, everyone else is singing, dancing, and getting healed. It's hard to imagine that anything other than a good time for all is the norm at the !Kung healing dance.

It is highly likely that our ancestors during the African Interregnum period were also enjoying social rituals involving dancing, chanting, and singing. These activities were probably present long before the supernatural. Along with being fun, the rhythms produced by these activities can have powerful analgesic and healing effects.[45] Adding the supernatural would have intensified these ritual experiences, making them even more effective.

A recent study compared supernatural meditation to secular meditation in terms of mood, anxiety reduction, and pain tolerance.[46] Volunteers were randomly assigned to one of three groups practicing different meditative/relaxation techniques. One group concentrated on a spiritual phrase such as "God is love" or "God is peace," while another used a more secular mantra such as "I am happy" or "I am joyful." The third group—the control group—was simply given instructions on how to relax. After practicing their technique 20 minutes a day for two weeks, subjects were tested on measures of anxiety, mood, and pain tolerance. Pain tolerance was measured by the amount of time volunteers could keep their hands in water of two degrees Celsius. Those who had been practicing spiritual meditation were able to keep their hands in the near-freezing water twice as long, on average, as those in the other groups. Additionally, the spiritual group showed greater anxiety reduction and mood elevation.

This effect has been replicated in another study where electric shock was delivered to both devout Catholics and atheist/agnostic volunteers. Both the religious and nonreligious subjects were pretested for equivalent levels of pain sensitivity. While the shock was administered, subjects sequentially viewed either a religious image or a similar nonreligious image. A significant increase in pain threshold was reported for the Catholic subjects when viewing the religious image. Furthermore, in the Catholic subjects who viewed the religious image, there was increased activity in an area of the brain known to be involved in the evaluation of sensory experiences, including the experience of pain.[47] Similar activation was not found for the nonreligious subjects. The results confirm the hypothesis that the sense of peace and compassion that often accompanies religious contemplation serves as a powerful force in pain reduction. Shamans exploit this analgesic force to dramatic effect, often performing great feats of pain endurance, to the amazement and delight of onlookers.

If ritual is good, then ritual infused with the supernatural is even better. During the African Interregnum our ancestors discovered exactly this: When they incorporated the supernatural into their already-established (and enjoyable) social rituals, those rituals became even more effective in promoting individual health benefits and community/social bonding. This, in fact, became the foundation for traditional forms of ritual healing.

As the supernatural world expanded, ritual retained its role as the touch-point between newly emerging supernatural concepts and the adult world. New gods and spirits meant new rituals to accommodate them. Among present-day traditional societies, for example, ancestor worship includes "exclusive" rituals performed by kin descendants; these are set apart from public rituals. Likewise, animal spirits involve rituals and sacrifices specifically dedicated to them or to a "master of animals" who is thought to control natural resources. Evidence in the archaeological record suggests that these types of rituals arose somewhat later than shamanistic healing rituals.[48]

The Soul

The soul represents another natural entry point for childhood imaginings to seep into adult cognition. Concepts of the soul are present in a wide variety of religions. Though there is some variability, the Abrahamic traditions (Judaism, Christianity, and Islam) share a common idea of the soul as being a person's immortal essence, capable of uniting with God after death. A similar concept, *jiwa*, is present in the Hindu and Jain traditions. This "soul" experiences cycles of reincarnation after an individual's death but has the potential to ultimately escape earthly existence for a higher one. Besides being widespread, the soul is also ancient. The religious beliefs of the ancient Egyptians included a complex notion of the human soul involving many distinct parts. The *ba* was probably the closest to our contemporary notion of the soul. The *ba* was the personality, character, or essence of the person and was thought to live on after death.

Recent studies have shown that both children and adults distinguish the soul from related concepts such as the mind and that the soul is regarded as having specifically spiritual functions. For example, children ages 7–12 claim that a religious ritual (baptism) specifically affects a person's soul, not his mind. Furthermore, children are significantly more likely to claim that the soul remains invariant over one's lifespan, while the mind changes, and that the soul is critical to spiritual or moral functions rather than cognitive functions. A similar pattern has been shown for college students, who claim that the soul (and not the mind) comes into existence at conception, survives death, and performs spiritual functions such as connecting one to God or providing an unchanging "essence" to one's existence.[49] Interestingly, these views of the soul are fairly consistent across various (but mostly Christian) religious denominations and are even prevalent among those who expressed little or no religious inclinations.

Why are soul concepts so prevalent? Two natural cognitive tendencies seem to be responsible: essentialist thinking and the inability to imagine death. Essentialist thinking refers to the tendency to think that natural kinds or categories are defined by some permanent set of internal properties. For example, if children are told that a horse has been disguised such that it looks exactly like a zebra and trained such that it behaves exactly like a zebra, they will still claim that it is "really" a horse. This claim is based on the notion that within the horse there is some fundamental "horseness" that remains unaffected by external changes. People are thought of similarly. An individual's unique personality is often treated as an essential characteristic of the person—something that defines the person and remains unaltered even if the person changes her hairstyle, loses an arm in a boating accident, or learns to ride a unicycle. But why would this essence be thought of as immortal? [50]

Psychologist Jesse Bering has done a number of studies showing that humans have a very difficult time imagining death. In one study, subjects who self-identified as "extinctivists" (they claimed that all aspects of conscious functioning, including what is popularly thought of as the "soul," cease upon death) were queried about a fictitious case of a man killed in car accident.[51] About a third of these subjects provided answers indicating that the emotions, desires, and thought processes of the deceased continued beyond death. In other words, though these subjects explicitly claimed that death was the end of all consciousness, they provided answers that implied the opposite.

The tendency to implicitly assume that some kind of psychological functioning continues after death, even while explicitly claiming otherwise, is most likely not a result of cultural learning but a natural product of our cognitive makeup, argues Bering. While we have experience with the cessation of certain bodily functions—we know what it is like to not see (when we sleep at night) or to not be tired (after having rested)—others are beyond our experience and even beyond our ability to imagine experiencing. Most significantly, we have no experience with not *experiencing*—as in having no conscious states, feelings, or desires. Even when we sleep, our minds continue to function, and we continue to experience dream states.

Thus, our ability to imagine death is woefully limited. The best we can do is to imagine death as a state where certain functions cease—we can't see or hear, we don't need to eat or rest, that painful ingrown toenail is gone, and so on—but, oddly, we are still aware of the absence of these experiences. We often think of death as the end of all suffering, but of course we could entertain this view only if we assume that in the dead state we are aware of the fact that we are not suffering. And this, of course, could be true only if we (at least implicitly) assume that our awareness has somehow survived death. It is our inability to imagine the "completeness" of death that makes it very easy to assume that some essence (soul) of the person must continue beyond death.

To further explore this issue, researchers presented 4- to 12-year-olds with a rather heartbreaking puppet show where a mouse, lost in the woods, ends up getting eaten by an alligator.[52] They reasoned that if the idea of an afterlife was the product of cultural learning and not an innate predisposition, then these assumptions should increase with age, as children get more exposure to cultural and religious teaching about souls and life after death. The children were asked a series of questions about the disposition of the deceased mouse: Does the mouse know that he is no longer alive? Does he want to go home? Can he see where he is? Does he still love his mother? Does his brain still work? Is he still hungry?

As children got older, the tendency to attribute any functions to the dead mouse declined. Moreover, the range of functions ascribed to the dead mouse narrowed, beginning with biological and perceptual functions. Most of the youngest children understood that upon death the mouse's brain and eyes stopped working. As children got older, their tendency to assume that mental and emotional functions also ceased increased as well. The authors argued that this pattern is actually contrary to what one would expect if children's afterlife beliefs are primarily a function of cultural/ religious indoctrination. As children mature and have increasing exposure to religious ideas and education, their afterlife beliefs actually narrow and become less overtly superstitious. However, this change does not mean that these beliefs disappear. Around half of the school-aged children continued to claim that the mouse still loved his mother and wanted to go home. Furthermore, using measures of implicit knowledge, Bering has shown that the tendency to assume that some psychological functions persist past death pervades the thinking of most adults.[53]

These findings do not, however, mean that culture plays no role in the formation of people's afterlife concepts. Culture very likely channels and accentuates natural cognitive predispositions. For example, Bering and his colleagues found that while Catholic school students showed the same developmental pattern in afterlife beliefs as secular students, their tendency to attribute mental and emotional states to dead agents was even stronger. Additionally, other research has found that for Vezo children of rural Madagascar, the mental functions attributed to the ancestors were those specifically relevant to their cultural role. Thus, the ancestors were more likely to be ascribed specific knowledge states, such as knowing their spouse's name and the location of their house, and specific emotional states, such as missing their children, than to be ascribed general knowledge and emotional states.[54]

In sum, both children and adults appear to be naturally inclined to think of individuals as defined by an unchanging essence or soul that accounts for their unique personality. Both children and adults find it very hard to envision the complete cessation of all conscious experience that defines death. This provides a natural entry point for childhood conceptions of immortal souls to make their way into the adult cognition. Even though an adult may explicitly claim to believe that all functions end at death, the idea of a personal essence that persists beyond death makes intuitive sense. In our evolutionary past, where that intuition could serve an adaptive function—as in postulating an ancestor who knows whether tribal traditions are being faithfully followed or not—it stood a good chance of being accepted into the adult social context.

Imagining Gods That Matter

> The counterintuitive properties of gods that actually matter to people are social in orientation, practical in nature, and a little less grandiose than those that are spectacularly theological in presentation. . . . In every culture the gods that matter know the truth, keep watch, witness what is done in private, divine the causes of events, and see inside people's minds.[55]

If religion represents a supernaturalizing of social life, then we would expect that the gods we envision would reflect the social worlds we inhabit. Whether it is a hunter-gatherer band or a Fortune 500 boardroom, the interpersonal relationships, political maneuverings, and social intrigues are probably not all that dissimilar. Some folks win with charm, and others just want to be feared; some people matter, and others not so much.

On a day-to-day basis, the president of my university has little relevance to my work life. Occasionally he surfaces, announcing a new initiative or a recent big donation, but other than that he is mostly just an earnest-looking image on a brochure, a signature on a memo filed long ago. Homage-wise, he requires only hearty applause at the annual university convocation.

Though seemingly far lower on the power scale, the office secretary is a much higher-maintenance deity. Privy as she is to the various feudings and indiscretions within my department, as well as my own weaker-moment rantings about university policy and personnel, appeasing her weighs much more heavily on my daily routine than appeasing the president does.

So it is with the "real" gods. They are as motley a cast of characters as those inhabiting our social circles, and our attitude and behavior toward them varies with their practical relevance. Cross-culturally, gods and spirits run the personality spectrum—some inviting and warm, others nasty and menacing.[56] This observation alone calls into question the notion that religion arose primarily to provide us with comfort against a dangerous world or to assuage our fears about death and suffering. Religion may do this to some degree (just as our personal relationships can), but religion may also add to those fears (again, just as our personal relationships can).

Moreover, some gods, like some university presidents, are high and mighty yet garner little regular attention. For example, the Fang are a traditional people living in Cameroon (West Africa). For them, the earth and the sky are the products of Mebeghe—a great creator-god. Alas, despite Mebeghe's undisputed grandeur, he is of little daily concern, and no rituals or sacrifices are made on his behalf. Instead, the many spirits, witches, and demons who populate the forests are of much greater practical consequence and therefore require regular ritual attention.[57] Just as with people, the gods who matter are the gods whose interests seem to intersect with our own on a daily basis. Like the ever-observant department secretary, these "gods who matter" are believed to possess strategically important information about us and our relationships. Across the globe, these "interested" gods are often ancestors or natural spirits whose well-being is intertwined with that of the tribe or with some resource or patch of land vital to the tribe's survival.

All of this reinforces the notion that when childhood supernatural imaginings were incorporated into adult religious life, that incorporation followed certain social/cognitive constraints. These constraints made the gods ones with whom we could socially interact, and while this proves problematic for academic theology, it is essential for practical religious belief. For one thing, this means, rather oddly, that the gods' "omniscience" and magical powers are actually limited in socially relevant ways. For example, although people claim that God is omniscient and omnipresent, they often describe him (or her) as having limited attentional capacities, such as saying that God would handle two simultaneously unfolding crises sequentially based on need (first saving a man's life, and then helping a woman find her purse).[58] Additionally, even though God knows everything, some of what he knows seems so much more relevant to his "omniscience" than other things. For example, it seems far more important for an all-knowing God to know that I desire revenge for a perceived injustice than to know that I prefer honey ham to turkey for lunch. For purposes of encouraging healthy interpersonal restraint, we need a God whose omniscience is focused on the former rather than the latter. In other words, he needs to know everything so that he can at least know the strategically important things that encourage group cooperation.

Furthermore, Bering provides evidence that our representations of supernatural agents are often implicitly constrained by our experience.[59] Since omniscience and unlimited attentional capacities are beyond our experience, we have difficulty successfully attributing these powers to God. A god with unimaginable capacities becomes difficult to relate to. Instead, we need God to be pretty much as we are—only better. As with any really good relational partner, I need to somehow think that when I'm praying to God he is listening exclusively to me and not to 5 million others as well. Similarly, when he's sorting out all those petitions, we need to think that he uses really good (Godlike) judgment—putting food for the starving at the top and the new bike for the rich kid down the line.

Cognitive studies show that supernatural agent concepts are typically minimally counterintuitive rather than just odd.[60] This means that by and large, a supernatural agent retains the usual qualities that we expect of humans or animals, but with at least one critical violation. This violation makes supernatural agents interesting, while preserving their comprehensibility. Thus, the Virgin Mary is, generally speaking, a typical member of her category: human females. She works, worries, washes, eats, sleeps, visits relatives, gets married, and so forth. She does, however, have one striking categorical violation: She can become pregnant without sex. Oddities, on the other hand, are just exceptionally strange category members, such as a man with a third nipple or a woman who collects old truck tires. A minimally counterintuitive category member is therefore easy to remember. This gives them an advantage in cultural transmission and survival—one reason that religious myths and characters are enduring. But the distinctiveness of minimally counterintuitive concepts is balanced by enough sundry predictability that these gods, spirits, and other supernatural agents are also ones with whom we can form relationships.

The Evolution of Religious Imagination

The fundamental hypothesis guiding this chapter is that imagination evolved as a mechanism for preparing children for the adult social world.

The evolutionary progression of that imaginative capacity can be summarized as follows:

1. Our oldest hominin ancestors probably had imaginative capacities at least as complex as those found in nonhuman primates—overzealous agency attribution and the assumption of a rationally ordered world.

2. Toolmaking demands suggest that by about half a million years ago, hominins possessed an "intermediate" imaginative capacity—beyond that of nonhuman apes, but not yet approaching modern human abilities.

3. The general increase in social complexity associated with the Interregnum period selected for significantly expanded imagination in children since those children grew into more socially competent adults.

4. These increasingly imaginative adults did not simply drop their childhood visions as they matured, but instead found creative, adaptive, and socially relevant ways to incorporate them into their adult lives.

5. This incorporation began as a "healing force" that made preexisting social rituals more intense and effective.

6. Further elaborations on the supernatural world in the form of immortal souls, spirits, gods, and ancestors proved adaptive since these provided a supernatural layer of social scrutiny that promoted social cohesion and cooperation.

7. All these ongoing supernatural incorporations were constrained by social/cognitive factors that ensured that supernatural agent concepts would be socially relevant.

6

Before and After the Interregnum

The Evolution of the Two "Modes" of Religion

Whitehouse's Two Modes of Religion

Anthropologist Harvey Whitehouse argues that religion exists in two modes: imagistic and doctrinal.[1] The imagistic mode is characterized by infrequent, emotionally charged rituals that create the conditions for strong social bonding among participants (e.g., a group enduring a painful initiation ceremony). This mode encourages private reflection on emotionally arousing events. Its effects typically remain localized and personalized, not conducive to widespread transmission. By contrast, the doctrinal mode facilitates the efficient spread of religious beliefs across a broad population. It does this by stressing frequent, stylized rituals that encourage the rote storage of a common set of actions, stories, and teachings (e.g., the Catholic mass, where the story of Jesus' last meal is reenacted and his message of sacrifice is revisited). While the doctrinal mode is an efficient tool for transmission, it can also lose its force through tedium. Thus, both modes are believed necessary for a religion to remain vital: the imagistic providing the individual motivation to participate in religious activities, the doctrinal to establish a common set of ideals and behaviors.

Whitehouse contends that the imagistic mode is historically more ancient, probably dating as far back as the "religious" cave art of the Upper Paleolithic. I agree, but I suggest that the ritual and emotional roots of the imagistic mode run far deeper than the Upper Paleolithic—to well before the African Interregnum. Conversely, the foundations for the doctrinal mode emerge much later. To understand the social/cognitive raw materials out of which our ancestors fashioned religion, we have to look at events prior to the Interregnum. To understand what our ancestors did with the religion they created, we have to look at what happened afterward.

Before the Interregnum: The Social and Ritual Roots of Religion

The story as it stands so far begins with the emergence of anatomically modern humans about 200,000 ybp. Around 100,000 ybp these ordinary hominins were banished from the Levant and began their transformative Interregnum in Africa. About 30,000 years later they emerged from this Interregnum more sophisticated both cognitively and socially. A key part of that cognitive/social sophistication was religion. The religion that emerged during the African Interregnum did not just spring forth from nothing; it was built on already existing hominin capacities. Those capacities clustered in two areas: social emotions and social rituals. Prior to the "real," supernaturalized religion that emerged during the African Interregnum, there was a foundational nonsupernatural "proto-religion." Social emotions and social rituals were the groundwork of this proto-religion.

Although our knowledge about religion becomes increasingly tenuous and speculative as we plumb deeper into our evolutionary history, it does not lose all rational mooring. We are anchored by three grounding assumptions: (1) Religion emerges out of social evolution, (2) emotion and ritual form two necessary and fundamental elements of religion, and (3) the religious capacity of our hominin ancestors prior to anatomically modern humans must fall somewhere within the boundaries set by the emotional and ritual capacities of nonhuman apes, on the one hand, and anatomically modern humans, on the other. Or to put it another way: Chimpanzees don't have religion; humans do. Social emotions and social rituals are fundamental, necessary components of religion. Can we identify the emotional and ritual "soil" from which specifically *religious* emotions and rituals took root in our hominin ancestors?

Religion and Emotion

I speak not now of your ordinary religious believer, who follows the conventional observances of his country. . . . We must make search rather for the original experiences which were the pattern-setters to all this mass of suggested and imitated conduct. These experiences we can only find in individuals for whom religion exists not as a dull habit, but as an acute fever.[2]

The quote above is from William James's *Varieties of Religious Experience*. James understood something about religion: that religion is not philosophy. Philosophy is largely confined to ivory-tower seminar rooms, but religion can be found in nearly every living room—or just about anywhere else you might care to look. Religion is not just (or even primarily) an intellectual pursuit; it is emotional. In fifteenth- and sixteenth-century Spain, entire villages would engage in near-hysterical communal weeping, often in conjunction with Holy Week processions or as a show of piety and remorse over their sins, which they believed might be causing a drought or other misfortune. Something similar occurs today during the festival of La Tirana de Tarapaca in Chile, where thousands of frenetic dancers dressed in monstrous masks whirl themselves to near exhaustion while others make agonizing procession on bended knee to the altar of the Blessed Virgin. Among traditional peoples in Papua New Guinea, certain initiation rites are so traumatic that Whitehouse labeled them "rites of terror." The trauma serves an important function, however, instilling a powerful sense of solidarity among the participants.[3]

Nearly a century ago German theologian Rudolf Otto used the Latin phrase *mysterium tremendum et fascinans* to describe the personal encounter with God.[4] For Otto, coming face to face with the Divine was characterized by rational incomprehensibility and inexpressibility (mystery), over-whelming power and awe-inspiring presence (*tremendum*), and a simultaneous reaction of fear and irresistible attraction (*fascinans*). Religion is about many things, but cold detachment is not one of them. Religion is emotion—often powerful, unspeakable emotion, as Otto contends.

Chimpanzees do not have religion, but read carefully the following description of their encounter with a python, as related by Bill Wallauer, a videographer at the Gombe reserve in Tanzania:

[W]hen a single individual or group of chimpanzees encounters a python (even a small one), the reaction is remarkable. One would expect the chimps to issue alarm calls to warn others. . . . Predictably, the chimpanzees do issue a specific vocalization called a snake wraa, but when it is uttered, the group often draws near, to stare at the snake. Some climb above if possible for a better look. Typical facial expres-sions are those of fear and curiosity. Physical reassurance contact is often made (especially mutual embracing), and eye contact among individuals is frequent. After tens of minutes, members finally begin to disperse. Some individuals however (Skosha and Apollo, for instance) show exaggerated and prolonged interest. Both call time and again even after the other individuals have moved well away. I have seen both stay and stare and call for as long as 30 minutes.[5]

Note the unmistakable fright. But also note how it mingles with an irresistible attraction. No, this is not Otto's *mysterium tremendum et fascinans*, but it is vaguely reminiscent of it. The roots of religious emotion are in primate emotions, especially those social emotions that bind us to one another and form the essential glue of community.

Social Emotions

By and large, social animals have a more elaborate set of emotional responses and expressions than more solitary ones do. The contrasting social lives of prosimian primates (lemurs, lorises, aye-ayes, etc.) and their simian cousins (monkeys and apes) is instructive. Generally prosimians are solitary, nocturnal creatures, whereas monkeys and apes are highly social, living in groups ranging from small family units to communities of 50 or more. Prosimians are also far less emotionally expressive than simians. Prosimian facial muscles are primarily designed for just biting and chewing; they provide for the display of only a few rudimentary emotional expressions, such as fear, anger, and affection. The facial musculature of monkeys and apes is far more complex, allowing for a much wider range of facial expressions.[6] Thus, as creatures become more social, their range of emotional expression (and likely experience) increases as well. This suggests that emotions play an important role in organizing and regulating social relationships. Indeed, apes and monkeys have specific emotional displays that are used to establish rank, repair damaged relationships, and convey intent—for example, signifying whether a smack on the head is intended as punishment or play.

The positive relationship between emotional complexity and sociability is further confirmed by the considerable overlap between the emotional lives of humans and our simian relatives. Many socially relevant emotions seen in humans have counterparts in monkeys and apes. For example, Frans de Waal has documented evidence for empathy, pride, and a primitive sense of fairness in monkeys and apes. Emotional contagion—where the expression of an emotion in one organism makes another susceptible to experiencing that same emotion—may form the foundation on which many of these social emotions, especially empathy, are built. Emotional contagion also represents another point of similarity between the social/emotional lives of humans and nonhuman apes. A recent study showed that laughter could become contagious among orangutans in the same way that it can in humans. "What is clear now is the building blocks of positive emotional contagion and empathy . . . evolved prior to humankind. Such [a] mechanism of empathy is likely to help us to form and maintain social bonds," said psychologist Marina Davila Ross, leader of the study.[7]

Finally, some of the primate/human overlapping emotional territory appears to have direct religious significance. Jane Goodall has reported that chimpanzees occasionally engage in extended and emotive "rain dance" or "waterfall" displays. Stewart Guthrie interprets these displays as a simian form of "anthropomorphizing," where the chimp reacts to the thunder or waterfall as if it were another threatening ape. In this behavior he sees the primordial seeds of the pervasive human tendency to anthropomorphize nature, which for him forms the basis of religion.[8]

Blessed Are the Peacemakers

A central function of religion is maintaining intragroup stability and cohesion (love thy neighbor, do not covet thy neighbor's wife). Our primate relatives share a similar emotional concern. For example, some monkeys and apes engage not just in direct reconciliation (where two combatants make peace), but also in triadic reconciliation, in which family members of the combatants "make peace" after a conflict. Suppose a dominant female monkey launches an attack on a subordinate. Afterward, members of the subordinate's family may approach the attacking dominant with appeasing gestures. This appears to reestablish good relations not just between the aggressor and the original victim, but between the aggressor and the victim's entire family.

Third-party mediation is also present among chimpanzees. Juveniles and adult females will sometimes facilitate reconciliations between fighting males by actively trying to bring the two together. Loud, celebratory hooting may ensue if they are successful and the formerly warring males embrace. Alpha males sometimes play what is called the "control role" within their communities. That is, they actively intervene in order to defuse any potential conflicts before they threaten the stability of the group. These alpha males are often more "popular" than those who use violence to maintain their status. Jane Goodall reports how, during a power struggle, group members actively rallied against the re-ascent of a formerly despotic alpha male.[9]

All of this suggests that some primates show emotional concern over the quality of their social life. Ultimately, this concern may be self-serving in the sense that maintaining within-group harmony is individually beneficial. However, "self-serving" and "selfish" are not identical. Even if a concern for the group serves self-interests, it is still a concern for the group.

All of this suggests that the emotions that lie at the heart of a religious sense of community were established deep in the primate brain prior to the onset of hominin evolution.

Sociologist Jonathan Turner argues that the evolution of complex social emotions was essential to the survival of the earth's few remaining ape species. In his book *On the Origins of Human Emotions*, Turner focuses specifically on the social differences between (Old World) monkeys and apes. Monkeys, he concludes, have strong social mechanisms for forming large groups. Chief among these mechanisms is the strict social ranking of females based on their family lines (matrilines) and the social ranking of males based on size and physical combat. Ten million years ago, as the African forests receded and dried out, monkeys used these mechanisms to bind themselves together into larger groups, which provided increased security against the threats inherent to life in a more open environment. Baboons, which can congregate into supergroups of over 100 or so, are a prototypical example of this.[10]

Apes, however, could not rely on these same organizing structures. In most ape species, females leave their natal groups at maturity, thus subverting well-organized matrilines. Furthermore, males are either solitary (as in orangutans) or have far more fluid social ranking systems (as with chimpanzees and bonobos) than do monkeys. Lacking the social mechanisms for creating larger, more secure groups, most ape species went extinct. The few who did survive had to evolve a unique strategy for organizing larger social groups: a repertoire of intense social emotions. This was especially true for that particular branch of the ape lineage that was fully committed to life in the open—the genus *Homo*.

How Ritual Tamed the Emotions

Jonathan Turner extends his argument on the role of emotions in the evolution of ape societies by pointing to the critical role of ritual in regulating and directing emotions during interpersonal encounters.[11] Social emotions such as empathy, sympathy, affection, admiration, shame, pride, and guilt compel us to seek out others and establish, reinforce, or repair interpersonal connections. However, these emotions can often get overwhelmed by the more basic survival-relevant emotions, such as fear or anger. Ritual tames and contains the fight-or-flight emotions, giving social emotions "room" to flourish.

The fact that humans are such widely successful social creatures would appear to provide prima facie validation for the power of emotions as a social glue. Maybe so, but a million years ago, this was not so obviously in the cards. Emotion, it turns out, is a volatile fuel with which to power your social engine. Observations across a wide variety of nonhuman primate species show (rather surprisingly, maybe) that most aggressive encounters appear to erupt spontaneously, without provocation. An especially dangerous situation is where one is in close proximity to a larger, more dominant group member. Among monkeys, a dominant female may launch an unprovoked attack just to remind the subordinate who's in charge. Among chimpanzees, playful juveniles run the risk of getting an unpleasant beating if they romp too close to a larger male. Female elk, deer, and moose must always be wary when large, aggressive males approach. Regulating dangerous emotions during these tense encounters is one of ritual's main functions.

In each of the examples above, specific rituals are used to regulate the dominant-subordinate interactions, such that danger is minimized. For instance, there are occasions where a more dominant female monkey may want to gain close proximity to a subordinate for purposes of grooming or to gain access to the female's infant. She will use a specific call—a grunt or girney—to signal peaceful intent. Primatologist Joan Silk reports that subordinate females are 30 times less likely to be attacked if the approaching dominate grunted or girneyed than if she remained silent. Furthermore, a grunt or girney often preceded a grooming session. These calls acted as reliable signals of peaceful intentions. The juvenile chimpanzee can let the larger male know that he just playing by using a stereotypic arm-raising gesture. Finally, we have already seen how male elk, deer, and moose use the "low stretch" approach to reassure tense females.[12]

Human social rituals are similar in many respects—they regulate and tame defensive emotions so that social interactions do not spin out of control. Recall the Yanomamo peacemaking ritual or the drum matches among the Ammassalik. In both these instances, ritual served as the restraining mechanism for explosive emotions. Homer provides another "classic" example of this. Consider Odysseus's dilemma in book 6 of the *Odyssey*. He has arrived shipwrecked on the land of the Phaiakians. Though Odysseus is a hero and warrior king, he hardly looks the part as he lies battered and naked on the shore. The Phaiakian Princess Nausikaa arrives on the shore with her entourage. Odysseus is desperate to solicit her help, but he has the wherewithal to understand that a disheveled male stranger (naked, no less!) approaching a teenage princess can only be regarded as a threat. How to make the approach? Homer picks up the tale:

> On seeing one so unkempt and so begrimed with salt water, the others scampered off along the spits that jutted out into the sea, but the daughter of Alkinoos stood firm, for Athena put courage into her heart and took away all fear from her. She stood right in front of Odysseus,

and he doubted whether he should go up to her, throw himself at her feet, and embrace her knees as a suppliant, or stay where he was and entreat her to give him some clothes and show him the way to the town. In the end he deemed it best to entreat her from a distance in case the girl should take offence at his coming near enough to clasp her knees, so he addressed her in honeyed and persuasive language. "O queen," he said, "I implore your aid—but tell me, are you a goddess or are you a mortal woman? If you are a goddess and dwell in heaven, I can only conjecture that you are Zeus's daughter Artemis, for your face and figure resemble none but hers."

Note that Odysseus first considers a grand behavioral ritual: He will throw himself at her feet and embrace her knees. Certainly this gesture (assuming that he could pull it off) would have effectively communicated his friendly desires. However, to get close enough to do it would have required Odysseus to rush up to her unexpectedly and grab her legs before she could flee. He shrewdly chooses another option—something more akin to a monkey's approach grunt. He calls to her from afar, addressing her as queen, and praises her beauty. There is far more to this flattery than meets the eye (ear?). Because of their shared cultural heritage, Nausikaa would have been immediately put at ease upon hearing that Odysseus thinks her to be Artemis. Artemis was more than just a goddess; she was a militantly virginal goddess. She dealt brutally with any man who threatened her virginity, often killing those who (even unintentionally) saw her naked.

All of these examples underscore two important aspects of ritual. First, a critical function of ritual is to initiate and extend positive social interactions. An approaching stranger could easily elicit a defensive reaction, either fight or flight. But proper ritual can smooth the approach. The approacher says, "I mean you no harm," and an interaction may follow. Second, one of the common circumstances for employing ritual is during dominant-subordinate encounters. Long before Moses was removing his sandals before the burning bush, monkeys and apes were making appeasement gestures to keep peace with the alpha male.

The Evolution of Social Rituals

The fact that social rituals are found among a range of different species suggests that this behavior has a deep evolutionary history. The notion that our hominin ancestors would have been engaging in social rituals is therefore quite plausible. At what point, however, did these rituals achieve a level of sophistication that would approach the religious ceremonies of hunter-gatherers or other traditional societies?

Homo heidelbergensis inhabited the Boxgrove site (England) more than 500,000 ybp. Either they were big-game hunters or, more conservatively, they had the ability to secure first access to the carcasses of big-game animals such as hippos, horses, and deer. In his study of the evolution of language, archaeologist Steven Mithen concludes that these hominins probably did not possess language but very likely engaged in "singing and dancing" around a freshly killed animal.[13] The prospect of stomachs soon to be filled by tasty meat would have been an occasion for great celebration:

> We can readily imagine that those at Boxgrove were relieved [at the site of a horse carcass], happy and excited by their work. Hence, we should envision rhythmic Early Human movements around the carcass and melodic vocalizations merging into something close to what we would recognize as dance and song.[14]

The reason Mithen can be confident they were singing and dancing together is that all the prerequisites for such behavior can be found in our primate relatives. Monkeys and apes (as well as numerous other animals) engage in rituals of social bonding involving specific actions and sounds that often induce a relaxed state of mind conducive to positive affiliation.

Suppose two gelada baboons are feeding in close proximity to one another. They will use rhythmic back-and-forth calls to reassure each other that neither means harm. As mentioned earlier, rituals of welcoming and social reaffirmation are present among many primates, including spider monkeys, chimpanzees, and bonobos (and the latter two are our closest primate relatives). Upon reuniting with fellow group members, they will engage in ritualized "greeting" behaviors such as mutual embraces, kissing, group pant-hooting, and grooming. These behavioral and vocal greeting rituals help to reestablish social bonds and reinforce the social hierarchy among community members.[15]

These examples indicate that rituals of social bonding that involve both vocal and behavioral elements are pervasive throughout the primate order and therefore would have been present in the chimpanzee/human common ancestor. However, one feature that appears to be just beyond nonhuman primate capacity is the ability to move rhythmically together as a group. Indeed, there are no recorded instances of wild chimpanzees doing anything that resembles stepping, marching, dancing, or otherwise moving in rhythm together. There is only one account of what might be considered rhythmically coordinated community motor activity among captive chimpanzees.

At his research station at Tenerife, on the Canary Islands, Wolfgang Kohler reported that while playing, a group of chimpanzees began to "march in an orderly fashion in a single file around and around the post. . . . a rough approximate rhythm develop[ed] and they tend[ed] to keep time with one another."[16] Kohler remarked that nothing he had seen before from the chimps so strongly reminded him of the dancing of some primitive tribes. To some degree, however, it appears that the chimpanzees' primitive dance benefited from emulating humans. Kohler goes on to describe how he could encourage their dance by stamping his foot rhythmically and how they typically halted their dance (with great disappointment) when his stamping ceased. Thus, the ability to rhythmically coordinate group-level movements appears to be something just beyond the abilities of chimpanzees, something that emerged along the hominin line.

As their social and cognitive capacities grew, hominins elaborated on primate social rituals, making them increasingly sophisticated and effective. One way in which they elaborated on them was to make them increasingly rhythmic and coordinated. It appears that only humans spontaneously engage in rhythmically coordinated body movements aimed at enhancing social cooperation. Historian William McNeill has written extensively about the "muscular bonding" that occurs among marching soldiers and drill team members. Thus, it was only along the hominin evolutionary branch that social rituals evolved into the singing, chanting, and dancing so prevalent in human societies.[17]

A final element of hominin social rituals that has deep roots in primate history is the ability to alter consciousness through ritual behavior. There is evidence indicating that primates achieve a state of consciousness conducive to social bonding through ritual activity. During grooming, for example, opiates are released in the brains of macaque monkeys. These opiates affect the "groomee," causing relaxation and tension reduction. This appears to be one of the reasons that grooming is so pervasive and effective as a social bonding mechanism. Ritual behavior can also work in the opposite direction, mentally preparing one for conflict. Goodall describes how a young male chimpanzee, challenging for ascendancy in the social hierarchy, ritualistically "rocked" himself into an agitated state (the human equivalent of a pregame "psych-up") prior to a raucous aggressive display. Similarly, male mandrills will sometimes consume the iboga root, which appears to have a powerful excitatory effect on them, in preparation for conflicts with other males. All of this should not be surprising, given that evidence of altered states of consciousness has been found in animals with far less complex nervous systems, such as rats and rabbits.[18]

Thus, all the elements for social rituals that alter consciousness, enhance social bonding, and promote mental rejuvenation were already present in our hominin ancestors long before the African Interregnum. Missing, of course, was the supernatural element—the element added during this period. By adding it, our ancestors intensified these rituals, making them all the more powerful and functional.

Religion did not invent new emotions when it emerged; it simply acted innovatively on the suite of social emotions already present, combining in sometimes novel ways the emotions and behaviors already adapted for social living. As our ancestors' social world become increasingly complex, primate community concern evolved into hominin guilt and shame. As the hominin social world became supernaturalized, guilt and shame were reinforced with rules of taboo and divine laws of behavior, giving these emotions cosmic significance. As fear and wonder mixed with admiration, religious awe and worship (*mysterium tremendum*) took shape.

Religion did not invent ritual either. But as emotions evolved to take on religious significance, ritual evolved to take on supernatural significance. Religious ritual not only accessed and regulated religiously relevant emotions, but also organized and directed those emotions in order to maintain constructive human-divine relationships. Approaching the gods can be as scary for humans as approaching an aggressive male is for a potential female mate. It is unsurprising that these encounters are heavily ritualized. We will now look in more detail at how ritual and emotion evolved together and at the motor/cognitive requirements necessary to make the transition from nonhuman primate emotions and rituals to uniquely human religious emotions and rituals.

Getting Control of the Ritual

The ability to move rhythmically together as a group appears to be just beyond nonhuman primate capacity. It is exactly this type of social ritual that is essential if primate ritual is to become religious ritual. The name for this type of activity is *group mimesis*. Neuroscientist Merlin Donald defines mimesis as the ability to consciously recall and refine motor routines. In mimesis, an organism voluntarily calls to mind a movement pattern and attempts to emulate it.[19] This is essential if a movement pattern is to be practiced and refined. So when a human practices a golf swing or tennis backhand, she is engaging in mimesis. Group mimesis simply extends this process from individuals to groups, as when soldiers practice marching together or synchronized swimmers practice their routines.

While it is not uncommon for humans to spend countless hours shooting a basketball, skipping rope, or hitting a tennis ball against a wall, there is very little evidence that animals engage in this sort of deliberate practice. As Donald succinctly puts it: "Baboons throw projectiles in a fight, but they don't systematically practice and improve their throwing skill."[20] Why not? Donald explains:

You cannot rehearse what you cannot recall. If an animal depends entirely upon environmental triggers to remember when and what to rehearse, skill development becomes extremely difficult, since the animal cannot self-trigger the memories supporting the skill, and effectively hangs in suspended animation until the environment provides the cues needed for retrieval of a given response-pattern. Trainers of apes have had to cope precisely with this limitation; for instance, it often takes thousands of trials to establish a reliable signing response in a chimpanzee.[21]

This difference is really a difference in consciousness. Deliberate practice of the sort described by Donald requires a level of consciousness that is simply beyond nonhuman animals.[22] So when and how did hominins evolve the capacity to consciously control motor movements such that they could engage in group mimesis? The best evidence we have for that is found in the tools they left behind and the motor skills necessary for their creation.

Mimesis and the Evolution of Tools

The earliest stone tools are the Oldowan industry, dating to about 2.5 million ybp. They are simply small sharp flakes broken from a core stone. Though there is no evidence that apes can create Oldowan-type tools in the wild, captive apes have created similar tools. Most researchers agree that Oldowan tools do not represent a major intellectual advance in terms of representational ability. In other words, the Oldowan toolmaker (called a knapper) probably did not have a conceptual plan or image guiding the tool construction process. Instead, the toolmaker was simply trying to create a sharp edge that would fulfill a cutting or scraping need. However, recent work does suggest that Oldowan tools require a level of motor control and timing that exceeds that of nonhuman apes. Some finds from the Lokalelei site of West Turkana, Kenya (about 2.3 million ybp), even suggest that Oldowan knappers could affect minor repairs on a core as it was being shaped. However, it is doubtful that Oldowan toolmakers needed to engage in deliberate, consciously monitored practice in order to perfect their toolmaking skill.[23]

The situation changes with the emergence of the next major toolmaking industry, called the Acheulean (about 1.4 million ybp). The emblematic tool of the Acheulean is the hand axe, which was created by trimming flakes around the sides of a core, producing a teardrop-shaped, roughly symmetrical implement. Unlike Oldowan tools, hand axe construction (especially later hand axes, which emerged around 0.5 million years ago) would have required considerable investment in time and energy: The toolmaker would have gone through a series of flaking iterations before completing the final product. Archaeologists Tom Wynn has argued that the late Acheulean hand axe maker, unlike his Oldowan counterpart, could not focus solely on the shape of the tool's edge. Instead, he had to understand how flakes trimmed from one part of the stone affected the tool's overall shape.[24] This would have required the knapper to hold in mind multiple perspectives of the tool as it was being created. Thus, the late Acheulean hand axe may provide us with the first evidence of hominin motor behaviors guided by a mental image—the first step toward skill acquisition via deliberate practice.

While this claim has met with some skepticism, recent studies of hand axe construction offer support for this assertion. The late Acheulean hand axe is not an easy tool to make—only one genus (*Homo*) has mastered it. Evidence from contemporary stone-knappers suggests that this skill could not have been acquired without deliberate practice. Modern-day knappers attempting to reproduce late Acheulean hand axes usually require months to years of practice before achieving an acceptable level of skill. Among the few traditional societies where stone-knapping is still present, years of apprenticeship are required for skill development. For example, stone-knappers from Khambat (India) usually begin training at age 10–12 and will spend anywhere from 3 to 10 years in apprenticeship. Among the Kim-Yal of New Guinea, the craftsmen who produce stone hand axe–like implements (adzes) are exclusively older males. Their apprenticeship begins at age 12 or 13, and 10 years or so is typically required to achieve the highest levels of adze-making skill.[25] Along with the technical difficulties, the hand axe also requires a considerable amount of sheer strength and bravery. Serious and sometimes fatal injuries were probably not uncommon among Acheulean hand axe makers. Stone tool experts Kathy Schick and Nicholas Toth comment:

> We know from experience that the injuries produced in quarrying massive flakes from boulder cores can be formidable, especially if one is scantily clad. We suspect that death due to loss of blood from a severed artery was probably not unknown in Acheulean times. Accidental injuries from flaking stone may have been one of the most common "occupational hazards" during these times.[26]

Given the time and effort required for skill development among contemporary stone knappers, it seems reasonable to assume that Acheulean hand axe makers would have required similar practice and training in perfecting their skills. Evidence of this practice may be present in various forms in the archaeological record.

Archaeologist Ofer Bar-Yosef notes that discarded cores from many Middle Paleolithic (250,000–35,000 ybp) sites show an interesting temporal pattern of flake removal: The technique used to remove the last flakes is often different from the one used to remove earlier ones.[27] He speculates that (among other possibilities) old cores were used for skill acquisition. Youngsters may have used discarded cores to practice flake removal, or a master may have used old cores to teach novices.

In her studies with modern hand axe makers, Vicky Winton has found that highly skilled knappers produce hand axes with a consistent proportional relationship between the tool's length and thickness. Among less skilled knappers, the length-to-thickness ratio is more variable. Assessing this ratio in ancient hand axes provides a potential measure of the skill level of the artisan. Hand axes unearthed from the Lower/Middle Paleolithic site of Dickett's Field, United Kingdom, have a generally consistent length-to-thickness ratio, while those from the Wolvercote site are more variable. This suggests that skilled knappers predominated at the former site, while a more variable range of skill levels was present at the latter.[28] A variable length-to-thickness ratio among a set of hand axes could very well indicate knappers working their way toward greater expertise.

At many sites where hand axes have been found, hundreds of them show no sign of use. If they weren't being used, why were they being made? One possibility is that they were used not as tools, but as indicators of toolmaking competence. This competence may have played an important function in mate selection. A male who could produce a high-quality hand axe may have been signaling his industriousness, skill, and overall mate quality—his good genes—to local females. The hundreds of unused hand axes could indicate male hominins practicing their skill. This interpretation fits nicely with the ethnographic evidence cited earlier from the Kim-Yal, where hand axe–like implements are the domain of mature males. Furthermore, these implements often carry symbolic and even sacred meaning as ritual exchange items and bride-wealth payments.[29]

By 300,000 ybp, highly refined, regionally variant, and often aesthetically pleasing hand axes are present. These hand axes suggest that local traditions in tool production had emerged and that the tool itself was now being appreciated as a signal of one's skill and cultural identity. This evidence is complemented by that of composite tools, which were also emerging at about this same time. Like hand axe construction, composite tool manufacture makes special demands on the cognitive system. The assembly process requires the craftsman to consciously plan a sequence of motor actions while actively monitoring the progress of each stage. From all this we can draw the conclusion that by 500,000–300,000 ybp, hominins had the conscious capacity to deliberately practice and refine motor routines: mimesis.[30]

It is also notable that this time frame intersects with Robin Dunbar's work on the evolution of language. Dunbar has documented a close connection between neocortex size and group size among primates, which suggests that social complexity was a key factor driving brain evolution.[31] In order to successfully navigate an increasingly complicated social landscape, primates required ever more brain power. By around 500,000 ybp, however, archaic hominins had reached a critical transition point. Group sizes were exceeding what could be successfully regulated using the typical mode of primate social bonding—grooming. Grooming takes time, and there simply would not have been enough hours in the day for enough group members to engage in mutual grooming to prevent the group from splintering apart.

Thus, about half a million years ago, archaic hominins were forced to invent new strategies for social bonding. Dunbar argues that their solution was vocal grooming—the beginnings of language in the form of idle group-based conversation (gossiping). This early language was probably not the fully developed, syntactically complex language we know today, but instead some protolanguage that worked in conjunction with gesture.[32] Thus, the conscious capacity that allowed for group-coordinated movements was very likely complemented by newly emerging vocalizations—singing and chanting accompanied marching and dancing.

Other Evidence of Ancient "Religion" in the Archaeological Record

By about 500,000 ybp hominins possessed a degree of conscious motor control that would have allowed for group mimetic rituals. In other words, they could have done something unprecedented among primates—danced, chanted, and marched in a rhythmically coordinated fashion. Along with this evidence, the archaeological record provides at least three other lines of evidence suggesting that group-based nonutilitarian rituals were also present at or around this time and that they may even have been accompanied by a murky "spiritual sense." Considered individually, each of these lines of evidence is questionable, and they do not convince me of the presence of "religion" as we understand it. But they do reinforce the notion that community rituals of some form were very likely present in archaic hominins and these rituals formed the foundational base on which later religious rituals could be erected. Each shall be discussed in turn.

Cannibalism

Among many hunter-gatherer societies, eating the flesh, especially the brain, of another was (is) tantamount to ingesting her spirit. This practice applied not just to enemies, but also (and more importantly) to relatives and fellow tribe members. A family or fellow tribe member might be consumed so that his strength and skills would forever remain within the tribe. For example, among the Wari' of South America it is considered far more respectful and compassionate to consume a loved one so that she is literally reincorporated into the tribe than to permit the remains to decay.[33]

Homo erectus skulls unearthed from the Zhoukoudien site near Beijing suggest that cannibalism among hominins may date back as far as half a million years. Many of these skulls were apparently broken open from the bottom, similar to the practices of more recent cannibals, suggesting that extraction and consumption of the brain might have been the goal. Even more intriguing is a *Homo erectus* skull found in Bodo, Ethiopia, dating to around 600,000 ybp. This skull contains 25 stone-tool cut marks, presumably incurred when the skin was removed. Facial skin removal would seem to have little practical purpose and therefore hints at possible symbolic or ritual significance.

Other skulls with possible evidence of defleshing have been found at Klasies River in South Africa (about 100,000 years old) and Herto, Ethiopia (about 160,000 years old). Similar finds strongly indicative of cannibalism and possible ritual (multiple skulls with broken bases and/or cut marks) have been documented at Neanderthal sites in Kapina, Croatia, and Abri Moula in southeastern France. In many of these instances, cranial fracturing from natural processes or cannibalism resulting from nutritional stress cannot be ruled out. Even so, the possibility remains that some of this activity represents some form of death-relevant ritual behavior that is hundreds of thousands of years old.[34]

Red Ochre and Other Early "Symbols"

Red ochre is a soft iron oxide that easily pigments other surfaces. Among hunter-gatherers, red ochre is used extensively in rituals and carries significant symbolic meaning. Some have argued that red's symbolic importance rises to the level of a universal human archetype, representing such things as blood, sex, life, and death. Evidence of red ochre and other mineral pigments dates as far back as 300,000 ybp. For example, archaeologists have unearthed from the Twin Rivers site in Zambia over 300 pieces of variously colored mineral pigments dated anywhere from 270,000 to 170,000 ybp. The pigments appear to have been intentionally transported to the site from remote locations and show evidence of deliberate modification. Though red ochre and other mineral pigments can have various uses, evidence from many of these finds suggests ritual rather than practical use.[35]

It is not until about 100,000 ybp that we have evidence of artifacts being painted with red ochre, presumably to enhance their appearance and meaningfulness. Prior to this, hominins probably painted themselves using red ochre and other mineral pigments. A 77,000-year-old red ochre cobble—carefully engraved with crosses—from Blombos Cave, South Africa, may represent the oldest piece of "art" on record. The presence of red ochre in the archaeological record, coupled with the effort being expended for its acquisition, suggests that its value exceeded whatever utilitarian function it might have had.[36]

Apart from the presence of ochre, there are a few scattered examples of what might be symbolic artifacts dating from 100,000 years ago or more. A three-million-year-old jasper cobble in the form of a human face was uncovered from a site near Makapansgat, South Africa. The nearest source for this item was 10 kilometers from the recovery site, leaving open the possibility that it was intentionally transported, presumably by a hominin who was intrigued by its anthropomorphic quality. A similar anthropomorphized artifact was found at Berekhat Ram in the Golan Heights. This was a 233,000-year-old human-figure-shaped stone that showed evidence of intentional modification. Finally, many items recovered from late Lower and Middle Paleolithic sites (from 300,000 to 35,000 years ago) contain what appear to be intentional zigzagging, parallel, or radiating markings that may represent visual experiences of altered states of consciousness.[37]

Deep Cave Rituals

A few Neanderthal deep cave sites provide possible evidence for ritual behavior. About a quarter of a kilometer deep in the Bruniquel Cave of southwestern France, Neanderthals apparently arranged broken stalagmites into two circles, one of which surrounded the remains of a fire. These remains have been dated to around 50,000 years ago. Additionally, Hayden has made a spirited case for bear-cult rituals at the Neanderthal site of Regourdou Cave in southwestern France. Remains of a bear skull, bones, and other possibly intentionally arranged and manipulated materials dated to between 60,000–70,000 years old have been found here. Other deep cave sites associated with Neanderthals may also have been locations of ritual activities.[38]

None of the evidence reviewed above is conclusive. However, note that much of it clusters within the 500,000–100,000 ybp time window. This roughly corresponds to the evidence for deliberate practice discussed earlier. Taken in total, it strongly suggests that some manner of behavior transcending purely practical concerns was present by around 500,000 ybp.

Group Rituals of Social Bonding

> As the dancer loses himself in the dance, as he becomes absorbed in the unified community, he reaches a state of elation in which he feels himself filled with energy or force immediately beyond his ordinary state, and so finds himself able to perform prodigies of exertion.[39]

By about 500,000 ybp, hominins were very likely engaging in social rituals that involved rhythmically coordinated group-level motor movements—swaying, dancing, and marching—and this was accompanied by newly emerging vocal signals: singing, calling, and chanting. These rituals facilitated group bonding and social cohesion. Hundreds of thousands of years ago, those hominids who managed to create more socially cohesive groups may very well have had a distinct selective advantage over their more isolated, individualistic counterparts. There is ethnographic evidence that offers support for this idea. In his studies of the Venda people of southern Africa, John Blacking found that communal dancing and music-making actually increased during times of plenty compared to times when resources were scarcer. He argued that it was when individuals and clans were most able to pursue self-interests at the expense of the larger group that community-scale cooperative activities became most urgent.[40] Group mimesis was essential for keeping the group together when (transient) prosperity threatened to pull it apart.

Prior to about 100,000 ybp, none of these group-based mimetic rituals need have included the supernatural. However, given that we have already found evidence of altered states of consciousness in nonhuman primates and other animals, it is highly likely that these rituals involved the attainment of an ecstatic mental state that enhanced social cohesion among the participants. These were group-mimetic, consciousness-altering rituals of social bonding. Late Lower and early Middle Paleolithic hominins (about 500,000–250,000 ybp) were gathering around a campfire or at the site of a freshly killed animal, and together they would dance, march, sing, and chant. The steady rhythmic movement would bring about an altered state of consciousness that would both "feel good" and enhance group solidarity. The modern-day analogues to these rituals are found in purely secular mimetic activities such as group dance (square dancing, for example), marching, drill team, some team sports, participatory spectator events (rock concerts, football games, etc.) and possibly some fraternity/sorority rituals.[41]

William McNeill contends that such rhythmic, group-coordinated actions bring about a euphoric state and a "muscular bonding" among participants that serve to enhance group cohesion and cooperation. Indeed, this feeling of "muscular bonding" is probably the result of chemical changes that can occur in conjunction with social rituals of this type. McNeill describes "muscular bonding" as "[a] strange sense of personal enlargement, a sort of swelling out, becoming bigger than life, thanks to participation in collective ritual, [a] euphoric fellow-felling."[42] This is very much what I envision these hominins experiencing.

Physically and emotionally engaging group-coordinated activities were the essence of "religion" prior to African Interregnum. These were the already-present rituals to which our ancestors added supernaturalism. Though the supernatural intensified these rituals, it did not fundamentally alter them. The psychological effects of group-based religious rituals and secular group-coordinated activities are similar. Both activities can bring about deindividuation, or the loss of a sense of personal identity as one becomes enmeshed in the crowd. Community-based rituals, whether secular or religious, encourage the release of brain opiates that promote social bonding. Moreover, activities that synchronize motor and respiratory functions among individuals (whether secular or religious in nature) correlate positively with measures of empathy and can lead to enhanced social bonding and cooperation.[43] Adding the supernatural intensified these effects, but the foundation—ecstatic social rituals of social bonding—was already present.

After the Interregnum: The Foundations of Doctrinal Mode

To complete our evolutionary story, we need to add one more piece to the puzzle. Religion involves more than just ecstatic rituals that promote social bonding—the imagistic mode discussed earlier. Religion also involves the doctrinal mode—stories and teachings that define a tribe and its place in universe.

Earlier I described something called the "Upper Paleolithic revolution model." This was the theoretical idea that modern human behavior and cognition did not reach full blossom until about 35,000 ybp, when we see, in Europe, an explosion of symbolic art and artifacts, sophisticated tools, and ritualized burial sites. While more recent evidence has shown that there was an incremental run-up to the Upper Paleolithic, it still appears that a cognitive/social tipping point was achieved around this time. Indeed, the Upper Paleolithic is the point at which we have the first convincing evidence of two cognitive attributes critical in the evolution of religion: language and episodic memory.

While the evolution of language has been and continues to be a source of great controversy, many experts in the field see the burst of symbolic artifacts and rapid pace of innovation characteristic of the Upper Paleolithic as indicative of "full-blown" language (as opposed to some form of more primitive protolanguage).[44] This "full-blown" language possessed a complex syntax that allowed for such things as communicating in the past and future tenses, and recursion—the ability to imbed clauses and create multifaceted concepts.

Episodic memory is a time-sensitive memory that allows people to recall and reexperience life events in their original (albeit subjective) context. So, for example, recalling the rules of baseball (three strikes, you're out; four balls, take first base, etc.) is qualitatively different from remembering that time in Little League when you struck out, losing the big playoff game. The latter memory, complete with the associated agony of a 10-year-old, is a personal one, a unique moment in one's life history. The former is simply a dispassionate fact whose origin is now irrelevant and forever lost.

As with language, episodic memory is a complicated and controversial topic. Recent studies have shown that certain birds and some primates appear to have some elements of a time-based memory. For example, scrub jays and squirrel monkeys appear capable of anticipating that they will eat certain foods or will be thirsty in the future.[45]

However, the degree to which this time-based memory is comparable to human episodic memory is debatable. A number of researchers have argued that the human capacity to code and retrieve memories in their temporal context is unique—a defining characteristic of human cognition. The degree to which our hominin ancestors possessed a time-sensitive memory system is, again, a matter of great discussion.[46] However, with the Upper Paleolithic we have the first evidence of time-relevant artifacts, indicating that some threshold was crossed in terms of the hominin ability to think about and conceptualize time. The Upper Paleolithic marks the first evidence of food storage pits, calendar-like timekeeping devices, and remote hunting technologies such as snares, traps, and weirs.[47] These devices suggest that during the Upper Paleolithic hominins were thinking about time differently than before.

These new elements—language and episodic memory—provide for a new aspect of religion: narratives and mythologies. Creation myths, tales of gods and heroic ancestors, and stories of tribal history and the tribe's connection to the divine world are all common characteristics of traditional religions.[48] The emergence of full-blown language and episodic memory would have provided the necessary cognitive apparatus for the construction and transmission of these culturally important religious elements. My hypothesis is that these elements emerged during the Upper Paleolithic, after shamanistic healing rituals had already been in place for 10,000 years or more. If the evidence from the Tsodilo Hills and Fumane Cave gives us a time frame of 70,000–35,000 ybp for the emergence of shamanism, then evidence of ancestor worship in the form of ritual burial with elaborate grave goods, I believe, marks the first "hard" evidence of religious narratives and myths.

Ancestor Worship and Narrative Formation

Earlier I discussed evidence that some hunter-gatherer societies of the Upper Paleolithic had moved from being purely egalitarian to transegalitarian or complex. These complex hunter-gatherers were more sedentary and used more sophisticated hunting technologies to gather surpluses of seasonally abundant resources. Surplus resources created a more stratified society, with elites laying claim to the resource-rich territories and the lion's share of the surpluses generated from those territories. It was these "elites" who were typically laid to rest with elaborate ceremony and lavish grave offerings as both a testament to their standing during life and as preparation for their role as powerful ancestors in the afterlife. The elaborate burial sites of the Upper Paleolithic provide evidence of the presence of this elite class and of the emergence of ancestor worship. While there is some evidence of intentional burial prior to the Upper Paleolithic, the evidence of burials unambiguously associated with grave goods such as body adornments (headdresses, beaded necklaces, armbands) and hunting weapons increases significantly in Upper Paleolithic.[49] This supports the notion that this form of religious practice emerged later than shamanism.

There are good reasons to suspect that the emergence of an elite social class and ancestor worship could not have been accomplished without compelling myths or narratives about the supernatural. Convincing members of a close-knit and traditionally egalitarian society that you and your family should be the beneficiaries of special privileges is no easy task. Anthropologist Christopher Boehm points out how hunter-gatherer egalitarianism is aggressively enforced by coalitions that vigorously resist attempts at individual domination.[50] To gain and maintain their status in the face of this opposition, social elites had to appeal to the supernatural.

It was their family link to powerful ancestors that justified their elevated status. The benevolent proprietorship that these ancestors generously extended over resource-rich territories was crucial for the survival and prosperity of the entire tribe. To maintain good relations with these ancestors, their earthly kin had to perform certain rituals and sacrifices. This special connection to powerful ancestors brought with it certain "legitimate" privileges. Thus, if my great-great-grandfather (now a divine ancestor) is responsible for sending the salmon downstream every year, and only I can communicate with him (through a certain exclusive ritual), then it is right that I be allowed a larger tent and more wives than anyone else in the tribe. Social stratification becomes an outgrowth of the demands of powerful ancestors—demands that must be met in order to ensure the entire tribe's prosperity and security.[51]

By appealing to the supernatural, resource-holding elites cloaked their status in divine legitimacy. This divine legitimacy may have functioned as an effective countermeasure against aggressive egalitarianism. However, this divine legitimacy did not come for free. Community rituals often serve as a restraining force against high-status individuals' exploiting others within the group. Mayan priests and kings, for example, were required to engage in ritualized acts of brutal self-mutilation, puncturing their penises or tongues and tugging objects through the open wounds, as signals of their divine worthiness. The divine ancestors fractured the community and, paradoxically, held it together at the same time. To accomplish this would seem to require a compelling, unifying myth.[52]

Evidence of ancestor worship, therefore, necessarily brings with it evidence of religious myth. There must be some reason *why* the ancestors are being worshipped, and this reason must be compelling enough to justify the social inequities associated with complex hunter-gatherers. Ancestor cults entail the construction of a conceptual framework for the supernatural, or, to put it another way, a coherent theological narrative connecting the ancestors, the supernatural, and the earthly realm. Its elements would go something like this: (1) The supernatural world exists (a holdover from early shamanism), (2) the ancestors reside in the supernatural world after death, (3) the ancestors can affect conditions of their former earthly tribe, (4) the ancestors maintain a special relationship with their kin descendants in the tribe, (5) the ancestors must be placated by certain rituals and sacrifices performed by their kin descendants so as to maintain their good favor, which is beneficial for both their direct kin and the tribe as a whole. From this skeletal framework, more elaborate stories and myths explaining why all this is true, how it originated in the history of the tribe, and other important cultural lessons and "facts" can be constructed to create a compelling story passed on from generation to generation. The full flowering of the narrative element in religion provides the cultural myth that sustains the tribe against social disintegration and buffers individuals against the inevitable travails of life.

Two other lines of evidence also suggest that ancestor worship was present during the middle of the Upper Paleolithic. While the ancestors provided wealth, descendants were necessary to ensure it. Thus, as might be expected, the Upper Paleolithic also provides evidence of an increasing concern with progeny and fertility. Nearly 200 "Venus" figurines—small artifacts carved in ivory, bone, or stone depicting naked, headless, female forms with exaggerated breasts, buttocks, and abdomens—have been unearthed and dated to the Upper Paleolithic, many concentrated around the time of 23,000–25,000 ybp. Other sculpted, carved, and graphic depictions of naked females and female body parts as well as phallic symbols have also been found. Given the amount of effort and resources required to create these images, the likelihood that they simply represent "Stone Age pornography" seems remote. Instead, as numerous researchers have argued, they more likely reflect concerns over fertility and childbearing. Furthermore, the Upper Paleolithic marks the first time in history that a substantial number of females were buried with elaborate grave goods, indicating an elevation in their social status. This would be expected if fertility and progeny were becoming increasingly valued.[53]

Evidence of exclusive rituals is also present during the Upper Paleolithic. One of the unique and puzzling aspects of Upper Paleolithic cave art is the fact that much of it is located in remote, isolated cave chambers. Many spectacular examples of cave art are in relatively open, accessible areas; nevertheless, it is intriguing how frequently cave artists intentionally selected tiny, tight, difficult-to-reach recesses for their work. Some painted chambers can only be accessed after a mile-long trek through frigid waters (Montespan Cave), a harrowing climb up a sheer rock face (Nerja Cave in Spain), a 16-foot rope descent (the shaft at Lascaux), or a 200-meter climb after traversing a 450-meter passage (Salon Noir at Niaux Cave in France). While the larger, more accessible cave sites were likely used for community-wide rituals, these remote sites were probably used for exclusive rituals and/or individual "vision quests." Exclusive rituals where elite tribe members offer sacrifice to powerful deceased ancestors are a common characteristic of ancestor-worshipping societies.[54]

Popular vs. Elite Religion: Setting the Stage for Paganism

Deep cave sites, in combination with the evidence for elaborate burials and fertility concerns, suggest that the Upper Paleolithic marks the emergence of something new in religion: exclusive rituals that existed alongside community-wide ones. The exclusive rituals were held in deep cave sites and were reserved for social elites. It was here that the elites communed with their powerful ancestors and offered them special forms of worship and sacrifice on behalf of the entire community. In more open, accessible venues, the entire community would gather for public rituals involving feasting, dancing, and other group-mimetic activities.[55] This division laid the groundwork for future ones characterizing classic paganism, such as the high gods or state gods of the ruling classes versus the minor gods of the field and forest; exclusive temple-based rituals versus public feasts and festivals; state-sponsored cults versus familial or domestic ones, and so forth. The highly mythologized and socially stratified religion that would characterize the first great civilizations was taking shape.

Summary

The pieces of our evolutionary puzzle are now falling into place. Unlike their ape cousins who clung to the dwindling tropical forests, our bipedal ancestors opted for life in the open, where there was increased pressure for larger social groups as protection against predation. Larger social groups deepened the social emotions. Additionally, social emotions were complemented by increasingly group-based, rhythmically coordinated social rituals. These group-based rituals were facilitated by the development of increased motor control. The motor skills necessary for sophisticated tool manufacture selected for hominins capable of consciously practicing and refining motor routines, and group mimesis began to emerge.

Sometime starting around 500,000 ybp, archaic *Homo sapiens* were gathering fairly regularly around campfires, hunting kills, and other venues to dance, clap, sing, and chant in unison. At times they may have painted their bodies with red ochre and other pigments, heightening the ritual's drama. These group rituals brought on an ecstatic mental state that further enhanced social bonding. During the African Interregnum, the supernatural was added to these rituals and shamanism emerged. As egalitarian hunter-gatherers transitioned into more socially stratified complex hunter-gatherers, ancestor worship, religious myths and narratives, and basic foundations for classic paganism took form.

7

Religion Is (or Was) an Adaptation

Adze makers . . . speak of forgetting their wives, gardens and everything else while knapping, and emphasize that a man's hand will "grow heavy" and lose its skill without continual practice. Commitment to the craft is more, however, than just a duty or virtue. Knapping is also a great source of pleasure, and craftsmen often call out in excitement after successful flake removals. Adze making, which is always conducted as a group exercise, is an enjoyable and meaningful social activity.[1]

Why Making an Axe Is Like Believing in God

Langda villagers on the Indonesian island of West Papua (formerly Irian Jaya) gather together regularly to make a traditional axe-like stone tool called an adze. As is apparent from the description above, the delight they derive from communal adze-making is almost akin to a religious experience. It turns out that adze-making and religion have more in common than one might first suspect. Both are cultural adaptations that have fitness benefits. Both give the groups possessing them a competitive advantage over other groups. Finally, both exerted evolutionary pressure affecting the traits possessed by group members. In short, as cultural products, both religion and adze-making represent human adaptations and human-created selective forces.[2]

Culture as Adaptation

Imagine yourself as a small hairy primate scurrying about the forest, 50 million years ago. So many plants to munch on and so little time. Of course, many of the plants would prefer not to end up in your gut, so they have evolved natural defenses against being eaten. The toxins they produce can be dangerous, even deadly. Any hairy primate capable of quickly and efficiently distinguishing the good from the bad would certainly reap a significant fitness advantage. Natural selection operated on the taste mechanisms of leaf-eating hairy primates such that those plants fit to eat tasted good, while the dangerous ones tasted noxious and bitter (so much so that they were spat out before they could be digested). This highly adaptive mechanism persists in us today.

However, if you fell ill while visiting a traditional society in the Amazonian rain forest, you would probably do well to heed the advice of a local healer and eat the bitter-tasting plant that your naturally evolved taste defenses urge you to reject. Why? Because the healer knows something that you don't: that under the right circumstances, prepared properly, and in the correct dosage, the dangerous plant can have medicinal effects. Obviously the healer wasn't born knowing this. It was passed along as part of her traditional lore. In other words, it is an adaptive product of her culture. Culture can be adaptive—so adaptive that it can compel us to engage in behaviors that would appear contrary to our individual fitness interests.[3]

Culture can also create conditions that affect the evolution of the members who participate in that culture. Millennia ago, dairying arose as an important subsistence practice among most Europeans, many East Asians, and some Africans. The dairying culture made milk and milk products abundantly available as a reliable source of nutrition, thus offering a health and survival advantage to those capable of digesting it. However, in the many millions of years prior to dairying, milk was something that was provided exclusively by mother to infant and not part of the adult diet. Therefore, most humans, consistent with the rest of their mammalian counterparts, evolved to be lactose intolerant as adults. The single dominant gene responsible for the adult capacity to process milk sugar (lactose) became selectively advantageous in dairying cultures. Today, we descendants of these dairying peoples happily carry this gene and enjoy four varieties of cheese on our pizzas. Those derived from nondairying cultures, such as Native Americans, Pacific Islanders, and Far Easterners, retain the more ancient genetic pattern and are generally lactose intolerant as adults.[4]

The selective force of culture may even play a role in more complex human characteristics, such as intelligence. Anthropologists Gregory Cochran, Jason Hardy, and Henry Harpending stirred up controversy recently by presenting evidence that the intellectual prowess of Ashkenazi Jews was potentially due, at least in part, to the social selection pressures of medieval Europe, combined with Jewish cultural traditions against marrying outside the faith.[5] Medieval Christian society restricted Jews to a prescribed set of intellectually demanding professions, such as retail, money-lending, and estate management. The most successful in these professions had the highest rates of reproduction. This, along with low rates of intermarriage, favored the accumulation of traits associated with intellectual ability within the Jewish community. An unfortunate side effect of this selection, however, was the increased incidence of certain genetic disorders known to be especially prevalent in Ashkenazi Jews, such as Tay-Sachs and Gaucher's disease.

Finally, culture can affect basic perceptual and cognitive processes that were once thought to be invariant across human groups. Take, for example, the simple process of visually scanning a scene. Americans of European descent typically focus on the details of a scene, such as the eyes on a face or the style of shoe someone is wearing. East Asians more often focus on a scene's relational properties, such as how close together people are.[6] These differences can even be observed in eye movement patterns: Americans fixate more on specific objects, while Asians spend more time scanning back and forth between foreground and background. Though these perceptual differences vary based on context, they have been linked to some general cognitive and social differences often found between Americans and Asians. The origins of these differences may lie in very early socialization practices. American mothers use far more nouns and spend more time labeling objects for their children, whereas Japanese and Chinese mothers use more verbs and more readily engage children in social routines. Thus, from perceptual processing, to digestion, to intelligence, culture has been shown to be not only a human creation, but also a creative force on human evolution.

Back to the Adze

Social adze-making has been part of the culture of Langda villagers for centuries. As an essential element of the horticulturalist lifestyle, the adze offers a direct fitness advantage in terms of extracting resources from the environment. Dietrich Stout puts it directly: "The horticultural lifestyle of the Highlands would not have been possible without ground stone axes/adzes."[7] It is not hard to imagine that in the distant past other nonhorticulturalist groups may have occupied the same highland territories where the Langda villagers now reside. However, once adze technology emerged, the advantage it offered allowed adze-wielding groups to out-compete these other groups, who were either replaced by or absorbed into the horticulturalists' lifestyle.

Adze-making also has indirect fitness benefits in that the process of construction is profoundly social. It begins with a master-apprentice relationship that lasts for several years. It continues in the groups of variously experienced adze-makers who gather regularly to practice their skill, critique each other's efforts, exchange stories, and simply enjoy their craft and company. These groups provide an essential forum for the maintenance of tribal identity and the transmission of cultural values and traditions. Within this context, the adze has become more than just a tool. It is a symbol of a man's skill and commitment. Adzes are often exchanged as gifts, offered as bride-price payments, captured as war trophies, and used in ritual activities. The single adaptive activity of communal adze-making brings together a wide range of separate social/cognitive functions, including technical skill development, social learning, master-apprentice roles, knowledge of natural resources, spatial/motor coordination, group rituals, storytelling, role modeling, and so forth. Adze-making strengthens and coordinates all these separate functions, bringing them together into one social/cultural "package."

Though speculative, it is possible that in the distant past there were other horticulturalists for whom adze-making was a much more individualized affair. Though such groups may have once existed, they are now gone. Presumably they lost out in direct competition with social adze-makers, not because of a lesser ability to extract resources, but because they lacked the same degree of social cohesion, cooperative spirit, and commitment to traditional tribal values. Similarly, in our ancestral past, there very likely were purely "secular" human groups. But any evidence of them is gone when we look at traditional societies today, none of whom lacks a spiritual culture. Presumably, they lost out as well in competition with religious groups.

As a central element of culture, it is highly likely that adze-making has also served as a selective force on the individuals within the culture. More skilled adze-makers achieve higher social status, and higher status typically leads to greater reproductive success. Thus, the social, cognitive, and technical skills that support adze-making, and the genetics underlying those skills, are selectively favored in a social adze-making culture. It would be unsurprising to find that traits such as spatial reasoning, strong hands, keen observational skills, patience, deference to authority, and efficient task-relevant categorizing abilities (good rock vs. bad rock) are common among Langda men. However, given the complexities of adze-making, it makes little sense to have a dedicated adze-making module installed in one's head. The adze-making process is too variable based on context to be reduced to a repeatable algorithm. Choosing the right rocks, precisely controlling the force and angle of the flaking blow, making subtle adjustments to the ongoing flaking processes, evaluating the potential of the roughed-out shape, carefully sharpening the final edge—all these aspects of adze-making require careful judgment, experience, and conscious control.

Instead, it makes more sense to hone the wide range of social/cognitive faculties upon which adze-making is based (perceptual/motor skills, social learning skills, reasoning ability, knowledge of natural resources, relational and communicative skills, etc.) such that they are especially prepared to engage in a highly likely cultural activity—adze-making. Thus, we would expect to find that the adze-making social context had, over the course of many generations, left an imprint on the Langda villagers such that they are particularly suited to acquiring adze-making skill.

Religion as an Evolutionary By-Product

Most scholars who study the evolution of religion take the view that religion does not represent an adaptation, but instead arises as a by-product of the way our minds have evolved to operate.[8] By-products are incidental outcomes related to adaptations. The human belly-button, for instance, is not an adaptation. It is simply a remnant structure associated with an adaptation—the placental connection between mothers and their offspring. With a little imagination, one could concoct a plausible story about the adaptive significance of belly-buttons in our ancestral past: Parents and other adults took such delight in poking little baby belly-buttons while making high-pitched squeaky noises that the button itself became an important device for facilitating infant-caregiver bonding. Whatever merits (or demerits) this story might have, it does not change the fact that the original emergence of belly-buttons had nothing to do with infant-caregiver social bonding. Furthermore, any supposed adaptive function of belly-buttons must be empirically demonstrated, not simply assumed. For most researchers, religion-as-adaptation falls into the same category as belly-buttons-as-adaptations. How so?

It has often been argued that our ability to envision supernatural agents and forces probably arose from the human capacity for agency detection.[9] The evolutionary demands of the hominin social world selected for a hypervigilant form of agency detection. So when Thag catches Thor snooping around his cave, he assumes not that Thor was just innocently strolling about and happened to wander into his cave, but that Thor *wants* something, such as Thag's new spear or maybe his new wife. Attributing agency provides valuable predictive insight into future behavior (e.g., Thor is not be trusted). Because of this usefulness, it is actually adaptive for agency detection to be overextended as opposed to underextended. The slightest hint of footsteps outside the cave had better bring a swift and strong reaction out of Thag, otherwise Thor might run off with his valuables, which (if one of those happens to be his wife) could severely reduce his reproductive success. Hearing voices in the wind, seeing strangers in the shadows, feeling a threatening presence in a darkened room: While all of these are most likely mere illusions, a single instance of just one being real could be fatal. It is always more adaptive to overattribute agency than to underattribute—that is, better to be safe than sorry.

A hair-trigger agency detection mechanism is a useful adaptation. However, by virtue of its "hair-triggerness," this useful adaptation is also ripe for supernatural extension. Lacking an immediately obvious cause, natural events from the mundane (the rising sun, falling rain, singing birds) to the extraordinary (earthquakes, eclipses, diseases) represent prime candidates for inclusion into the domain of agency-attributed actions. So the rain falls because the ancestors want to help us grow our crops, or an epidemic rages through our village because the forests spirits are angry that we killed all the caribou. The important lesson here is that while our hyper-vigilant, overactive agency detection system is an adaptation, using this system as a basis for constructing supernatural explanations for natural events is (very likely) not—it's a by-product. It is a highly probable way of thinking, but not necessarily a mode of thinking specifically designed by natural selection to solve an adaptive problem. Religion takes naturally evolved mental and emotional systems and stretches and modifies them in highly probable ways, producing a set of beliefs and practices that many people find useful and convincing.

Now here is where a misunderstanding can occur. At the level of the individual mind, this model of religion is probably correct. Religion as a cultural adaptation in no way requires that individuals possess some kind of dedicated religious system, any more than adze-makers posses a dedicated adze-making system. Instead, religion, like social adze-making, is an adaptive trait, not within individuals but within societies. Religion is about relationships. It describes a particular way that individuals and communities relate to each other and to the world around them. It is a community-level way of relating that proved effective in dealing with the ecological and social challenges facing ancestral populations. As such, religion commandeers many different mental faculties, such as agency detection, the capacity for coalition-building, the capacity to experience ecstatic emotional states, ritual behavior, the ability to develop strong emotional attachments, and so on, and channels them into a set of highly effective, communally shared activities and beliefs.

However, locating religion's adaptive function at the cultural level does not mean that religion has not affected the human mind. Similar to adze-making, religion created a social environment where certain individual traits were favored—traits that made individuals more accommodating to religious culture. Thus, we would expect that the social/cognitive abilities that support religious beliefs and behaviors have been molded to be especially amenable to participating in and deriving benefits from a religious social environment.

What Is (or Was) Religion?

Before we can understand either the fitness advantage that religion offered or the selective environment that it created, we have to be clear on what is meant by "religion." In chapter 1, I reviewed some of the many definitions of religion that have been proposed over the years—a testament to the fact that (unlike with adze-making) it is not always easy to figure out when someone is doing "religion." This definitional problem is a key stumbling block for anyone wishing to make the adaptive case for religion.[10] Religion is a complex phenomenon involving rituals, beliefs, behaviors, attitudes, moral codes, institutional bureaucracies, and a range of different cognitive faculties and cultural traditions. Its complexity makes defining exactly what we mean by "religion" problematic. If we are not even sure what religion is, how can we link it to an environmental challenge for which it was an adaptive response?

Religion is complicated—the emphasis here being on the verb "is." Religion as we see it today is the product of many millennia of evolutionary history. Neither the Olympian pantheon nor the Roman magisterium was part of religion in our ancestral world. To understand religion as a cultural adaptation, we must understand what it was when it first emerged, and what kind of world it was born into. After all, religion did not arise to help modern humans adapt to the modern world any more than the adze did. Instead, both helped our ancestors deal with their ancestral worlds.

So what was religion originally? While we cannot be certain, the best evidence we have indicates that when religion first emerged, it was shamanism: supernatural rituals of individual and communal healing.

What Was Religion's Adaptive Function?

Shamanism arose to deal with the same ever-present ecological challenges that hominins had been facing for hundreds of thousands of years—maintaining group solidarity, dealing with illness and injury, and overcoming resource scarcity and competition. These ecological stressors intensified around 70,000 ybp, and shamanism proved to be more effective than other, older strategies in confronting these daunting challenges. Why? Because it introduced the supernatural as a "binding mechanism," harnessing togeth-er a number of separate social/cognitive capacities and directing them toward a single adaptive purpose: healing. These different capacities included the capacity to engage in ritual, the capacity to experience mental states such as ecstasy and altered states of consciousness, the capacity to form beliefs and expectations, and the capacity to form strong social bonds. Similar to adze-making, shamanism brought all these different functions together into single adaptive "package" that created unparalleled condi-tions for placebo healing effects. It did what I call *placebo consolidation*.

Shamanism built upon already-present aspects of hominin social life. For instance, social rituals that affected individuals' conscious states undoubtedly predated shamanism. However, a critical transition took place when our ancestors took social rituals that had incidental healing effects and turned them into healing rituals that called upon a supernatural force. To our ancestors, this force was probably not seen as "supernatural." Instead, it was very likely understood as simply another aspect of the natural world. It was the spiritual part of the natural world that humans accessed during sleep, hypnagogic states, and other altered states of consciousness associated with fatigue, deprivation, and mental or physical stress (conditions that were probably far more frequent for them than for us). By adding a supernatural element, however, shamanism made these rituals even more effective.

Because religion operated at the cultural level, it created social selec-tion pressures that left a mark on individual psyches. For tens of thousands of years, shamanistic healing rituals were the major form of health care available to our ancestors. Those of our ancestors best able to reap benefits from these rituals would have had an advantage over others. Getting the most from the rituals would have meant being able to successfully engage in social rituals, being able to achieve a health-enhancing altered state of consciousness, being able to experience ecstatic mental states, being able to believe in a healing power, being able to resolutely expect positive healing outcomes, and being able to create strong social bonds with others. This religious context selected for minds amenable to supernatural belief, pow-erful emotions, strong social bonds, and a need for ritual. Humans are designed not with a specific adaptive religious module, but instead with a mind prepared to engage in the myriad social/emotional/cognitive activi-ties that fall under what we call "religion."

Placebo Effects

The direct adaptive function of the adze was to facilitate resource extrac-tion from the environment. The direct adaptive function of shamanism was to enhance placebo health and healing effects. The term "placebo effects" refers to the positive health outcomes associated with the psychosocial context of treatment. Recent reviews of placebo effects have identified a number of factors that contribute to the effect, including (1) the suggestive context of treatment, (2) the expectancy and desire of the patient, and (3) the degree of somatic focus on symptoms.[11]

The suggestive context of treatment refers to the degree to which the patient is led to believe that treatment will be effective. For example, when patients are told that they will receive "a powerful pain-relieving agent," they report greater pain reductions than when they are told that there is a 50% chance that what they are receiving is an effective pain reliever. This occurs even when the same substance is given in both cases. The suggestive context of treatment can also be enhanced by inducing an altered state of consciousness wherein the patient is more amenable to suggestion. This helps to explain the effectiveness of hypnosis in some treatment contexts.[12]

Expectancy refers to the degree to which the patient believes that a treatment will be successful. While this subjective factor is often related to the context of treatment (a more confident, reassuring context can produce greater expectancy), it is separable from it. For example, in a double-blind study to assess an experimental surgical treatment for Parkinson's disease, patients were randomly assigned to either mesencephalic transplantation surgery or sham surgery. In 12-month follow-up assessments, the actual treatment assignment had negligible effects. Instead, it was the perceived treatment that made a difference. Patients who believed that they received the "real" surgical procedure showed significant improvements in both psychological (overall quality of life) and physical (motor control) outcomes. A similar result was found in studies comparing real acupuncture to sham acupuncture in the treatment of conditions such as migraine and tension headaches, chronic lower back pain, and osteoarthritis. Once again, regardless of whether patients received sham or real acupuncture, those who believed that acupuncture was an effective treatment and who expected to gain relief from it realized significantly greater benefits than those who did not.[13]

Health outcomes are also affected by the patient's desire for healing. In a pair of similar studies involving treatments for irritable bowel syndrome, the patient's desire for pain relief was measured and found to significantly affect the degree of placebo relief achieved.[14] All these studies demonstrate that a patient's belief can have significant effects on health outcomes regardless of the actual treatment he receives.

Finally, the phrase "somatic focus" refers to the extent to which a treatment leads a patient to selectively attend to certain areas of the body and monitor them for signs of improvement. Studies have shown that increases in placebo pain relief occur when patients are required to monitor their symptoms more frequently. This frequent monitoring seems to bias their attention toward any signs of improvement. Furthermore, placebo effects can be specifically targeted to particular locations on the body. In one study, subjects were given three different placebo creams applied to different areas of the forearm. They were told that the different creams varied in their analgesic power. When heat stimulation was applied, subjects reported the greatest pain on the area of the forearm where they believed the weakest analgesic cream was applied and the least pain where they believed the strongest cream was applied. Thus, both temporal and spatial precision seems to play a role in placebo outcomes.[15]

Along with these factors, social support is also critical in placebo effects. Numerous studies have shown that the degree of social support, either perceived or real, available to a patient can significantly affect health outcomes. For example, breast cancer patients randomly chosen to receive psychosocial intervention along with medical treatment were found to have higher survival rates and lower recurrences.[16]

The health benefits associated with greater social support are very likely due (at least in part) to improved immune system function. Among medical students given a hepatitis B vaccine, those scoring lowest on a psychometric test of loneliness (indicating strong social support networks) mounted the greatest immune system response to the vaccine. The depth and diversity of one's social support networks appear to be particularly important to health. In a study of over 275 healthy volunteers, Sheldon Cohen and colleagues found that those with broader, more extensive social ties among family, friends, work colleagues, and community members were less susceptible to upper respiratory infections and, when infected, were quicker to regain health and experienced fewer and less severe symptoms. Elevations in mood and stress relief are also consistently associated with more extensive social support networks. These factors are also known to positively affect immune system function and to improve health outcomes.[17]

Contextual Healing

It has been argued recently that the term "placebo effect" should be dropped from the scientific lexicon and replaced by the more precise term "contextual healing."[18] This term more accurately conveys the essence of this form of healing—that is, the powerful role that the social and psychological context of treatment plays in the maintenance and restoration of health. This psycho/social healing context can be reduced to two broad factors: (1) the environment, which includes the degree of social support available to the patient and how convincingly a treatment's efficacy is conveyed to the patient; and

(2) the patient's psychological state, which includes her confidence in the treatment, desire for healing, stress level, mood, state of suggestibility, and attentional biases toward signs of improvement.

The shamanistic healing rituals that emerged about 70,000 years ago created an unprecedentedly powerful psycho/social context for placebo healing. By invoking powerful supernatural healing forces and cloaking them in emotionally compelling consciousness-altering rituals, shamanistic healing rituals pointed both the psychological state of the individual and the supportive framework around the individual toward healing. This was the key adaptive transition to which I referred earlier—social rituals became healing rituals. These healing rituals harnessed and enhanced the placebo effect by creating an environment where people embedded within tightly cohesive social support networks believed in a powerful healing force. These factors were self-reinforcing in that they created a context for positive health and healing outcomes, and the outcomes strengthened the belief in the shamans and their rituals.

Religion and Placebo Consolidation: Empirical Evidence

If religion originally emerged as shamanistic rituals that offered an adaptive advantage through improved health and healing, then evidence of this should still be present today. The evidence falls into three categories: (1) religion's capacity for creating a context of belief in healing power, (2) religion's capacity for creating strong social support networks through highly cohesive and cooperative groups, and (3) religion's connection to health, healing, and longevity.

A Reason to Believe

By adding the supernatural, our ancestors took social rituals that had incidental healing effects and transformed them into evocative spectacles specifically designed to heal. This change actually made the rituals more effective. When supernatural belief is included in meditative or contemplative practices, anxiety is reduced, and significant increases in pain tolerance and mood elevation are found.[19]

Along with real increases in effectiveness, the dramatic and emotionally riveting nature of rituals that invoke the supernatural very likely created events that appeared miraculous to those involved. Miraculous or unexplainable events that are ascribed to supernatural forces can be effective in engendering belief in the supernatural. Furthermore, over time one's memory for the placebo effects becomes exaggerated, increasing the intensity of the belief in the supposed "healing power."[20] Finally, accounts of "miraculous" healing events from trusted sources (friends or family members) can often be as effective as direct experience in convincing someone of the power of supernatural or ritualistic healing. Thus, in our ancestral past, once shamans had developed an emotionally captivating way of presenting their healing "treatment," the beliefs motivating those treatments could become self-reinforcing as tales of healing were transmitted from person to person, band to band.

What would the shamanistic healing rituals of our Paleolithic ancestors have been like? The healing rituals of extant traditional societies provide the best guide. These practices are dramatic indeed, and it is not hard to imagine that they would have created a powerful context for placebo healing events. For example, during !Kung healing ceremonies, the shamans who channel healing power engage in feats of physical endurance and pain tolerance that undoubtedly leave observers awestruck. Richard Katz, who studied the !Kung and their healing traditions extensively, describes what the shaman-healer Kana does while in the trance-state called *kia*:

> Kana continues to walk around in the state of kia, like a tightrope walker. He is healing people who are sitting at the little fires on the outskirts of the dance fire. He . . . presses his hands in the area of the chest, flutters them, and moans. He then goes back to the central dance fire, picks up several reddish-orange coals, and rubs them together in his hands, then over his chest and under his armpits. The sparks fly. He drops the coals back into the fire just as the singers begin to scatter.[21]

Enduring self-inflicted pain as a demonstration of power is widespread among shamans. A traditional healer in Thailand plunges large needles through her cheeks and tongue. Healers and holy people from Japan, southeast Asia, and the Balkans are known to walk on hot coals and perform other acts of fire-immunity. Ascetics dedicated to the Hindu goddess Kali have themselves suspended high in the air on ropes attached to giant hooks embedded in their backs during the festival of Meenabharani. They swing about casting flower petals and blessings to onlookers below, impervious to what would seem to be incredible pain. Such feats of pain tolerance are often explainable in psycho/physical terms. This, however, does little to diminish the spell-binding effect the demonstration has on the audience (both presently and certainly in our Paleolithic past). Other types of shamanistic rituals are equally compelling.[22]

We have already encountered an example of an Inuit shamanistic ritual involving apparent soul flight, where the shaman traveled to the spirit world to confront the sea goddess Takanakapsaluk. Among the Innu people of Quebec and Labrador, a similar ritual—the shaking tent ceremony—was one of the most important of the harvesting season. A shaman (called a *kakushapatak*) sets up a conically shaped tent, whose size varies with the presumed spiritual power of the shaman. The tent serves as a "spiritual battlefield" where the shaman confronts animal spirits and rival shamans. Upon entering the tent, the shaman is bound hand and foot. Despite this, the tent begins to shake violently as the ritual reaches its climax—more violently, onlookers say, than any human could produce. Moreover, voices and rumblings emerge from the earth below.[23] As with the shamanistic feats of pain endurance, a perfectly natural explanation may be present for why people report the shakings and rumblings. However, this does little to reduce the gripping nature of the ritual.

Both folklorist David Hufford and psychologist/philosopher William James argued that it was the individual experience of the divine or of the supernatural imposing itself on everyday reality that lies at the root of all religious traditions. National surveys suggest that somewhere between 35% to 47% of the population have had some form of intense spiritual experience or encounter with a powerful spiritual force. Additionally, a fifth to a third of Europeans and even larger percentages of Americans report experiencing some type of anomalous event, such as ESP or contact with the dead. Often these experiences are intense and transformative and seem to elude logical explanation or description in ordinary language. These experiences often elicit and/or strengthen religious belief or belief in the supernatural.[24]

In his study of over 1,200 memories of personally experienced anomalous events—apparitions, out-of-body experiences, contacts with the dead—McClenon reports that in 33% of them, subjects cited supernatural or religious belief as an explanation for the event. The event often either reinforced already-present beliefs or proved pivotal in erasing earlier skepticism. Of the 40 accounts of paranormal dreams for which subjects provided a possible explanation, 90% were supernatural in nature (ESP, God, a deceased person). This was true even among a number of subjects who claimed to be nonbelievers. Nearly 50% of those who had experience some sort of anomalous event claimed that it had changed either their spiritual beliefs or their concept of the meaning of life.[25] Pulling all of these data together, it seems highly likely that the shamanic rituals of our ancestral past gave people a reason to believe in healing power. A reason to believe made placebo effects more likely to occur, which in turn made belief ever more intense and likely to spread.

Social Support

Social support is a key factor in placebo effects. While this factor is not inherently religious, there is evidence that religion is especially effective at creating high-quality social support networks. In one survey of nearly 3,000 people, even after controlling for a number of important social factors (age, income, martial status, employment, etc.), church attendance significantly predicted the number of non-kin social contacts, in-person contacts, telephone calls, and acts of instrumental support that a person received. Furthermore, the perceived quality of these relationships was strongly correlated with church attendance, indicating that for many people the most meaningful social support was found in their church communities. Among a sample of older African Americans, life satisfaction was closely connected to the number of friendships originating from church-related sources. When compared to secular groups such as bowling leagues or parent groups, church-affiliated groups in America have higher levels of within-group trust and commitment. Comparisons of religious and secular kibbutzim in Israel produce similar conclusions. Religious kibbutzim have significantly lower divorce rates and rates of adverse health events resulting from stressful life events. Study authors attribute these effects, in part at least, to stronger social support networks associated with religious ritual and belief.[26]

This is consistent with findings by sociologist Richard Sosis indicating that religious communes or kibbutzim are more cooperative and enduring than comparable secular ones. The level of trust Sosis found among the Jewish Haredi communities he studied was quite startling when considered against the norm of modern urban life:

> During my fieldwork among Haredi communities, I repeatedly observed invitations for meals, lodging, and rides by residents to unknown Haredi travelers. On several occasions, I witnessed cars being loaned to complete strangers, and interviews revealed a surprising number of interest-free loans offered and accepted between people who had previously not known each other.[27]

Natalie and Joseph Henrich report similar levels of cooperation and trust among the Chaldean community of Detroit, Michigan. But this trust was predicated on being an accepted member of the community, which required two essential traits: speaking the language and belonging to the Chaldean Church. Nearly all Chaldeans agreed that leaving the Chaldean Church meant that one was effectively excluded from the community.[28]

All of this supports the hypothesis that in our evolutionary past, belief in the supernatural emerged as an additional layer to human social life. This spiritual layer served as an ever-present set of social "eyes," motivating adherence to group norms and discouraging insidious individualism. As discussed earlier, the fear of critical social judgment is one of the most effective mechanisms of social control. And as we will see later, considerable empirical evidence shows that religious people tend to be more conforming and more adherent to social norms and tend to exercise greater self-restraint than nonreligious people.[29] The supernatural has proven to be an effective means of constructing highly cohesive and cooperative groups. The social support these groups offer to their members enhances placebo health and healing effects.

Religion and Health

As far back as written records can be found, religion has been connected to health and health care, and illness has been understood in spiritual terms. The book of Exodus in the Hebrew Scriptures has Moses instructing the people of Israel: "Worship the Lord your God, and he will bless your bread and your water. I [the Lord your God] will take away all sickness out of your midst. None shall miscarry or be barren in your land. I will grant you a full span of life" (Ex. 23:25–26). Religious ritual was part of the health and healing practices of all of humanity's earliest civilizations, including those of ancient Egypt, Mesopotamia, China, the Indus Valley, and the later Greco-Roman world. Often these rituals involved practices that induced a hypnotic state of consciousness. The health/religion relationship remained intact through the European Middle Ages, and it was only with the eighteenth-century Enlightenment that a purely mechanistic view of bodily function began to emerge.[30]

There has been considerable discussion concerning the role of religion in health and healing. Numerous studies have provided evidence that religious people are healthier and happier, live longer, and recover faster from illness and surgery. For example, religious beliefs have been found to predict positive outcomes following hip and heart surgery, and the degree of strength and comfort that one receives from religion is associated with faster recovery and greater longevity following heart surgery. However, the findings are not always consistent. Spiritual beliefs had no correlation with recovery from spinal surgery, and religious involvement does not have a significant impact on the survival rates of most cancer patients. The general pattern appears to be that religion typically has modest positive effects on health and healing, but with many exceptions and inconsistencies. Again, this is not surprising, given that religion enhances placebo effects, which are positive but which only go so far—all the placebo in the world isn't going to save you if you've been stomped on by a woolly mammoth.[31]

What is relatively uncontroversial is the connection between religion and mental/emotional well-being. In a recent review of over 100 studies addressing the religion/well-being connection, Harold Koenig and colleagues found that 79% reported positive correlations. Furthermore, over 80% of the reviewed studies found a positive correlation between religion and increased hope and optimism, and no published study has found religious people to be less optimistic than nonreligious. Intrinsic religious commitment and active involvement in organized religious activities are associated with lower rates of depression. For example, religious involvement and belief among older men are associated with reduced incidence of depression and predictive of fewer depressive symptoms in six-month follow-ups. Among those diagnosed with depression, greater intrinsic religiosity was predictive of a 70% increase in the speed of symptom remission.[32]

A general enhancement of well-being typically pays off in longevity. Twelve of 13 studies addressing religion and longevity (i.e., 92% of the studies) have found positive associations, and many of these studies find that the association remains significant even after controlling for a variety demographic, social, behavioral, and health-related factors. For example, one study followed over 5,000 people in Alameda County, California, for nearly three decades. After adjusting for multiple potentially confounding predictors of survival, this study concluded that religious involvement was associated with a 23% reduction in the likelihood of dying during the study period. Using a similar format, Koenig and colleagues followed about 4,000 randomly selected older adults for six years and found that frequent religious attendance predicted a 28% reduction in mortality. An even larger study followed over 20,000 Americans ages 18–65 for nine years, and concluded that those who attended religious services at least once a week lived an average of seven years longer than nonattendees. Finally, a retrospective comparison of religious versus secular kibbutzim matched on a range of socioeconomic, educational, demographic, and prior health factors found a significantly lower mortality rate for the religious kibbutzim members. Over a 10-year period, the religious kibbutzim averaged 5.67 deaths per 1,000 person-years for men and 2.33 for women. For the secular kibbutzim, the averages were 9.96 for men and 6.34 for women.[33]

A good deal of heat has been generated about religion and health—much of it focusing on whether the positive effects of religion are attributable to "religion itself" or the many potentially health-enhancing factors associated with religion, such as increased social support, healthier lifestyles, moral codes, hope and optimism, and a sense of purpose. While teasing apart these individual factors has important scientific relevance, it misses a critical point: All of these so-called confounding factors, bound together by rituals and beliefs, *are religion itself!* Religion was the mechanism by which all these placebo-relevant factors were consolidated. Religion's adaptive function was (and in many respects still is) placebo consolidation, and that function still resonates today. So while optimism, healthy lifestyles, strong social support networks, the belief in healing power, and the expectation of positive outcomes are in no way available only to religious people, being a part of a religious community plays an important role in making them more readily available. By bringing them together in a coherent, compelling way (by virtue of a supernatural narrative and emotion-laded rituals), religion made placebo healing a potent cultural force, and that force continues to echo even in modern times.

Placebo and the Brain

Neurochemical and brain imaging research attributes placebo effects (in part, at least) to the nervous system's capacity to release pain-relieving chemicals in response to the expectation of healing. In other words, when the patient believes that a treatment will have a positive result, pain-relieving chemicals—brain opiates—are released into the nervous system. The brain systems involved in this response include broad areas of the frontal and prefrontal cortex, including those involved in working memory, attention, and the emotional interpretation of stimuli. These areas are part of the brain's evaluative network, which constructs an "anticipatory conceptual framework" prior to the activation of the opiate system. To put it more simply, this is where the patient "believes" in healing, and where that belief causes pain-blocking opiates to be released into the nervous system. The brain's opiate system, in turn, has been shown to modulate immune system activity.[34]

These findings very likely provide the biochemical mechanisms behind many of the positive health benefits associated with religion. Note that the peak of this cascading system of biochemical connections is the cognitive-evaluative system of the prefrontal cortex. That the highest brain centers of the neocortex stand at such a critical junction supports the notion that the consciously controlled aspects of placebo effects are evolutionarily quite new, and very likely unique to the human species.

The Religious Advantage

Religion offered health and healing advantages to our ancestors. An important part of this advantage was due to the increased social support and group solidarity associated with groups that practice religious rituals. However, increased social cohesion and cooperation had advantages extending beyond just health and well-being. These advantages included more effective strategies for accessing and sharing resources, a greater capacity for coordinated action, and a deeper sense of commitment to group norms. This made religious groups more competitive than nonreligious groups when there was direct conflict over resources.

During the African Interregnum, intergroup interactions became increasingly common as human groups expanded their ranges in search of ever more scarce and widely scattered resources. Genetic evidence indicates that around this time, a particular subset of the human population expanded precipitously, absorbing or replacing other human groups in Africa. Thereafter, they trekked out of their home continent and globally displaced all remaining hominin forms.[35] These were the first and only hominins to leave archaeological evidence of religion in their wake. This may help to explain why religion turns out to be one of the very few cultural universals of the human species.

The competitive advantage of religious groups relative to others is borne out by a number of recent empirical findings. Sociologist Richard Sosis has done extensive research examining how religion serves as a mechanism of social cohesion.[36] By requiring members to engage in costly ritual behaviors and to profess belief in unverifiable supernatural claims, religion effectively filters out uncommitted, less trustworthy group members. Religious "badges" (as Sosis calls them) such as regular attendance at worship services, a distinctive style of dress, claiming that Mary was forever a virgin, and abstinence from alcohol, dancing, or nonkosher foods are singularly effective in "marking" those who can be trusted to treat other group members in accordance with a mandated moral code.

Indeed, groups bounded by religion have been found to be more stable and cohesive compared to secular groups. In his comparison of religious versus secular communes, Sosis found that religious communes were about four times more likely to survive than their secular counterparts. Furthermore, the most enduring of the religious communes were those that made the greatest personal demands on their members, such as requiring them to abstain from meat or to give up all material possessions. This was not true, however, among secular communes. This same pattern was found when comparing Israeli kibbutzim. Religious kibbutzim have outlasted secular ones, remaining economically viable while secular ones have gone bankrupt. Furthermore, the most cooperative and successful of the religious kibbutzim have been those with the most demanding ritual requirements. This is consistent with work mentioned earlier showing that American church groups exhibited higher levels of intragroup trust and commitment than other nonreligious social groups.[37]

Historically, one of religion's primary functions was fostering social cohesion. Biologist David Sloan Wilson provides a number of diverse examples of this, including the Calvinism that spared sixteenth-century Geneva from destructive factionalism, the culture-preserving effects of Judaism among the far-flung diasporas, and the Bali water temple system, which for centuries successfully regulated water use among competing villages. In each case, religion helped preserve social integrity against centrifugal forces. Cross-cultural analyses have shown that as societies become larger, more complex, and more threatened by external forces, their tendency to believe in moralizing gods also increases. Recent history provides numerous instances where religion has provided a potent mechanism for what sociologist Steve Bruce calls "cultural defense"—maintaining group identity in the face of hostile forces. The Catholic Church in Poland and Lithuania during Soviet domination, the Iranian Shiite revolt against Western influence, and the numerous immigrant religious subcultures that emerge in host countries are prime examples of this.[38]

Finally, the external threats facing groups and group identity are not always social in nature. Biologist Randy Thornhill and his student Cory Fincher have found that global religious diversity is directly proportional to the level of parasites and other infectious diseases present in a region (this being true even after other confounding factors are accounted for). Put simply, religion and religious diversity are far more prominent in tropical regions than in temperate ones. This, they argue, is a response to the increased threat of disease in tropical regions. The boundaries effectively marked by religious belief and ritual serve to discourage interaction with out-group members who might carry foreign parasites against which the in-group members' immune systems are ineffective.[39]

Religion and Reproductive Success

Religious "marking" also has important implications for successful mate selection and reproduction. Anthropologist William Irons asked Honduran men what they were looking for in a wife. They expressed a clear preference for a regular churchgoer. It turns out that these men were often away from home because of work and perceived churchgoing women as more faithful. The connection between religious involvement and mate selection has been further demonstrated in a recent study that found that the attitudes most strongly correlated with church attendance were those pertaining to sex, sexual behavior, and family life. The authors concluded that one's attitudes and lifestyle regarding sex, marriage, and family are just as likely to be the *cause* for one's religious involvement as the *result* of it. For someone with traditionalist attitudes about sex and marriage, the religious environment is not only a welcoming one, but also a good place to find a similarly minded mate. Indeed, it seems to work. Rates of promiscuity and extramarital sexual relations are typically lower among religious people. Additionally, religious people tend to have relatively stable, happy

TABLE 7.1   Average number of children born to women in the United States and
Europe, broken down by frequency of attendance at religious
services (adapted from Frejka & Westoff, 2008)

Women Aged 18–44 Church Attendance	United States	All of Europe	Western Europe
At least once a week	1.63	1.59	2.16
Less than once a month or never	1.22	1.19	1.16

Women Aged 35–44 Church Attendance			Western Europe
At least once a week			3.26
Less than once a month or never			1.8

marriages, compared to the nonreligious, who are more likely to be unmarried or divorced.[40]

All of this affects bottom-line reproduction. Across the globe, religious people are more fruitful than nonreligious people. A recent analysis comparing demographic trends in the United States and Europe found a consistent pattern of increasing fertility associated with increasing religiosity. Table 7.1 summarizes just a portion of the data.[41]

The authors summarize their findings bluntly: "It is obvious that in practically all countries/regions and among all denominations, the more devout have more children."[42] As can be seen from the table, in both Europe and the United States, women who attend church at least once a week have anywhere from .4 to 1 more child on average than those who attend more sporadically or not at all. In general these fertility differences were even more extreme when looking at women between the ages of 35–44, where in Western Europe frequent churchgoers had nearly 1.5 more children on average than non-churchgoers. Fertility differences between secular and religious Jews have compelled political sociologist Eric Kaufmann to suggest that the replacement of a majority secular population with a more religious one appears inevitable in Israel and many other industrialized nations:

> In Israel, for instance, fertility rates among the ultra-Orthodox rose from an already staggering 6.49 children per woman in 1980–82 to 7.61 during 1990–96; among other Israeli Jews, it declined from 2.61 to 2.27. All told, the ultra-Orthodox are on track to comprise at least a quarter of the under-17 population by 2025. . . .. if the secular West doesn't

relearn the habit of having children, they will soon be replaced by religiously-committed natives and religious immigrants.[43]

Kaufmann's assessment is echoed by Phillip Longman, who in his recent book, *The Empty Cradle*, predicted dire consequences to the global economy and dramatic social upheavals if current demographic trends continue:

> On our current course, more and more of the world's population will be produced by people who believe they are (or who in fact are) commanded by a higher power to procreate. . .. Demographic conditions today suggest that a cultural transformation of similar proportions [to that which transformed ancient Rome from a pagan to Christian empire] may be in store if secularists increasingly avoid the growing economic costs of raising children.[44]

In sum, a reasonably strong body of literature indicates that religion is tightly linked to the enhancement of social cohesion and that this social cohesion contributes to the health, well-being, and reproductive success of its members—both today and in our Paleolithic past.

How Religion Affected the Brain

While those most able to benefit from health-enhancing rituals were more likely to pass along their traits to subsequent generations, successfully participating in religious ritual cannot be reduced to a simple algorithm. The particulars of the rituals, beliefs, and emotions would have been far too variable to have been formulaically specified. Identifying the right "religious" inputs and structuring the appropriate ritualized responses have to be learned through culture, not genetically implanted in individual minds.

Thus, we would not expect to find a specific "god module" in the brain. Rather, we would expect to find minds possessing a suite of traits that make the beliefs and rituals associated with religion particularly attractive and psychologically/emotionally satisfying. As a selective force, religion has left its imprint on the human mind in at least three ways: (1) in our range of conscious experience, (2) in childhood imaginative capacities, and (3) in our capacity for symbolic thought. Each of these traits was honed by our ancestral religious environment and serves to make religious belief and behavior particularly attractive to most humans.

Expanded Conscious Experience

Shamanistic healing rituals always involve achieving a health-enhancing altered state of consciousness. In our ancestral past, those with minds most able to achieve this conscious state would have been in a position to reap more health and healing benefits from the rituals. Thus, we would expect the human species to be set at a population norm of deeper, more intense subjective conscious experience compared to other species. In other words, our capacity for altered states is greater (set at a higher norm) than that of other species.

While there is evidence for altered states of consciousness in other species, it seems a pretty safe bet that no creature matches us when it comes to the range and depth of our subjective conscious states. A rather glaring flaw in this reasoning could be that the capacity for experiencing altered states of consciousness had little to do with shamanism and much more to do with simply having a big brain with an expanded neocortex. However, Neanderthals had brains roughly the same as ours, if not slightly larger. Yet among Neanderthals we find no evidence of image-making, cave art, abstract artifacts, ritual burial, or other remains suggestive of supernatural beliefs. It was this difference that led archaeologist David Lewis-Williams to conclude that their consciousness was different from that of *Homo sapiens*, such that experiences, images, and "encounters" they may have had in altered states could not be integrated into a meaningful narrative that was applicable to everyday life. Thus, for a human, a dream where a dead relative appears would be interpreted as an important message from the spirit world. For a Neanderthal, the dream was forgotten by morning.[45]

Lewis-Williams's notion is speculative, to be sure. However, as we saw in chapter 4, some cognitive difference separated humans from Neanderthals, and to date, searching for the origins of that difference in toolmaking, hunting efficiency, diet, habitat range, adaptation to harsh environments, and other related factors has produced very little of substance.[46] But we have already reviewed considerable evidence indicating that the root of the difference between Neanderthals and AMH was cultural. *Homo sapiens* were doing something culturally that Neanderthals were not—they were engaging in rituals that taxed their working memory capacity. This expanded both their social worlds and their consciousness. *Homo sapiens*'s consciousness had the capacity to envision the supernatural and meaningfully incorporate it into their lives, while Neanderthals did not—and that made an adaptive difference.

Childhood Imagination

The second imprint that religion left on our minds can be found in our capacity for imagination. Tens of thousands of years of religious culture played a significant role in giving us highly imaginative children. In chapter 5, we saw that (1) childhood imagination evolved to prepare children for the cognitive complexities of the adult social world, and (2) by virtue of the supernaturalization of the adult social world, childhood imagination acquired at least four supernatural features—omniscient agents, magical causation, imminent justice, and promiscuous teleology. Each of these features prepared children to deal cognitively with an adult world where supernatural players and forces were as relevant to everyday social functioning as other humans were.

As children matured, each of these supernatural features found its culturally appropriate niche. Childhood imagination provided a more complete explanation for the characteristics common in adult religious thinking than alternative theories dealing only with hyperactive agency detection and anthropomorphism. Our imagination actually helped us deal with an inevitable prospect that was unimaginable: the complete loss of consciousness associated with death. Imagining an immortal soul proved to be an intuitively appealing way of dealing with death.

Symbolic Thought and the Very Essence of Being Human

The last imprint left by religion is nothing less than the very heart of what it means to be human. The famous anthropologist Roy Rappaport titled his last book *Ritual and Religion in the Making of Humanity.*[47] As the title implies, Rappaport argued that religious ritual was, in no small way, responsible for the very essence of our humanness. I believe this at least as strongly as he did, but for different reasons. Ritual behavior was crucial in the evolution of the working memory capacity necessary for symbolic thought. During the Interregnum, our ancestors were forced to construct intergroup trade alliances in order to more efficiently exploit increasingly scarce and scattered resources. Social rituals, including rituals of initiation, cooperation, reconciliation, and healing, were the backbone of these relationships. To one degree or another all these rituals involved or came to involve a supernatural element. Furthermore, all of these rituals taxed working memory capacity, such that those with greater working memory capacity were at an advantage in reaping resource-, status-, and health-enhancing rewards from the rituals. It was this modest but significant increase in working memory that provided the cognitive foundation for our ability to think symbolically.

If it is our extraordinary capacity for symbolic thought that makes us cognitively unique, then it is ritual that made us so. For centuries philosophers and theologians have debated whether it was God that created man, or man that created God. That debate will surely not end. The evidence, however, points to the conclusion that it was religion that made us human.

8

Religion and Morality

Earlier we saw that the origins of morality were rooted in the concepts of "kin selection," "reciprocal altruism," "indirect reciprocity," and "cultural group selection." Over the course of evolution, nature found ways of getting selfish organisms to set aside immediate self-interest in order to aid family, reap a returned favor later, gain benefits through reputation, or gain the benefits associated with being part of a well-organized, cooperative group. Since this "enlightened self-interest" falls well short of true "selflessness," how can it be seen as the roots of morality? Morality has to start somewhere, and the first step is to put larger interests ahead of immediate self-interest.

It is also crucial to recognize the inherently social nature of morality. Kin selection, reciprocal altruism, indirect reciprocity, and cultural group selection (and, indeed, morality itself) are irrelevant to a solitary organism. The need to regulate ourselves so as to live peaceably among others is a prerequisite for moral evolution. Morality naturally arises out of social life. As social life becomes more complex—moving from immediate family, to extended kin, to tribal community, and so forth—the "larger interests" that impinge on self-interest become increasingly remote and abstract. Thus, morality becomes increasingly complex. If religion represents a "supernaturalizing" of social life, then there should be a connection between religion and morality. The crux of that connection is found in the greater cohesiveness that religion brought to group life. Achieving this cohesiveness meant more effective means of motivating people to set aside individual interests for group-level ones.

Take losing weight as an analogy. The conditions for losing weight are actually quite simple: One needs to expend more energy through exercise than one takes in through eating. But motivating someone to do this is not always easy. Promises of sex or money might be effective motivators and might spell the difference between success or failure. Now let's be clear: Just as religion is not necessary for morality, promises of sex or money are not necessary for weight loss. But those promises might help motivate people to follow the "rules" of weight loss. What sex and money are to losing weight, religion is to moral behavior—not that religion promises sex and money for being moral, but it does promise things, and it does motivate.

Is Religion Irrelevant to Morality?

Recently it has been fashionable to deny any sort of connection between religion and morality.[1] Since recent research has established the natural origins of morality, religion has been rendered superfluous to morality and moral development. Morality comes naturally to us. Those of our ancestors who were untrustworthy, irresponsible, undependable, and egregiously selfish suffered social ostracism and the resulting negative fitness consequences. Our natural moral sense simply arises out of our deeply social nature—a sufficient degree of personal morality is merely a prerequisite to getting along with others. None of this requires religion. Furthermore, there are certainly enough examples of nonreligious people who have lived highly moral lives and, conversely, of great evil perpetrated in the name of religion to make the case that religion is not essential to morality.

This reasoning is sound as far as it goes. What our evolutionary history has taught us, however, is that it does not go far enough. Our natural moral sense allows us to get along with others. But it does not motivate us to engage in collective action. For this, we need adherence to group norms, and nothing encourages adherence to group norms like religion. There may be times when our natural moral sentiments—our "gut" sense of right and wrong—lead us in directions contrary to what the group needs for effective action. For example, student appeals are an end-of-semester ritual at my university. I am routinely confronted with sad stories of misfortune and death (some of which I'm sure are true). As much as my heart may go out to a hard-luck student, there are university policies that must be followed. Since following the group norm may not always "feel right," a strong motivator is often needed so that individuals don't just make up the rules as they go along. Thus, while it is true that our moral sentiments arise quite naturally from social life, translating those sentiments into moral action often requires a motivator. If we look at the basic moral sentiments, we can easily see how religion acts a motivating force for each of them.

Moral psychologist Jonathan Haidt provides evidence that our moral emotions fall along five fundamental axes: harm/care, fairness/reciprocity, in-group/loyalty, authority/respect, and purity/sanctity.[2] Each of these axes has roots that extend deep into primate and hominin social evolution. The authority/respect axis, for example, has its origins in the hierarchically structured groups that characterize nearly all primate species. While dominants have certain privileges over subordinates, they are also expected to assume certain responsibilities, such as protection of the group. Subordinates sometimes "rebel" against a dominant who is too brutal or tyrannical. Likewise, the fairness/reciprocity axis has its roots in our primate and hominin history of within-group reciprocal relationships, where repaying favors and maintaining a good reputation go hand in hand with identifying and avoiding cheaters.

Religion takes these axes and "spiritualizes" them, providing a supernatural incentive for following norms relevant to each axis. For example, ancestor worship is intimately intertwined with respect for tradition and authority (Haidt's authority/respect axis). In most traditional societies, worshipping the ancestors *is* respecting them and upholding their traditions. As hunter-gatherer bands coalesced into tribes, shamans became priests who bestowed supernatural authority on chiefs and kings, thus adding another divine dimension to the authority/respect axis. Taboo, that ubiquitous feature of nearly every traditional society, is often focused on issues of purity (the purity/sanctity axis)—what to eat, when sexual relations are appropriate, what to say or not say. Religion addresses the in-group/loyalty axis using divine commandments designed to maintain in-group stability (no coveting your neighbor's wife or property) and regulate out-group relations (no intermarriage with the infidels). By adding a spiritual aspect to these axes, religion directs gut-level moral sentiments in specific ways, encouraging collective interests over self-interest and thus facilitating effective group action.

Supernatural Inhibition

It has been argued that traditional religions were not moral systems and thus that any connection between religion and morality is of recent and not evolutionary origin. While it is true that traditional religions did not codify any set of holy laws such as the Decalogue or Dharmasastras, it is an oversimplification to see them as entirely irrelevant to morality. A central focus of nearly all traditional religions is taboo—a set of supernaturally ordained behavioral prohibitions. Often these prohibitions deal with foods that cannot be eaten or words that cannot be spoken (names of the dead, for example). Among the Lohorung Rai of Nepal, it is taboo for a new mother to eat pork, buffalo meat, or anything spicy. Instead, chicken, eggs, honey, rice, and broth are considered proper foods. Furthermore, mother and her newborn must remain secluded in the home for the first five days or so after birth. It is taboo for someone to touch the mother or for her to touch the home's hearth. Among the Karuks of the American Northwest, merely gazing upon the fires where the first salmon of the season would be cooked was strictly prohibited and believed to bring bad luck and a poor catch.[3]

While these taboos may seem arbitrary or even quaint, they effectively encourage personal restraint, respect for tradition, and cooperative behavior. For example, for the Lohorung Rai, a mother and her newborn are in a transitional status. Until ritually introduced to the ancestors—a ceremony done five days after birth for girls, six days for boys—the mother and her newborn are thought to be threatening in that they could easily arouse supernatural anger. Hence the taboos. However, during this transitional stage, all ancestral rituals are suspended for all families in the home village, thus involving the entire community in the fate of mother and her newborn. Likewise, with the Karuk, no fishing was allowed until all ritual ceremonies had been concluded. Avoiding even gazing on the fires helped ensure that no one would encroach upon the ritual control of the fishing season. This control helped to keep competing communities from overfishing the stocks and destroying the very resource central to their survival. Taboo served as the first step toward moral restraint—the ability to regulate behavior so as to put larger interests above self-gratification. Indeed, a recent wide-ranging review has concluded that one of religion's main morally relevant functions is to facilitate the development of personal self-control.[4]

Building on earlier theoretical and empirical work, Dominic Johnson and Jesse Bering have recently proposed that a major adaptive function of religion in our ancestral world was as an inhibitor of self-destructive selfish acts.[5] While these acts might very well have been beneficial to an individual in the short term, they would have had negative long-term fitness consequences resulting from damage to reputation and social isolation. So even though Thor is confident that he can "get away" with having an affair with Thag's wife, he resists the temptation out of fear of divine retribution. Although Thor has sacrificed a short-term mating opportunity, he may gain a greater long-term advantage through the material and social rewards of having kept his reputation clear of any suspicion.

Of course, all of this turns critically on the likelihood of Thor's getting caught. In our ancestral past, Johnson and Bering argue that this likelihood would have been pretty great, given the close-knit, gossipy nature of hunter-gatherer groups and the tendency of violators to overestimate their ability to get away with socially deviant acts. Furthermore, there is considerable evidence from both psychological and economic studies that fear of punishment is more effective than the promise of rewards in motivating prosocial behavior. In traditional cultures, the fear of illness—which is seen as divine retribution for sin—often serves as a disincentive for antisocial behavior.[6]

If religion offered a fitness advantage through constructive self-inhibition, then we should be able to identify empirical evidence supporting the idea that religious people tend to inhibit themselves from antisocial or immoral acts to a greater extent than nonreligious people. Indeed, numerous studies have found connections between religion and the avoidance of such antisocial behaviors as substance abuse, delinquency, and criminality in both adults and adolescents. With regard to alcohol abuse, avoidance was highest among those religious denominations that specifically condemn alcohol, suggesting that religious doctrine was not trivial in promoting self-restraint. Religion also appears to reduce levels of promiscuity and extramarital sexual relations. This finding may help explain why the religious tend to have relatively stable, happy marriages, while the nonreligious are more likely to be divorced.[7]

Psychologist Peter Benson concludes his review of religion and antisocial behavior by pointing directly to religion's role in discouraging self-destructive behaviors by "promoting environmental and psychological assets that constrain risk-taking" and "[using] a system of norms and values that favor personal restraint." It is this "personal restraint," coupled with the tendency of religious people to be service-minded, that may account for religion's role in promoting community harmony. Indeed, studies have shown that religious communities are often more cohesive and enduring than comparable secular ones, and the extent to which a religion emphasizes supernatural agency appears to be at least partially responsible for this effect.[8]

Recently, two researchers did a comprehensive review of the religion/self-control literature. They found "strong evidence" of a positive relationship between religion and self-control. Furthermore, religion was closely connected to the personality traits of Agreeableness and Conscientiousness, which, in the view of many personality theorists, are the basic building blocks of self-control. While acknowledging the limits of the data, the authors nevertheless conclude that religion, self-control, and self-regulation are "intimately related."[9]

One empirical study demonstrates that religion may in fact *cause* increased self-control in individuals.[10] The study made use of the priming effect often found in cognitive science studies. Priming is where the visual presentation of one word can facilitate the processing of another. So suppose someone is sitting before a computer screen where either words (such as "fork") or nonword letter combinations ("cmktd") are being presented. The person's task is simply to press one button on the keyboard if a word is presented and a different button if a nonword is presented. The experimenter measures the person's reaction time—how long it takes the person to press the key after the word or nonword is presented. The important finding is that a word such as "fork" will have a significantly faster reaction time if a related word such as "spoon" is presented just before it, rather than a nonrelated word such as "frog" or a nonword letter combination such as "cmktd." It is said that "spoon" primed recognition of "fork." This finding tells us something about how words are represented in the person's head—"fork" and "spoon" are "close together," while "frog" and "fork" are "farther apart." Significantly, this priming effect can be found even if we present "spoon" so quickly that the person has no conscious awareness of it—this is called "subliminal priming."

Using this procedure, researchers subliminally presented subjects with words that dealt with either sin (e.g., drugs, illicit sex) or religion (e.g., Bible, prayer, God). After these words, subjects were required to identify words that were again related to either sin or religion. The researchers found that subliminal presentation of sin-related words led to significantly faster recognition of religion-related words. In other words, in the same way that presenting "spoon" makes someone faster at recognizing "fork," presenting a word such as "drugs" made someone faster at recognizing a word such as "prayer." The opposite pattern was found when religious words were followed by sin-related words. So when "prayer" is presented first (subliminally), it actually makes one *slower* at recognizing a word such as "drugs." The authors interpreted these findings as evidence that subjects automatically recruit religious concepts as mechanisms of self-control in the face of temptation and that religious concepts implicitly inhibit access to sin-related concepts. In other words, when faced with sin ("drugs"), people reflexively think about religion ("prayer") as means of dealing with the temptation. Furthermore, thinking about religion actually makes it difficult to bring other sinful concepts to mind. Or as the old Irish nuns used to say, "Five Hail Marys will take your mind off sex, young Molly."

Self-control is undoubtedly an important aspect of morality, and in our ancestral past, religion's major contribution to morality was probably in promoting self-restraint (through taboo) and, to a lesser extent, encouraging self-sacrificial acts.[11] If a religious social environment natu-rally strengthens morality, then we should continue to see evidence of that today. I will review this evidence shortly. However, in order to pro-vide a theoretical framework for understanding this evidence, we must first spend some time defining morality and looking at the recent research addressing the issue of the moral faculty.

Defining Morality

Traditionally, morality has been understood as a set of rules for guiding behavior. At least as far back as Aristotle, morality has also been viewed as a set of character virtues—honesty, courage, temperance, and so on—that incline one toward honorable behavior and contribute to human flourish-ing. More recently, philosophers and social scientists have investigated morality as the reasoning process behind an ethically justifiable conclusion or action (Why is it right for Hans to steal the medicine for his ailing wife?). For current purposes, all three of these aspects of morality—rules, virtues, and reasoning—are relevant. Morality is here defined as *the cultivation and application of virtue*. In this definition, the "cultivation of virtue" refers to the development of character traits that motivate moral action, while the "application of virtue" refers to both an understanding of moral rules and proper reasoning about which rules apply in what situations. Thus, in agreement with moral philosopher Linda Zagzebski, I hold that morality is motivational (wanting to do what's right), cognitive (knowing what the right thing is), and behavioral (possessing the skills to execute the right action).[12]

It is also important to acknowledge that morality evolved as a means of organizing local, often kin-based social relationships.[13] Thus, for the vast majority of our evolutionary history, morality was applied narrowly—it pertained exclusively to how other members of the tribe were to be treated. The same moral regard was not extended to the members of other tribes. The ease with which out-group members have been dehumanized and bru-talized throughout human history is the legacy of this evolutionary origin. The fact that religion has served as reinforcement for this within-group morality helps to explain why religion has often exacerbated between-group wars and violence. The idea of religiously based universal love is a relatively recent one in the history of religion and remains much more of an ideal toward which people strive than a routinely practiced reality. Like-wise, while it obviously seems more moral to be universalistic than tribalis-tic, it is not easily done, given our basic nature and the cultural differences often encountered when defining "right" and "wrong."

The Moral Faculty

The phrase "moral faculty" refers to the notion that humans have a natural proclivity toward the development of moral emotions, reasoning, and behavior. The moral faculty is thought to be one of a collection of "intuitive ontologies"—competencies that emerge spontaneously over the course of normal human development. Other such competencies include skills such as language, face perception, numerical reasoning, categorization, and some motor skills (running and jumping, for example).[14]

While moral thinking shares many features in common with these other competencies, its closest kinship is thought to be with language. For example, over the course of development, infants and children show an evolved hypersensitivity to both linguistic and moral information— picking up quickly on the verbal labels used to name objects and the key features of actions and events that make them "good" or "bad." More significantly, both morality and language are partially universal and partially culture-specific. Languages, for example, are obviously different from each other. Yet beneath these differences, they all have certain universals, such as a system of grammar that allows the embedding of clauses.[15]

So too with morality. There are fundamental moral principles that appear to be universal, but the application of these principles varies with culture. For example, all parents are expected to care for and nurture their children; neglect of one's offspring is universally condemned. However, there are conditions when abandonment might be morally permissible that vary from culture to culture. Among many hunter-gatherers, those conditions might be when the infant is weak and sickly and food is scarce, while in Western societies it might be when the mother is a cocaine-addicted teenager and an adoptive couple is readily available. Other moral universals with culture-specific variations include a bias for regarding intended harm as more culpable than unintended harm, and a concern for equity in reciprocal exchanges.[16]

These naturally emerging competencies are commonly characterized by a broadly normal distribution of abilities.[17] By this I mean that most people's ability develops to an average level of competence, and only a few people are either functionally impaired or superlatively skilled. For example, consider language skills. The vast majority of people are linguistically competent (to varying degrees). Far smaller numbers are either linguistically impaired (abused/neglected children, familial dyphasics, etc.) or extraordinarily capable (great orators, prize-winning playwrights and novelists, etc.). Or consider running and jumping. To varying degrees, nearly all humans can run and jump; small numbers, however, are either functionally impaired (e.g., cerebral palsy or spina bifida victims) or highly skilled (e.g., Olympic sprinters or NBA basketball players).

The same type of distribution should characterize moral functioning. While the vast majority develop competent moral skills—they get along in society and form close personal relationships—a rare few should be either incompetent (sociopaths, psychopaths)[18] or extraordinarily capable (moral "experts"). Thus, an important implication of the moral faculty is the idea that moral expertise exists (actually or potentially) in the population. Studying moral experts and the process whereby moral expertise is acquired can provide valuable insights into the human moral sense.

Moral Expertise

The idea that morality is a perfectible natural ability is not new. In his *Nicomachean Ethics*, Aristotle contends that the virtuous person makes right behavior a habit and that this habit can be learned:

> Moral virtue comes about as a result of habit. . . . Neither by nature, then, nor contrary to nature do the virtues arise in us; rather we are adapted by nature to receive them, and are made perfect by habit. . . . the virtues we get by first exercising them, as also happens in the case of the arts. . . . men become builders by building and lyre players by playing the lyre; so too we become just by doing just acts, temperate by doing temperate acts, brave by doing brave acts.[19]

Others, including Thomas Aquinas and Thomas Jefferson, followed in this tradition. Jefferson claimed that our moral sense may be "strengthened by exercise as may a particular limb of the body."[20] These analogies to physical development are instructive. Just as one can develop physical skills to an elite level (such as a pro-caliber golf swing, or an Olympic-level backstroke), one can develop expert-level moral skills.

Recent research offers at least three empirical lines of support for the notion that moral skills can be perfected with practice. First, self-control is central to virtuous behavior, and self-control exhibits features analogous to a muscle. For example, it can suffer "fatigue"—when two sequential tasks require self-control, performance on the second declines. More importantly, self-control also exhibits long-term "strengthening" with exercise—subjects required to practice acts of self-control over a two-week period performed better on a follow-up self-control task. Furthermore, motivation can also heighten self-control.[21] These studies have religious implications. Religious practices that require self-discipline (attending church rather than sleeping in, not taking the Lord's name in vain) and religious ideas that motivate self-restraint (salvation, eternal damnation, divine judgment) may over time strengthen the self-control muscle, facilitating moral behavior. It may be the strengthening of this muscle in religious people that accounts, at least in part, for the reductions in delinquency, substance abuse, and extra-marital affairs discussed earlier.

A second line of evidence involves the development of wisdom. From a research perspective, wisdom can be understood as a type of skill-based expert knowledge relevant to priority-setting and dealing effectively with life's complexities. Wisdom can be enhanced through social interaction and observation. For example, one study found that subjects' performance on dilemmas used to measure wisdom improved significantly when they were allowed to work collaboratively on them with others, followed by a period of reflection. This was true even if the collaboration was entirely internal, that is, conversing with a wise "inner voice" (as is not uncommon in prayer).[22] Thus, religious or spiritual practices that encourage insightful reflection can serve as effective strategies for wisdom development and the moral insights that this development entails.

A third line of evidence can be found in intervention programs with at-risk children. Programs designed to increase children's empathetic awareness, social skills, self-control, and social problem solving have been found to significantly reduce discipline and delinquency problems in three- and five-year follow-up assessments.[23]

Collectively, these studies show that certain practices enhance morally relevant character traits or abilities such as self-control, wisdom, social intelligence, and empathy. Furthermore, the practices that fortify these abilities are common in religious settings. Thus, religion's behavioral obligations and proscriptions, motivational concepts, and meditative rituals may act as morality-enhancers by cultivating self-control, empathy, and social reasoning. While biological endowment plays a role in the development of these abilities, training is also essential.

The Acquisition of Skilled Performance and Expertise

Modern research on the development of expertise can be traced back to the pioneering work of Dutch chess master and psychologist Adrianus de Groot, who found that chess experts were far superior to novices in their ability to select the best moves after a brief examination of the chessboard. In succeeding decades, studies have scrutinized expertise in a wide range of sports, professions, and other activities including everything from computer programming to cricket. This body of literature has concluded that a particular activity, called deliberate practice, is essential to the acquisition of expertise, and the extent of deliberate practice is directly related to the ultimate level of skill attained.[24]

Deliberate Practice

Deliberate practice is a unique form of activity, distinguishable from both work and play, where goal-directed, concentrated effort is expended in order to improve specific mental and physical skills. It has three important characteristics:

1. The critical evaluation of one's current skill state against that of a more skilled model
2. The constant focus on the elevation, not just maintenance, of skill
3. The maintenance of conscious, voluntary control over the target behavior

EVALUATION OF CURRENT SKILL STATE AGAINST MORE SKILLED MODEL Future chess grand masters improve their skills by spending countless hours studying the games of past masters.[25] While studying a game, they predict the grand master's moves in various situations. When their predictions differ from the master's actual move, they review the chessboard in order to uncover what the master saw that they had missed. Through repeated analysis, review, and self-critical evaluation, future chess experts train themselves to "see" and "think" like grand masters. Whatever the specific skill, constant self-monitoring and self-evaluation (often with the aid of a teacher or coach) are necessary in order to progress.

While early stages of skill acquisition focus on emulating the model, later stages shift to producing desired outcomes. In other words, as mental and physical skills develop, one increasingly concentrates on results.[26] Thus, at first, a tennis novice closely watches a model's backhand and concentrates on properly executing the movement. Then, as the movement becomes more natural, the novice's concentration shifts to hitting the ball to a particular spot.

FOCUS ON ELEVATION, NOT JUST MAINTENANCE, OF SKILL Elevating skill often involves repetitious exercises, but deliberate practice is more than mindless repetition. Once a skill has been acquired, there is a natural tendency toward automation. At this point, repetitious, less rigorous practice is usually enough to maintain one's skill. Deliberate practice, however, requires that the individual resist complete automation by constantly challenging himself with new goals and more effective behaviors.[27] Expert pianists, for example, often purposely rehearse an already-learned piece at an excruciatingly slow tempo, thus forcing themselves to concentrate on individual notes and the relationships among them.

MAINTENANCE OF CONSCIOUS CONTROL OVER BEHAVIOR Moving from a current skill level to a higher one requires that potential experts retain some degree of conscious control over target behaviors. This control allows experts to respond effectively to unexpected circumstances or (in the case of sports) the responses of competitors. A study using expert pianists nicely demonstrated this "retention of control."[28] In the course of playing a memorized piece, the pianists were unexpectedly required to skip every other measure, or play with only one hand, or even transpose the piece into another key. Despite these changes and the novel movement patterns they entailed, the accuracy of the pianists' performance remained high. Thus, they were not just running off automated motor routines; rather, they were flexibly controlling stored knowledge to meet changing task demands.

Along with these three core features, K. Anders Ericsson has identified some other important characteristics of deliberate practice.[29] It involves activity that is at a difficulty level appropriate but challenging to the individual's current skills. It provides informative feedback concerning the individual's success in attaining new skill levels. And it provides opportunities for the repetition of new skills, along with the correction of errors as skills are being learned.

It is important to recognize that while we typically think of "practice" as a motor activity, expertise develops along both cognitive and behavioral lines. For example, an expert chess player or computer programmer engages in deliberate practice just as a soccer player or swimmer might, even though the former activities are more mental and the latter more physical. Deliberate practice applies to all forms of expertise because, at bottom, expertise is about recognizing critical patterns and adaptively responding to them. The chess player recognizes a pattern on the board and responds with a move, just as the soccer player recognizes a pattern in the action of play and responds with a pass or a shot. Developing moral expertise may be more akin to chess than soccer, but it too involves identifying relevant patterns in the environment and responding to them in effective ways.

Three important points emerge concerning deliberate practice and expertise. First, deliberate practice is necessary for skill acquisition, though it may or may not be sufficient. Second, what separates elite performers from average performers is the effort and duration of deliberate practice. The average person drops deliberate practice for a less rigorous, more repetitious form of practice once an acceptable level of competence is achieved. Experts continue deliberate practice for a much longer time, possibly indefinitely, in order to advance skill to a superlative level. Finally, deliberate practice requires effort and focused attention. So demanding is this activity that only a few hours of it can be sustained in a day's time before rest is required.[30]

To achieve expertise, one must engage in deliberate practice. Therefore, if one is to achieve moral expertise, then one must engage in deliberate "moral practice." But where and how does this type of practice take place?

Why Be a Moral Expert?

Deliberate practice is demanding. For some pursuits, rewards in money and fame can motivate people to make the effort necessary to develop expertise. There are few obvious rewards, however, for moral expertise. Studies have shown that religion can be a strong motivator.[31] The fact that nearly all religions link moral conduct with rewards and punishments in this life or the next makes them potentially potent moral motivators. Thus, the religiously devout should be more likely to expend energy monitoring, analyzing, and critiquing their moral lives, resulting in the elevation of their moral skills.

It is important, however, not to confuse this elevation of moral skill with morality per se. Religion is not necessary for morality. A secular environment can produce competent moral skills just as a religious one can. Again, consider the language analogy. Given a healthy biological endowment and rearing environment, a child will naturally develop competent linguistic skills. The same is true for moral abilities—that is what the moral faculty is all about. However, just as there are only a select few who hone their linguistic skills to the point of being a Pulitzer Prize nominee, only a few will hone their moral skills to an analogous level. It is here that religion becomes relevant.

Also, it is important to reiterate that religion's role has typically been as a reinforcer of within-group moral standards. How laudable those standards are may be a matter of perspective. Religion certainly has its share of universally admired moral paragons: Mohandas Gandhi, Martin Luther King Jr., and Mother Teresa come to mind. But suicidal terrorists and medieval inquisitors might also be or have been viewed as moral experts by those of their in-group. The expertise being honed may not always be "moral" in the universalist sense.

Religion as Deliberate Moral Practice

Though religious rituals and practices vary widely, a number of underlying commonalities strongly suggest that religion is an effective venue for deliberate moral practice. Nearly all of the global religions have some moral standard to which members are expected to adhere or aspire. That standard may be embodied in the life and deeds of an individual (Jesus, Buddha), an authoritative set of laws or teachings (the Torah, the Dharmasastras), or the collective example set by a tradition's holy people (Christian saints, Jewish sages, gurus, bodhisattvas, etc.). Furthermore, religion surrounds these standards and role models with powerful rituals and injunctions, creating a particularly effective social learning context.[32]

Second, nearly all religions require members to regularly engage in self-critical reflection on their success or failure in adhering to this standard. For example, weekly Mass attendance is obligatory for faithful Catholics, and the Mass begins with the Penitential Rite, in which members call to mind their sins and ask for forgiveness. Synagogue worship among Jews includes the Amidah or Shemona Esrei prayer, in which one approaches God offering praise and requesting forgiveness. Faithful Muslims pray five times daily. This practice, called Salat, is not just for worship but to keep the believer safe from social wrong and moral deviancy (Qur'an 29:45). Recited before each prayer is the sura al-Fatiha, a verse from the Qur'an asking for God's mercy and guidance to follow the right path. Christian, Jewish, and Muslim worship services also include some form of authoritative preaching by a priest, minister, rabbi, or imam. Often this preaching examines some aspect of the religion's moral teaching and how that teaching should be practiced in daily life.

Finally, nearly all religions offer opportunities for acts of self-sacrifice, either through required monetary giving (*zakat* in the Muslim tradition, tithing in the Christian tradition) or through acts of volunteerism (working in soup kitchens, visiting the sick and elderly, working on church committees). In the Sikh tradition, a central element of community worship is *langar*—where the faithful gather in the temple to prepare and serve vegetarian food for free to others regardless of race, religion, or caste.

Thus, common to the practice of most major religions are the key elements of deliberate practice:

1. Regular evaluation of moral behavior against a standard
2. Continual study of the moral standard in order to elevate moral skill
3. Conscious deliberation over both moral shortcomings and strategies for overcoming them
4. Opportunities to consciously exercise moral action in the community

This is not to say that all devotees engage these elements with the seriousness necessary to promote real moral growth. For many, the rituals become routinized and lose their force. The important point, however, is that the rituals provide the means and opportunity for deliberate "moral practice."

Individually, the elements listed above do not make religion unique. Secular moral teachings and models could be substituted and studied in place of strictly religious ones. Furthermore, numerous secular groups engage in charitable acts. Religion's uniqueness is that it combines these characteristics and requires that members practice them on a regular basis. By way of highlighting this, consider the following question: Are there any purely secular groups that require members to (1) gather regularly to evaluate their moral behavior against some agreed-upon standard,

(2) listen to lessons and exhortations designed to deepen their understanding of that moral standard and motivate them to more effectively put the moral standard into action, and (3) practice their moral precepts through organization-sponsored charity and volunteerism? Even if such secular groups exist, it seems a safe bet that they pale in size and influence compared to the world's religions. Thus, simply by virtue of "market dominance," the search for a setting conducive to the development of moral expertise will almost inevitably lead to a religious one. This leads to a testable hypothesis: Given that deliberate practice sharpens skills and religion appears to provide the elements for the deliberate practice of moral skills, then is religion more likely to produce moral expertise?

Religion and Moral Expertise: A Study of Moral Exemplars

One way to test this hypothesis is to identify moral experts and see whether religious people dominate their ranks. Anecdotally, the most commonly cited moral paragons—Gandhi, Mother Teresa—are often religious. To my knowledge, only one empirical study has attempted to identify and analyze moral experts, or what the authors called "moral exemplars." Psychologists Ann Colby and William Damon worked with a panel of 22 scholars to establish a set of criteria for identifying people who were living morally "outstanding" lives. The panel included a diverse collection of moral philosophers, theologians, historians, professional ethicists, and social scientists. Once the criteria had been established, the panel nominated people whom they believed fulfilled the criteria. In the end, the panel selected 24 "moral exemplars" for intensive study (one of whom was forced to drop out prior to completion of the study).[33]

Curiously, none of these exemplars stood out in terms of moral reasoning capacity; instead, it was their character and behavior that made them extraordinary. For our purposes, however, the most important finding from the study was this: For 19 of the 24 moral exemplars (about 80%), religion was a significant force behind their moral attitudes and actions. This finding surprised the authors: "Almost 80% of the exemplars attributed their core value commitments to their religious faith. This was an intriguing and unexpected finding—our nominating criteria, after all, reflected nothing that was directly religious in nature."[34]

Interpreting this study is tricky. On the one hand, it suggests that when scholars attempt to identify people who embody "moral excellence," they, like the general public, tend to converge on religious people. Thus, there may be more than just coincidence behind the religion/moral paragon connection. On the other hand, given that 90% or more of Americans claim to believe in God, then finding that *only* 80% of moral exemplars are religious is actually below what one should expect. This percentage, however, may not be the appropriate comparison figure. America's prevailing religious ethos makes claiming belief easy and socially advantageous. A fairer comparison, some might contend, would be just those classified as "intrinsically" religious—a number well below 80%.[35] In any case, the current study, though suggestive, needs replication in a more religiously skeptical social context, such as Western Europe, before being convincing.

Religion and Moral Expertise: The Moral Virtues

Psychologists Christopher Peterson and Martin Seligman conducted an extensive cross-cultural, sociohistorical analysis to identify personality traits that were universally admired as morally virtuous. This analysis involved examination of the world's wisdom literature, including Confusion and Taoists texts from China, the Buddhists and Hindu texts from South Asia, the Platonic and Aristotelian writings from Greece, the biblical Wisdom texts, the Jewish Sage writings, and Islamic wisdom literature. General patterns found in these texts were then compared to more recent psychological and philosophical theories (Freud, Erickson, James Rachels, theories of intelligence, evolutionary psychology). In the end, they identified six traits as universally admired moral virtues, which they called the "High Six." Each of these moral virtues is expressed through a number of character strengths, the specific psychological/behavioral routes by which a moral virtue is displayed. Here are the "High Six":[36]

1. *Wisdom*: Cognitive strengths that entail the acquisition and use of knowledge. Character strengths of wisdom: creativity, curiosity, open-mindedness, love of learning, and perspective.
2. *Courage*: Emotional strengths that involve the exercise of will to accomplish goals in the face of opposition. Character strengths of courage: bravery, persistence, integrity, and vitality.
3. *Humanity*: Interpersonal strengths that involve tending and befriending others. Character strengths of humanity: love, kindness, and social intelligence.
4. *Justice*: Civic strengths that underlie healthy community life. Character strengths of justice: citizenship, fairness, and leadership.
5. *Temperance*: Strengths that protect against excess. Character strengths of temperance: forgiveness, humility, prudence, and self-regulation.
6. *Transcendence*: Strengths that forge connections to the larger universe and provide meaning. Character strengths of transcendence: appreciation of beauty and excellence, gratitude, hope, humor, and spirituality.

The religion/moral expertise hypothesis predicts that religion would contribute positively to the development of these moral virtues. A brief survey of each moral virtue and some of the associated character strengths is largely supportive of the hypothesis.

One virtue, transcendence, has clear religious implications. It is noteworthy that a trait so intimately connected with religion would be among those recognized as universally admired moral virtues. It suggests that there may be something intrinsic to religion that is universally seen as virtuous. Additionally, many of the character strengths associated with transcendence, such as gratitude, hope, and a sense of purpose, are facilitated by religious involvement.

For example, gratitude, as a stable personality characteristic, has been positively correlated with an array of religious/spiritual variables. The hope engendered by religious faith is an important factor in the generally positive association between religion and well-being. Finally, religion's capacity to instill a sense of purpose in people's lives remains potent even in the most religiously indifferent societies. Icelandic adolescents high in religious participation perceive the world as a more coherent place than those low in religious participation, even though Iceland's rate of church attendance is about 2%, the lowest among Nordic nations.[37] While the other moral virtues are more "secular," religion continues to play a significant role in their development.

WISDOM Peterson and Seligman define wisdom (as expressed through perspective) as the ability to give good counsel to others, and having ways of looking at the world that makes sense to oneself and others. Psychologists Ursula Staudinger and Paul Baltes measured wisdom using a series of social dilemmas. They found that subjects' performance on the dilemmas improved when they were allowed social collaboration, along with a time period for reflective integration (they spoke with others about the content of the dilemma and were subsequently allowed time to think about the interaction). The results showed that the positive effect of the social collaboration/reflective integration condition was present even when the social collaboration was entirely internal—that is, subjects were allowed to have a mental conversation with a "wise other." In many religious traditions, prayer is construed as a "conversation" with God. To the extent that religious rituals and teachings encourage reflective prayer when facing difficult choices, they may be facilitating the development of wisdom. The fact that religion typically forms the backbone of any culture's storehouse of collective wisdom would also seem to attest to the strong connection between religion and wisdom-building.[38]

COURAGE (AS MEASURED BY THE CHARACTER STRENGTH OF BRAVERY) Sociologist Rodney Stark argues that courage played a major role in the early growth of Christianity. Christians, far more so than pagans, were willing to remain in Rome during a plague and care for the sick, helping their own members to survive while at the same time attract-ing converts. In their study of moral exemplars, Colby and Damon used "a willingness to risk one's self interest for the sake of one's moral principles" as a selection criterion. Unsurprisingly, all of their moral exemplars had endured some hardship in the course of remaining true to their moral ide-als. These hardships included the voluntary abrogation of material or financial gain, estrangement from family and friends, loss of jobs, and the threat of physical harm. Given that the vast majority of these exemplars were religiously motivated, it seems reasonable to assume that religion played some role in inspiring the courage necessary for them to face these hardships. Interestingly, however, nearly all of the exemplars (21) disa-vowed being courageous. Instead, they attributed their actions to a sense of duty based on an unwavering moral certainty.[39]

HUMANITY (AS MEASURED BY LOVE AND SOCIAL INTELLI-GENCE) According to Peterson and Seligman, the moral virtue of human-ity is exhibited through love and social intelligence. These strengths should contribute to the success of long-term social relationships. Thus, if religion builds humanity (by making people more loving and socially intelligent), then we might expect religious people to have more satisfying and success-ful marriages than those who are not religious. Empirical evidence sup-ports this expectation. Both church attendance and the personal relevance of religion are positively correlated with marital satisfaction. Religious cou-ples communicate more effectively and use better conflict resolution strate-gies than nonreligious couples. Rates of domestic violence and martial infidelity are typically lower among religious couples, while their divorce rates run anywhere from 13 to 16 percentage points lower as well. In gen-eral, religious people are more likely to get married, stay married, and pro-vide a stable supportive atmosphere for successful child-rearing.[40]

HUMANITY (AS MEASURED BY KINDNESS OR COMPASSION) In their now famous "Good Samaritan" study, social psychologists John M. Darley and C. Daniel Batson found that less than half of seminary students were willing to stop and aid a debilitated man, suggesting that religion and compassion were not tightly connected. In more recent years, however, Batson and colleagues have produced evidence that the "quest" religious orientation might be a foundation for universal compassion. The quest ori-entation is a "seeking" orientation, defined by an openness to questioning and an appreciation of wonder and mystery. This attitude is often contrast-ed with the "intrinsic" orientation—describing true, committed believers—and the "extrinsic" orientation—describing those who participate in religion for practical, utilitarian purposes. Questers, unlike the other orien-tations, appear to be more likely to offer aid based on another's need rather than a desire to appear helpful.[41]

JUSTICE (AS MEASURED BY CITIZENSHIP) One way that the moral virtue of justice is put into practice is through citizenship—the exercise of social responsibility. Numerous studies have shown that religious people engage in more charitable giving and volunteerism than do nonreligious. This is especially true when it comes to religious-based charities and causes and may even be the case for purely secular ones, though this is more controversial. The religious also rate high in other areas of citizenship, including voting, political involvement, and political knowledge. Furthermore, religion and religious institutions contribute positively to the "social capital" that strengthens a healthy community.[42] Stephen Monsma concludes his review by noting the following:

> These findings reveal that religiously committed people who give and volunteer are also active citizens. As such, they may constitute the chief exemplars of civic responsibility. Those, who by several measures, are religiously active and committed are the citizens who are likeliest to give to and volunteer for religiously based community causes. Moreover, they give and volunteer to about the same extent as the irreligious respondents do to secularly based community causes. . . . As a rule, religionists live out more facets of civic responsibility than do the irreligious.[43]

TEMPERANCE (AS MEASURED BY FORGIVENESS AND HUMILITY) While there is evidence that religious people place a higher value on forgiveness and tend to think and reason more about forgiveness than do nonreligious people, establishing a relationship between religion and the actual act of forgiving has been more challenging. Some studies have found that increased religiosity is positively correlated with self-reports of forgiving, increased motivation to forgive, and a decreased tendency to harbor resentment. Religion's role, however, appears to be stronger in terms of a general tendency to forgive as opposed to the likelihood of forgiving any specific transgression (referred to as the "religion-forgiveness discrepancy").[44]

A recent review of the forgiveness literature tentatively concludes that "religious individuals are, in general, slightly more forgiving than are less religious people, although the association is rather small." Interestingly, in Colby and Damon's study of moral exemplars, the three most forgiving of the 24 exemplars were all devoutly religious, while the three least forgiving were all nonreligious. Finally, a second character strength associated with temperance—humility—has also been shown to be positively connected with religiousness, especially those categorized as "quest" religionists.[45]

TEMPERANCE (AS MEASURED BY SELF-CONTROL) Religion is a major promoter of constructive self-restraint, and studies addressing this

is evidence that fundamentalist beliefs among both Jews and Christians are associated with a greater likelihood of child abuse. Furthermore, when religion can be cited as justification for aggression, perpetrators may be compelled to even greater levels of violence.[53] All of this reinforces the fact that religion is a multifaceted phenomenon that can interact in complex and not always positive ways with different individuals under different circumstances.

Secular Groups and the Development of Moral Expertise

Religion's negative effects suggest that it may have some weakness in transmitting certain aspects of morality. Could secular environments provide an alternative venue for the development of moral expertise? Well-known skeptic Michael Shermer has argued that science provides evidence of a cosmos of increasing complexity.[54] This inspiring image, coupled with an ethic of enlightened happiness and liberty—always seeking one's happiness and liberty in concert with the happiness and liberty of others—could provide the basis for a potent secular morality. In principle, secular groups could adopt this ideal as their moral standard and exemplify it through practical lessons, stories, and specific rules of behavior. Some elements of this may already be present in certain civic or environmental groups. Regular meetings of these groups might provide opportunities for moral review, refinement, and practice.

Furthermore, though a setting might technically be secular, an intermingling of religious and secular values and practices may still be present. Many workplace environments include regular (and often ritualized) gatherings to invigorate employee morale, review important policies or standards, and deal with ethical issues such as customer satisfaction or employee relations. Moral experts within these groups (some of whom may be religiously trained) could provide role models for others' edification.

These examples show that secular environments are certainly not bereft of morality or the opportunities for moral learning. However, one would suspect that the moral lessons of secular groups are more narrowly drawn, compared to those of religious groups. For example, a civic or environmental group will likely confine its morality to civic or environmental concerns. Workplace ethics deals with workplace issues. Indeed, it is nearly impossible to find a meaning system more comprehensive than religion.[55] Along with the challenges of establishing agreement on moral principles and gathering regularly to review and reflect upon those principles, secular environments must ensure that their moral training addresses the full range of human experiences.

Religion and Morality: Summary

A social environment with religion provides a level of moral motivation and opportunities for moral enhancement not typically available otherwise. If morality is a naturally emerging and *perfectible* competency, then the elements required for the elevation of that competency (deliberate practice) appear to be present in the world's religious traditions.

An important cautionary note is order, however. The evolutionary relationship between religion and morality has always been one where religion reinforces within-group moral standards. The notion of religiously based universal love or universal moral regard is only a very recent invention. The moral expertise being honed in some religious settings may not be a universalist one. One person's moral expert may be another's religious fanatic. Religion has been a part of our social world for tens of thousands of years. Only very recently has the novel idea of raising children in an entirely secularized, religion-free world arisen. No, contrary to what ardent believers contend, these "children of the Enlightenment" are not doomed to amorality. However, they probably are less likely to have among their ranks moral experts of the Gandhi variety or fanatics of the Osama Bin Laden variety. A secular future is very likely one less prone to zealotry, more prone to narcissistic indifference. Time will tell whether or not this is more adaptive.

9

Religion's Past and Future

Here's the story of religion in three acts.

Act 1

Around 500,000 ybp, our ancestors had the ability to sing, dance, and chant together. These groupwide activities often brought on an ecstatic mental state that served to enhance social bonding. Sometime between 200,000 and 150,000 ybp, anatomically modern humans (*Homo sapiens sapiens*) emerged in Africa. About 100,000 ybp, they made their first venture out of Africa into the Levant region of the Middle East. Sometime shortly after 100,000 years ago, they abandoned the Levant and retreated back to Africa.

The major evidence for act 1[1] is threefold: (1) Nonhuman primates have a wide repertoire of social emotions and rituals, and their rituals sometimes bring about an altered state of consciousness; (2) the conscious motor control necessary for the creation of late Acheulean hand axes and composite tools indicates that by at least 500,000 ybp hominins could engage in group coordinated rituals—singing and dancing; and (3) evidence of red ochre and defleshing of skulls around this time suggests the existence of group ritual behavior among hominins.

Act 2, Scene 1

During the African Interregnum (roughly 90,000–60,000 ybp), ecological degradation associated with rapid climate changes and possibly the massive Toba eruption forced our ancestors to undergo a social revolution. They formed increasingly larger, more complex social groups and established unprecedented intergroup trading alliances. The singing and dancing rituals of their predecessors were not enough to handle the demands of this more complicated social world.

Our ancestors expanded their social life to include rituals of initiation, trust-building, reconciliation, and shamanistic healing. These rituals taxed attention and working memory, making greater working memory capacity advantageous for survival and reproduction. This set the stage for the emergence of symbolic thinking and other uniquely human forms of cognition.

The major evidence for act 2, scene 1 is threefold. (1) Ethnographic and comparative evidence indicate that rituals of social bonding are extensive among traditional societies and widespread in the animal kingdom, including among our primate relatives. (2) The first archaeological evidence of expanded trading networks emerges at this time. (3) Neuroscience evidence indicates that ritual behavior requiring focused attention and the inhibition of prepotent responses activates brain areas essential to working memory.

Act 2, Scene 2

As the hominin social world became increasingly complex, more imaginative children had a fitness advantage because they grew into more socially intelligent adults. The supernatural elements of childhood imagination became incorporated into the adult world because they enhanced the intensity and efficacy of social rituals. The supernatural was first added as a healing force in rituals of social bonding, creating shamanistic healing rituals. These rituals proved highly effective for both healing and social bonding purposes. Over time, more and more elements of childhood supernatural imagination were incorporated into the adult social world because of social bonding effects (supernatural social scrutiny increases social cohesion), ritual enhancement effects (supernatural elements add drama and potency to rituals), and intuitive appeal (the plausibility of an immortal soul). Ultimately these additive advantages gave "religious" hominin groups a decisive edge over more "secular" groups, which eventually went extinct.

The major evidence for act 2, scene 2, is fourfold. (1) Developmental research indicates that childhood imagination facilitates social intelligence. (2) Archaeological and ethnographic evidence suggest that shamanism is humanity's oldest form of religion, possibly extending back to the time of the Interregnum. (3) Psychological and medical research strongly connect religious belief and ritual to health benefits through placebo effects. (4) Sociological research indicates that groups bonded by religious belief and ritual are more trusting, cooperative, and enduring than secular groups.

Act 3

Somewhere between 50,000 and 30,000 ybp, ancestor worship emerged, and, with it, the first religious myths and narratives. These narratives justified the inequities of increasingly stratified societies and laid the groundwork for the "elite versus popular" religious distinction of classic paganism.

The major evidence for act 3 is archaeological. Innovations present with the onset of the Upper Paleolithic, such as sophisticated tools, cave art, food storage pits, time-keeping devices, and abstract figurines, indicate that full-blown language and episodic memory were present by this time. Elaborate burials and artifacts reflecting fertility concerns emerge predominantly during the Upper Paleolithic, indicating that ancestor worship was present. Ancestor worship and the social inequities it entails require compelling myths and narratives to justify and sustain them.

Testing the Model

I hope that the story I have told is an interesting one. But to be science, it has to be more than just interesting; it must be testable as well. Five general testable predictions flow from the model. Within each of these general predictions there are a number of more specific hypotheses, some of which already have corroborative evidence.

General Prediction 1: Emotional bonding precedes supernaturalism. The model I have outlined claims that the first stage in the evolution of religion was a stage of intense social bonding brought on by group mimetic activities that affected the participants' conscious state. This preceded any notions of the supernatural. Supernatural agency, initially in the form of a healing force and later in the form of watchful ancestors, gods, and spirits, was grafted onto already-existing consciousness-altering social rituals. Therefore, emotional rituals of social bonding are a more basic and primary aspect of religion than specific supernatural concepts. This can be tested in a number of ways.

If my hypothesis is correct, one would expect that the parts of the brain used for social bonding are of older evolutionary origin that those needed for agency detection. Evidence to date is consistent with this prediction: More "primitive" subcortical areas have been implicated in both emotional functioning and ecstatic experiences, while areas of the neocortex, especially the prefrontal cortex, are involved in agency detection.[2]

Comparative work adds further support to this pattern. Social emotions are fairly widespread among many nonhuman animals. However, agency detection appears to be restricted to apes and possibly just humans.[3] Finally, since according to the proposed model, supernaturalism was added to rituals of social bonding and did not replace them, we would expect that the brain areas activated by group-based religious ritual (such as rhythmic chanting and dancing) would be similar to those associated with secular group-based activities such as square dancing and marching band, especially where it involves older, subcortical structures.

While this particular prediction still awaits testing, the psychological effects of the two have been found to be similar. For example, both community religious rituals and secular group-coordinated activities can bring about deindividuation, or the loss of a sense of personal identity as one becomes enmeshed in the crowd. Community-based rituals, whether secular or religious, encourage the release of brain opiates that promote social bonding. Moreover, group-synchronized activities (whether secular or religious in nature) correlate positively with measures of empathy and lead to greater social cooperation.[4]

General Prediction 2: Shamanism precedes ancestor worship. The model argues that shamanistic healing rituals were the first "supernatural" aspects of human existence. Only after shamanism did ancestor worship come into being. This position has a number of testable implications. First: Ethnographically, we should find evidence of shamanism to be more widespread than evidence of ancestor worship. This does appear to be true. While both are widespread, there appears to be only one documented example of a traditional society without shamanism (the Siriono of Bolivia). But ancestor cults are relatively less frequent. For many traditional people in North American and Australia, though the ancestors may be present, their role is rather minor.[5] This issue certainly needs to be looked at more closely and systematically; however, presently the data seem to conform to the prediction of the model.

Relatedly, this model would predict that shamanism is more basic, in the sense that it can stand alone, without language or other cultural supports. Again, there is some evidence to support this contention. In chapter

4, we saw how the compelling nature of a ritual, not any specific ideology, is really the key to its healing power. Thus, a Muslim could find healing in a Christian-based ritual, provided she "bought into" the ritual's power. Furthermore, language too appeared to be only tangential to the ritual. Ancestor worship, however, is different. It needs a story to work and therefore is much more dependent on cultural supports.

Furthermore, the model predicts that shamanism or the more shamanistic elements of religion (dramatic ritual, ecstatic emotional states, etc.) are more directly related to fitness-enhancing benefits (physical and psychological well-being) than other elements of religion, such as myths or dense theologies. A number of observations offer support for this hypothesis. For instance, though shamanistic practices vary widely across the globe, they always include some type of *healing*, and this healing is always accomplished with ritualized alterations of consciousness. Furthermore, though today the shaman is seen as a rare, gifted individual, there is reason to suspect that they were far more prevalent in the past. Among the !Kung, for example, it is estimated that half the men and a third of the women are (or were) shamans. Recent studies confirm that meditative practices can have health benefits. The fitness benefits of subsequent elements of religion were likely more indirect (if present at all), operating through group-level factors such as increased stability and cooperation.[6]

Finally, the archaeological record offers possible avenues for testing the sequence. Already I have noted that the earliest evidence of shamanism is older than the evidence for ancestor worship. However, as is often the case with archaeological remains, pinning down the correct interpretation for the data is a challenge. Deep cave sites where evidence of consciousness-altering rituals took place could indicate shamanism, or could indicate exclusive rituals directed at ancestors. Ethnographic evidence can sometimes favor one interpretation over another. For example, ancestor worship is more common among complex hunter-gatherers than among egalitarian hunter-gatherers. Thus, archaeological evidence relevant to the social structure may help to clarify the likely type of ritual taking place in any associated deep cave sites.

General Prediction 3: Ritual enhances working memory capacity. I have argued that ritual behavior was critical in the formation of more complex social arrangements and in the emergence of uniquely human cognition. This claim is falsifiable. Suppose, for example, that evidence of intergroup trade networks comparable to those of Cro-Magnons is found among Neanderthals. Two possibilities arise from this finding: (1) Neanderthals engaged in complex social rituals without achieving modern cognition, or (2) Neanderthals created intergroup trade networks without complex social rituals. Either of these implications is damaging and potentially falsifying to the model. A corollary to this would be that among traditional societies where more extensive intergroup relations are noted, more sophisticated and demanding social rituals would also be present.

A second implication of the model is that ritualized behavior serves as an effective mechanism for freeing up working memory capacity, which can then be allocated for greater inhibitory control. If so, one would predict that ritual improves performance under conditions of high stress. There is already evidence supporting this prediction in the area of athletic performance.

A number of studies have demonstrated that ritual behavior, in the form of performance routine, leads to better performance in a number of different sports. For example, basketball players who maintain their established pre-free-throw routines have been found to be significantly more accurate on subsequent free-throws than those who deviate from their routines. This difference has been attributed to the fact that pre-performance routines serve to eliminate distractions, reduce anxiety, and build confidence by focusing attention on a series of well-rehearsed, productive cues and away from negative thoughts that disrupt execution of practiced motor patterns.[7]

Brain imaging studies comparing novice athletes to experts have revealed significant differences in the brain areas activated during preperformance routines. Specifically, subcortical areas associated with emotions were significantly more active in novices, whereas areas associated with focused attention and response inhibition were more active in experts. The authors of these studies argue that these patterns indicate that the experts possess a superior ability to maintain attentional focus while inhibiting detrimental emotional responses.[8] Although not measured in the brain imaging studies, a reasonable assumption would be that part of the experts' success is due to their ability to more effectively execute their preperformance rituals.

General Prediction 4: Religion is fitness-enhancing. The model I propose is based firmly on the notion that religion represents an evolutionary (cultural) adaptation that offered fitness benefits in the ancestral past. Chapter 7 reviewed considerable evidence in support of the hypothesis that religion brought together the various factors involved in placebo health and healing effects, including (1) the suggestive context of treatment, (2) the expectancy and desire of the patient, (3) the bias of the patient toward signs of improvement, and (4) social support.

The model makes the rather mundane prediction that evidence for religion's positive health effects will continue to accrue, with the specific effects being increasingly tied to the four placebo factors listed above. For example, religion should increasingly be found to have positive benefits because it creates a powerful suggestive context for treatment and because it fosters strong social support mechanisms. However, this model would also make the prediction that the specific placebo pathway by which religion has its positive effects will vary for different individuals in different contexts. In other words, religion's critical role in health and healing is that it makes placebo factors more available to devotees than to skeptics. In a sense, devotees can pick and choose which of the placebo factors best suits their circumstances, whereas skeptics are less likely to have these placebo options available to them.

A second, related line of testing can be found in the physical, psychological, and social benefits that accrue from the avoidance of self-destructive behaviors due to concerns over supernatural monitoring. A good deal of evidence in support of this hypothesis has already been presented. For example, in chapter 8 we saw that rates of substance abuse, criminality, delinquency, divorce, extramarital sexual affairs, and promiscuity are lower among religious people. Furthermore, religious groups tend to be more cohesive, enduring, and trusting than secular ones. A prediction still to be tested is whether the health benefits most directly associated with self-restraint are primarily motivated by concerns over supernatural monitoring. A chief reason that religious people exercise greater self-restraint should be because they believe they are under social scrutiny even when they are ostensibly alone.

General Prediction 5: Tests arise from evolutionary specificity. The proposed evolutionary sequence is specific enough to lend itself to testing and potential falsification. I argue that religion arose at a particular time (around 70,000 ybp) and place (Africa) for a specific reason (as a cultural adaptation for enhancing health and increasing group competitiveness in the wake of the ecological stressors). Any archaeological evidence definitively contradicting these specifics would be damaging and potentially falsifying.

For example, evidence of trading networks or shamanistic rituals among Neanderthals prior to their contact with Cro-Magnons would be damaging to the current model. Second, the current model contends that the subpopulation of African AMH who created extended trading networks and religion were the same as the AMH who ventured out of Africa and took over the world. Any evidence suggesting otherwise would again be damaging to the model. On the positive side, this model predicts that the evidence of religion in the form of abstract artifacts and deep cave ritual sites will continue to grow in the African archaeological record, with dates for such finds clustering around 70,000 ybp and certainly not being any older than 100,000 ybp.

What the Past Says About the Future

> If our social universe, our network if you will, grows larger than 150
> we must begin to deal with some of them as categories: bankers, Mon-
> tagues and Capulets, Republicans and Democrats, and so on.[9]

This book has primarily been about the past. But does the past tell us anything about the future? I think it does. Religion arose about 70,000 ybp at a
time of increasing social complexity. It is no coincidence that social markers
such as body ornaments or local tool types emerged at this same time as
well. As Coolidge and Wynn observe in the quote above, social categories
were being constructed at this time in order to deal with the expanding
social world. Thus, a style of bead told others what tribe you were in and
what rank you held.

But who needs a visible marker to know that you are the family elder
or the chief's daughter? Certainly not the family or the tribe itself. Monkey
troops don't need body ornaments to know who the alpha male or the
daughter of the highest-ranking female is. Marking social categories using
a visible sign is necessary not for immediate family or close friends, but for
midrange social players—those who occupy the space between intimates
and strangers.[10] These "social intermediates" are the ones with whom a
profitable relationship might be established if a basis for trust can be found.
A common style of bead or a shared belief in a healing power just might be
beginnings of such trust. An important lesson of the past is that religion
emerged within the context of constructing midrange social networks. This
feature has significance for religion's future.

Is Religion Still Adaptive?

Religion arose for two major reasons: (1) It enhanced mental and physical
health, and (2) it enhanced group cooperation and coordination. There is
plenty of evidence that these adaptive functions persist even today. As we
saw in chapters 7 and 8, religious people today are happier and healthier
than their nonreligious counterparts, and religious communities are more
cooperative and enduring. Of even greater significance is that the final tally
of adaptiveness—reproductive success—also seems to be heavily skewed
in favor of the religious. This alone would suggest that religion continues
to serve an adaptive function. This seems to confirm what some researchers
have argued—that religion is so deeply ingrained in the human psyche that
it is all but impossible to eliminate.[11] My conclusion is more nuanced. Yes,
there will always be some vague "spiritual" sense in the human mind. But
religion requires more than this. Religion is relational, and relationships

require effort. Religion is a rather easy relationship for humans to fall into, but it is not an inevitable one. Relationships have costs. They impose obligations and limit personal freedoms and desires. The critical question for religion's future is one not of adaptiveness, but of costs and benefits.

In the past, religion was well worth the cost. Yes, the ancestors could be a nuisance, but they gave the tribe its identity and values. Rituals could be trying, but they were also exhilarating and unifying. But in the modern world, is the cost still worth it? Ritual healing is replaced by modern medicine. Secular laws and social conventions replace tribal traditions and customs. Getting up early for church on Sunday is not going to bring rain for the crops, fix the aging Oldsmobile, or get next week's report written, so why bother? Increasingly, the modern world tends to accentuate the costs of supernatural relationships while reducing their benefits. Thus, it is not surprising that in much of the developed world, traditional religious practice has declined and public life is far more secular than in the past. Whether societies necessarily secularize as they modernize is a contentious issue. However, the factors conducive to an increasingly secularized public sphere are often ones integral to the regulation of midrange relationships.

When Does Religion Cost Too Much?

Sociologist Steve Bruce has summarized the various factors associated with secularization in the West.[12] These include (1) rational social organization, (2) social diversity, (3) economic growth, (4) individualism, (5) science and technology, and (6) social welfare.

RATIONAL SOCIAL ORGANIZATION Western societies are based on social contracts where one agrees to do X and in return another agrees to do Y (e.g., I'll fix the toilet, you pay me $50/hour; You vote for me and I'll lower taxes). Ironically, the rise of monotheism, with its contractual obligations between the one God and his people ("Worship the Lord your God, and I will give you long life on this promised land"), actually encouraged the creation of more rationally, contract-based social structures. In time, though, the social and economic benefits of a better-organized society became attributed to the rational organization itself, detached from any supernatural significance. In other words, you don't necessarily need God to make society run efficiently.

SOCIAL DIVERSITY Urban centers are typically a diverse collection of varied ethnic, religious, and ideological groups. To avoid conflicts and navigate effectively through the typical Western, egalitarian urban world, the religious believer must often banish her views from the public sphere or adopt a "watered-down," more relativistic version of religion fit for public consumption. In either case, religious absolutism and certainty are replaced by relativism and timidity—a retreat that makes the total abandonment of religion that much easier.

ECONOMIC GROWTH The economic growth characteristic of Western societies has brought increasing prosperity to an ever larger segment of the population. Widespread prosperity raises the cost of ascetic religious practices. As these practices become increasingly unpopular with believers, religious organizations are forced to deemphasize or drop them entirely, causing religion to lose its "otherworldly" distinctiveness. As religion accommodates more and more to affluence, its members become progressively more indistinguishable in behavior and belief from their nonreligious neighbors.

INDIVIDUALISM The rise of Protestantism in the West brought with it an emphasis on the individual believer's relationship with God rather than community-based rituals and beliefs. This more "individualized" view of religion increasingly pushed religion out of the public sphere and further into an exclusively private one.

SCIENCE AND TECHNOLOGY Expanding scientific knowledge steadily eroded the credibility of many supernatural religious concepts. As our understanding of and (to some degree) control over the natural world increased, the need to appeal to supernatural forces was reduced or eliminated. Farmers no longer offer sacrifice to Demeter or request a blessing of the field for the "assurance" of a good harvest; instead, fertilizers, pesticides, and other agri-technologies provide this assurance.

SOCIAL WELFARE As governments increasingly usurped services once provided predominantly by religion (health care, education, charity), religion became increasingly marginalized and socially "optional" rather than central.[13]

These factors provide a profile of a society where, for many people, religion simply costs too much. This society is one where (1) people are relatively prosperous, thus reducing group-based competitiveness; (2) government services and technology provide assurances against calamity and suffering; (3) people regularly interact with and need to get along with others of different social/cultural backgrounds; (4) these "intergroup" interactions are personally and materially beneficial and are largely regulated by secular laws and customs. Thus, for the average well-off Westerner, many midrange social relationships—work colleagues, fellow parents, the family doctor, the kid's music teacher—can be effectively regulated using secular signals of professional competence (board certification, membership in the Better Business Bureau) rather than religious/cultural signals of personal virtue (regular church attendance). These secularly assured relationships provide the security and stability that was once obtainable only through religiously bonded communities and tribes. This effectively narrows religion's "practical niche," thus exaggerating its costs while minimizing its benefits.

For example, in America, sociologists have found that claiming to be a Mormon increases a girl's prospects of landing a babysitting job.[14] The assumption that Mormon girls adhere to strict norms of honesty, abstinence, and responsibility gives them a competitive advantage in the marketplace. This advantage operates most critically within that midrange social context—a person is most likely to need a babysitter when she can't find a family member to watch the kids, and she is most likely to search for babysitters among a "pool" of girls with whom she has some familiarity. Thus, in a competitive babysitting environment, Mormon girls can offset the costs of their religion with the benefits of babysitting jobs. However, if the babysitting environment is made less competitive—for example, if the government provides publicly funded, quality-assured services—then the "Mormon advantage" is largely lost.

Secular Europe and the Midrange Social Context

By many measures, Europe is a generally less competitive culture than America and a far less religious one as well. There is another curious cultural difference between Europe and America: Political philosopher Francis Fukuyama observed that countries such as Spain, France, and Italy have a long-standing tradition of weak "intermediate" social groups existing between the family and the state. In fact, Alexis de Tocqueville claimed that in pre-Revolutionary France "it would have been impossible to find . . . even ten men used to acting in concert and defending their interests without appealing to the central power for aid." Given its historical entanglements with the state, religion was part of the central, not local, authority. So even in a rural French village, it was not unheard-of for the church to control local credit unions, agricultural cooperatives, and educational institutions. Furthermore, clergy often instructed villagers on how to vote. Against this backdrop, the French—along with the Spaniards and Italians—often found themselves highly suspicious of any social groupings outside of the immediate family. With trust being reserved exclusively for blood kin, religion's natural niche—constructing midrange social alliances—was a narrow, inhospitable one. Americans, by contrast, have a more endearing history with their local clubs and show greater trust in them.[15]

A comparison of American, German, and Swedish social groups (bowling leagues, church choirs, parent groups) found that American groups were characterized by higher intragroup trust than European groups. This result replicated an earlier finding comparing America and Japanese social groups: It was only in the U.S. groups that the longer a person was in the group, the more others in the group trusted him. Interestingly, among the American groups, the very highest levels of trust and personal commitment were found in church groups.[16]

Furthermore, unlike Europe—where sectarianism is anathema—America has a long history of cultural enclaves ("Chinatown," "Little Italy"), which often serve as stepping-stones for immigrant assimilation.[17] Thus, American culture is one where local groups play an important role in providing critical services in a competitive environment. In this context, religion continues to serve as an important mechanism for forging mid-range social relationships. The girl I can trust with the kids or the mechanic I can trust with the car is likely to be someone from my church—especially if I'm new in town or new to the country. In this setting, where the local social world is relatively competitive, getting up early for Sunday services and following strict group norms still have high market value.

All of this suggests that what makes religion valuable to believers is entirely located in religion's practical, worldly benefits. This, of course, is not entirely true. To many believers, the most important benefits of religion are those associated with a relationship with God—eternal life, the forgiveness of sins, a sense of divine purpose, hope in the future. Even if religion did not provide a practical payback, these believers would continue to be active participants. However, for these people, it is the firm belief in these "otherworldly" rewards that serves to offset what would otherwise be prohibitive costs. Religion will probably never entirely die out because there will likely always be believers whose cost/benefit calculations grant heavy weight to "otherworldly" factors. Whether religion retains a prominent place in public life, however, probably depends more on those for whom earthly factors are predominant.

Does Religion Require Competition?

The preceding discussion suggests that for religion to thrive there must be competition—especially intergroup competition. This really should not be surprising. If religion is an adaptation, then of course it evolved out of competition. All evolutionary adaptations have their origin in competition; and where competition is most intense, the adaptation's advantages are seen most clearly. This is probably why religion and intergroup conflict are often so closely associated with each other. However, competition can play out in varied, sometimes unexpected forms. As we saw earlier, cooperation can actually be a means of competing. Compared to Europe, America is more competitive and more religious. This competition is largely that of a relatively unregulated, freewheeling marketplace, not of intergroup violence. This, however, is enough for religion to find a useful niche—and whether societies and governments can sustain all the factors necessary to deprive religion of this niche is also an open question.[18]

Is it possible, though, to envision a religion that does not require competition? The global religions see themselves as possessing something capable of uniting all people. Nothing motivates people to adhere to group norms quite like religion. Often these norms serve to define a people— which necessarily means setting them apart from others (the Jews are the ones who don't eat pork, the Sikhs are the ones who wear turbans). Humans need their groups, so the idea that exclusive norms can (or even should) be eliminated is foolhardy. Most religions, however, do have overlapping norms that can serve to unite. Furthermore, these inclusive norms often pass empirical muster as being genuinely beneficial for individuals and their communities.

Universal Religious Norms: Compassion, Self-Restraint, and Service

Nearly all the major global religions promote teachings in three areas: compassion for others, restraining desire, and serving the community. For example, in Mahayana Buddhism, compassion takes the form of Tara, the goddess of compassion and the mother of all Buddhas. Additionally, in this tradition, bodhisattvas are enlightened ones who out of compassion for others have chosen to remain in the world and aid in its spiritual development. In Islam, Allah is known as Al-Rehman, or The Compassionate, and *zakat* (charity to the less fortunate) is one of Islam's Five Pillars. The Sermon on the Mount and the parable of the Good Samaritan stand as two of Christianity's great expressions of compassion.

Self-restraint is embodied in nearly all religious traditions in the form of divine laws or commandments that the faithful must follow. Practicing Jews have over 600 laws to which they are bound. The path to enlightenment for Jain holy persons requires ascetic renunciation of all violence, lying, possessions, and sexual relations. Finally, in the Christian tradition, service is exemplified by Jesus washing the feet of his followers and commanding that the greatest among them must serve the least (John, chapter 13). Central to Sikh worship is *langar*, the communal meal provided to all who wish to partake, regardless of caste or status.

Not only are they stressed by nearly every major religion, but practicing compassion, self-restraint, and service can also have empirically verifiable benefits to both individuals and communities. Consider, for example, the fact that those who exercise compassion in the form of forgiveness have reduced cortisol levels. Cortisol is a physical indicator of stress that, when elevated, can have deleterious effects on immune system function. The self-restraint expressed in religious injunctions appears to play an important role in protecting adolescents from drug abuse and delinquency. Furthermore, most religions place a high value on marriage and fidelity within marriage. Studies have shown that stable, high-quality marriages provide both physical and psychological benefits to those involved. Finally, service in the form of volunteerism, community and civic involvement, and church membership are important indicators of community health. Thus, religious doctrines requiring the practice of compassion, self-restraint, and service need not simply be accepted on authority (as may be sufficient for the devout) but can be defended rationally because of their empirically established effects in promoting individual happiness and community health.[19]

Religion is paradoxical. It emerged out of intergroup competition, yet it has a remarkable power to unite. It sets people apart from one another, yet can also draw vastly different people together. Long ago we envisioned relationships with spiritual beings. In one sense these relationships were very mundane—they served practical human needs. The practical side of these relationships is also the source of their power to divide us, to pit one group against another. The divine side is in their capacity to quietly but persistently call us to transcend ourselves and find common ground for trust.

Notes

INTRODUCTION

1. See Dow, 2006; or Atran, 2002, pp. 13–15.
2. Weeden, Cohen, & Kenrick, 2008.
3. Atran, 2002, p. 14.
4. Atran, 2002, p. 14.
5. Rappaport, 1968, 1999; Connors, 2000; Lansing, 1991.
6. Fehr, Fischbacher, & Gächter, et al., 2002; Gintis, 2000; Richerson & Boyd, 2005; Sterelny, 1996.
7. Durkheim, 1912/1965.
8. Lawson & McCauley, 1990; McCauley & Lawson, 2002.
9. Boyer, 2001, p. 261.
10. Atran, 2002, p. 14.
11. James, 1902; Baruss, 2003, pp. 189–190; Hood, Spilka, Hunsberger, & Gorsuch, 1996, p. 247.
12. Farthing, 1992, pp. 442–443.
13. Azari, Missimer, & Seitz, 2005; Beauregard & Paquette, 2006; Newberg, Alavi, et al., 2001; Newberg, Pourdehnad, Alavi, & d'Aquili, 2003.
14. See Azari, 2006, for discussion.
15. Wallace, 1966, pp. 52–67.
16. Adams, 2001; Dugatkin, 2001; Richerson & Boyd, 2001.

17. Cheney & Seyfarth, 2007; Goodall, 1986; Silk, 2001; de Waal, 1990.

18. Azari, 2006; James, 1902; Otto, 1923.

19. Atran, 2002, pp. 226–227; Bird-David, 1999, pp. 257; Brightman, 1993, pp. 2, 103, 187; Connors, 2000; Eder, 1999, pp. 296; de Waal Malefijt, 1968; Hallowell, 1975; Worl, 1999, pp. 63.

20. Atran, Medin, Lynch, et al., 2002; Atran, Medin, Ross, et al., 1999; see also Atran, 2002, pp. 219–227, 271–273; Brightman, 1993, pp. 76, 110, 186.

21. Provine, 1989, p. 253.

22. James, 1896/1956, pp. 23–24.

23. James, 1896/1956, p. 28.

24. Buber, 1970; Haught, 2008.

25. Camus, 1955; Haught, 2003; Russell, 1961.

26. See, for example, Churchland, 1994, pp. 67–72; also Velmans, 2000.

CHAPTER 1

Parts of this chapter were adapted from M. J. Rossano (2001), Artificial intelligence, religion, and community concern, *Zygon: Journal of Religion and Science, 36,* 57–75.

1. Account taken from Arlington National Cemetery Web site, www.arlingtoncemetery.net/hcenochjr.htm (accessed 10/2/08), and a National Public Radio report, www.npr.org/templates/story/story.php?storyId=93677504 (accessed 10/2/08).

2. Frank, 1988.

3. "Hominin" refers to all the species that emerged along the evolutionary branch that ultimately led to modern humans (*Homo sapiens sapiens*). Thus, such species as *Homo habilis, Homo erectus,* and *Homo neanderthalensis* (Neanderthals) are all hominins. Hominin has replaced the older term "hominids" in paleoanthropological literature.

4. Archaeological: Dickson, 1990; Hayden, 2003; Lewis-Williams, 2002. Anthropological: Atran, 2002; Hinde, 1999; McClenon, 2002. Primatological: King, 2007. Cognitive: Boyer, 2001; Tremlin, 2006. Neuroscientific: d'Aquili & Newberg, 1999; Newberg, d'Aquili, & Rause, 2001.

5. Aggressive atheists: Dawkins, 2006; S. Harris, 2007; Hitchens, 2007; Stenger, 2007. Atheist critics: Haught, 2008; McGrath, 2007; McGrath & McGrath, 2007.

6. Anderson, Reid, & Jennings, 1992; Headey et al., 2002; Siegel, 1990.

7. Dawkins, 2003, p. 147; 2006, p. 31.

8. Dawkins, 2003, pp. 8–10.

9. Calzato, van den Wildenberg, & Hommel, 2008.

10. Calzato, van den Wildenberg, & Hommel, 2008, p. 2.

11. Tillich, 1948, p. 57.

12. Haught, 2003, p. 130.

13. Murphy & Ellis, 1996; Prager & Telushkin, 1975.

14. Haught, 2003.

15. See, for example, Dawkins, 2003, pp. 146–151.

16. For a fuller discussion see Rossano, 2007b.

17. Horton, 1960, p. 211.

18. Frazer, 1890/1941, p. 50.

19. Bruce, 2002, p. 2.

20. Argyle & Beit-Hallahmi, 1975, p. 1; Stark, 1999, p. 270.

21. In order: Dollahite, 1998, p. 5; Zinnbauer & Pargament, 2005, p. 35; Bellah, 1970, p. 2; Clark, 1958, p. 22; James, 1902, p. 53.

22. Whitehead, 1925, p. 92.

23. Buber, 1970; Hill & Hall, 2002.

24. First quote, Haught, 2008, p. 46; second quote, Greeley, 1981, p. 18.

25. Gallup & Jones, 1989; Kirkpatrick & Shaver, 1992; see also Kirkpatrick, 2005a, pp. 53–54; review of religion/attachment literature can be found in Kirkpatrick, 2005a. Another line of research supportive of the "religion-as-relationship" approach can be found in Doug Oman and Carl Thoresen's work showing that people learn from "spiritual role models" in ways analogous to how they learn from human role models: see Oman & Thoresen, 2007; 2003.

26. Positive effects of secure attachments in children and adults: Ainsworth, 1985; Hazan & Zeifman, 1999. Positive effects of secure attachments to God: Baker & Gorsuch, 1982; Entner, 1977; Kahoe, 1974; Kirkpatrick & Shaver, 1992; Rowatt & Kirkpatrick, 2002; Strickland & Shaffer, 1971; Ventis, 1995. Relational aspects of religion central to religion's positive effects: Galanter, 1989; Pollner, 1989; Poloma & Gallup, 1991.

27. Catholic teenagers: Spilka, Addison, & Rosensohn, 1975. Fourth graders: Jubis, 1991. Adolescent boys: Krol, 1982. Female seminarians and nuns: Potvin, 1985; Vergote & Tamayo, 1981.

28. Kirkpatrick & Shaver, 1992. Religious conversion: Granqvist, 1998; Kirkpatrick & Shaver, 1990; Lohmann, 2003.

29. Parenting style and deities: Lambert, Triandis, & Wolf, 1959; Rohner, 1975. Hinduism: Bowker, 1997, pp. 32–37; Hiebert, 1992.

30. Kirkpatrick, 2005a, p. 73.

31. Compensation: Kirkpatrick & Shaver, 1990. Correspondence: Granqvist, 1998; Granqvist & Hagekull, 1999; Kirkpatrick & Shaver, 1992; James, 1902.

32. Granqvist & Hagekull, 1999.

33. Kirkpatrick, 1992. See also discussion in Hill & Hall, 2002; Weiss, 1974, 1986.

34. Exline & Rose, 2005, p. 317–318; Exline & Martin, 2005.

35. Forgiving God: Exline, 2004. Repairing the God-human relationship: Exline & Rose, 2005, pp. 318–319; Virkler & Virkler, 1986; Shulman, 1993.

36. Hardman, 2000, 2004.

37. Twenty-third Psalm and PET scan: Azari, Missimer, & Seitz, 2005.

38. Beauregard & Paquette, 2006. Studies of meditative practices: Lazar, Bush, et al., 2000; Lazar, Kerr, et al., 2005; Lou et al., 1999. SPECT studies: Newberg, Alavi, et al., 2001; Newberg, Pourdehnad, Alavi, & d'Aquili, 2003.

39. Activation in prefrontal and inferior parietal/superior temporal cortices: Azari, Missimer, & Seitz, 2005; Beauregard & Paquette, 2006; Lazar, Bush, et al., 2000; Lazar, Kerr, et al., 2005; Newberg, Alavi, et al., 2001; Newberg, Pourdehnad, Alavi, & d'Aquili, 2003. Prefrontal and social cognition: Adolphs, 1999; Amodio & Frith, 2006. Superior temporal/inferior parietal and social cognition: Adolphs, 1999; Blakemore, et al., 2003; Gallagher & Frith, 2003.

40. Schjoedt, Stødkilde-Jørgensen, Geertz, & Roepstorff, 2009.

41. Azari, 2006 (see esp. pp. 43–44); Kapogiannis, Barbey, Su, Zamboni, Krueger, & Grafman, 2009.

CHAPTER 2

This chapter is adapted in part from M. J. Rossano (2007a), Supernaturalizing social life: Religion and the evolution of human cooperation, *Human Nature, 18,* 272–294.

1. H. J. Deacon, 1989; Ingman, Kaessman, Paabo, & Gyllensten, 2000; Ke et al., 2001; McDermott et al., 1996; McDougall, Brown, & Fleagle, 2005; Stringer, 1996; Underhill et al., 2001; T. D. White et al., 2003.

2. Shea, 2006.

3. Kessin & Van Lookeren Campagne, 1992; Matsuda & Harada, 1990.

4. Wild dogs, jackals, and hyenas: Malcolm & Marten, 1982; Moehlman, 1979; Owens & Owens, 1984. Birds: Woolfendon & FitzPatrick, 1984. Lionesses: Packer, Lewis, & Pusey, 1992.

5. Hamilton, 1964. Social insects: Ratnieks, 1988; Oldroyd, Smolenski, Cornuet, & Corzier, 1994. Humans: Borgerhoff Mulder, 1991; Cronk, 1991.

6. Wilkinson, 1984; DeNault & McFarlane, 1995.

7. Chimpanzees: de Waal & Luttrell, 1988; Boesch & Boesch-Achermann, 2000; Nishida, Hasegawa, Hayaki, Takahata, & Uehara, 1992. Monkeys: de Waal & Berger, 2000. Hauser's critique: Hauser, 2006, pp. 383–392.

8. Alexander, 1987.

9. Guppies: Dugatkin & Alfieri, 1991. Chimpanzees: Goodall, 1992; Melis, Hare, & Tomasello, 2007. Humans: Cohen & Vandello, 2001; Engelmann & Fischbacher, 2002; Hawkes & Bird, 2002; Milinski, Semmann, & Krambeck, 2002.

10. Cooperation increases significantly in repeated encounters: see Cooper, DeJong, Forsythe, & Ross, 1996; Poundstone, 1992. However, higher-than-expected levels of cooperation are also present in one-off encounters: see Cooper et al., 1996; Henrich & Henrich, 2007, pp. 111–112.

11. Cooperation in ultimatum game: Carpenter, Burks, & Verhoogen, 2005; Fehr & Fischbacher, 2003; Forsythe, Horowitz, Savin, & Sefton, 1994; Roth, Prasnikar, Okuno-Fujiwara, & Zamir, 1991. Cultural variation in ultimatum game: Henrich, McElreath, et al., 2006; Henrich, Boyd, et al., 2001.

12. Fehr & Gächter, 2005; Fehr & Fischbacher, 2004.

13. Henrich & Henrich, 2007, pp. 144–155.

14. Williams, 1966.

15. Fehr, Fischbacher, & Gächter, 2002; Gintis, 2000; Richerson & Boyd, 2005; Sober & Wilson, 1998; Sterelny, 1996.

16. R. C. Kelly, 1985.

17. North America and New Guinea: Jorgensen, 1980; Keeley, 1996; Soltis, Boyd, & Richerson, 1995. Global survey of hunter-gatherers: Ember, 1978.

18. Gurerk, Irlenbusch, & Rockenbach, 2006.

19. Mellars, 2006. Red ochre: Barham, 2000, 2002; Kuhn & Stiner, 2007, p. 46. Beads: Vanhaeren et al., 2006.

20. Darwin, 1871, p. 166.

21. Boyd, Gintis, Bowles, & Richerson, 2003; Gurerk et al., 2006; Sethi & Somanathan, 1996; Sterelny, 2003, pp. 125–137.

22. Better behavior when being watched: Andreoni & Petrie, 2004; Burnham & Hare, 2007; Buss, 1980; Diener & Srull, 1979; Duval, 1976; Hoffman, McCabe, & Smith, 1996; Kleck et al., 1976; Rege & Telle, 2004. Effects on self-perception: Baumeister & Tice, 1984; Tice, 1992.

23. Burnham & Hare, 2007.

24. Bateson, Nettle, & Roberts, 2006. For quote see www.sciencedaily.com/releases/2006/06/060628091247.htm (accessed 5/6/09).

25. Shariff & Norenzayan, 2007.

26. Shariff & Norenzayan, 2007, pp. 807–808.

27. Ghosts: Bering, McLeod, & Shackelford, 2005; Fish: Milinski & Rockenbach, 2007.

28. Indirect reciprocity: Alexander, 1987; Hunting as display: Gurven et al., 2000; Hawkes & Bird, 2002; Honor cultures: Cohen & Vandello, 2001; W. Miller, 1990.

29. Engelmann & Fischbacher, 2002; Milinski et al., 2002; Nowak & Sigmund, 1998; Wedekind & Milinski, 2000.

30. Henrich, Boyd, et al., 2001; Roth et al., 1991.

31. Boehm, 1999, 2000; Hawkes & Bird, 2002; Lee, 1979.

32. Bingham, 1999. Ape/monkey throwing: van Lawick-Goodall, 1968; Calvin, 1993; Westergaard, Liv, Haynie, & Suomi, 2000. Hunter-gatherer throwing: Corballis, 2002, p. 79; Isaac, 1992.

33. Skully, 1997.

34. Costly moralistic punishment: Fehr & Gächter, 2002; Fehr & Tyran, 1996. Need to punish cheaters: Boyd et al., 2003; Fehr & Fischbacher, 2003.

35. Cycles of drought: Alley, 2000, pp. 118–126. Toba: Ambrose, 1998b. Genetics and population expansion: Mellars, 2006. Symbolism: Henshilwood, d'Errico, Vanhaeren, van Niekerk, & Jacobs, 2004; Henshilwood & Sealy, 1997; Henshilwood et al., 2002.

36. Minkel, 2006.

CHAPTER 3

This chapter is adapted in part from M. J. Rossano (2007a), Supernaturalizing social life: Religion and the evolution of human cooperation, *Human Nature, 18,* 272–294.

1. Klein & Edgar, 2002; Mellars, 1996; Stringer & Gamble, 1993.

2. Settlement sites: Bar-Yosef, 2000; Dickson, 1990, pp. 84–92, 180–189; Hoffecker, 2002, pp. 129, 136; Stringer & Gamble, 1993, pp. 154–158. Trade networks: Adler, Bar-Oz, Belfer-Cohen, & Bar-Yosef, 2006.

3. Burials: O'Shea & Zvelebil, 1984; Vanhaeren & d'Errico, 2005. Prestige objects: Hayden, 2003, p. 130.

4. Gradual emergence of modern cognition: McBrearty & Brooks, 2000. Beads: Henshilwood et al., 2004, 2002; Vanhaeren et al., 2006. Trade networks: H. J. Deacon & J. Deacon, 1999; Ambrose, 1998a.

5. Genetics: Behar et al., 2008; Mellars, 2006; Religion and human society: Rappaport, 1999.

6. Rossano, 2007b.

7. Kuper, 1961, pp. 192–193.

8. Hardman, 2004.

9. "Traditional" religions in this instance are being contrasted with "book" religions; the two differ along a number of dimensions. Traditional religions tend to see nature, food, dance, and nearly all human activities as sacred or potentially sacred. Traditional religions tend to emphasize ecstatic experiences as central to religion and tend to deemphasize any sort of articulated moral code. Traditional religions tend not to be exclusive and to acknowledge other systems as valid. Finally, while book religions often emphasize the afterlife and union with a deity beyond the grave, traditional religions tend to see life as the most central mystery and concern. For more thorough discussions see Hayden, 2003, pp. 5–12; Howells, 1948, pp. 2–5; or Rappaport, 1999, p. 325. It should be noted, however, that these distinctions are not strict dichotomies, and there are degrees of overlap between the systems.

10. Ancestor worship is widespread: Harvey, 2000; Eliade & Couliano, 1991; Lee & Daly, 1999. Parrinder quote: Parrinder, 1976, p. 24. Kwaio: Keesing, 1982. Efe Pygmies: Sawada, 2001. Native Americans, Australians, and ancestors: Eliade & Couliano, 1991, pp. 199–200; Hayden, 2003, p. 184; Hultkrantz, 1967; p. 129.

11. Hayden, 2003, pp. 237–240.

12. Butzer, 1971, p. 463; Dahlberg & Carbonell, 1961; Hayden, 2003, pp. 122–131; O'Shea & Zvelebil, 1984; T. D. Price & Brown, 1985; Vanhaeren & d'Errico, 2005; see review in Dickson, 1990, pp. 84–92, 180–189.

13. Hunting technologies: Hoffecker, 2002, pp. 179–184, 239–243. Food storage: Soffer, 1989. Prime territories: R. White, 1985.

14. Ancestors and complex hunter-gatherers: Freedman, 1965, 1970. Tlingit: Oberg, 1973.

15. Sungir: R. White, 1993. Dolní Věstonice: Klima, 1988. Saint-Germain-la-Rivière: Vanhaeren & d'Errico, 2005. Burials and ancestor worship: Hayden, 2003, p. 239; Sandarupa, 1996.

16. Lepinski Vir: Srejovic & Babovic, 1983; Srejovic & Letica, 1978; see also Hayden, 2003, pp. 159–164. Sannai Maruyama: Iizuka, 1995. Skateholm and Bredasten: M. Larsson, 1985–1986; L. Larsson, 1987–1988. Honoring the dead: Hayden, 2003, p. 162.

17. Platvoet, 1993.

18. Cited in Parrinder, 1976, pp. 57, 65.

19. Keesing, 1982.

20. Lohorung Rai: Hardman, 2000. Interested parties: Boyer, 2001; Harvey, 2000; Lee & Daly, 1999.

21. African tribes: Parrinder, 1976. Australian aboriginals: Hume, 2000.

22. Berndt & Berndt, 1964, p. 188; Parrinder, 1976, p. 59; Radin, 1937, p. 14; Woodward, 2000.

23. M. J. Field, 1961, p. 145; Kuper, 1961, pp. 192–193.

24. Mithen, 2003, pp. 130–131.

25. Shamanism strictly speaking: Campbell, 1983. Shamanism as universal: Lee & Daly, 1999, p. 108; Townsend, 1999; Vitebsky, 2000, pp. 55–56. Among traditional societies only the Siriono of Bolivia appeared not to have shamanistic practices when first contacted.

26. Definition of shaman: Campbell, 1983, p. 157; Guenther, 1999, p. 427. Shamanism as oldest form of religion: Halifax, 1982; Guenther, 1999; Lee & Daly, 1999; Winkelman, 1990.

27. !Kung San healing dances: Katz, 1982. San rock art: Lewis-Williams, 2002, p. 140; R. White, 2003, pp. 152–173.

28. Cave art and shamanism: Dowson & Porr, 1999; Eliade, 1972; Halifax, 1982; Hayden, 2003; Lewis-Williams, 1986, 2002. Three-tiered cosmos: Lewis-Williams, 2002, p. 144. Cave handprints: Lewis-Williams, 2002, pp. 216–220.

29. Hayden's review: Hayden, 2003, pp. 143–145, 148–151. Caves as gateways to the underworld: Clottes & Lewis-Williams, 1998; Campbell, 1983; Lewis-Williams, 2002; pp. 169–170, 209. Infrequent use of caves: Clottes, 1992; de Beaune, 1995. Isolated spaces and ecstatic states: Campbell, 1983. Animal depictions as shamanic hallucinations: Dowson & Porr, 1999; Lewis-Williams, 1986. Bizarre symbols and graphics: Lewis-Williams & Dowson, 1988. (These symbols have been argued to reflect the "entoptic" visual experiences of altered states. Entoptic experiences result from quasi-random activity of neurons in the visual system resulting in images of parallel lines, grid patterns, concentric arcs, and similar patterns.) Handprints/footprints of children: Clottes, 1992; Owens & Hayden, 1997.

30. Soul flight: Townsend, 1999; Vitebsky, 2000; Winkelman, 1999. Part-human/part-animal images: de Beaune, 1998; Dickson, 1990. (These images are called therianthropic images or therianthropes.) Lion-headed man: Freeman & Echegaray, 1981.

31. Sorcerer: Dickson, 1990, p. 115. Bird-man of Lascaux: Davenport & Jochim, 1988; Dickson, 1990, pp. 131–135.

32. Balter, 2000; Vitebsky, 2000.

33. Townsend, 1999.

34. Lewis-Williams, 2002, pp. 138–143, 164–176.

35. Social function of shamanism: Townsend, 1999, pp. 446, 450. Hultkranz quote: Hultkrantz, 1973, p. 34.

36. Violations of taboo arouse supernatural anger: Lee & Daly, 1999, p. 59. Vitebsky quote: Vitebsky, 2000, p. 63.

37. Quote taken from Vitebsky, 2000, p. 62, based on account from Rasmussen, 1929, pp. 123–129.

38. Townsend, 1999, p. 443.

39. Vitebsky, 1993.

40. Natural spirits common cross-culturally: Guenther, 1999, p. 426; Harvey, 2000; Hayden, 2003, pp. 105–106; Hultkrantz, 1967, 1994; Lee & Daly, 1999, p. 310. Animal spirits and early civilizations: Atran, 2002, p. 67. African Pygmies and animal spirits: Boyer, 2001, p. 69; Sawada, 2001.

41. Cave art, masculine/feminine motifs: Leroi-Gourhan, 1968. Lion chapel: Begouen & Clottes, 1986–1987. Bear chamber: Chauvet, Deschamps, & Hillaire, 1995, p. 42.

42. Dolní Věstonice: Vandiver, Soffer, Klima, & Svoboda, 1989; Hayden, 2003 p. 134. Natural spirits and UP religious practices: Bahn & Vertut, 1988; Clottes & Lewis-Williams, 1998; Leroi-Gourhan, 1968.

43. Hunting as exchange: Atran, 2002, pp. 226–227; Brightman, 1993, pp. 2, 103, 187; Lee & Daly, 1999, pp. 63, 257, 296. Persuasion and rituals: Connors, 2000; Hallowell, 1975; de Waal Malefijt, 1968. Master of animals: Brightman, 1993, pp. 91–93; Hultkrantz, 1967, p. 59; Lee & Daly, 1999, pp. 257, 264, 296; Nilsson, 1950; Reichel-Dolmatoff, 1978, pp. 291–292; Sawada, 2001.

44. Brightman, 1993, pp. 76, 110, 186.

45. Alvard, 1994; Brightman, 1993 pp. 281–291; Connors, 2000; Nelson, 1993; Stearman, 1994.

46. Connors, 2000; Swezey & Heizer, 1993.

47. Bunting, 1997; Connors, 2000, p. 146.

48. Lansing, 1991.

49. Lansing, 1991, p. 124.

50. Frontinus, 1961, p. 405.

51. W. H. Walker, 2001; Rappaport, 1968.

CHAPTER 4

This chapter is adapted in part from M. J. Rossano (2009), Ritual behaviour and the origins of modern cognition, *Cambridge Archaeological Journal, 19*, 243–256, and M. J. Rossano (2007c), Did meditating make us human? *Cambridge Archaeological Journal, 17*, 47–58.

1. Rapid climate changes: Alley, 2000, pp. 118–126. Toba: Ambrose, 1998b.

2. Petraglia et al., 2007.

3. Ambrose, 1998b; Behar et al., 2008; Mellars, 2006.

4. Wiessner, 1982.

5. Ambrose, 1998a; Henshilwood et al., 2004; Vanhaeren et al., 2006.

6. Ambrose's analysis: Ambrose & Lorenz, 1990. Troop-to-tribe transition: Ambrose, 2002, p. 22.

7. Campsites: Bar-Yosef, 2000; Dickson, 1990, pp. 84–92, 180–189; Hoffecker, 2002, pp. 129, 136; Stringer & Gamble, 1993, pp. 154–158. Social stratification: Hayden, 2003, pp. 122–131; Mellars, 1996; Vanhaeren & d'Errico, 2005. Trade networks: Adler et al., 2006; Feblot-Augustins, 1999; Gamble, 1999, pp. 242, 360–362, 382–383; Taborin, 1993; Stringer & Gamble, 1993, pp. 210–211.

8. Defining ritual: Bell, 1997, pp. 138–169; Rappaport, 1999, p. 24. Baboon scrotum-grasping: Smuts & Watanabe, 1990; Whitham & Maestripieri, 2003.

9. de Waal, 1990; R. D. Guthrie, 2005, p. 68; Silk, 2001.

10. Monkey grunting: Silk, 2001. Brain opiates: Keverne, Martinez, & Tuite, 1989.

11. Reunion rituals: Goodall, 1986; de Waal & Lanting, 1997; van Roosmalen & Klein, 1988, p. 515. Baboon vocalizations: Richman, 1987. Chimpanzee reconciliation: de Waal, 1990.

12. Smuts & Watanabe, 1990.

13. de Waal & Johanowicz, 1993.

14. David Brooks, op-ed column, *New York Times*, 6/17/08.

15. Symbols as markers of modern cognition: Henshilwood & Marean, 2003. Ratcheting effect of culture: Richerson & Boyd, 2005, pp. 107–108.

16. Morwood, 2002, pp. 19, 42–43, 78.

17. My discussion of symbolism is based on the distinctions articulated by philosopher C. S. Peirce: see Hawkes, 1932, or T. W. Deacon, 1997, pp. 75–92, for good discussions.

18. Coolidge & Wynn, 2001, 2005; Wynn & Coolidge, 2003, 2004.

19. Kane & Engle, 2002.

20. Tomasello, Carpenter, Call, Behne, & Moll, 2005, esp. pp. 680–681.

21. Innovative Neanderthals: Langley, Clarkson, & Ulm, 2008. Culture and cognition: Barnes, 2000.

22. Cognition and social engagement: Ybarra et al., 2008. Neuroscience and social reasoning: Adolphs, 1999; Amodio & Frith, 2006; Mitchell, 2008; Nee, Berman, Moore, & Jonides, 2008. Neuroscience and toolmaking: Stout & Chaminade, 2007; Stout, Toth, Schick, & Chaminade, 2008.

23. Frontal lobe, working memory, direction of attention: Curtis & D'Esposito, 2003; Duncan et al., 2000; D'Esposito, Kirkby, van Horn, Ellmore, & Berman, 1999; Gray, Chabris, & Braver, 2003. Frontal lobe and inhibitory control: Brass, Derrfuss, Forstmann, & von Cramon, 2005; Derrfuss, Brass, & von Cramon, 2004; Hester, Murphy, & Garavan, 2004; A. M. Kelly, Hester, Foxe, Shpaner, & Garavan, 2006. Right frontal critical to self-control: Ingvar, 1994; Knoch & Fehr, 2007; Sanfey, Rilling, Aronson, Nystrom, & Cohen, 2003; Stuss, Binns, Murphy, & Alexander, 2002. Two areas of the frontal lobe are most critical—the dorsolateral prefrontal cortex and the anterior cingulate cortex. Inhibitory control involves these areas plus areas of the inferior parietal and inferior frontal cortices.

24. Beauregard, Levesque, & Bourgouin, 2001.

25. Lieberman, Hariri, Jarcho, Eisenberger & Brookheimer, 2005; Olsson, Ebert, Banaji, & Phelps, 2005.

26. A. M. Kelly et al., 2006.

27. Mirsky, 1937.

28. Chagnon, 1968.

29. Rappaport, 1999, p. 79.

30. Rites of passage in 70% of societies: Alcorta, 2006; Lutkehaus & Roscoe, 1995. Severity of initiations and external threats: Young, 1965; Hayden, 2003, pp. 104–105; Sosis, 2006, p. 82. Costly signaling theory: Sosis, 2006.

31. Hand/footprints in caves: Clottes, 1992. Deep caves as ritual venues: see summary in Hayden, 2003, pp. 148–50. Altered states and adolescent initiation ceremonies: Owens & Hayden, 1997; Pettitt, 1946.

32. Female initiations: Knight, Power, & Watts, 1995; Power, 1998, pp. 122–125. Male initiations: Catlin, 1867; Glucklich, 2001; McCauley, 2001; Whitehouse, 1996. Mandan Sun dance: Catlin, 1867.

33. Hayden, 2003, p. 32.

34. Brain opiates: Frecska & Kulcsar, 1989. Synchronized activity and cooperation: Wiltermuth & Heath, 2009.

35. Shamanism as healing: McClenon, 2002. !Kung healing dances: Katz, 1982.

36. McClenon, 1997, 2002.

37. Winkelman, 1990; see McClenon, 2002, p. 67.

38. See McClenon, 2002, pp. 67–71.

39. Katz, 1982, p. 138; Morgan, 1973; S. C. Wilson & Barber, 1978; for review see McClenon, 2002, pp. 93–96.

40. Katz, 1982, pp. 49–55; Bowers & LeBaron, 1986; Brown, 1992; see McClenon, 2002, pp. 46–67, or Newberg & Lee, 2006, pp. 50–51 for review; Newberg, 2006.

41. Goodall, 1986; Hayden, 2003; Jolly & White, 1995, p. 345; Lewis-Williams, 2002; Trinkaus, 1983, pp. 409–411.

42. Majno, 1975; Sigerist, 1987.

43. Palmer, 1979; see McClenon, 2000; McClenon, 2002, pp. 70, 132–135, 150–151.

44. Neuroscience studies of prayerful/meditative practices: Azari et al., 2001; Beauregard & Paquette, 2006; Lazar, Bush, et al., 2000; Lazar, Kerr, et al., 2005; Lutz, Greischar, Rawlings, Ricard, & Davidson, 2004; Lou et al., 1999; Newberg, Alavi, et al., 2001; R. K. Wallace, Benson, & Wilson, 1971. These studies have employed both neuroimaging and EEG techniques, finding that the dorsolateral prefrontal cortex and anterior cingulate cortex are two key areas consistently activated. Long-term structural/function brain changes due to meditation: Carter, et al., 2005; Lazar, Kerr, et al., 2005; Slagter, et al., 2007. Increase in AVP: Newberg, 2006.

45. E.g., Smith & Jonides, 1994.

46. Klein, 1995; Klein & Edgar, 2002.

47. Kirschner & Gerhart, 2005; Jablonka & Lamb, 1995; West-Eberhard, 2003.

48. Jablonka & Lamb, 1995; Simpson, 1953.

49. Waddington, 1942.

50. Defining an encultured ape: Call & Tomasello, 1996. Deferred imitation in encultured apes: Bjorklund & Rosenberg, 2005. Review of encultured ape abilities: see Tomasello & Call, 1997, pp. 390–395.

51. Jablonka & Lamb, 2005, pp. 158–176. This is not the only possible mechanism. Kirschner & Gerhart (2005) argue for another called "facilitated variation," where mutations are still random but developmental constraints bias which genetic changes are likely to be expressed in the phenotype.

52. Domesticating silver foxes: Belyaev, 1979. Belyaev's appeal to epigenetic changes was consistent with Waddington's explanation of his fruit fly experiment although he used the term "genetic assimilation." Short term evolution and epigenetic changes: Jablonka & Lamb, 2005, p. 274.

53. Hours-old infants imitating: T. M. Field, Woodson, Greenberg, & Cohen, 1982; Kugiumutzakis, 1988; Meltzoff & Moore, 1977. Baby imitation is provocative, not reflexive: Nagy & Molnar, 2004; see also Reddy, 2008, pp. 52–55.

54. Ape baby imitation: Ferrari et al., 2006; Myowa-Yamakoshi, Tomonaga, Tanaka, & Matsuzawa, 2004; Myowa, 1996. Mother-infant dance: Trevarthen, 1979, p. 347.

55. Tronick, Als, & Adamson, 1979.

56. Keller, Scholmerich, & Eibl-Eibesfeldt, 1988.

57. Ross & Lollis, 1987; Tronick, 2003; Tronick, Als, Adamson, Wise, & Brazelton, 1978; see also Reddy, 2008, pp. 72–77.

58. Bruner, 1975.

59. Haviland & Lelwica, 1987; Hobson, 2004, p. 37.

60. Apes don't do protoconversation: Tomasello et al., 2005. Autism and proto-conversation: Carpenter, Pennington, & Rogers, 2002; Hobson, 2004, pp. 45–46.

61. Mother-infant rituals and theory of mind: Stern, 2000; Tomasello, 1988. Child neglect: Curtiss, 1977. First two years: Hobson, 2004; Greenspan & Shanker, 2004.

62. Hobson, 2004, pp. 48–49.

63. "Ritually capable" and incapable mothers: Kogan & Carter, 1996; Trevarthen & Aitken, 1994; Tomasello, 1988.

64. Adler et al., 2006; d'Errico, 2003; Grayson & Delpech, 2003; Sorensen & Leonard, 2001.

65. Feblot-Augustins, 1999; Stringer & Gamble, 1993, pp. 210–211.

CHAPTER 5

1. Atran, 2006; J. L. Barrett, 2000; Boyer, 2001; S. Guthrie, 1993.

2. P. L. Harris, 2000, p. 192; Hauser, 2006, p. 203; Zwaan & Radvansky, 1998.

3. Redefining objects in play: P. L. Harris, 2000, pp. 11–13. Counterfactuals: Harris, German, & Mills, 1996.

4. Mulcahy & Call, 2006; Osvath & Osvath, 2008; Cheney & Seyfarth, 2007, p. 279.

5. Baron-Cohen, 2005.

6. Accidental vs. intentional acts: Call, Hare, Carpenter, & Tomasello, 2004; Call & Tomasello, 1998. Beliefs and inferences: Tomasello et al., 2005.

7. Csibra & Gergely, 1998; Csibra, Gergely, Biro, Koos, & Brockbank, 1999; Gergely & Csibra, 2003; Woodward, 1998.

8. S. C. Johnson, 2000, 2003.

9. Vervet alarm calls: Seyfarth & Cheney, 1986. Infant chimpanzees: Uller, 2004. Baboons: Cheney & Seyfarth, 2007, pp. 91–95. Rhesus monkeys: Harlow & Zimmerman, 1959.

10. Harris's summary: P. L. Harris, 2000. Fantasy vs. reality: Dierker & Sanders, 1996; P. L. Harris, 2000, pp. 60–65; Sharon & Woolley, 2004. Pretend play and physical causation: P. L. Harris, 2000, pp. 13–17. Magic: Woolley, Browne, & Boerger, 2006.

11. Playing trains: Dunn & Dale, 1984, p. 141. Updating mental models: P. L. Harris, 2000, pp. 11–13.

12. Connolly & Doyle, 1984; P. L. Harris, 2000, pp. 30–31; Howes, 1988; Lalonde & Chandler, 1995.

13. Positive effects of imaginary companions: Singer & Singer, 1990; Taylor & Carlson, 1997; Taylor, 1999; Taylor, Carlson, Maring, Gerow, & Charley, 2004. Imaginary companions and language skills: Bouldin, Bavin, & Pratt, 2002; Roby & Kidd, 2008. Teenagers: Seiffge-Krenke, 1993, 1997.

14. Autism: Baron-Cohen et al., 1996.

15. Woolley, 1995.

16. Woolley, 1995.

17. Dias & Harris, 1988, 1990; Leevers & Harris, 1999, 2000.

18. P. L. Harris, 2000, pp. 110–115; Leevers & Harris, 1999.

19. Oatley, 1999; Mar, Oatley, Hirsh, dela Paz, & Peterson, 2006; Rinck & Bower, 1995.

20. Freud, 1927; Piaget, 1929.

21. J. L. Barrett, Newman, & Richert, 2003.

22. God and false belief: J. L. Barrett, Richert, & Driesenga, 2001; Richert & Barrett, 2005. Cross-cultural: Knight, Sousa, Barrett, & Atran, 2004. God as "pre-pared" concept: J. L. Barrett & Richert, 2003.

23. Knight, 2008.

24. Phelps & Woolley, 1994; see also P. L. Harris, 2000, pp. 164–165; Rosengren & Hickling, 1994.

25. P. L. Harris, 2000, pp. 162–166; Rosengren & Hickling, 1994.

26. Bering & Parker, 2006.

27. DeLoache, Miller, & Rosengren, 1997.

28. Age-related declines in magical thinking: Rosengren & Hickling, 1994; Woolley, Phelps, Davis, & Mandell, 1999. Prayer: Woolley, 2000, pp. 121–125. Evil essence: Nemeroff & Rozin, 1994.

29. Gill, Hadaway, & Marler, 1998; S. Walker, 1999.

30. Piaget, 1932/1965, pp. 258, 251.

31. Jose, 1990.

32. Fein, 1976.

33. P. L. Harris & Nunez, 1996; Nunez & Harris, 1998.

34. See discussion in P. L. Harris, 2000, pp. 134–139, 156–159.

35. Bibace, Dillon, & Saragin, 1999; Raman & Winer, 2004; Siegal, 1988.

36. Promiscuous teleology: Kelemen, 1999a, 1999c, 2004. Hunter-gatherers anthropomorphizing: Gubser, 1965; Marks, 1976; Mithen, 1996, p. 168; Silberbauer, 1981; see also discussion by H. C. Barrett, 2005, pp. 456–457. Fate and Destiny in Western Europe: Deridder, Hendriks, Zani, Pepitone, & Saffioti, 1999; Pepitone & Saffioti, 1997.

37. Piaget, 1929; Looft & Bartz, 1969.

38. Why rocks are pointy: Kelemen, 1999b. Fundamentalists and nonfunda-mentalists: Evans, 2001. That these patterns have been replicated among elementary school children in West London (Kelemen & DiYanni, 2005) suggests that American religiosity is not required for the emergence of teleological thinking in young children. See also Gelman & Kremer, 1991; Petrovich, 1997.

39. Kelemen, 2004.

40. By saying "invented" I do not intend to pass any metaphysical judgment on the reality or nonreality of the gods. More precisely, what is being "invented" here is the *idea* of the supernatural (and the gods therein). Whether this idea corre-sponds to anything objective in the universe I leave for others to sort out.

41. Symmetrical tools: This argument has been made for some Acheulean hand axes, especially those emerging around a half million ybp. Gowlett, 1992; Wynn, 1996. hand axe critic: McPherron, 2000. Composite tools: Ambrose, 2001; McBrearty & Tryon, 2006.

42. Stout & Chaminade, 2007; Stout, Toth, Schick & Chaminade, 2008.

43. Parish, 2004, p. 163, quote from a high-caste Newar (Hindu) informant.

44. Katz, 1982, pp. 43–44.

45. Mithen, 2006, pp. 95–101, 151, 235–236.

46. Wachholtz& Pargament, 2005.

47. Wiech et al., 2008. A significant increase in activation of the ventrolateral prefrontal cortex was observed while viewing the religious image.

48. Hayden, 2003, esp. pp. 146–166.

49. Richert & Harris, 2006, 2008.

50. Bering, 2006; Gelman, 2003; Hirschfeld & Gelman, 1999; Richert & Harris, 2008.

51. Bering, 2002.

52. Bering & Bjorklund, 2004.

53. Bering, 2005, p. 421.

54. Catholics: Bering, Hernández-Blasi, & Bjorklund, 2005. Vezo: Astuti & Harris, 2008.

55. Tremlin, 2006, pp. 111, 115.

56. S. Guthrie, 1993.

57. Boyer, 2001.

58. J. L. Barrett, 1998; J. L. Barrett & Keil, 1996.

59. Bering, 2002.

60. Atran, 2002, pp. 100–107; Barrett, 2000; Boyer, 2001, pp. 79–81; Boyer & Ramble, 2001; Kelly & Keil, 1985; Norenzayan & Atran, 2002.

CHAPTER 6

This chapter is adapted in part from M. J. Rossano (2003), Expertise and the evolution of consciousness, *Cognition, 89*, 207–236, and M. J. Rossano (2006), The religious mind and the evolution of religion, *Review of General Psychology, 10*, 346–364.

1. Whitehouse, 1995.

2. James, 1902, pp. 24–25.

3. Medieval Spain: Christian, 1982. Chile: Echevarria, 1963. Rites of Terror: Whitehouse, 1996. Trauma and solidarity: Atran, 2002, pp. 161–166.

4. Otto, 1923.

5. Wallauer's account can be found at www.janegoodall.org/chimp_central/chimpanzees/behavior/rain_dance.asp (accessed 5/20/09).

6. Chevalier-Skolnikoff, 1973.

7. Empathy, pride, a sense of fairness: de Waal, 1996; de Waal & Berger, 2000. Laughing orangutans: Ross, Menzler, & Zimmermann, 2008; Ross quote from www.dailymail.co.uk/pages/live/articles/technology/technology.html?in_article_id=505634&;in_page_id=1965 (accessed 5/19/09).

8. Goodall, 1986; S. Guthrie, 1993, p. 52.

9. Third-party mediation and male control role: see de Waal, 1996, pp. 203–204, 128–132; 241 note 36; Goodall, 1992, p. 139.

10. J. H. Turner, 2000. Baboons: Fleagle, 1999.

11. Spontaneous violence in apes/monkeys: Walters & Seyfarth, 1987; J. H. Turner, 2000, pp. 44–45, 54–55.

12. Monkey grunts: Silk, 2001. Chimpanzee arms up: Pika, Liebal, Call, & Tomasello, 2005. Reconciliation: de Waal, 1990.

13. Big game hunters at Boxgrove: Parfitt & Roberts, 1999. Singing and dancing: Mithen, 2006, pp. 195–196.

14. Mithen, 2006, p. 195.

15. Baboons: Richman, 1987. Greeting rituals: Goodall, 1986; van Roosmalen & Klein, 1988, p. 515.

16. Kohler, 1927, pp. 314–316, quote from p. 315.

17. Only humans have rhythm: Atran, 2002, p. 171. Muscular bonding: McNeill, 1995.

18. Grooming and brain opiates: Keverne, Martinez, & Tuite, 1989. Psyched-up chimps: Goodall, 1971, pp. 112–114. Mandrills: Samorini, 2002, p. 58. Altered states in other animals: Hoskovec & Svorad, 1969; Prince, 1982; Volgyesi, 1969.

19. Donald, 1991, 1999.

20. Animals don't practice: Donald, 1993, 1999; Rossano, 2003; Stout, 2005. Donald quote: Donald, 1993, p. 152.

21. Donald, 1999, p. 143.

22. Rossano, 2003.

23. Oldowan tools: Semaw et al., 1997. Apes and Oldowan tools: Toth, Schick, Savage-Rumbaugh, Sevcik, & Rumbaugh, 1993; Wright, 1972. Oldowan tools not an intellectual advance: Toth, 1985; Wynn, 1996, 2002. Oldowan tools and motor control: Pelegrin, 2005; Roche, 2005.

24. Wynn, 1981, 2002.

25. Hand axe critics: Jones, 1979; McPherron, 2000. Practice required to make hand axe: Edwards, 2001; Winton, 2005. Khambat (India): Bril, Roux, & Dietrich, 2005; Roux & David, 2005. Kim-Yal: Stout, 2005.

26. Schick & Toth, 1993, p. 237.

27. Bar-Yosef, 2006, pp. 309–310.

28. Winton, 2005.

29. Hundreds of unused hand axes: Klein & Edgar, 2002, p. 107; Kohn & Mithen, 1999; Stringer & Andrews, 2005, p. 225. Hand axes as male quality display: Kohn & Mithen, 1999. Kim-Yal: Stout, 2005.

30. Pretty hand axes: Schick & Toth, 1993, pp. 282–283. Composite tools: Ambrose, 2001; Haidle, in press; McBrearty & Tryon, 2006. Donald (1991) has argued for an even more liberal estimate of the emergence of mimesis, contenting that it would have been present with *Homo erectus* by least 1 million ybp.

31. Dunbar, 1992, 1996.

32. Bickerton, 1995; Corballis, 2002; Donald, 1999; Mithen, 2006.

33. Conklin, 2001; Hogg, 1966; Sanday, 1986.

34. Chinese skull: Hayden, 2003, pp. 96–97; Weidenreich, 1943. Bodo skull: R. S. White, 1986. South African skull: Klein & Edgar, 2002, p. 16; Singer & Wymer, 1982. Herto skull: T. D. White et al., 2003. Neanderthals: DeFleur, Dutour, Valladas, & Vandermeersch, 1993; DeFleur, White, Valensi, Slimak, & Cregut-Bonnoure, 1999. Nutritional stress: Arsuaga et al., 1997; Binford & Ho, 1985.

35. Red ochre use by hunter-gatherers: Power & Watts, 1996. Red's symbolism: E. O. James, 1957; Marschack, 1981; Wreschner, 1980. Red ochre in archaeological

record: Barham, 2002; J. D. Clark & Brown, 2001; de Lumley, 1969; Roebroeks, 1984. Twin Rivers site: Barham, 2000, 2002. Practical and symbolic use of red ochre: Bahn & Vertut, 1988; Keeley, 1978, 1980; Knight, Power, & Watts, 1995; Watts, 2002. Barham, 2002, p. 187, notes that the wide variety of different pigments found at the Twin Rivers site argues against purely practical use.

36. Artifacts painted with ochre: Bednarik, 1995. Body painting: Kuhn & Stiner, 2007, p. 46. Blombos cave artifact: Henshilwood & Sealy, 1997; Lewis-Williams, 2002, pp. 98–99.

37. Three-million-year-old jasper cobble: Dart, 1974. Berekhat Ram: d'Errico & Nowell, 2000; Marschack, 1997. Zigzagging artifacts: Bednarik, 1995; Horowitz, 1964; Kluver, 1942. These may be the entoptic visual experiences discussed in chap. 3; see chap. 3, n. 30.

38. Bruniquel Cave: Rouzaud, Soulier, & Lignereux, 1996. Regourdou Cave: Hayden, 2003, pp. 108–115. Other cave sites: Galerie Schoepflin at Arcy-sur-Cure in France (Farizy, 1990; Baffier & Girard, 1998); Congnac and Grotta della Barura (Lorblancher, 1999).

39. Radcliff-Brown, 1922, pp. 252–253.

40. Blacking, 1973.

41. Donald, 1991.

42. Brain opiates: Frecska & Kulcsar, 1989. McNeill quote: McNeill, 1995, p. 2.

43. Deindividuation: d'Aquili & Newberg, 1999, pp. 95–103; Watson, 1973. Brain opiates: Frecska & Kulcsar, 1989; Prince, 1982. Synchronized activities and social bonding: Levenson, 2003; Wiltermuth & Heath, 2009.

44. Bickerton, 1995; Corballis, 2002; Klein & Edgar, 2002; Mithen, 2006; Noble & Davidson, 1996. Corballis sees the Upper Paleolithic as marking the emergence of fully autonomous speech, as opposed to a vocal/manual combined communication system. For him this move would have freed the hands for more effective manufacturing, pedagogy, and cultural transmission, which in turn accounts for the explosion of artwork, symbolic artifacts and sophisticated tools of the Upper Paleolithic (see Corballis, 2002, pp. 194–200).

45. Birds/primates and time-based memory: Clayton & Dickinson, 1998, 1999; Clayton, Yu, & Dickinson, 2001, 2003; Menzel, 1999; Schwartz & Evans, 2001. Monkeys and birds anticipate future states: Correia, Alexis, Dickinson, & Clayton, 2007; Naqshbandi & Roberts, 2006.

46. Episodic memory as uniquely human: Conway, 1995; Suddendorf & Corballis, 1997; Tulving, 1983. Hominins and episodic memory: Whitehouse argues that the imagistic mode activates episodic memory, while the doctrinal activates semantic and procedural memory. Thus, it may have been a more limited form of episodic memory that mediated the imagistic experiences of our hominin ancestors of 500,000 years ago or so. Fully human episodic memory allowed for a deeper, more reflective analysis of those imagistic experiences, setting the conditions for the creation of stories and myths out of them.

47. d'Errico & Cacho, 1994; Hoffecker, 2002, pp. 161, 171, 189, 225, 254; Marschack, 1991; Soffer, 1989; Stringer & Andrews, 2005, p. 167.

48. Campbell, 1969.

49. Riel-Salvatore & Clark, 2001. See especially comment by Davidson & Noble.

50. Boehm, 1999.

51. Woodward, 2000.

52. Ritual as a restraining force on elites: V. W. Turner, 1969. Mayan kings: Schele & Freidel, 1990.

53. Venus figurines and phallic symbols: Eliade, 1958; Gamble, 1982; Harding, 1976; Hayden, 2003, p. 154; Hutton, 1991; Rice, 1982; Soffer, 1985; Wymer, 1982. Female burials: Harrold, 1980; Vanhaeren & d'Errico, 2005.

54. Deep caves, exclusive rituals, and ancestor worship: Hayden, 2003, pp. 142–153; Lewis-Williams, 2002, pp. 228–267; Woodward, 2000.

55. This proposal is consistent with that of Dickson (1990, p. 199), who argues that the Upper Paleolithic ushered in a move from shamanistic cults to communal cults of greater social complexity. Hayden (2003, pp. 209–211) has also argued for a popular/elite distinction emerging in Upper Paleolithic religion.

CHAPTER 7

1. Stout, 2005, p. 334.

2. For a good discussion of culture as adaptation see Richerson & Boyd, 2005, esp. chaps. 1 and 2.

3. This example was inspired by Richerson & Boyd, 2005, p. 11.

4. Simoons, 1970.

5. G. Cochrane, Hardy, & Harpending, 2006.

6. Nisbett & Miyamoto, 2005.

7. Stout, 2005, p. 333.

8. Atran, 2002, 2006; Boyer, 2001; Kirkpatrick, 2006; S. Guthrie, 1993.

9. Atran, 2002; Boyer, 2001; S. Guthrie, 1993; Tremlin, 2006.

10. Kirkpatrick, 2006, pp. 165–166.

11. Colloca & Benedetti, 2005; D. D. Price, Finniss, & Benedetti, 2008.

12. Suggestive context of treatment: Vase, Riley, & Prince, 2002. Hypnosis: Bowers & LeBaron, 1986; Brown, 1992.

13. Parkinson's research: McRae et al., 2004. Acupuncture: Bausell et al., 2007 ; Linde et al., 2007.

14. Vase, Robinson, Verne, & Price, 2003; Verne, Robinson, Vase, & Price, 2003.

15. Monitoring symptoms: Geers, Helfer, Weiland, & Kosbab, 2006; Vase Robinson, Verne, & Price, 2005. Placebo creams: Price et al., 1999.

16. Spiegel, Bloom, Kraemer, & Gottheil, 1989; Fawzy, Kemeny, et al., 1990; Fawzy, Fawzy, et al., 1993.

17. Hepatitis research: Kiecolt-Glaser, Garner, & Spelcher, 1984. Upper respiratory infections: S. Cohen, Doyle, Skoner, Rabin, & Gwaltney, 1997. For reviews see S. Cohen, 2001; Koenig & Cohen, 2001b, pp. 124–127.

18. Miller & Kaptchuk, 2008.

19. Wachholtz & Pargament, 2005; Wiech et al., 2008; see chap. 5.

20. Miracles strengthen faith: McClenon, 2002, pp. 145–147. Memory effects: De Pascalis, Chiaradia, & Carotenuto, 2002; Price et al., 1999.

21. Katz, 1982, p. 71.

22. Thailand: McClenon, 2002, pp. 5–6. Southeast Asia/Balkans: McClenon, 2002, p. 71; Thompson, 1966. Hindu ascetics: Powell, 1914. Psycho/physical explanations: Margolis, Domangue, Ehleben, & Shrier, 1983; Patterson, Burns, Everett, & Marvin, 1992.

23. L. M. Turner, 1879/1984.

24. Hufford, 1982; James, 1902. Surveys of spiritual experiences: Baruss, 2003, pp. 189–190; Hood et al., 1996, p. 247; for summary see McClenon, 2002, p. 109. Experiences strengthen belief: Targ, Schlitz, & Irwin, 2000; Wagner & Ratzeberg, 1987.

25. Memories of anomalous events: McClenon, 2000; McClenon, 2002, p. 120. Life-changing experiences: Palmer, 1979.

26. Survey of 3,000: Ellison & George, 1994. African Americans: Ortega, Crutchfield, & Rushing, 1983. Church groups in America: Stolle, 2001. Religious kibbutzim: Anson, Carmel, Bonneh, Levenson, & Maoz, 1990; Kark et al., 1996.

27. Sosis, 2006, p. 67.

28. Henrich & Henrich, 2007, pp. 180, 204.

29. Rossano, 2007a, 2008.

30. Religious healing in ancient civilizations: Majno, 1975; Sigerist, 1987. Hypnosis: Mac Hovec, 1975. Mechanistic view of body: Solomon, 2001.

31. See reviews in Koenig, McCullough, & Larson, 2001; Koenig & Cohen, 2002. Hip and heart surgery: Contrada et al., 2004; Oxman, Freeman, & Manheimer, 1995; Pressman, Lyons, Larson, & Strain, 1990. Spinal surgery and cancer: Hodges, Humphrey, & Eck, 2002; Loprinzi et al., 1994; Ringdal, Gotestam, Kaasa, Kvinnsland, & Ringdal, 1996. Exceptions and inconsistencies: Sloan & Bagiella, 2002.

32. Religion and well-being, optimism and depression: Koenig, McCullough, & Larson, 2001, pp. 117, 215, 135. Religion and depression: Koenig et al., 1992; Koenig, George, & Peterson, 1998.

33. Religion and longevity: Glass et al., 1999; Goldman et al., 1995; Hummer et al., 1999; Koenig et al., 1999; Oman & Reed, 1998. Strawbridge et al., 1997. Kibbutzim study: Kark et al., 1996.

34. Benedetti, 1996; Grevert, Albert, & Goldstein, 1983; Petrovic, Kalso, Peterson, & Ingvar, 2002. Note: the specific brain areas involved appear to be the anterior cingulate cortex, the orbital frontal cortex, and the anterior insula. In addition, during the anticipatory phase prior to the onset of the placebo analgesic response, broad areas of the prefrontal cortex are active, including the dorsolateral, orbital, rostral medial, and anterior prefrontal cortices (Lieberman et al., 2005; Wagner et al., 2004). Brain's opiate system and immune function: Sibinga & Goldstein, 1988.

35. Mellars, 2006.

36. For a recent review see Sosis, 2006.

37. Sosis, 2000; Sosis & Bressler, 2003; Sosis & Ruffle, 2003; Stolle, 2001.

38. Wilson, 2002. Moralizing gods: Roes & Raymond, 2003. Cultural defense: Bruce, 2002, pp. 31–34.

39. Fincher & Thornhill, 2008.

40. Honduran men: Irons, 2001, p. 304. Church attendance and attitudes about sex: Weeden, Cohen, & Kenrick, 2008. Promiscuity: Benson, Donahue, & Erickson,

1989; see also review in Spilka et al., 2003, pp. 428–432. Happy marriages: Bock & Radelet, 1988; Filsinger & Wilson, 1984; Gruber, 2005.

41. Table adapted from table 5, p. 23 of Frejka & Westoff, 2008.

42. Frejka & Westoff, 2008, p. 29.

43. Kaufmann, 2007, www.sneps.net/uploadsepk/JQR%20Demography.pdf (accessed 5/21/09).

44. Longman, 2004, p. 35.

45. Evidence for altered states in other species is reviewed in Rossano, 2006. Neanderthals: Mellars, 1996; Lewis-Williams, 2002 (see esp. p. 94).

46. Adler et al., 2006; Clark & Riel-Salvatore, 2006; Eren, Greenspan, & Sampson, 2008; Sorensen & Leonard, 2001.

47. Rappaport, 1999.

CHAPTER 8

This chapter is adapted in part from M. J. Rossano (2008), The moral faculty: Does religion promote "moral expertise"? *International Journal for the Psychology of Religion, 18,* 169–194, and M. J. Rossano (2003), Expertise and the evolution of consciousness, *Cognition, 89,* 207–236.

1. Hauser, 2006; Sharpe, 2007. For example, in his book *Moral Minds,* Harvard psychologist Marc Hauser (2006, p. xx) says: "I will argue this marriage between morality and religion is not only forced but unnecessary, crying out for a divorce."

2. Haidt & Joseph, 2004; Haidt & Graham, 2006; Haidt & Bjorklund, in press.

3. Traditional religion as moral system: Campbell, 1969; Eliade, 1959; Rappaport, 1999. Lohorung Rai: Hardmann, 2000. Karuks: Connors, 2000.

4. McCullough & Willoughby, 2009.

5. D. P. Johnson & Bering, 2006. Earlier work: D. P. Johnson, 2005; Johnson & Kruger, 2004; Roes & Raymond, 2003.

6. Violators overestimate themselves: Robinson & Darley, 2004. Fear of punishment stronger motivator than rewards: Baumeister, Bratslavsky, Finkenauer, & Vohs, 2001; Fehr & Gächter, 2002; Ostrom, Walker, & Gardner, 1992; Yamagishi, 1986. Illness as punishment: Murdock, 1980.

7. Religion and antisocial behaviors: Jang & Johnson, 2001; Koenig, McGue, Krueger, & Bouchard, 2007; Merrill, Salazar, & Gardner, 2001; see review in Spilka, Hood, Hunsberger, & Gorsuch, 2003, pp. 422–428. Religion and alcohol abuse: J. K. Cochrane, 1993. Promiscuity/extramarital sex: Benson, Donahue, & Erickson, 1989; see also review in Spilka et al., 2003, pp. 428–432. Religion and marriage: Bock & Radelet, 1988; Filsinger & Wilson, 1984; Gruber, 2005.

8. Benson, 1992, quotes from pp. 218 and 216, respectively. Religious communities more cohesive/enduring: Sosis, 2000; Sosis & Bressler, 2003; Sosis & Ruffle, 2003. Importance of supernatural agency: D. P. Johnson, 2005.

9. McCullough & Willoughby, 2009. (Note: One of the important limitations cited is the correlational nature of much of the data. Quoted words: pp. 86, 88.).

10. Fishbach, Friedman, & Kruglanski, 2003.

11. Baumeister & Exline, 1999.

12. Zagzebski, 1996, pp. 113–115.

13. Durkheim, 1912/1965; Irons, 2001; Kirkpatrick, 2005b; Krebs, 2005; Richerson & Boyd, 2001; Ridley, 1996; Rossano, 2007a; Wilson, 2002.

14. Moral faculty: Broom, 2003; Hauser, 2006; Joyce, 2006; Krebs, 2005; Ridley, 1996; Sober & Wilson, 1998. Intuitive ontologies: Boyer & Barrett, 2005.

15. Moral faculty and language: Hauser, 2006, pp. 36–37, 112, 156. Hypersensitivity to language and moral information: Baldwin, Markman, Bill, Desjardins, & Irwin, 1996; P. L. Harris & Nunez, 1996; Markman & Hutchinson, 1984; Nunez & Harris, 1998.

16. Hauser, 2006, pp. 122–131; Henrich et al., 2001; O'Neill & Petrinovich, 1998.

17. Geary, 2005, pp. 257, 334–335.

18. Blair, 1995; Blair, Jones, Clark, & Smith, 1997.

19. Aristotle, 350 BCE, book 2, chap. 1.

20. Jefferson, 1787/1955, p. 15.

21. Self-control as muscle: Baumeister & Exline, 1999; Muraven, Baumeister, & Tice, 1999; Muraven & Baumeister, 2000. Motivation and self-control: Muraven & Slessareva, 2003.

22. Wisdom as skill-based knowledge: Baltes & Staudinger, 2000; Emmons, 2000; Oman & Thoresen, 2003; Staudinger & Baltes, 1996. Wisdom study: Staudinger & Baltes, 1996.

23. Interventions with at-risk children: CPPRG, 2002; Ialongo, Poduska, Werthamer, & Kellam, 2001.

24. Studies on expertise: Chess: Charness, 1989; Chase & Simon, 1973; de Groot, 1946. Medical diagnosis: Elstein, Shulman, & Sprafka, 1990. Computer programming: Adelson & Soloway, 1985; Jeffries, Turner, Polson, & Atwood, 1981. Music: Ericsson, Krampe, & Tesch-Romer, 1993; Sloboda, 1991. Cricket: Lamb & Burwitz, 1988; McLeod & Jenkins, 1991. Table tennis: Bootsma & van Weiringen, 1990. Snooker: Abernathy, Neal, & Koning, 1994. Volleyball: Allard & Starks, 1980. Reviews: Ericsson, 2002; Ericsson & Lehmann, 1996.

25. Charness, Krampe, & Mayr, 1996.

26. Zimmerman, 2002.

27. Anderson, 1987; Ericsson, 2002, p. 29.

28. Lehmann & Ericsson, 1997.

29. Ericsson, 1996.

30. Deliberate practice necessary but perhaps not sufficient: Ericsson & Charness, 1994; Sternberg, Grigorenko, & Ferrari, 2002. Experts continue deliberate practice: Ericsson, 2002. Deliberate practice is hard work: Ericsson, Krampe, & Tesch-Romer, 1993.

31. Few rewards for moral experts: Colby & Damon, 1992, pp. 67–69. Religion as strong motivator: Bushman, Ridge, Das, Key, & Busath, 2007; Mayer & Sharp, 1962; Nielsen, 2002; Rosen, 1950; Wuthnow, 1994.

32. See Oman & Thoresen, 2003, for discussion.

33. Colby & Damon, 1992.

34. Colby & Damon, 1992, pp. 78–80, 279–281; quote from p. 78. Colby and Damon's methodology: Used 22 "expert" nominators from diverse political, religious, and sociocultural (race, gender, religious, geographic) backgrounds. Included

historians, theologians, philosophers, ethicists, and social scientists. The goal was to develop a general definition of moral exemplar that would "include morally committed people, while excluding fanatics, hypocrites, and self-promoting careerists" (p. 28). The authors wanted to be "confident" that their chosen moral exemplars "met a clear and relatively impartial criteria for having lived a morally outstanding life" (pp. 28–29). In the end the panel agreed on the following set of criteria (pp. 29–32):

1. A sustained commitment to moral ideals or principles that include a generalized respect for humanity; or a sustained evidence of moral virtue. (Designed to exclude one-time heroes as well as fanatics and those who exacerbate group-based tensions.)
2. A disposition to act in accord with one's moral ideals or principles, implying also a consistency between one's actions and intentions and between the means and ends of one's actions. (Designed to ensure that expressed moral ideals were consistent with moral actions and effects. Intending to do good and actually doing good were necessary.)
3. Willingness to risk one's self-interest for the sake of one's moral values. (When morality collides with self-interest, the exemplar chooses the moral ideal.)
4. A tendency to be inspiring to others and thereby to move them to moral action. (Emphasizes the social nature of morality. Moral exemplars must have positive salutary effect on those around them, although the actual scale of that effect is not critical.)
5. A sense of realistic humility about one's own importance relative to the world at large, implying a relative lack of concern for one's own ego. (Requires that moral exemplar maintain focus on their mission not on themselves.)

After establishing criteria, members of the panel nominated individuals whom they believed fulfilled the criteria. Eighty-four nominations were initially made (if one assumes that the authors were part of the panel, that means on average each panelist nominated between 3–4 individuals). Authors report that the original 84 nominees "varied greatly in occupation, income, gender, race, ethnicity, religion, education, political orientation, moral mission, and public visibility" (p. 32).

The original 84 were reduced to 23 because some were impossible to contact, and of those contacted only 28 were willing to be interviewed, and of these one died, three did not have time, and one did want details of his or her life made public. Authors report (p. 33) that the final sample of 23 "was no different in composition from the nominee group of 84."

Characteristics of the group: age range: 35–86; education: 8th grade to PhD, MD, and JD; occupation: corporate CEOs, clergy, physicians, teachers, innkeeper, journalist, charity workers, heads of nonprofits, leaders of social movements; 10 men, 13 women; 17 whites, 4 African Americans, 2 Latinas; from all geographic regions of the country (United States).

The 23 were interviewed extensively by the authors regarding key personal and moral events in their lives; also, goals, values, worldviews, life assumptions, life histories, especially events, relationships, and experiences that shaped their lives. Interviews also focused on how the exemplars developed their moral commitment and sustained it through difficult times. They were also asked about their understanding of their work and lives, explanations for choices they had made, and interpretations of critical life experiences.

Some might contend that despite using a diverse panel of so-called experts to identify moral exemplars, the degree of subjectivity in this study is so great that it renders it worthless. I disagree. The study possesses all the inherent limitations found in case study research, and one must therefore be cautious not to overinterpret it. But it still provides useful information. Take an analogy: If you wanted to know whether a certain art school produced great artists (not just popular artists), how would you study it? Getting together a panel of diverse art experts, having them draw up a set of criteria for what makes art "great," and then having them identify art that fulfills that criteria does not seem (to me at least) to be a completely useless exercise—especially if the experts are entirely blind to the study's purpose. If the art school in question really does produce "great" artists, then we might expect that a nontrivial portion of the identified "great" art would be from artists who attended the school. Should this be the last statement on the matter? Certainly not, but what we learn from it should not be ignored either.

35. Establishing percentages for the Intrinsic, Extrinsic, and Quest religious orientations is not simple, because the categories are not necessarily mutually exclusive. Gordon Allport, the originator of the Intrinsic/Extrinsic distinction, expected no more than 10% of the population to be true Intrinsics (see Kirkpatrick & Hood, 1990, p. 452).

36. Peterson & Seligman, 2004, pp. 29–30.

37. Gratitude: McCullough, Emmons, & Tsang, 2002. Hope: Snyder, Sigmon, & Feldman, 2002. Sense of purpose: Bjarnason, 1998; Verweij, Ester, & Nauta, 1997.

38. Definition for wisdom: Peterson & Seligman, 2004, p. 29. Wisdom study: Staudinger & Baltes, 1996. Religion as backbone of culture's wisdom: In Eastern traditions, for example, the writings of Confucius, Lao-tzu, and Buddhist texts hold prominence as canonical sources of wisdom. Likewise, in the West any list of Great Books is typically populated with religious writings such as books from the Bible (Ecclesiastes, Proverbs, etc.) or the writings of Augustine, Aquinas, Maimonides, Dante, and others. Furthermore, even the writings of Plato and Aristotle, though not overtly religious, assume a divine realm that gives order and purpose to existence.

39. Stark, 1996, pp. 83–94; Colby & Damon, 1992, p. 29.

40. Marital satisfaction: Mahoney, Pargament, Tarakeshwar, & Swank, 2001. Communication and conflict resolution: Brody, Stoneman, Flor, & McCrary, 1994; Mahoney et al., 1999. Divorce rates: Ellison, Bartkowski, & Anderson, 1999; Fergusson, Horowood, Kershaw, & Shannon, 1986; Mahoney et al., 2001; see review in Mahoney & Tarakeshwar, 2005. Stable environment for children: Strawbridge, Shema, Cohen, & Kaplan, 2001.

41. Good Samaritan study: Darley & Batson, 1973. Quest and compassion: Batson, Eidelman, Higley, & Russell, 2001; Batson, Floyd, Meyer, & Winner, 1999; see, however, Goldfried & Miner, 2002. Quest/intrinsic/extrinsic: Bateson, Shoenrade, & Ventis, 1993.

42. Religion and charity: see reviews in Brooks, 2003, and Monsma, 2007. Religion as social capital: see Social Capital Survey, 2001, www.cfsv.org/communitysurvey/results2.html (accessed 6/25/07).

43. Monsma, 2007, p. 26.

44. Religious people place higher value on and think more about forgiveness: Enright, Santos, & Al-Mabuk, 1989; McCullough & Worthington, 1999; Rokeach, 1973. More motivation to forgive: Gorsuch & Hao, 1993; Mullet, Barros, Frongia, Usai, Neto, & Shafihi, 2003. Religion-forgiveness discrepancy: McCullough & Worthington, 1999; Tsang, McCullough, & Hoyt, 2005.

45. Review of forgiveness literature: McCullough, Bono, & Root, 2005, quote from p. 399. Colby and Damon's (1992) most/least forgiving, pp. 276–278. Humility and "quest" religion: Cline & Richard, 1965; Rowatt, Ottenbreit, Nesselroade, & Cunningham, 2002.

46. Religion and antisocial behavior: Koenig, McGue, Krueger, & Bouchard, 2007; see review in Spilka, Hood, Hunsberger, & Gorsuch, 2003, pp. 422–428. Religion and risky sex: Benson, Donahue, & Erickson, 1989; also see review in Spilka et al., 2003, pp. 428–432. Religion and happy marriages: Bock & Radelet, 1988; Filsinger & Wilson, 1984; Gruber, 2005.

47. Sosis, 2000; Sosis & Bressler, 2003; Sosis & Ruffle, 2003.

48. Bias sampling: Hill, 2005, pp. 45–46. Cross-cultural replication: McCullough & Willoughby, 2009, p. 87.

49. Interpretive challenges: Hill, 2005. Review of religion and family life: Mahoney & Tarakeshwar, 2005, quote from p. 186. Religion/forgiveness discrepancy: McCullough & Worthington, 1999.

50. Brody et al., 1994; McCullough et al., 2002; Gruber, 2005.

51. Original sin and divine punishment: Ano & Vasconcelles, 2005; Exline, 2002; Pargament et al., 1990; Pargament, Koenig, Tarakeshwar, & Hahn, 2001. Obsessive fasting: Wulff, 1991, pp. 63–64.

52. Extrinsic religion and prejudice: see review in Donahue & Nielsen, 2005; Morrison & Morrison, 2002. Fundamentalism and authoritarianism: Altemeyer & Hunsberger, 2005.

53. Religion and honesty: Donahue & Nielsen, 2005. Religious students cheat more: Guttman, 1984. Fundamentalism and child abuse: Bottoms, Nielsen, Murray, & Filipas, 2004; Shor, 1998. Religion and violence: Bushman et al., 2007.

54. Shermer, 2005.

55. Emmons, 2005; Silberman, 2005.

CHAPTER 9

This chapter is based in part on M. J. Rossano (2007b), Religion on which the devout and skeptic can agree, *Zygon: Journal of Religion and Science, 42,* 301–315.

1. For the sake of simplicity I'm breaking the Interregnum period into two substages. This does not mean that what I describe in scene 1 necessarily preceded scene 2. I think all these events were unfolding together, although not necessarily at the same pace.

2. Subcortical regions important to emotions and religious experiences: Mandell, 1980; Ramachandran & Blakeslee, 1998, pp. 177–179; Winkelman, 1997,

2002. Areas of the limbic system appear to be important here. Winkelman (1997, 2002), for example, attributes the altered state of consciousness associated with ritual to high-voltage, slow-frequency activity of the hippocampal-septal region, acting as a "driver" synchronizing activity across the frontal lobe. D'Aquili and Newberg (1999) attribute the ritually induced ecstatic state to sympathetic/parasympathetic "spillover" effects. This refers to the fact that during intense ritual, the typical antagonistic relationship between these systems (where activity in one system necessarily subdues activity in the other) is violated and the overstimulation of one system paradoxically activates the other. In either case, the brain areas involved are relatively old (from an evolutionary standpoint). By contrast, areas of the brain associated with agency detection include the prefrontal cortex, the paracingulate cortex, and the medial temporal cortex (Amodio & Frith, 2006; Gallagher & Frith, 2003; Sabbagh, 2004).

3. Heyes, 1998; Povinelli, 2000; Tomasello, Call, & Hare, 2003; Tomasello et al., 2005.

4. Deindividuation: d'Aquili & Newberg, 1999, pp. 95–103; Watson, 1973. Brain opiates: Frecska & Kulcsar, 1989; Prince, 1982. Synchronized activity and cooperation: Levenson, 2003; Wiltermuth & Heath, 2009.

5. Hayden, 2003, p. 184; Hultkrantz, 1967, p. 129.

6. Shamanism and healing: McClenon, 2002; Winkelman, 1992. Shamans among the !Kung: Lewis-Williams, 1982. Selling spiritual prowess: Lowie, 1963, p. 175. Health benefits of meditation: Davidson et al., 2003; Orme-Johnson & Herron, 1997.

7. Preperformance routines and sports: Czech, Ploszay, & Burke, 2004; Gayton, Cielinsky, Francis-Kineston, & Hearns, 1989; Lobmeyer & Wasserman, 1986; Lonsdale & Tam, 2007; Southard & Amos, 1996. Free-throws: Lonsdale & Tam, 2007. Preperformance routines and directed attention: Boucher & Crews, 1987; Lindor & Singer, 2000; Weinberg & Gould, 2003.

8. Brain imaging studies: Kim et al., 2008; Milton, Solodkin, Hlustik, & Small, 2007. Areas associated with emotions: the posterior cingulate and the amygdala. Areas active in experts: the anterior cingulate, along with areas in the temporal and parietal lobes. Inhibition in experts indicated by significantly reduced response in the posterior cingulate and amygdala.

9. Coolidge & Wynn, 2009, p. 240.

10. Kuhn, Stiner, Reese, & Gulec, 2001.

11. E.g., Atran, 2002, 278–279; Newberg, d'Aquili, & Rause, 2001.

12. Bruce, 2002, pp. 1–36.

13. Tellingly, church attendance in Europe corresponds roughly inversely to the degree of social welfare benefits (Alesina & Angeletos, 2002; Verweij, Ester, & Nauru, 1997; World Values Survey, 1997). There are other factors as well that contribute to secularization, especially with regard to why Europe is so much more secular than the United States, including historical differences: In Europe, traditional national churches have long been associated with the aristocracy and antidemocratic elements in society (e.g., Franco's Fascists in Spain; de Tocqueville, 1835/1990; Martin, 1969, p. 122). In the United States, churches historically have been more closely associated with the aspirations of new immigrants, the underprivileged,

and the rural poor (Finke & Starke, 1992; Wacker, 2000). In addition, there are marketplace differences: Europe has a history of national churches, while America, with its historical separation of church and state, has a more competitive religious marketplace, prompting churches to work harder to attract and retain contributing members (Finke & Stark, 2000).

14. Boyer, 2001, p. 151, or Frank, 1994, p. 207.

15. *Europe as less competitive*: European social welfare has closed income gaps, reduced poverty, and created a generally less competitive social climate, relative to the United States. Estimates of redistributive transfers average about 22–25% of GDP across Europe, compared to about 14% in the United States. One outcome of this is that the poverty rate in the United States tends to be about triple (18–20%) that in Europe (5–8%: Alesina & Angeletos, 2002). Socioeconomic differences are augmented by attitudinal differences as well. According to the *World Values Survey* 71% of Americans believe that individual effort could raise one out of poverty, while only 40% of Europeans do. While only 16% of Americans believe that one's income and success are largely due to luck, 25% of Europeans do. Additionally, while most objective measures of social mobility show only modest advantages for the United States compared to Europe, both Americans and Europeans perceive America to be a substantially more mobile society (Checchi, Ichino, & Rustichini, 1999; Fields & Ok, 1999; Gottshalck & Spolaore, 2002). Thus, relative to Europe, America is a more economically stratified society, where movement up (and down) the economic ladder is seen as being readily attainable and where primary responsibility for that movement is attributed to individual effort and initiative rather than government intervention. This would suggest that by and large, American is a more internally competitive society than Europe is. *Europe as less religious*: Over 90% of Americans believe in God or a "higher power," and around 45% of the population attends religious services weekly (Gallup & Lindsay, 1999; Greeley, 1992). In terms of both behavior and belief, most Western countries have turned decidedly irreligious. For example, only 23% of Belgians, 19% of Western Germans, 13% of the British, 10% of the French, 3% of Danes, and only 2% of Icelanders claim to be regular church attendees (Verweij, Ester, and Nauta, 1997; see also Bruce, 2002, pp. 60–74). The percentage of the Britons who claim to believe in a personal God has dropped from 43% in the 1940s to somewhere around 26% in 2000 (Bruce, 2002, p. 138). Furthermore, belief in life after death now stands at around 46% for Italians, 43% for the French, and only 35% for Scandinavians (Gallup, 1979). Hell as a concept has fallen on hard times: only 28% of the British worry about it as a possible final destination (Greeley, 1995). *Weak intermediate social groups in Spain, France, and Italy*: Fukuyama, 1995, pp. 55–56. De Tocqueville quote: De Tocqueville, 1955, p. 206. *Local church control in France*: Lambert, 1989.

16. Comparison of American, German, Swedish groups: Stolle, 2001. American and Japanese groups: Yamagishi & Yamagishi, 1994.

17. Europe's aversion to sectarianism: A general European aversion to religious sectarianism tightly constrains religion's place in the public sphere. This aversion is reflected most glaringly in the French policy of *laicité* (secularism). While constitutionally guaranteeing religious freedom, *laicité* also makes religion strictly a private matter. The Republic takes it as its duty to ensure that no dangerous

sect develops under the name of religion that could threaten individual liberties (*anticommunautarisme*). Sectarian (or perceived sectarian) groups such as the Amish or Scientologists exist on the fringes of legality. France may be more aggressively secular than other European nations, but the ability of religious subcultures to sustain themselves across Europe is severely limited by social, political, and structural factors (see Bruce, 2002, pp. 145–150). The status of Scientology in Germany, for example, has been an ongoing controversy (Paige-English, 1997).

18. Stark and Iannaccone (1994) argue that the competitive marketplace is, in fact, the key to understanding European secularization. America has a competitive religious marketplace where churches work hard to attract and retain paying members. Europe has a long history of state-supported church monopolies, which have made churches lazy and unresponsive to their congregations.

19. Forgiveness and cortisol levels: Berry & Worthington, 2001; Sapolsky, 1993. Religion and delinquency: Jang & Johnson, 2001; Merrill, Salazar, & Gardner, 2001. Happy marriages: Combs, 1991; Gallo, Troxel, Matthews, & Kuller, 2003; Lillard & Waite, 1995; Myers, 2001; Wilson & Oswald, 2002. Religion as social capital: see Social Capital Survey, 2001.

References

Abernethy, B. (1987). Anticipation in sport: A review. *Physical Education Review, 10,* 5–16.

Abernethy, B., Neal, R. J., & Koning, P. (1994). Visual-perceptual and cognitive differences between expert, intermediate, and novice snooker players. *Applied Cognitive Psychology, 18,* 184–211.

Adams, E. S. (2001). Threat displays in animal communication: Handicaps, reputations, and commitments. In R. M. Neese (Ed.). *Evolution and the capacity for commitment* (pp. 99–119). New York: Russell Sage Foundation.

Adelson, B., & Soloway, E. (1985). The role of domain expertise in software design. *IEEE Transactions on Software Engineering, 11,* 1351–1360.

Adler, D. S., Bar-Oz, G., Belfer-Cohen, A., & Bar-Yosef, O. (2006). Ahead of the game: Middle and Upper Paleolithic hunting behaviors in the Southern Caucasus. *Current Anthropology, 47,* 89–118.

Adolphs, R. (1999). Social cognition and the human brain. *Trends in Cognitive Sciences, 3,* 469–479.

Aiello, L. C. (1996). Terrestriality, bipedalism and the origin of language. In W. C. Runciman, J. Maynard-Smith, & R. I. M. Dunbar (Eds.), *Evolution of social behaviour patterns in primates and man* (pp. 269–290). Oxford: Oxford University Press.

Ainsworth, M. D. S. (1985). Attachments across the lifespan. *Bulletin of the New York Academy of Medicine, 61,* 792–812.

Alcorta, C. S. (2006). Religion and the life course: Is adolescence an "experience expectant" period for religious transmission? In P. McNamara (Ed.), *Where God and science meet, vol. 2* (pp. 55–79). Bridgeport, CT: Praeger.

Alcorta, C. S., & Sosis, R. (2006). Ritual, emotion, and sacred symbols: The evolution of religion as an adaptive complex. *Human Nature, 16*, 323–359.

Alesina, A., & Angeletos, G.-R. (2002). Fairness and redistribution: US versus Europe. National Bureau of Economic Research, working paper #9502.

Alexander, R. D. (1987). *The biology of moral systems.* New York: Aldine de Gruyter.

Alexander, R. D. (1989). Evolution of the human psyche. In P. Mellars & C. Stringer Princeton (Eds.), *The human revolution: Behavioural and biological perspectives on the origins of modern humans* (pp. 455–513). Princeton, NJ: Princeton University Press.

Allard, F., & Starkes, J. L. (1980). Perception in sport: Volleyball. *Journal of Sport Psychology, 2*, 14–21.

Alley, R. B. (2000). *The two-mile time machine: Ice cores, abrupt climate change, and our future.* Princeton, NJ: Princeton University Press.

Altemeyer, B., & Hunsberger, B. (2005). Fundamentalism and authoritarianism. In R. F. Paloutzian & C. L. Park (Eds.), *Handbook of the psychology of religion and spirituality* (pp. 378–393). New York: Guilford Press.

Alvard, M. S. (1994). Conservation by native peoples: Prey choice in a depleted habitat. *Human Nature, 5*, 127–154.

Ambrose, S. H. (1998a). Chronology of the later stone age and food production in East Africa. *Journal of Archaeological Science, 25*, 377–392.

Ambrose, S. H. (1998b). Late Pleistocene population bottlenecks, volcanic winter, and the differentiation of modern humans. *Journal of Human Evolution, 34*, 623–651.

Ambrose, S. H. (2001). Paleolithic technology and human evolution. *Science, 291*, 1748–1752.

Ambrose, S. H. (2002). Small things remembered: Origins of early microlithic industries in Subsaharan Africa. In R. Elston & S. Kuhn (Eds.), *Thinking small: Global perspectives on microlithic technologies* (pp. 9–29). Archaeological Papers of the American Anthropological Association #12.

Ambrose, S. H., & Lorenz, C. G. (1990). Social and ecological models for the Middle Stone Age in Southern Africa. In P. Mellars (Ed.), *The emergence of modern humans* (pp. 3–33). Edinburgh: University of Edinburgh Press.

Amodio, D. M., & Frith, C. D. (2006). Meeting of minds: The medial frontal cortex and social cognition. *Nature Reviews: Neuroscience, 7*, 268–277.

Anderson, W. P., Reid, C. M., & Jennings, G. L. (1992). Pet ownership and risk factors for cardiovascular disease. *Medical Journal of Australia, 157*, 298–301.

Andreoni, J., & Petrie, R. (2004). Public goods experiment without confidentiality: A glimpse into fund-raising. *Journal of Public Economics, 88*, 1605–1623.

Ano, G. G., & Vasconcelles, E. B. (2005). Religious coping and psychological adjustment to stress: A meta-analysis. *Journal of Clinical Psychology, 61*, 1–20.

Anson, O., Carmel, S., Bonneh, D. Y., Levenson, A., & Maoz, B. (1990). Recent life events, religiosity, and health: An individual or collective effect. *Human Relations, 43*, 1051–1066.

Aquinas, St. Thomas. (1268). *Summa contra gentiles*. www2.nd.edu/Departments/ Maritain/etext/gc.htm (accessed 11/4/08).

Argyle, M., & Beit-Hallahmi, B. (1975). *The social psychology of religion*. London: Routledge.

Arieti, J. A., & Wilson, P. A. (2003). *The scientific and the divine: Conflict and reconciliation from ancient Greece to the present*. New York: Rowman and Littlefield.

Aristotle (350 BCE). *Nichomachean Ethics*. Translated by W. D. Ross. Retrieved March 8, 2007. www.constitution.org/ari/ethic_00.htm.

Arsuaga, J. L., Martinez, I., Gracia, A., Carretero, J. M., Lorenzo, C., Garcia, N., et al. (1997). Sima de los Huesos (Sierra de Atapuerca, Spain): The site. *Journal of Human Evolution, 33*, 109–127.

Astuti, R., & Harris, P. L. (2008). Understanding mortality and the life of the ancestors in rural Madagascar. *Cognitive Science, 32*, 713–740.

Atran, S. (2002). *In gods we trust*. Oxford: Oxford University Press.

Atran, S. (2006). The cognitive and evolutionary roots of religion. In P. McNamara (Ed.), *Where God and science meet*, Vol. 1 (pp. 181–207). Westport, CT: Praeger.

Atran, S., Medin, D., Lynch, E., Vapnarsky, V., Ucan Ek', E., Coley, J., et al. (2002). Folkecology, cultural epidemiology, and the spirit of the commons: A garden experiment in the Maya Lowlands, 1991–2001. *Current Anthropology, 43*, 421–450.

Atran, S., Medin, D., Ross, N., Lynch, E., Coley, J., Ucan Ek', E., et al. (1999). Folkecology and commons management in the Maya Lowlands. *Proceedings of the National Academy of Sciences of the United States of America, 96*, 7598–7603.

Atran, S., & Norenzayan, A. (2004). Religion's evolutionary landscape: Counterintuition, commitment, compassion, and communion. *Behavioral and Brain Sciences, 27*, 713–770.

Augustine, Saint (1982). *The literal meaning of Genesis*. Trans. John Hammond Taylor. In Johannes Quasten et al. (Eds.), *Ancient Christian writers, vol. 41–42*. New York: Newman Press.

Azari, N. P. (2006). Neuroimaging studies of religious experience: A critical review. In P. M. McNamara (Ed.), *Where God and science meet*, Vol. 2 (pp. 33–54). Westport, CT: Praeger.

Azari, N. P., Missimer, J., & Seitz, R. J. (2005). Religious experience and emotion: Evidence for distinct cognitive neural patterns. *International Journal for the Psychology of Religion, 15*, 263–281.

Azari, N. P., Nickel, J. P., Wunderlich, G., Niedeggen, M., Hefter, H., Tellmann, L., et al. (2001). Neural correlates of religious experience. *European Journal of Neuroscience, 13*, 1649–1652.

Baffier, D., & Girard, M. (1998). *Les caverns D'Arcy-sur-Cure*. Paris: La Maison des Roches.

Bahn, P., & Vertut, J. (1988). *Images of the ice age*. Leicester: Windward.

Baker, M., & Gorsuch, R. (1982). Trait anxiety and intrinsic-extrinsic religiousness. *Journal for the Scientific Study of Religion, 21*, 119–122.

Baldwin, D. A., Markman, E. M., Bill, B., Desjardins, R. N., & Irwin, J. M. (1996). Infant's reliance on social criterion for establishing word-object relations. *Child Development, 67*, 3135–3153.

Balter, M. (2000). Paintings in Italian cave may be oldest yet. *Science, 290*, 419–421.

Baltes, P. B., & Staudinger, U. M. (2000). Wisdom: A metaheuristic (pragmatic) to orchestrate mind and virtue toward excellence. *American Psychologist, 55*, 122–136.

Barham, L. (2000). *The Middle Stone Age of Zambia, south-central Africa.* Bristol: Western Academic and Specialist Press.

Barham, L. (2002). Systematic pigment use in the Middle Pleistocene of South-Central Africa. *Current Anthropology, 43*, 181–190.

Barnes, M. H. (2000). *Stages of thought.* New York: Oxford University Press.

Baron-Cohen, S. (2005). The empathizing system: A revision of the 1994 model of the mindreading system. In B. J. Ellis & D. F. Bjorklund (Eds.), *Origins of the social mind* (pp. 468–492). New York: Guilford Press.

Baron-Cohen, S., Cox, A., Baird, G., Swettenham, J., Drew, A., Nightingale, N., et al. (1996). Psychological markers of autism at 18 months of age in a large population. *British Journal of Psychiatry, 168*, 158–163.

Barrett, H. C. (2005). Cognitive development and the understanding of animal behavior. In B. J. Ellis & D. F. Bjorklund (Eds.), *Origins of the social mind* (pp. 438–467). New York: Guilford Press.

Barrett, J. L. (1998). Theological correctness: Cognitive constraints and the study of religion. *Method & Theory in the Study of Religion, 11*, 325–339.

Barrett, J. L. (2000). Exploring the natural foundations of religion. *Trends in Cognitive Neuroscience, 4*, 29–34.

Barrett, J. L., & Keil, F. C. (1996). Anthropomorphism and God concepts: Conceptualizing a non-natural entity. *Cognitive Psychology, 31*, 219–247.

Barrett, J. L., Newman, R., & Richert, R. A. (2003). When seeing does not lead to believing: Children's understanding of the importance of background knowledge for interpreting visual displays. *Journal of Cognition and Culture, 3*, 91–108.

Barrett, J. L., & Richert, R. A. (2003). Anthropomorphism or preparedness? Exploring children's God concepts. *Review of Religious Research, 44*, 300–312.

Barrett, J. L., Richert, R., & Driesenga, A. (2001). God's beliefs versus mother's: The development of nonhuman agent concepts. *Child Development, 72*, 50–65.

Baruss, I. (2003). *Alterations of consciousness.* Washington, DC: American Psychological Association.

Bar-Yosef, O. (2000). A Mediterranean perspective on the Middle/Upper Palaeolithic Revolution. In C. B. Stringer, R. N. E. Barton, & J. C. Finlayson (Eds.), *Neanderthals on the Edge* (pp. 9–18). Oxford: Oxbow.

Bar-Yosef, O. (2006). Between observations and models: An eclectic view of Middle Paleolithic Archaeology. In E. Hovers & S. L. Kuhn (Eds.), *Transitions before the transition* (pp. 305–325). New York: Springer.

Bar-Yosef, O., Vandermeersch, B., Arensburg, B., Belfer-Cohen, A., Goldberg, P., Laville, H., Meignen, L., Rak, Y., Speth, J. D., Tchernov, E., Tillier, A.-M., & Weiner, S. (1992). The excavations in Kebara Cave, Mt. Carmen. *Current Anthropology, 33*, 497–550.

Bateson, M., Nettle, D., & Roberts, G. (2006). Cues of being watched enhance cooperation in a real-world setting. *Biology Letters, 2*, 412–414.

Batson, C. D., Eidelman, S. H., Higley, S. L., & Russell, S. A. (2001). "And who is my neighbor?": II. Quest religion as a source of universal compassion. *Journal for the Scientific Study of Religion, 40*, 39–50.

Batson, C. D., Floyd, R. B., Meyer, J. M., & Winner, A. L. (1999). "And who is my neighbor?": Intrinsic religion as a source of universal compassion. *Journal for the Scientific Study of Religion, 38*, 31–41.

Batson, C. D., Shoenrade, P., & Ventis, W. L. (1993). *Religion and the individual*. New York: Oxford University Press.

Baumeister, R. F., Bratslavsky, E., Finkenauer, C., & Vohs, K. D. (2001). Bad is stronger than good. *Review of General Psychology, 5*, 323–370.

Baumeister, R. F., & Exline, J. J. (1999). Virtue, personality, and social relations: Self-control as the moral muscle. *Journal of Personality, 67*, 1165–1194.

Baumeister, R. F., & Tice, D. M. (1984). Role of self-presentation and choice in cognitive dissonance under forced compliance: Necessary or sufficient causes? *Journal of Personality and Social Psychology, 46*, 5–13.

Bausell, R. B., Lao, L., Bergman, S., Lee, W. L., & Berman, B. M. (2007). Is acupuncture analgesia expectancy effect? Preliminary evidence based on participants perceived assignment: Two placebo-controlled trials. *Evaluation and the Health Professions, 28*, 9–26.

Beatty, A. (1999). *Varieties of Javanese religion*. Cambridge: Cambridge University Press.

Beauregard, M., Levesque, J., & Bourgouin, P. (2001). Neurocorrelates of conscious self-regulation of emotion. *Journal of Neuroscience, 21, RC 165*, 1–6.

Beauregard, M., & Paquette, V. (2006). Neural correlates of mystical experience in Carmelite nuns. *Neuroscience Letters, 405*, 186–190.

Bednarik, R. (1995). Concept-mediated marking in the Lower Paleolithic. *Current Anthropology, 36*, 605–634.

Begouen, R., & Clottes, J. (1986–1987). Le grand félin des trois-frères. *Antiquités Nationales, 18–19*, 109–113.

Behar, D. M., Villems, R., Soodyall, H., Blue-Smith, J., Pereira, L., et al. (2008). The dawn of human matrilineal diversity. *American Journal of Human Genetics, 82*, 1130–1140.

Bell, C. (1997). *Ritual: Perspectives and dimensions*. Oxford: Oxford University Press.

Bellah, R. N. (1970). *Beyond belief*. New York: Harper and Row.

Belyaev, D. K. (1979). Destabilizing selection as a factor in domestication. *Journal of Heredity, 70*, 301–308.

Benedetti, F. (1996). The opposite effects of the opiate antagonist naloxone and cholecsytokinin antagonist proglumide on placebo analgesia. *Pain, 64*, 535–543.

Benson, H., & Klipper, M. Z. (1976). *The relaxation response*. New York: Harper-Torch.

Benson, H., & Stark, M. (1997). *Timeless healing*. New York: Scribner.

Benson, P. L. (1992). Religion and substance abuse. In J. F. Shumaker (Ed.), *Religion and mental health* (pp. 211–220). New York: Oxford University Press.

Benson, P. L., Donahue, M. J., & Erickson, J. A. (1989). Adolescence and religion: A review of the literature from 1970 to 1986. *Research in the Social Scientific Study of Religion, 1*, 151–179.

Berger, T. D., & Trinkaus, E. (1995). Patterns of trauma among the Neandertals. *Journal of Archaeological Science, 22*, 841–852.

Bering, J. (2002). Intuitive conceptions of dead agents' minds: The natural foundations of afterlife beliefs as phenomenological boundary. *Journal of Cognition and Culture, 2*, 263–308.

Bering, J. M. (2005). The evolutionary history of an illusion: Religious causal beliefs in children and adults. In B. J. Ellis & D. F. Bjorklund (Eds.), *Origins of the social mind* (pp. 411–437). New York: Guilford Press.

Bering, J. M. (2006). The folk psychology of souls. *Behavioral and Brain Sciences, 29*, 453–462.

Bering, J. M., & Bjorklund, D. F. (2004). The natural emergence of reasoning about the afterlife as a developmental regularity. *Developmental Psychology, 40*, 217–233.

Bering, J. M., Hernández-Blasi, C., & Bjorklund, D. F. (2005). The development of "afterlife" beliefs in secularly and religiously schooled children. *British Journal of Developmental Psychology, 23*, 587–607.

Bering, J. M., McLeod, K. A., & Shackelford, T. K. (2005). Reasoning about dead agents reveals possible adaptive trends. *Human Nature, 16*, 360–381.

Bering, J. M., & Parker, B. D. (2006). Children's attributions of intentions to an invisible agent. *Developmental Psychology, 42*, 253–262.

Berndt, R. M., & Berndt, C. N. (1964). *The world of the first Australians*. Chicago: University of Chicago Press.

Berry, J. W., & Worthington, E. L. (2001). Forgivingness, relationship quality, stress while imagining relationship events, and physical and mental health. *Journal of Counseling Psychology, 49*, 287–310.

Bibace, R., Dillon, J. J., & Saragin, J. (1999). Toward a co-existence of causal reasoning about illness in children and adults. In R. Bibace, J. Dillon, & B. N. Dowds (Eds.), *Advances in applied developmental psychology* (pp. 27–36). Stamford, CT: Ablex.

Bickerton, D. (1995). *Language and human behavior*. Seattle: University of Washington Press.

Biederman, J., Monuteaux, M. C., Doyle, A. E., et al. (2004). Impact of executive function deficits and attention-deficit hyperactivity disorder on academic outcomes in children. *Journal of Consulting and Clinical Psychology, 72*, 757–766.

Binford, L. R., & Ho, C. K. (1985). Taphonomy at a distance: Zhoukoudian, "the cave home of Beijing man"? *Current Anthropology, 26*, 413–442.

Bingham, P. M. (1999). Human uniqueness: A general theory. *Quarterly Review of Biology, 74*, 133–169.

Bird-David, N. (1999). "Animism" revisited. *Current Anthropology* (supplement) *40*, S67–S92.

Bjarnason, T. (1998). Parents, religion, and perceived social coherence: A Durkheimian framework for adolescent anomie. *Journal for the Scientific Study of Religion, 37*, 742–754.

Bjorklund, D. F., & Rosenberg, J. S. (2005). The role of developmental plasticity in the evolution of human cognition. In B. J. Ellis & D. F. Bjorklund (Eds.), *Origins of the social mind* (pp. 45–75). New York: Guilford.

Blacking, J. (1973). *How musical is man?* Seattle: University of Washington Press.

Blair, R. J. R. (1995). A cognitive developmental approach to morality: Investigating the psychopath. *Cognition, 57,* 1–29.

Blair, R. J. R., Jones, L., Clark, F., & Smith, M. (1997). The psychopathic individual: A lack of responsiveness to distress cues. *Psychophysiology, 34,* 192–198.

Blakemore, S. J., Boyer, P., et al. (2003). The detection of contingency and animacy from simple animations in the human brain. *Cerebral Cortex, 13,* 837–844.

Bock, E. W., & Radelet, M. L. (1988). The marital integration of religious independents: A reevaluation of its significance. *Review of Religious Research, 29,* 228–241.

Boehm, C. (1999). *Hierarchy in the forest.* Cambridge, MA: Harvard University Press.

Boehm, C. (2000). Conflict and the evolution of social control. *Journal of Consciousness Studies, 7,* 79–101.

Boesch, C., & Boesch-Achermann, H. (2000). *The chimpanzees of the Taï Forest: Behavioral ecology and evolution.* Oxford: Oxford University Press.

Bootsma, R. J., & Van Wieringen, P. C. W. (1990). Timing an attacking forehand in table tennis. *Journal of Experimental Psychology: Human Perception and Performance, 16,* 21–29.

Borgerhoff Mulder, M. (1991). Behavioral ecology of humans: Studies in foraging and reproduction. In J. R. Krebs & N. B. Davies (Eds.), *Behavioral ecology* (pp. 69–98). London: Blackwell.

Bottoms, B. L., Nielsen, M. E., Murray, R., & Filipas, H. (2004). Religion related child physical abuse: Characteristics and psychological outcome. *Journal of Aggression, Maltreatment and Trauma, 8,* 87–114.

Bouldin, P., Bavin, E. L., & Pratt, C. (2002). An investigation of the verbal abilities of children with imaginary companions. *First Language, 22,* 249–264.

Boutcher, S. H., & Crews, D. J. (1987). The effect of preshot attentional routine on a well-learned skill. *International Journal of Sport Psychology, 18,* 30–39.

Bowers, K. S., & LeBaron, S. (1986). Hypnosis and hypnotizability: Implications for clinical intervention. *Hospital and Community Psychiatry, 37,* 457–467.

Bowker, J. (1997). *World religions: The great faiths explored and explained.* New York: DK Publishing.

Boyd, R., Gintis, H., Bowles, S., & Richerson, P. J. (2003). The evolution of altruistic punishment. *Proceedings of the National Academy of Sciences of the United States of America, 100,* 3531–3535.

Boyer, P. (2001). *Religion explained.* New York: Basic Books.

Boyer, P., & Barrett, H. C. (2005). Domain specificity and intuitive ontology. In D. M. Buss (Ed.), *The handbook of evolutionary psychology* (pp. 96–118). New York: Wiley.

Boyer, P., & Lienard, P. (2008). Ritual behaviour in obsessive and normal individuals. *Current Directions in Psychological Science, 17,* 291–294.

Boyer, P., & Ramble, C. (2001). Cognitive templates for religious concepts: Cross-cultural evidence for recall of counter-intuitive representations. *Cognitive Science, 25,* 535–564.

Brass, M., Derfuss, J., Forstmann, B., & von Cramon, D. Y. (2005). The role of the inferior frontal junction in cognitive control. *Trends in Cognitive Science, 9,* 314–316.

Bretherton, I. (1989). Pretense: The form and function of make believe play. *Developmental Review, 9*, 383–401.

Brightman, R. A. (1993). *Grateful prey: Rock Cree human-animal relationships.* Berkeley: University of California Press.

Bril, B., Roux, V., & Dietrich, G. (2005). Stone knapping: Khambhat (India), a unique opportunity? In V. Roux & B. Bril (Eds.), *Stone knapping: The necessary conditions for uniquely hominin behaviour* (pp. 53–71). Cambridge, UK: McDonald Institute.

Brody, G. H., Stoneman, Z., Flor, D., & McCrary, C. (1994). Religion's role in organizing family relationships: Family processes in rural, two-parent, African-American families. *Journal of Marriage and the Family, 56*, 878–888.

Brooks, A. C. (2003). Religious faith and charitable giving. *Policy Review, 121*, 39–50.

Broom, D. M. (2003). *The evolution of morality and religion.* Cambridge: Cambridge University Press.

Brown, D. P. (1992). Clinical hypnosis research since 1986. In E. Fromm & M. R. Nash (Eds.), *Contemporary hypnosis research* (pp. 427–458). New York: Guilford Press.

Bruce, S. (2002). *God is dead: Secularization in the West.* London: Blackwell.

Bruner, J. S. (1975). The ontogenesis of speech acts. *Journal of Child Language, 2*, 1–19.

Buber, M. (1970). *I and thou.* New York: Scribner.

Bunting, R. (1997). *The Pacific raincoast: Environment and culture in an American Eden, 1770–1900.* Lawrence: University of Kansas Press.

Burnham, T., & Hare, B. (2007). Engineering human cooperation: Does involuntary neural activation increase public goods contributions in adult humans? *Human Nature, 18*, 88–108.

Bushman, B. J., Ridge, R. D., Das, E., Key, C. W., & Busath, G. L. (2007). When God sanctions killing; Effect of scriptural violence on aggression. *Psychological Science, 18*, 204–207.

Buss, A. H. (1980). *Self-consciousness and social anxiety.* San Francisco: W. H. Freeman.

Butzer, K. W. (1971). *Environment and archaeology.* Chicago: Aldine Atherton.

Byrne, R. W., & Whiten, A. (1997). Machiavellian intelligence. In A. Whiten & R. W. Byrne (Eds.), *Machiavellian intelligence II: Extensions and evaluations* (pp. 1–24). Cambridge: Cambridge University Press.

Call, J., Hare, B., Carpenter, M., & Tomasello, M. (2004). "Unwilling" versus "unable": Chimpanzees' understanding of human intentional action. *Developmental Science, 7*, 488–498.

Call, J., & Tomasello, M. (1996). The effects of humans on the cognitive development of apes. In A. E. Russon, K. A. Bard, & S. T. Parker (Eds.), *Reaching into thought: The minds of the great apes* (pp. 371–403). New York: Cambridge University Press.

Call, J., & Tomasello, M. (1998). Distinguishing intentional from accidental actions in orangutans (*Pongo pygmaeus*), chimpanzees (*Pan troglodytes*) and human children (*Homo sapiens*). *Journal of Comparative Psychology, 112*, 192–206.

Calvin, W. H. (1993). The unitary hypothesis: A common neural circuitry for novel manipulations, language, plan-ahead, and throwing. In K. R. Gibson &

T. Ingold (Eds), *Tools, language, and cognition in human evolution* (pp.230–250). Cambridge: Cambridge University Press.

Calzato, L. S., van den Wildenberg, W. P. M., & Hommel, B. (2008). Losing the big picture: How religion may control visual attention. *PLoS One, 3,* e3679. doi:10.1371/journal.pone.0003679.

Campbell, J. (1969). *The masks of God: Primitive mythology.* New York: Penguin Books.

Campbell, J. (1983). *The way of animal powers. Historical atlas of world mythology* (vol. 1). San Francisco: Harper and Row.

Camus, A. (1955). *The myth of Sisyphus and other essays.* New York: Vintage Books.

Carey, J. (1992). *The intellectuals and the masses.* London: Faber and Faber.

Carpenter, J., Burks, S., & Verhoogen, E. (2005). Comparing students to workers: The effects of social framing on behavior in distribution games. In J. Carpenter, G. Harrison, & J. List (Eds.), *Field experiments in economics* (pp. 261–290). Greenwich, CT: JAI Press.

Carpenter, M., Pennington, B. F., & Rogers, S. J. (2002). Interrelations among social-cognitive skills in young children with autism and developmental delays. *Journal of Autism and Developmental Disorders, 32,* 91–106.

Carter, O. L., Presti, D. E., Callistemon, C., Ungerer, Y., Lui, G. B., & Pettigrew, J. D. (2005). Meditation alters perceptual rivalry in Buddhist monks. *Current Biology, 15,* R412.

Catlin, G. (1867). *O-kee-pa: A religious ceremony and other customs of the Mandans.* London: Trubner.

Chagnon, N. (1968). *Yanamamo: The fierce people.* New York: Holt, Rinehart, Winston.

Chalmers, D. (1996). *The conscious mind.* New York: Oxford University Press.

Charness, N. (1989). Expertise in chess and bridge. In D. Klahr & K. Kotovsky (Eds.), *Complex information processing: The impact of Herbert A. Simon* (pp. 183–208). Hillsdale, NJ: Erlbaum.

Charness, N., Krampe, R., & Mayr, U. (1996). The role of practice and coaching in entrepreneurial skill domains: An international comparison of life-span chess skill acquisition. In K. A. Ericsson (Ed.), *The road to excellence* (pp. 51–80). Mahwah, NJ: Erlbaum.

Chase, W. G., & Simon, H. A. (1973). The mind's eye in chess. In W. G. Chase (Ed.), *Visual information processing* (pp. 215–281). New York: Academic Press.

Chauvet, J., Deschamps, E. B., & Hillaire, C. (1995). *La grotte Chauvet.* Paris: Seuil.

Checchi, D., Ichino, A., & Rustichini, A. (1999). More equal and less mobile? Education financing and intergenerational mobility in Italy and the US. *Journal of Public Economics, 74,* 351–393.

Cheney, D. L., & Seyfarth, R. M. (2007). *Baboon metaphysics: The evolution of the social mind.* Chicago: University of Chicago Press.

Chevalier-Skolnikoff, S. (1973). Facial expressions of emotions in nonhuman primates. In P. Ekman (Ed.), *Darwin and facial expressions* (pp. 11–90). New York: Academic Press.

Christian, W. A. (1982). Provoked religious weeping in early modern Spain. In J. Davis (Ed.), *Religious organization and religious experience* (pp. 97–114). London: Academic Press.

Churchland, P. M. (1994). *Matter and consciousness*. Cambridge, MA: MIT Press.

Clark, G. A., & Riel-Salvatore, J. (2006). Observations on systematics in paleolithic archaeology In E. Hovers & S. L. Kuhn (Eds.), *Transitions before the transition: Evolution and stability in the Middle Paleolithic and Middle Stone Age* (pp. 29–56). New York: Springer.

Clark, J. D., & K. Brown (2001). The Twin Rivers Kopje, Zambia: Stratigraphy, fauna, and artifacts. *Journal of Archaeological Science, 28*, 305–330.

Clark, J. D., Oakley, K. P., Wells, L. W., & McClelland, J. A. C. (1947). New studies on Rhodesian Man. *Journal of the Royal Anthropological Society, 77*, 4–33.

Clark, W. H. (1958). How do social scientists define religion? *Journal of Social Psychology, 47*, 143–147.

Clayton, N. S., & Dickinson, A. (1998). Episodic-like memory during cache recovery by scrub jays. *Nature, 395*, 272–278.

Clayton, N. S., & Dickinson, A. (1999). Memory for the content of caches by scrub jays (*Aphelocoma coerulescens*). *Journal of Experimental Psychology: Animal Behavioral Processes, 25*, 82–91.

Clayton, N. S., Yu, K. S., & Dickinson, A. (2001). Scrub jays (*Aphelocoma coerulescens*) form integrated memories of the multiple features of caching episodes. *Journal of Experimental Psychology: Animal Behavioral Processes, 27*, 17–29.

Clayton, N. S., Yu, K. S., & Dickinson, A. (2003). Interacting cache memories: Evidence of flexible memory use by scrub jays. *Journal of Experimental Psychology: Animal Behavioral Processes, 29*, 14–22.

Cline, V. B., & Richard, J. M. (1965). A factor-analytic study of religious belief and behavior. *Journal of Personality and Social Psychology, 1*, 569–578.

Clottes, J. (1992). L'archaeologie des grottes ornées. *La Recherche, 239*, 52–61.

Clottes, J., & Lewis-Williams, D. (1998). *The shamans of prehistory: Trance and magic in painted caves*. New York: Abrams Press.

Cochrane, C. N. (1940). *Christianity and the classical culture*. Oxford: Oxford University Press.

Cochrane, G., Hardy, J., & Harpending, H. (2006). Natural history of Ashkenazi intelligence. *Journal of Biosocial Science, 38*, 659–693.

Cochrane, J. K. (1993). The variable effects of religiosity and denomination on adolescent self-reported alcohol use by beverage type. *Journal of Drug Issues, 23*, 479–491.

Cohen, D., & Vandello, J. (2001). Honor and "faking" honorability. In R. Nesse (Ed.), *Evolution and the capacity for commitment* (pp. 163–185). New York: Russell Sage Foundation.

Cohen, S. (2001). Psychosocial stress, social networks, and susceptibility to infection. In H. G. Koenig & H. J. Cohen (Eds.), *The link between religion and health* (pp. 101–123). Oxford: Oxford University Press.

Cohen, S., Doyle, W. J., Skoner, D. P., Rabin, P. S., & Gwaltney, J. M. (1997). Social ties and the susceptibility to the common cold. *Journal of the American Medical Association, 277*, 1940–1944.

Colby, A., & Damon, W. (1992). *Some do care: Contemporary lives of moral commitment*. New York: Free Press.

Collins, F. S. (2006). *The language of God*. New York: Free Press.

Colloca, L., & Benedetti, F. (2005). Placebos and painkillers: Is mind as real as matter? *Nature Reviews: Neuroscience, 6*, 545–552.

Conduct Problems Prevention Research Group (2002). Evaluation of the first 3 years of the fast track prevention trial with children at high risk for adolescent conduct problems. *Journal of Abnormal Child Psychology 30*, 19–35.

Conklin, B. A. (2001). *Consuming grief: Compassionate cannibalism in an Amazonian society.* Austin: University of Texas Press.

Connolly, J. A., & Doyle, A.-B. (1984). Relation of social fantasy play to social competence in preschoolers. *Developmental Psychology, 20*, 797–806.

Connors, S. M. (2000). Ecology and religion in Karuk orientations toward the land. In G. Harvey (Ed.), *Indigenous religions* (pp. 139–151). London: Cassell.

Contrada, R. J., Goyal, T. M., Cather, C., Rafalson, L., Idler, E. L., & Krause, T. J. (2004). Psychosocial factors in outcomes of heart surgery: The impact of religious involvement and depressive symptoms. *Health Psychology, 23*, 227–238.

Conway, M. A. (1995). *Flashbulb memories.* Hove, UK: Erlbaum.

Coolidge, F. L., & Wynn, T. (2001). Executive functions of the frontal lobes and the evolutionary ascendancy of *Homo sapiens. Cambridge Archaeological Journal 11*, 255–260.

Coolidge, F. L., & Wynn, T. (2005). Working memory, its executive functions, and the emergence of modern thinking. *Cambridge Archaeological Journal 15*, 5–26.

Coolidge, F. L., & Wynn, T. (2009). *The rise of Homo sapiens: The evolution of modern thinking.* New York: Wiley-Blackwell.

Coombs, R. H. (1991). Marital status and personal well-being: A literature review. *Family Relations, 40*, 97–102.

Cooper, R., DeJong, D. V., Forsythe, R., & Ross, T. W. (1996). Cooperation without reputation: Experimental evidence from Prisoner's Dilemma games. *Game and Economic Behavior, 12*, 187–218.

Corballis, M. C. (2002). *From hand to mouth: The origins of language.* Princeton, NJ: Princeton University Press.

Correia, S. P. C., Alexis, D. M., Dickinson, A., & Clayton, N. S. (2007). Western Scrub-Jays *(Aphelocoma californica)* anticipate future needs independently of their current motivational state. *Current Biology, 17*, 856–861.

Cronk, L. (1991). Human behavioral ecology. *Annual Reviews of Anthropology, 20*, 41–75.

Csibra, G., & Gergely, G. (1998). The teleological origins of mentalistic action explanation: A developmental hypothesis. *Developmental Science, 1*, 255–259.

Csibra, G., Gergely, G., Biro, S., Koos, D., & Brockbank, M. (1999). Goal attribution without agency cues: The perception of "pure reason" in infancy. *Cognition, 72*, 237–267.

Cunningham, W. A., Johnson, M. K., Raye, C. L., Gatenby, J. C., Gore, J. C., & Banaji, M. (2004). Separable neural components in the processing of Black and White faces. *Psychological Science, 15*, 806–813.

Curtis, C. E., & D'Esposito, M. (2003). Persistent activity in the prefrontal cortex during working memory. *Trends in Cognitive Science, 7*, 415–423.

Curtiss, S. (1977). *Genie: A psycholinguistic study of a modern-day "wild child."* New York: Academic Press.

Czech, D. R., Ploszay, A. J., & Burke, K. L. (2004). An examination of the maintenance of preshot routines in basketball free throw shooting. *Journal of Sport Behavior, 27,* 323–329.

d'Aquili, E., & Newberg, A. B. (1999). *The mystical mind.* Minneapolis: Fortress Press.

Dahlberg, A. A., & Carbonell, V. M. (1961). The dentition of the Magdalenian female from Cap Blanc, France. *Man, 61,* 49–50.

Dart, R. A. (1974). The waterworn Australopithecene pebble of many faces from Makapansgat. *South African Journal of Science, 70,* 167–169.

Darwin, C. (1871). *The descent of man and selection in relation to sex.* London: John Murray.

Davenport, D., & Jochim, M. A. (1988). The scene in the shaft at Lascaux. *Antiquity, 62,* 558–562.

Davidson, R. J., Irwin, W., Anderle, M. J., & Kalin, N. H. (2003). The neural substrates of affective processing in depressed patients treated with Venlafaxine. *American Journal of Psychiatry, 160,* 64–75.

Davidson, R. J., Kabat-Zinn, J., Schumacher, J., Rosenkrantz, M., Muller, D., Santorelli, S. F., et al. (2003). Alterations in brain and immune function produced by mindfulness meditation. *Psychosomatic Medicine, 65,* 564–570.

Davies, P. (1993). *The mind of God.* New York: Simon & Schuster.

Dawkins, R. (1998). *Unweaving the rainbow.* New York: Houghton Mifflin.

Dawkins, R. (2003). *A devil's chaplain.* New York: Houghton Mifflin.

Dawkins, R. (2006). *The God delusion.* New York: Houghton Mifflin.

Deacon, H. J. (1989). Late Pleistocene paleoecology and archaeology in the southern Cape. In P. Mellars & C. B. Stringer (Eds.), *The human revolution: Behavioral and biological perspectives on the origin of modern humans* (pp. 547–564). Edinburgh: Edinburgh University Press.

Deacon, H. J., & Deacon. J. (1999). *Human beginnings in South Africa: Uncovering the secrets of the Stone Age.* Cape Town, SA: David Philips.

Deacon, T. W. (1997). *The symbolic species.* New York: Norton.

de Beaune, S. (1995). *Les hommes au temps de Lascaux.* Paris: Hachette.

de Beaune, S. (1998). Chamanisme et prehistoire. *L'Homme, 147,* 203–219.

d'Errico, F. (2003). The invisible frontier: A multiple species model for the origin of behavioral modernity. *Evolutionary Anthropology, 12,* 188–202.

d'Errico, F., & Cacho, C. (1994). Notation versus decoration in the Upper Palaeolithic: A case study from Tossal de la Rocca, Alicante, Spain. *Journal of Archaeological Science, 21,* 185–200.

d'Errico, F., & Nowell, A. (2000). A new look at the Berekhat Ram figurine: Implications for the origin of symbolism. *Cambridge Archaeological Journal, 10,* 123–167.

D'Esposito, G., Kirkby, B. S., van Horn, J. D., Ellmore, T. M., & Berman, K. F. (1999). Context-dependent, neural system-specific neurophysiological concomitants of ageing: Mapping PET correlates during cognitive activation. *Brain, 122,* 963–979.

Defleur, A., Dutour, O., Valladas, H., & Vandermeersch, V. (1993). Cannibals among the Neanderthals. *Nature, 362,* 214.

Defleur, A., White, T., Valensi, P., Slimak, L., & Cregut-Bonnoure, E. (1999). Neanderthal cannibalism at Moula-Guercy, Ardeche, France. *Science, 286,* 128–131.

de Groot, A. D. (1946). *Thought and choice and chess*. The Hague, Netherlands: Mouton.

Dehaene, S. (2001). *The cognitive neuroscience of consciousness*. Cambridge, MA: MIT Press.

Deichmann, U. (1966). *Biologists under Hitler*. Cambridge, MA: Harvard University Press.

DeLoache, J. S., Miller, K. F., & Rosengren, K. S. (1997). The credible shrinking room: Very young children's performance with symbolic and nonsymbolic relations. *Psychological Science, 8*, 308–313.

de Lumley, H. (1969). A Paleolithic camp at Nice. *Scientific American, 220*, 42–50.

Dembski, W. A. (1998). *The design inference*. Cambridge: Cambridge University Press.

DeNault, L. K., & McFarlane, D. A. (1995). Reciprocal altruism between male vampire bats (*Desmondus rotundus*). *Animal Behavior, 49*, 855–856.

Denenberg, V. H., & Rosenberg, K. M. (1967). Non-genetic transformation of information. *Nature, 216*, 549–550.

De Pascalis, V., Chiaradia, C., & Carotenuto, E. (2002). The contribution of suggestibility and expectation to placebo analgesia phenomenon in an experimental setting. *Pain, 96*, 393–402.

Deridder, R., Hendriks, F., Zani, B., Pepitone, A., & Saffioti, S. (1999). Additional cross-cultural evidence on the selective usage of nonmaterial beliefs in explaining life events. *European Journal of Social Psychology, 29*, 435–442.

Derrfuss, J., Brass, M., & von Cramon, D. Y. (2004). Cognitive control in the posterior frontolateral cortex: Evidence from common activations in task coordination, interference control, and working memory. *NeuroImage, 23*, 604–612.

de Tocqueville, A. (1835/1990). *Democracy in America*. New York: Vintage Books.

de Tocqueville, A. (1955). *The old regime and the French Revolution*. New York: Doubleday Anchor.

de Waal, F. B. M. (1990). *Peacemaking among primates*. Cambridge, MA: Harvard University Press.

de Waal, F. B. M. (1996). *Good natured*. Cambridge, MA: Harvard University Press.

de Waal, F. B. M., & Berger, M. L. (2000). Payment for labour in monkeys. *Nature, 404*, 563.

de Waal, F. B. M., & Johanowicz, D. L. (1993). Modification of reconciliation behavior through social experience: An experiment with two macaque species. *Child Development, 64*, 897–908.

de Waal, F. B. M., & Lanting, F. (1997). *Bonobo: The forgotten ape*. Berkeley: University of California Press.

de Waal, F. B. M., & Luttrell, L. M. (1988). Mechanisms of social reciprocity in three primate species: Symmetrical relationship characteristics or cognition? *Ethology and Sociobiology, 9*, 101–118.

de Waal Malefijt, A. (1968). *Religion and culture*. Prospect Heights, IL: Waveland Press.

Dias, M., & Harris, P. L. (1988). The effect of make-believe play on deductive reasoning. *British Journal of Developmental Psychology, 6*, 207–221.

Dias, M., & Harris, P. L. (1990). The influence of the imagination on reasoning in young children. *British Journal of Developmental Psychology, 8*, 305–318.

Dickson, B. D. (1990). *The dawn of belief.* Tucson: University of Arizona Press.

Diener, E., & Srull, T. K. (1979). Self-Awareness, psychological perspective, and self-reinforcement. *Journal of Personality and Social Psychology, 37*, 413–423.

Dierker, L. C., & Sanders, B. (1996). Developmental differences and individual differences in children's ability to distinguish reality from fantasy. *Imagination, Cognition, and Personality, 16*, 25–49.

Dollahite, D. C. (1998). Fathering, faith, and spirituality. *Journal of Men's Studies, 7*, 3–15.

Donahue, M. J., & Nielsen, M. E. (2005). Religion, attitudes, and social behavior. In R. F. Paloutzian & C. L. Park (Eds.), *Handbook of the psychology of religion and spirituality* (pp. 274–291). New York: Guilford Press.

Donald, M. (1991). *Origins of the modern mind.* Cambridge, MA: Harvard University Press.

Donald, M. (1993). Human cognitive evolution: What we were, what we are becoming. *Social Research, 60*, 143–170.

Donald, M. (1999). Preconditions for the evolution of protolanguage. In M. C. Corballis & S. E. G. Lea (Eds.), *The descent of mind* (pp. 138–154). Oxford: Oxford University Press.

Dossey, L. (1997). *Healing words: The power of prayer and the practice of medicine.* New York: HarperOne.

Dow, J. W. (2006). The evolution of religion: Three anthropological approaches. *Method and Theory in the Study of Religion, 18*, 67–91.

Dowson, T., & Porr, M. (1999). Special objects—special creatures: Shamanic imagery and Aurignacian art. In N. Price (Ed.), *The archaeology of shamanism* (pp. 165–177). London: Routledge.

Dugatkin, L. A. (2001). Subjective commitment in nonhuman animals: What should we be looking for, and where should we be looking. In R. M. Neese (Ed.). *Evolution and the capacity for commitment* (pp. 120–137). New York: Russell Sage Foundation.

Dugatkin, L. A., & Alfieri, M. (1991). Guppies and the TIT FOR TAT strategy: Preference based on past interaction. *Behavioral Ecology and Sociobiology, 28*, 243–246.

Dukas, H., & Hoffman, B. (1979). *Albert Einstein: The human side.* Princeton, NJ: Princeton University Press.

Dunbar, R. I. M. (1992). Neocortex size as a constraint on group size in primates. *Journal of Human Evolution, 20*, 469–493.

Dunbar, R. I. M. (1996). *Grooming, gossip and the evolution of language.* Cambridge, MA: Harvard University Press.

Duncan, J., Seitz, R. J., Kolodny, J., Bor, D., Herzog, H., Ahmed, A., Newell, F. N., & Emslie, H. (2000). A neural basis for general intelligence. *Science, 289*, 457–460.

Dunn, J., & Dale, N. (1984). "I Daddy": 2-year-olds' collaboration in joint pretend with sibling and with mother. In I. Bretherton (Ed.), *Symbolic play: The development of social understanding* (pp. 131–158). Orlando, FL: Academic Press.

Durkheim, É. (1912/1965). *The elementary forms of the religious life.* Trans. Joseph Ward Swain. New York: Free Press.

Duval, S. (1976). Conformity on a visual task as a function of personal novelty on attitudinal dimensions and being reminded of the object status of self. *Journal of Experimental Social Psychology, 12*, 87–98.

Echevarria, J.-U. (1963). *Fiesta de la Tirana de Tarapaca.* Valparaiso, Chile: Ediciones Universitaria de Valparaiso.

Eder, J. F. (1999). Batak. In R. B. Lee & R. Daly (Eds.), *The Cambridge encyclopedia of hunters and gatherers* (pp. 294–297). Cambridge: Cambridge University Press.

Edwards, S. W. (2001). A modern knapper's assessment of the technical skills of the late Acheulean biface workers at Kalambo Falls. In J. D. Clark (Ed.), *Kalambo Falls prehistoric site, vol. 3* (pp. 605–611). Cambridge: Cambridge University Press.

Ehrman, B. D. (1999). *Jesus: Apocalyptic prophet of the new millennium.* Oxford: Oxford University Press.

Eliade, M. (1958). *Patterns in comparative religion.* London: Sheed and Ward.

Eliade, M. (1959). *The sacred and the profane.* New York: Harcourt Brace Jovanovich.

Eliade, M. (1972). *Shamanism: Archaic techniques of ecstasy.* London: Routledge and Kegan Paul.

Eliade, M., & Couliano, I. P. (1991). *The Eliade guide to world religions.* San Francisco: HarperCollins.

Ellison, C. G., Bartkowski, J. P., & Anderson, K. L. (1999). Are there religious variations in domestic violence? *Journal of Family Issues, 20*, 87–133.

Ellison, C. G., & George, L. K. (1994). Religious involvement, social ties, and social support in a southeastern community. *Journal for the Scientific Study of Religion, 33*, 46–61.

Elstein, A. S., Shulman, L. S., & Sprafka, S. A. (1990). Medical problem solving: A ten-year retrospective. *Evaluation and the Health Professions, 13*, 5–36.

Ember, C. R. (1978). Myths about hunter-gatherers. *Ethnology, 17*, 439–448.

Emmons, R. A. (2000). Is spirituality an intelligence? Motivation, cognition, and the psychology of ultimate concern. *International Journal for the Psychology of Religion, 10*, 3–26.

Emmons, R. A. (2005). Striving for the sacred: Personal goals, life meaning and religion. *Journal of Social Issues, 61*, 731–745.

Engelmann, D., & Fischbacher, U. (2002). Indirect reciprocity and strategic reputation building in an experimental helping game. Working Paper 132, Institute for Empirical Research in Economics, University of Zurich.

Enright, R. D., Santos, M. J., & Al-Mabuk, R. (1989). The adolescent as forgiver. *Journal of Adolescence, 12*, 99–110.

Entner, P. (1977). Religious orientation and mental health. *Dissertation Abstracts International, 38*(4-B), 1949.

Eren, M. I., Greenspan, A., & Sampson, C. G. (2008). Are Upper Paleolithic blade cores more productive than Middle Paleolithic discoidal cores? A replication experiment. *Journal of Human Evolution, 55*, 952–961.

Ericsson, K. A. (1996). The acquisition of expert performance. In K. A. Ericsson (Ed.), *The road to excellence* (pp. 1–50). Mahwah, NJ: Erlbaum.

Ericsson, K. A. (2002). Attaining excellence through deliberate practice: Insights from the study of expert performance. In M. Ferrari (Ed.), *The pursuit of excellence through education* (pp. 21–56). Mahwah, NJ: Erlbaum.

Ericsson, K. A., & Charness, N. (1994). Expert performance: Its structure and acquisition. *American Psychologist, 49*, 725–747.

Ericsson, K. A., Krampe, R., & Tesch-Romer, C. (1993). The role of deliberate practice in the acquisition of expert performance. *Psychological Review, 100*, 363–406.

Ericsson, K. A., & Lehmann, A. C. (1996). Expert and exceptional performance: Evidence on maximal adaptations on task constraints. *Annual Review of Psychology, 47*, 273–305.

Evans, E. M. (2001). Cognitive and contextual factors in the emergence of diverse belief systems: Creation versus evolution. *Cognitive Psychology, 42*, 217–266.

Exline, J. J. (2002). Stumbling blocks on the religious road: Fractured relationships, nagging vices, and the inner struggle to believe. *Psychological Inquiry, 13*, 182–189.

Exline, J. J. (2004). Anger toward God: A brief overview of existing research. *Psychology of Religion Newsletter, 29*, 1–8.

Exline, J. J., & Martin, A. (2005). Anger toward God: A new frontier in forgiveness research. In E. L. Worthington Jr. (Ed.), *Handbook of forgiveness* (pp. 73–88). New York: Routledge.

Exline, J. J., & Rose, E. (2005). Religious and spiritual struggles. In R. F. Paloutzian & C. L. Park (Eds.), *Handbook of the Psychology of Religion* (pp. 315–330). New York: Guilford.

Farizy, C. (1990). Du Mousterien au Chatelperronien à Arcy-sur-Cure. *Memoires du Musée de Prehistoire, Île-de-France, 3*, 281–289.

Farthing, G. W. (1992). *The psychology of consciousness*. New York: Prentice-Hall.

Fawzy, F. I., Fawzy, N. W., Hyun, C. S., Elashoff, R., Guthrie, D., Fahey, J. L., & Morton, D. L. (1993). Malignant melanoma: Effects of an early structured psychiatric intervention, coping, and affective state on recurrence and survival 6 years later. *Archives of General Psychiatry, 50*, 681–689.

Fawzy, F. I., Kemeny, M. E., Fawzy, N. W., Elashoff, R., Morton, D. L., Cousins, N., & Fahey, J. L. (1990). A structured psychiatric intervention for cancer patients. II: Changes over time in immunological measures. *Archives of General Psychiatry, 47*, 729–735.

Feblot-Augustins, J. (1999). Raw material transport patterns and settlement systems in the European Lower and Middle Paleolithic: Continuity, change, and variability. In W. Roebroeks & C. Gamble (Eds.), *The Middle Paleolithic occupation of Europe* (pp. 193–214). Leiden: University of Leiden Press.

Fehr, E., & Fischbacher, U. (2003). The nature of human altruism. *Nature, 425*, 785–791.

Fehr, E., & Fischbacher, U. (2004). Third party sanction and social norms. *Evolution and Human Behavior, 25*, 63–87.

Fehr, E., Fischbacher, U., & Gächter, S. (2002). Strong reciprocity, human cooperation, and the enforcement of social norms. *Human Nature, 13*, 1–25.

Fehr, E., & Gächter, S. (2002). Altruistic punishment in humans. *Nature, 415*, 137–140.

Fehr, E., & Gächter, S. (2005). Egalitarian motive and altruistic punishment (reply). *Nature, 433*, E1–E2.

Fehr, E., & Tyran, J.-R. (1996). Institutions and reciprocal fairness. *Nordic Journal of Political Economy, 67*, 133–144.

Fein, D. (1976). Just world responding in 6–9 year old children. *Developmental Psychology, 12*, 79–80.

Fergusson, D. M., Horwood, L. J., Kershaw, K. L., & Shannon, F. T. (1986). Factors associated with reports of wife assault in New Zealand. *Journal of Marriage and the Family, 48*, 407–412.

Ferrari, P. F., Visalberghi, E., Paukner, A., Fogassi, L., Ruggiero, A., & Suomi, S. J. (2006). Neonatal imitation in rhesus macaques. *PLOS Biology, 4*, e302.

Field, M. J. (1961). *Religion and medicine of the Ga people*. Oxford: Oxford University Press.

Field, T. M., Woodson, R., Greenberg, R., & Cohen, D. (1982). Discrimination and imitation of facial expressions by neonates. *Science, 218*, 179–181.

Fields, G., & Ok, E. (1999). Measuring movements of income. *Econometrica, 66*, 455–471.

Filsinger, E. E., & Wilson, M. R. (1984). Religiosity, socioeconomic rewards, and family development: Predictors of marital adjustment. *Journal of Marriage and the Family, 46*, 663–670.

Fincher, C. L., & Thornhill, R. (2008). Assortative sociality, limited dispersal, infectious disease and the genesis of the global pattern of religion diversity. *Proceedings of the Royal Society, B, 275*, 2587–2594.

Fishbach, A., Friedman, R. S., & Kruglanski, A. W. (2003). Leading us not into temptation: Momentary allurements elicit overriding goal activation. *Journal of Personality and Social Psychology, 84*, 296–309.

Fleagle, J. G. (1999). *Primate adaptation and evolution*. San Diego: Academic Press.

Flinn, M. V., Geary, D. C., & Ward, C. V. (2005). Ecological dominance, social competition, and coalitional arms races: Why humans evolved extraordinary intelligence. *Evolution and Human Behavior, 26*, 10–46.

Forsythe, R., Horowitz, J. L., Savin, N. E., & Sefton, M. (1994). Fairness in simple bargaining experiments. *Games and Economic Behavior, 6*, 347–369.

Fortes, M. (1959). *Oedipus and Job in west Africa*. Cambridge: Cambridge University Press.

Frank, R. (1994). *Microeconomics and behavior*. New York: McGraw-Hill.

Frank, R. H. (1988). *Passion within reason*. New York: Norton.

Frazer, J. G. (1890/1941). *The golden bough: A study of magic and religion*. New York: Macmillan.

Frecska, E., & Kulcsar, Z. (1989). Social bonding in the modulation of the physiology of ritual trance. *Ethos, 17*, 70–87.

Freedman, M. (1965). *Lineage organization in Southeastern China*. New York: Athlone Press.

Freedman, M. (1970). Ritual aspects of Chinese kinship and marriage. In M. Freedman (Ed.), *Family and kinship in Chinese society* (pp. 164–179). Stanford, CA: Stanford University Press.

Freeman, L. G., & Echegaray, G. (1981). El Juyo: A 14,000-year-old sanctuary from Northern Spain. *History of Religions, 21*, 1–19.

Frejka, T., & Westoff, C. F. (2008). Religion, religiousness, and fertility in the US and in Europe. *European Journal of Population, 24*, 5–31.

Freud, S. (1927). *The future of an illusion*. New York: Norton.

Frontinus, S. J. (1961). *De aquae ductu urbis Romae.* Trans. by Charles Bennett. Cambridge, MA: Harvard University Press.

Fukuyama, F. (1995). *Trust.* New York: Free Press.

Galanter, M. (1989). *Cults: Faith, healing, and coercion.* New York: Oxford University Press.

Gallagher, H. L., & Frith, C. D. (2003). Functional imaging of "theory of mind." *Trends in Cognitive Sciences, 7,* 77–83.

Gallo, L. C., Troxel, W. M., Matthews, K. A., & Kuller, L. H. (2003). Marital status and quality in middle-aged women: Associations with levels and trajectories of cardiovascular risk factors. *Health Psychology, 22,* 453–463.

Gallup, G. (1979). Religion at home and abroad. *Public Opinion,* March–May.

Gallup, G., & Jones, S. (1989). *One hundred questions and answers: Religion in America.* Princeton, NJ: Princeton Religious Research Center.

Gallup, G., Jr., & Lindsay, D. M. (1999). *Surveying the religious landscape.* Harrisburg, PA: Morehouse.

Gamble, C. (1982). Interaction and alliance in Paleolithic society. *Man, 17,* 92–107.

Gamble, C. (1999). *The Upper Paleolithic societies of Europe.* Cambridge: Cambridge University Press.

Gayton, W. F., Cielinski, K. L., Francis-Keniston, W. J., & Hearns, J. F. (1989). Effects of preshot routine on free throw shooting. *Perceptual and Motor Skills, 68,* 317–318.

Geary, D. C. (2005). *The origin of mind.* Washington, DC: American Psychological Association.

Geers, A. L., Helfer, S. G., Weiland, P. E., & Kosbab, K. (2006). Expectations and placebo response: A laboratory investigation into the role of somatic focus. *Journal of Behavioral Medicine, 29,* 171–178.

Gelman, S. A. (2003). *The essential child: Origins of essentialism in everyday life.* New York: Oxford University Press.

Gelman, S. A., & Kremer, K. E. (1991). Understanding natural cause: Children's explanations of how objects and their properties originate. *Child Development, 62,* 396–414.

Gergely, G., & Csibra, G. (2003). Teleological reasoning in infancy: The naive theory of rational action. *Trends in Cognitive Science, 7,* 287–292.

Gill, R., Hadaway, C. K., & Marler, P. L. (1998). Is religious belief declining in Britain? *Journal for the Scientific Study of Religion, 37,* 507–516.

Gintis, H. (2000). Strong reciprocity and human sociality. *Journal of Theoretical Biology, 206,* 169–179.

Glaser, R., Rabin, B., Chesney, M., Cohen, S., & Natelson, B. (1999). Stress-induced immunomodulation: Implications for infectious disease? *Journal of the American Medical Association, 281,* 2268–2270.

Glass, T. A., Mendes de Leon, C., Marottoli, M. A., & Berkman, I. F. (1999). Population based study of social and productive activities as predictors of survival among elderly Americans. *British Medical Journal, 319,* 478–485.

Glucklich, A. (2001). *Sacred pain.* New York: Oxford University Press.

Goldfried, J., & Miner, M. (2002). Quest religion and the problem of limited compassion. *Journal for the Scientific Study of Religion, 41,* 685–695.

Goldman, N., Korenman, S., & Weinstein, R. (1995). Marital status and health among the elderly. *Social Science and Medicine, 40*, 1717–1730.

Goleman, D. (1997). *Emotional intelligence*. New York: Bantam Books.

Goodall, J. (1971). *In the shadow of man*. Boston: Houghton Mifflin.

Goodall, J. (1986). *The chimpanzees of Gombe*. Cambridge, MA: Harvard University Press.

Goodall, J. (1992). Unusual violence in the overthrow of an alpha male chimpanzee at Gombe. In T. Nishida et al. (Eds.), *Topics in primatology, vol. 1: Human origins* (pp. 131–142). Tokyo: University of Tokyo Press.

Goodenough, U. (1998). *The sacred depths of nature*. Oxford: Oxford University Press.

Gorsuch, R. L., & Hao, J. Y. (1993). Forgiveness: An exploratory factor analysis and its relationship to religious variables. *Review of Religious Research, 34*, 333–347.

Gottschalk, P., & Spolaore, E. (2002). On the evaluation of economic mobility. *Review of Economic Studies, 69*, 191–208.

Gould, S. J. (1999). *Rocks of ages: Science and religion in the fullness of life*. New York: Ballantine.

Gowlett, J. A. J. (1992). Tools—the Paleolithic record. In S. Jones, R. Martin, & D. Pilbeam (Eds.), *The Cambridge encyclopedia of human evolution* (pp. 350–360). Cambridge: Cambridge University Press.

Granqvist, P. (1998). Religiousness and perceived childhood attachment: On the question of compensation or correspondence. *Journal for the Scientific Study of Religion, 37*, 350–367.

Granqvist, P., & Hagekull, B. (1999). Religiousness and perceived childhood attachment: Profiling socialized correspondence and emotional compensation. *Journal for the Scientific Study of Religion, 38*, 254–273.

Gray, J. R., Chabris, C. F., & Braver, T. S. (2003). Neural mechanisms of general fluid intelligence. *Nature Neuroscience, 6*, 316–322.

Grayson, D. K., & Delpech, F. (2003). Ungulates and the Middle-to-Upper Paleolithic transition at Grotte, XVI (Dordogne, France). *Journal of Archaeological Science, 30*, 1633–1648.

Greeley, A. (1981). *The religious imagination*. New York: Sadler.

Greeley, A. (1992). Religion in Britain, Ireland, and the USA. In G. Prior & B. Taylor (Eds.), *British social attitudes: The 9th report* (pp. 51–70). Aldershot: Dartmouth.

Greeley, A. (1995). The good old days. In A. Greeley (Ed.), *Sociology and Religion* (pp. 256–276). New York: HarperCollins.

Green, B. (1998). *The elegant universe*. New York: Norton.

Greenfield, P. M., & Savage-Rumbaugh, E. S. (1990). Grammatical combination in *Pan paniscus*: Processes of learning and invention in the evolution and development of language. In S. T. Parker & K. R. Gibson (Eds.), *Language and intelligence in monkeys and apes* (pp. 540–578). Cambridge: Cambridge University Press.

Greenspan, S. I., & Shanker, S. G. (2004). *The first idea: How symbols, language, and intelligence evolved from our primate ancestors to modern humans*. Cambridge, MA: DaCapo Press.

Grevert, P., Albert, L. H., & Goldstein, A. (1983). Partial antagonism of placebo analgesia by naloxone. *Pain, 16*, 129–143.

Gruber, J. H. (2005). Religious market structure, religious participation, and outcomes: Is religion good for you? *Advances in Economic Analysis and Policy, 5,* article 5. Retrieved February 12, 2007, from www.bepress.com/bejeap/advances/vol5/iss1/art5.

Gubser, N. J. (1965). *The Nunamiut Eskimos: Hunters of caribou.* New Haven, CT: Yale University Press.

Guenther, M. (1999). From totemism to shamanism: Hunter-gatherer contributions to world mythology and spirituality. In R. B. Lee & R. Daly (Eds.), *Cambridge encyclopedia of hunters and gatherers* (pp. 426–433). Cambridge: Cambridge University Press.

Gurerk, O., Irlenbusch, B., & Rockenbach, B. (2006). The competitive advantage of sanctioning institutions. *Science, 312,* 108–111.

Gurven, M., Allen-Arave, W., Hill, K., & Hurtado, M. (2000). It's a wonderful life: Signally generosity among the ache of Paraguay. *Evolution and Human Behavior, 21,* 263–282.

Guthrie, R. D. (2005). *The nature of Paleolithic art.* Chicago: University of Chicago Press.

Guthrie, S. (1993). *Faces in the clouds: A new theory of religion.* New York: Oxford University Press.

Guttman, J. (1984). Cognitive morality and cheating behavior in religious and secular school children. *Journal of Educational Research, 77,* 249–254.

Haidle, M. N. (2009). How to think a spear. In S. A. de Beaune, F. L. Coolidge & T. Wynn (Eds.), *Cognitive archaeology and human evolution* (pp. 57–74). Cambridge: Cambridge University Press.

Haidt, J., & Bjorklund, F. (in press). Social intuitionists answer six questions about morality. In W. Sinnott-Armstrong (Ed.), *Moral psychology.* Oxford: Oxford University Press.

Haidt, J., & Graham, J. (2006). When morality opposes justice: Conservatives have moral intuitions that liberals may not recognize. *Social Justice Research, 20,* 98–116.

Haidt, J., & Joseph, C. (2004). Intuitive ethics: How innately prepared intuitions generate culturally variable virtues. *Daedalus, Fall,* 55–66.

Halifax, J. (1982). *Shaman: The wounded healer.* London: Thames and Hudson.

Hallowell, A. I. (1975). Ojibwa ontology, behavior, and world view. In D. Tedlock & B. Tedlock (Eds.), *Teachings from the American earth* (pp. 141–178). New York: Liveright.

Hamilton, W. D. (1964). The genetical evolution of social behavior, I and II. *Journal of Theoretical Biology, 7,* 1–52.

Hamlin, J. K., Wynn, K., & Bloom, P. (2007). Social evaluation by preverbal infants *Nature, 450,* 557–559.

Harding, J. R. (1976). Certain Upper Paleolithic "Venus" statuettes considered in relation to the pathological condition known as massive hypertrophy of the breasts. *Man, 11,* 271–272.

Hardman, C. E. (2000). Rites of passage among the Lohorung Rai of East Nepal. In G. Harvey (Ed.), *Indigenous religions* (pp. 204–218). London: Cassell.

Hardman, C. E. (2004). Emotions and ancestors: Understanding the experiences of Lohorung Rai in Nepal. In J. Corrigan (Ed.), *Religion and emotion* (pp. 327–349). Oxford: Oxford University Press.

Harlow, H. F., & Zimmerman, R. R. (1959). Affectional responses in the infant monkey. *Science, 130*, 421–432.

Harris, K. R., Danoff-Friedlander, B., Saddler, B., Frizzelle, R., & Graham, S. (2005). Self-monitoring of attention versus self-monitoring of academic performance: Effects among students with ADHD in the general education classroom. *Journal of Special Education, 39*, 145–156.

Harris, P. L. (2000). *The work of the imagination*. London: Blackwell.

Harris, P. L., German, T., & Mills, P. (1996). Children's use of counterfactual thinking in causal reasoning. *Cognition, 61*, 233–259.

Harris, P. L., & Nunez, M. (1996). Understanding of permission rules by preschool children. *Child Development, 67*, 1572–1591.

Harris, S. (2007). *Letter to a Christian nation*. New York: Knopf.

Harrold, F. B. (1980). A comparative analysis of Eurasian Paleolithic burials. *World Archaeology, 12*, 195–211.

Harvey, G. (2000). *Indigenous religions*. London: Cassell.

Haught, J. F. (2003). *Deeper than Darwin*. Boulder, CO: Westview.

Haught, J. F. (2008). *God and the new atheism*. Louisville, KY: Westminster John Knox Press.

Hauser, M. D. (2006). *Moral minds*. New York: HarperCollins.

Haviland, J. M., & Lelwica, M. (1987). The induced affect response: 10-week-old infants' responses to three emotional expressions. *Developmental Psychology, 23*, 97–104.

Hawkes, K., & Bird, R. B. (2002). Showing off, handicap signaling, and the evolution of men's work. *Evolutionary Anthropology, 11*, 58–67.

Hawkes, T. (1932). *Structuralism and semiotics*. Berkeley: University of California Press.

Hayden, B. (2003). *Shamans, sorcerers and saints: A prehistory of religion*. Washington, DC: Smithsonian Institution Books.

Hazan, C., & Zeifman, D. (1999). Pair bonds as attachments: Evaluating the evidence. In J. Cassidy & P. R. Shaver (Eds.), *Handbook of attachment: Theory, research, and clinical applications* (pp. 336–354). New York: Guilford Press.

Headey, B., Grabka, M., Kelley, J., et al. (2002). Pet ownership is good for your health and saves public expenditure too: Australian and German longitudinal evidence. *Australian Social Monitor, 4*, 93–99.

Henrich, J., Boyd, R., Bowles, S., Camerer, C., Fehr, E., Gintis, H., et al. (2001). In search of Homo economicus: Behavioral experiments in 15 small-scale societies. *American Economic Review, 91*, 73–78.

Henrich, J., McElreath, R., Barr, A., Ensminger, J., Barrett, C., Bolyanatz, A., et al. (2006). Costly punishment across human societies. *Science, 312*, 1767–1770.

Henrich, N., & Henrich, J. (2007). *Why humans cooperate*. Oxford: Oxford University Press.

Henshilwood, C., d'Errico, F., Vanhaeren, M., van Niekerk, K., & Jacobs, Z. (2004). Middle Stone Age shell beads from South Africa. *Nature, 304*, 404.

Henshilwood, C. S., d'Errico, F., Yates, R., Jacobs, Z., Tribolo, C., Duller, G. A. T., Mercier, N., Sealy, J. C., Valladas, H., Watts, I., & Wintle, A. G. (2002). Emergence of modern human behavior: Middle Stone Age engravings from South Africa. *Nature, 295*, 1278–1279.

Henshilwood, C. S., & Marean, C. W. (2003). The origin of modern human behavior: A critique of the models and their test implications. *Current Anthropology, 44*, 627–651.

Henshilwood, C. S., & Sealy, J. C. (1997). Bone artifacts from the Middle Stone Age at Blombos Cave, southern Cape, South Africa. *Current Anthropology, 38*, 890–895.

Hester, R., Murphy, K., & Garavan, H. (2004). Beyond common resources: The cortical basis for resolving task interference. *NeuroImage, 23*, 202–212.

Heyes, C. M. (1998). Theory of mind in nonhuman primates. *Behavioral and Brain Sciences, 21*, 101–148.

Hiebert, P. G. (1992). Conversion in Hinduism and Buddhism. In H. N. Malony & S. Southard (Eds.), *Handbook of religious conversion* (pp. 9–21). Birmingham, AL: Religious Education Press.

Hill, P. C. (2005). Measurement in the psychology of religion and spirituality. In R. F. Paloutzian & C. L. Park (Eds.), *Handbook of psychology of religion and spirituality* (pp. 43–61). New York: Guilford Press.

Hill, P. C., & Hall, T. W. (2002). Relational schemas in processing one's image of God and self. *Journal of Psychology and Christianity, 21*, 365–373.

Hinde, R. A. (1999). *Why gods persist*. London: Routledge.

Hirschfeld, L. A., & Gelman, S. A. (1999). How biological is essentialism? In D. L. Medin & S. Atran (Eds.), *Folkbiology* (pp. 403–446). Cambridge, MA: MIT Press.

Hitchens, C. (2007). *God is not great: How religion poisons everything*. New York: Twelve Books, Hachette Book Group.

Hobson, P. (2004). *The cradle of thought*. Oxford: Oxford University Press.

Hodges, S. D., Humphreys, S. C., & Eck, J. C. (2002). Effects of spirituality on successful recovery from spinal surgery. *Southern Medical Journal, 95*, 1381–1384.

Hoffecker, J. F. (2002). *Desolate landscapes: Ice-Age settlement in Europe*. New Brunswick, NJ: Rutgers University Press.

Hoffman, E., McCabe, K., & Smith, V. L. (1996). Social distance and other-regarding behavior in dictator games. *American Economic Review, 86*, 653–656.

Hogg, G. (1966). *Cannibalism and human sacrifice*. New York: Citadel Press.

Hood, R. W., Jr., Spilka, B., Hunsberger, B., & Gorsuch, R. (1996). *The psychology of religion*. New York: Guilford Press.

Horowitz, M. J. (1964). The imagery of visual hallucinations. *Journal of Nervous and Mental Diseases, 138*, 513–523.

Horton, R. (1960). A definition of religion and its uses. *Journal of the Royal Anthropological Institute of Great Britain and Ireland, 90*, 201–226.

Hoskovec, J., & Svorad, D. (1969). The relationship between human and animal hypnosis. *American Journal of Clinical Hypnosis, 11*, 180–182.

Howells, W. (1948). *The heathens: Primitive man and his religion*. New York: Doubleday.

Howes, C. (1988). Peer interaction of young children. *Monographs of the Society for Research in Child Development, 53*, 1, Serial #217.

Hufford, D. J. (1982). *The terror that comes in the night: An experience-center study of supernatural assault traditions*. Philadelphia: University of Pennsylvania Press.

Hultkrantz, A. (1967). *The religions of the American Indians*. Berkeley: University of California Press.

Hultkrantz, A. (1973). A definition of shamanism. *Temenos, 9*, 25–37.

Hultkrantz, A. (1994). Religion and environment among the Saami. In T. Irimoto & T. Yamada (Eds.), *Circumpolar religion and ecology* (pp. 347–374). Tokyo: University of Tokyo Press.

Hume, L. (2000). The dreaming in contemporary aboriginal Australia. In G. Harvey (Ed.), *Indigenous religions* (pp. 125–138). London: Cassell.

Hummer, R., Rogers, R., Nam, C., & Ellison, C. G. (1999). Religious involvement and U.S. adult mortality. *Demography, 36*, 273–285.

Humphrey, N. K. (1976). The social function of intellect. In M. Bateson & R. A. Hinde (Eds.), *Growing Points in Ethology* (pp. 303–318). Cambridge: Cambridge University Press.

Husserl, E. (1937/1999). *The crisis of European sciences and transcendental phenomenology*. Evanston, IL: Northwestern University Press.

Hutton, R. (1991). *The pagan religions of the ancient British Isles*. Oxford: Blackwell.

Ialongo, N., Poduska, J., Werthamer, L., & Kellam, S. (2001). The distal impact of two first-grade preventive interventions on conduct problems and disorder in early adolescence. *Journal of Emotional and Behavioral Disorders, 9*, 146–160.

Iizuka, T. (1995). *The kingdom of earth and wood: The San'nai Maruyama site*. Japan: Jomon Film Production Company.

Ingman, M., Kaessman, H., Paabo, S., & Gyllensten, U. (2000). Mitochondrial genome variation and the origin of modern humans. *Nature, 408*, 708–713.

Ingvar, D. H. (1994). The will of the brain: Cerebral correlates of willful acts. *Journal of Theoretical Biology, 171*, 7–12.

Irons, W. (2001). Religion as a hard-to-fake sign of commitment. In R. M. Nesse (Ed.), *Evolution and the capacity for commitment* (pp. 293–309). New York: Russell Sage Foundation.

Isaac, B. (1992). Throwing. In S. Jones, R. Martin, & D. Pilbeam (Eds.), *The Cambridge encyclopedia of human evolution* (p. 358). Cambridge: Cambridge University Press.

Jablonka, E., & Lamb, M. J. (1995). *Epigenetic inheritance and evolution*. Oxford: Oxford University Press.

Jablonka, E., & Lamb, M. J. (2005). *Evolution in four dimensions*. Cambridge, MA: MIT Press.

Jacobs, Z., Roberts, R. G., Galbraith, R. F., Deacon, H. J., Grun, R., Macay, A., et al. (2008). Ages for the Middle Stone Age of Southern Africa: Implications for human behavior and dispersal. *Science, 322*, 733–735.

James, E. O. (1957). *Prehistoric religion*. New York: Frederick A. Praeger.

James, W. (1896/1956). *The will to believe and other essays in popular philosophy*. New York: Dover.

James, W. (1902). *The varieties of religious experience*. New York: Longmans, Green.

Jang, S. J., & Johnson, B. R. (2001). Neighborhood disorder, individual religiosity and adolescent use of illicit drugs: A test of multilevel hypotheses. *Criminology, 39*, 109–144.

Jefferson, T. (1787/1955). Letter to Peter Carr, August 10. In J. P. Boyd (Ed.), *The papers of Thomas Jefferson* (p. 15). Princeton, NJ: Princeton University Press.

Jeffries, R., Turner, A. Polson, P., & Atwood, M. (1981). The processes involved in designing software. In J. A. Anderson (Ed.), *Cognitive skills and their acquisition* (pp. 255–284). Hillsdale, NJ: Erlbaum.

Johnson, D. P. (2005). God's punishment and public goods: A test of the supernatural punishment hypothesis in 186 world cultures. *Human Nature, 16,* 410–446.

Johnson, D. P., & Bering, J. M. (2006). Hand of God, mind of man: Punishment and cognition in the evolution of cooperation. *Evolutionary Psychology, 4,* 219–233.

Johnson, D. P., & Kruger, O. (2004). The good of wrath: Supernatural punishment and the evolution of cooperation. *Political Theology, 5,* 159–176.

Johnson, P. E. (1991). *Darwin on trial.* Washington, DC: Regnery Gateway.

Johnson, S. C. (2000). The recognition of mentalistic agents in infancy. *Trends in Cognitive Science, 4,* 22–28.

Johnson, S. C. (2003). Detecting agents. *Philosophical Transactions of the Royal Society of London, B, 358,* 549–559.

Jolly, A. (1966). Lemur social behaviour and primate intelligence. *Science, 153,* 501–506.

Jolly, C., & White, R. (1995). *Physical anthropology and archaeology.* New York: McGraw-Hill.

Jones, P. (1979). The effects of raw material on biface manufacture. *Science, 204,* 815–816.

Jorgensen, J. G. (1980). *Western Indians. Comparative environments, languages, and cultures of 172 western American Indian tribes.* San Francisco: W. H. Freeman.

Jose, P. E. (1990). Just world reasoning in children's imminent justice judgments. *Child Development, 61,* 1024–1033.

Joyce, R. (2006). *The evolution of morality.* Cambridge, MA: MIT Press.

Jubis, R. (1991). *An attachment-theoretical approach to understanding children's conceptions of God.* PhD diss., University of Denver, Denver, CO.

Kahoe, R. D. (1974). Personality and achievement correlates of intrinsic and extrinsic religious orientations. *Journal of Personality and Social Psychology, 29,* 812–818.

Kane, M. J., & Engle, R. W. (2002). The role of prefrontal cortex in working-memory capacity, executive attention, and general fluid intelligence: An individual-differences perspective. *Psychonomic Bulletin & Review 9,* 637–671.

Kapogiannis, D., Barbey, A. K., Su, M., Zamboni, G., Krueger, F., & Grafman, J. (2009). Cognitive and neural foundations of religious belief. *Proceedings of the National Academy of Science,* www.pnas.org_cgi_doi_10.1073_pnas.0811717106 (accessed 5/11/09).

Kark, J. D., Shemi, G., Friedlander, Y., Martin, O., Manor, O., & Blondheim, M. D. (1996). Does religious observance promote health? Mortality in secular vs. religious kibbutzim in Israel. *American Journal of Public Health, 86,* 341–346.

Kater, M. H. (1989). *Doctors under Hitler.* Chapel Hill: University of North Carolina Press.

Katz, R. (1982). *Boiling energy: Community healing among the Kalahari !Kung.* Cambridge, MA: Harvard University Press.

Kauffman, S. (1995). *At home in the universe.* Oxford: Oxford University Press.

Kaufmann, E. (2007). Shall the religious inherit the earth? *Jewish Quarterly, Autumn.* Available at www.sneps.net/uploadsepk/JQR%20Demography.pdf (accessed 5/21/09).

Ke, Y., Su, B., Song, X., Lu, D., Chen, L., Li, H., et al. (2001). African origin of modern humans in East Asia: A tale of 12,000 Y chromosomes. *Science, 292,* 1151–1153.

Keeley, L. (1978). Preliminary microwear analysis of the Me assemblages. In F. Van Noten (Ed.), *Les Chasseurs de Meer* (pp. 73–86). Brugge: De Temple.

Keeley, L. (1980). *Experimental determination of stone tool use: A microwear analysis.* Chicago: University of Chicago Press.

Keeley, L. H. (1996). *War before civilization.* Oxford: Oxford University Press.

Keesing, R. (1982). *Kwaio religion: The living and the dead in a Solomon Island society.* New York: Columbia University Press.

Kelemen, D. (1999a). The scope of teleological thinking in preschool children. *Cognition, 70,* 241–272.

Kelemen, D. (1999b). Why are rocks pointy? Children's preference for teleological explanations of the natural world. *Developmental Psychology, 35,* 1440–1453.

Kelemen, D. (1999c). Beliefs about purpose: On the origins of teleological thought. In M. C. Corballis & S. E. G. Lea (Eds.), *The descent of mind* (pp. 278–294). Oxford: Oxford University Press.

Kelemen, D. (2004). Are children "intuitive theists"? Reasoning about purpose and design in nature. *Psychological Science, 15,* 295–301.

Kelemen, D., & DiYanni, C. (2005). Intuitions about origins: Purpose and intelligence in children's reasoning about nature. *Journal of Cognition and Development, 6,* 3–31.

Keller, H., Scholmerich, A., & Eibl-Eibesfeldt, I. (1988). Communication patterns in adult-infant interactions in Western and non-Western cultures. *Journal of Cross-Cultural Psychology 19,* 427–445.

Kelly, A. M., Hester, R., Foxe, J. J., Shpaner, M., & Garavan, H. (2006). Flexible cognitive control: Effects of individual differences and brief practice on a complex cognitive task. *NeuroImage, 31,* 866–886.

Kelly, M., & Keil, F. (1985). The more things change. . . : Metamorphoses and conceptual structure. *Cognitive Science, 9,* 403–416.

Kelly, R. C. (1985). *The Nuer conquest: The structure and development of an expansionist system.* Ann Arbor: University of Michigan Press.

Kelly, R. L. (1995). *The foraging spectrum: Diversity in hunter-gatherer lifeways.* Washington, DC: Smithsonian Institution Press.

Kessin, R. H., & van Lookeren Campagne, M. M. (1992). The development of a social amoeba. *American Scientist, 80,* 556–565.

Keverne, E. B., Martinez, N. D., & Tuite, B. (1989). Beta-endorphin concentrations in cerebrospinal fluid of moneys influenced by grooming relationships. *Psychoneuroendocrinology, 14,* 155–161.

Kiecolt-Glaser, J. K., Garner, W., & Spelcher, C. (1984). Psychosocial modifiers immunocompetence in medical students. *Psychosomatic Medicine, 46,* 7–14.

Kim, J., Lee, H. M., Kim, W. J., Park, H. J., Kim, S. W., Moon, D. H., et al. (2008). Neural correlates of pre-performance routines in expert and novice archers. *Neuroscience Letters, 445,* 236–241.

King, B. J. (2007). *Evolving God: A provocative view on the origins of religion*. New York: Doubleday.

Kirkpatrick, L. (1992). Religious motivation and function conceptualized from an interpersonal relationships perspective. Paper presented at the annual convention of the American Psychological Association, Washington, DC, August.

Kirkpatrick, L. (1997). A longitudinal study of changes in religious belief and behavior as a function of individual differences in adult attachment style. *Journal for the Scientific Study of Religion, 36*, 207–217.

Kirkpatrick, L. (1998). God as a substitute attachment figure. *Personality and Social Psychology Bulletin, 24*, 961–973.

Kirkpatrick, L. A. (2005a). *Attachment, evolution, and the psychology of religion*. New York: Guilford Press.

Kirkpatrick, L. A. (2005b). Evolutionary psychology: An emerging new foundation for the psychology of religion. In R. F. Paloutzian & C. L. Park (Eds.), *Handbook of the psychology of religion and spirituality* (pp. 101–119). New York: Guilford Press.

Kirkpatrick, L. A. (2006). Religion is not an adaptation. In P. M. McNamara (Ed.), *Where God and science meet, Vol. 1* (pp. 159–179). Westport, CT: Praeger.

Kirkpatrick, L. A., & Hood, R. W. (1990). Intrinsic-Extrinsic religious orientation: The boon or bane of contemporary psychology of religion? *Journal for the Scientific Study of Religion, 29*, 442–462.

Kirkpatrick, L. A., & Shaver, P. R. (1990). Attachment theory and religion: Childhood attachments, religious beliefs, and conversion. *Journal for the Scientific Study of Religion, 29*, 315–334.

Kirkpatrick, L. A., & Shaver, P. R. (1992). An attachment-theoretical approach to romantic love and religious belief. *Personality and Social Psychology Bulletin, 18*, 266–275.

Kirschner, M. W., & Gerhart, J. C. (2005). *The plausibility of life*. New Haven, CT: Yale University Press.

Kleck, R. E., Vaughn, R. C., Cartwright-Smith, J., Vaughn, K. B., Colby, C. Z., & Lanzetta, J. T. (1976). Effects of being observed on expressive, subjective, and physiological responses to painful stimuli. *Journal of Personality and Social Psychology, 43*, 1211–1218.

Klein, R. G. (1995). Anatomy, behavior, and modern human origins. *Journal of World Prehistory, 9*, 167–198.

Klein, R. G., & Edgar, B. (2002). *The dawn of human culture*. New York: John Wiley & Sons.

Klima, B. (1988). A triple burial from the upper Paleolithic of Dolni Vestonice, Czechoslovakia. *Journal of Human Evolution, 16*, 831–835.

Kluver, H. (1942). Mechanisms of hallucinations. In Q. McNemar & M. A. Merrill (Eds.), *Studies in personality* (pp. 175–207). New York: McGraw-Hill.

Knight, C. D., Power, C., & Watts, I. (1995). The human symbolic revolution: A Darwinian account. *Cambridge Archaeological Journal, 5*, 75–114.

Knight, N. (2008). Yukatek Maya children's attributions of belief to natural and non-natural entities. *Journal of Cognition and Culture, 8*, 235–243.

Knight, N., Sousa, P., Barrett, J., & Atran, S. (2004). Children's attributions of beliefs to humans and God: Cross-cultural evidence. *Cognitive Science, 28*, 117–126.

Knoch, D., & Fehr, E. (2007). Resisting the power of temptations: The right prefrontal cortex and self-control. *Annals of the New York Academy of Science, 1104*, 123–134.

Koenig, H. G. (2001). The connection between psychoneuroimmunology and religion. In H. G. Koenig & H. J. Cohen (Eds.), *The link between religion and health: Psychoneuroimmunology and the faith factor* (pp. 11–30). New York: Oxford University Press.

Koenig, H. G., & Cohen, H. J. (2001a). *The link between religion and health: Psychoneuroimmunology and the faith factor*: Oxford: Oxford University Press.

Koenig, H. G., & Cohen, H. J. (2001b). Psychosocial factors, immunity, and wound healing. In H. G. Koenig & H. J. Cohen (Eds.), *The link between religion and health: Psychoneuroimmunology and the faith factor* (pp. 124–138). New York: Oxford University Press.

Koenig, H. G., Cohen, H. J., Blazer, D. G., Pieper, C., Meador, K. G., Shelp, F., et al. (1992). Religious coping and depression in elderly hospitalized medically ill men. *American Journal of Psychiatry, 149*, 1693–1700.

Koenig, H. G., George, L. K., & Peterson, B. L. (1998). Religiosity and remission from depression in medically ill older patients. *American Journal of Psychiatry, 155*, 536–542.

Koenig, H. G., Hays, J. C., Larson, D. B., George, I. K., Cohen, H. J., McCullough, M., et al. (1999). Does religious attendance prolong survival? A six-year follow-up study of 3,968 older adults. *Journal of Gerontology, 54A*, M370–M377.

Koenig, H. G., McCullough, M. E., & Larson, D. B. (2001). *Handbook of religion and health*. Oxford: Oxford University Press.

Koenig, L. B., McGue, M., Krueger, R. F., & Bouchard, T. J., Jr. (2007). Religiousness, antisocial behavior, and altruism: Genetic and environmental mediation. *Journal of Personality, 75*, 265–290.

Kogan, N., & Carter, A. S. (1996). Mother-infant re-engagement following the still-face: The role of maternal availability in infant affect regulation. *Infant Behaviour and Development, 19*, 359–370.

Kohler, W. (1927). *The mentality of apes*. New York: Harcourt Brace.

Kohn, M., & Mithen, S. (1999). Handaxes: Products of sexual selection? *Antiquity, 73*, 518–526.

Krebs, D. (2005). The evolution of morality. In D. M. Buss (Ed.), *The handbook of evolutionary psychology* (pp. 747–771). New York: Wiley.

Krol, J. (1982). Young people's image of father and its influence on their image of God [English translation]. *Roczniki Filozoficzne: Psychologia, 30*, 73–103.

Kropotkin, P. (1902). *Mutual aid: A factor in evolution*. London: Allen Lane.

Kugiumutzakis, G. (1988). Neonatal imitation in the intersubjective companion space. In S. Braten (Ed.), *Intersubjective communication and emotion in early ontogeny* (pp. 63–88). Cambridge: Cambridge University Press.

Kuhlmeier, V. A., Bloom, P., & Wynn, K. (2004). Do 5-month-old infants see humans as material objects? *Cognition, 94*, 95–103.

Kuhn, S. L., & Stiner, M. C. (2007). Paleolithic ornaments: Implications for cognition, demography, and identity. *Diogenes, 214*, 40–48.

Kuper, H. (1961). *An African aristocracy: Rank among the Swazi*. Oxford: Oxford University Press.

Lalonde, C. E., & Chandler, M. J. (1995). False belief understanding goes to school: On the social-emotional consequences of coming early or late to a first theory of mind. *Cognition and Emotion, 9*, 167–185.

Lamb, K. L., & Burwitz, L. (1988). Visual restriction in ball-catching: A re-examination of earlier findings. *Journal of Human Movement Studies, 14*, 93–99.

Lambert, W. W., Triandis, L. M., & Wolf, M. (1959). Some correlates of beliefs in the malevolence and benevolence of supernatural beings: A cross-societal study. *Journal of Abnormal and Social Psychology, 58*, 162–169.

Lambert, Y. (1989). From parish to transcendent humanism in France. In J. A. Beckford & T. Luckmann (Eds.), *The changing face of religion* (pp. 49–63). Newbury Park, CA: Sage Publications.

Langley, M. C., Clarkson, C., & Ulm, S. (2008). Behavioural complexity in Eurasian Neanderthal populations: A chronological examination of the archaeological evidence. *Cambridge Archaeological Journal, 18*, 289–307.

Lansing, J. S. (1991). *Priests and programmers: Technologies of power in the engineered landscape of Bali*. Princeton, NJ: Princeton University Press.

Larsson, L. (1987–1988). A construction for ceremonial activities from the late Mesolithic. *Archaeological Institute Papers 7*. Lund: University of Lund.

Larsson, M. (1985–1986). Bredasten: An early ertelolle site with a dwelling structure in South Scania. *Archaeological Institute Papers 6*. Lund: University of Lund.

Lawson, E. T., & McCauley, R. (1990). *Rethinking religion: Connecting culture and cognition*. Cambridge: Cambridge University Press.

Lazar, S. W., Bush, G., Gollub, R. L., Fricchione, G. L., Khalsa, G., & Benson, H. (2000). Functional brain mapping of the relaxation response and meditation. *NeuroReport, 11*, 1581–1585.

Lazar, S. W., Kerr, C. E., Wasserman, R. W., Gray, J. R., Greve, D. N., Treadway, M. T., et al. (2005). Meditation experience is associated with increased cortical thickness. *NeuroReport, 16*, 1893–1897.

Lee, R. B. (1979). *The !Kung San: Men, women, and work in a foraging society*. Cambridge: Cambridge University Press.

Lee, R. B., & Daly, R. (1999). Introduction: Foragers and others. In R. B. Lee & R. Daly (Eds.), *The Cambridge encyclopedia of hunters and gatherers* (pp. 1–22). Cambridge: Cambridge University Press.

Leevers, H. J., & Harris, P. L. (1999). Persisting effects of instruction on young children's syllogistic reasoning with incongruent and abstract premises. *Thinking and Reasoning, 5*, 145–173.

Leevers, H. J., & Harris, P. L. (2000). Counterfactual syllogistic reasoning in normal 4-year-olds, children with learning disabilities, and children with autism. *Journal of Experimental Child Psychology, 76*, 64–87.

Lehmann, A. C., & Ericsson, K. A. (1997). Expert pianists' mental representations: Evidence from successful adaptation to unexpected performance demands. *Proceedings of the Third Triennial ESCOM Conference* (pp. 165–169). Uppsala, Sweden: SLU Service/Reproenhenten.

Leroi-Gourhan, A. (1968). The evolution of paleolithic art. *Scientific American, 218*, 58–70.

Levenson, R. W. (2003). Blood, sweat, and fears: The autonomic architecture of emotion. In P. Ekman, J. J. Campos, R. J. Davidson, & F. B. M. de Waal (Eds.), *Emotions inside out* (pp. 348–366). New York: New York Academy of Sciences.

Levine, J. D., Gordon, N. C., & Fields, H. L. (1978). The mechanisms of placebo analgesia. *Lancet, 2,* 654–657.

Lewis-Williams, J. D. (1982). The economic and social context of southern San rock art. *Current Anthropology, 23,* 429–449.

Lewis-Williams, J. D. (1986). Cognitive and optical illusions in San rock art. *Current Anthropology, 27,* 171–177.

Lewis-Williams, J. D. (2002). *The mind in the cave.* London: Thames & Hudson.

Lewis-Williams, J. D., & Dowson, T. (1988). The signs of the times: Entoptic phenomena in Upper Paleolithic art. *Current Anthropology, 29,* 201–245.

Lidor, R., & Singer, R. N. (2000). Teaching preperformance routines to beginners. *Journal of Physical Education, Recreation, & Dance, 71,* 34–36.

Lieberman, M. D., Hariri, A., Jarcho, J. M., Eisenberger, N. I., & Brookheimer, S. Y. (2005). An fMRI investigation of race-related amygdala activity in African-American and Caucasian-American individuals. *Nature Neuroscience, 8,* 720–722.

Lillard, L. A., & Waite, L. J. (1995). "Til death do us part": Marital disruption and mortality. *American Journal of Sociology, 100,* 1131–1156.

Linberg, D. C. (1986). Science and the early church. In D. C. Lindberg & R. L. Numbers (Eds.), *God and nature: Historical essays on the encounter between Christianity and science* (pp. 19–48). Berkeley: University of California Press.

Linde, K., Witt, C. M., Streng, A., Weidenhammer, W., Wagenpfeil, S. et al. (2007). The impact of patient expectations on outcomes in four randomized controlled trials of acupuncture in patients with chronic pain. *Pain, 128,* 264–271.

Lobmeyer, D. L., & Wasserman, E. A. (1986). Preliminaries to free throw shooting: Superstitious behavior? *Journal of Sports Behavior, 9,* 70–78.

Lohmann, R. I. (2003). Turning in the belly: Insights on religious conversion from New Guinea gut feelings. In A. Buckser & S. D. Glazier (Eds.), *The anthropology of religious conversion* (pp. 109–121). New York: Rowman and Littlefield.

Lommel, A. (1967). *Shamanism: The beginning of art.* New York: McGraw-Hill.

Longman, P. (2004). *The empty cradle.* New York: Basic Books.

Lonsdale, C., & Tam, J. T. M. (2007). On the temporal and behavioural consistency of pre-performance routines: An intra-individual analysis of elite basketball players' free throw shooting accuracy. *Journal of Sports Sciences, 26,* 259–266.

Looft, W. R., & Bartz, H. (1969). Animism revisited. *Psychological Bulletin, 7,* 1–19.

Loprinzi, C. I., Laurie, J. A., Wieand, H. S., Krook, J. F., Novotny, P. J., Kugler, J. W., et al. (1994). Prospective evaluation of prognostic variables from patient-completed questionnaires. North Central Cancer Treatment Group. *Journal of Clinical Oncology, 12,* 601–607.

Lorblancher, M. (1999). *La Naissance de L'Art.* Paris: Editions Errance.

Lou, H. C., Kjaer, T. W., Friberg, L., Wildschiodtz, G., Holm, S., & Nowak, M. (1999). A 15O-H2o PET study of meditation and the resting state of normal consciousness. *Human Brain Mapping, 7,* 98–105.

Lowie, R. H. (1963). *Indians of the plains*. New York: American Museum of Natural History.

Lutkehaus, N. C., & Roscoe, P. B. (1995). *Gender rituals: Female initiation in Melanesia*. London: Routledge.

Lutz, A., Greischar, L. L., Rawlings, N. B., Ricard, M., & Davidson, R. J. (2004). Long-term meditators self-induce high-amplitude gamma synchrony during mental practice. *Proceedings of the National Academy of Sciences, 101*, 16369–16373.

Mac Hovec, F. J. (1975). Hypnosis before Mesmer. *American Journal of Clinical Hypnosis, 17*, 215–220.

Mahoney, A., Pargament, K. I., Jewell, T., Swank, A. B., Scott, E., Emery, E., & Rye, M. (1999). Marriage and the spiritual realm: The role of proximal and distal religious constructs in marital functioning. *Journal of Family Psychology, 13*, 1–18.

Mahoney, A., Pargament, K. I., Tarakeshwar, N., & Swank, A. (2001). Religion in the home in the '80s and '90s: A meta-analytic review and conceptual analysis of religion, marriage, and parenting. *Journal of Family Psychology, 15*, 559–596.

Mahoney, A., & Tarakeshwar, N. (2005). Religion's role in marriage and parenting in daily life and during family crises. In R. F. Paloutzian & C. L. Park (Eds.), *Handbook of the psychology of religion and spirituality* (pp. 177–195). New York: Guilford Press.

Majno, G. (1975). *The healing hand: Man and wound in the ancient world*. Cambridge: Cambridge University Press.

Malcolm, J. R., & Marten, K. (1982). Natural selection and the communal rearing of pups in African wild dogs (*Lycaon pictus*). *Behavioral Ecology and Sociobiology, 10*, 1–13.

Mandell, A. (1980). Toward a psychobiology of transcendence: God in the brain. In D. Davidson & R. Davidson (Eds.), *The psychobiology of consciousness* (pp. 379–464). New York: Plenum Press.

Mar, R. A., Oatley, K., Hirsh, J., dela Paz, J., & Peterson, J. B. (2006). Bookworms versus nerds: Exposure to fiction versus non-fiction, divergent associations with social ability, and the simulation of fictional social worlds. *Journal of Research in Personality, 40*, 694–712.

Margolis, C. L., Domangue, B. B., Ehleben, C., & Shrier, L. (1983). Hypnosis and the early treatment of burns: A pilot study. *American Journal of Clinical Hypnosis, 26*, 9–15.

Markman, E. M., & Hutchinson, J. E. (1984). Children's sensitivity to constraints on word meaning: Taxonomic vs. thematic relations. *Cognitive Psychology, 16*, 1–27.

Marks, S. A. (1976). *Large mammals and brave people: Subsistence hunters in Zambia*. Seattle: University of Washington Press.

Marschack, A. (1981). On Paleolithic ochre and the early uses of color and symbol. *Current Anthropology, 22*, 188–191.

Marschack, A. (1991). The Tai Plaque and calendrical notation in the Upper Palaeolithic. *Cambridge Archaeological Journal, 1*, 25–61.

Marschack, A. (1997). The Berekhat Ram figurine: A late Acheulian carving from the Middle East. *Antiquity, 71*, 327–337.

Matsuda, H., & Harada, Y. (1990). Evolutionary stable stalk to spore ratio in cellular slime molds and the law of equalization of net incomes. *Journal of Theoretical Biology, 147*, 329–344.

Mauro, J. (1991). *The friend that only I can see: A longitudinal investigation of children's imaginary companions*. PhD diss., University of Oregon.

Mayer, A., & Sharp, H. (1962). Religious preferences and worldly success. *American Sociological Review, 27*, 218–227.

McBrearty, A., & Brooks, A. (2000). The revolution that wasn't: A new interpretation of the origin of modern human behavior. *Journal of Human Evolution, 39*, 453–563.

McBrearty, S. & Tryon, C. (2006). From Acheulean to Middle Stone Age in the Kapthurin formation, Kenya. In E. Hovers & S. L. Kuhn (Eds.), *Transitions before the transition: Evolution and stability in the Middle Paleolithic and Middle Stone Age* (pp. 257–277). New York: Springer.

McCauley, R. N. (2001). Ritual, memory, and emotion: Comparing two cognitive hypotheses. In J. Andresen (Ed.), *Religion in mind* (pp. 115–140). Cambridge: Cambridge University Press.

McCauley, R. N., & Lawson, E. T. (2002). *Bringing ritual to mind: Psychological foundations of cultural forms*. Cambridge: Cambridge University Press.

McClenon, J. (1997). Shamanic healing, human evolution and the origin of religion. *Journal for the Scientific Study of Religion, 36*, 345–354.

McClenon, J. (2000). Content analysis of an anomalous memorate collection: Testing hypotheses regarding universal features. *Sociology of Religion, 61*, 155–169.

McClenon, J. (2002). *Wondrous healing: Shamanism, human evolution and the origin of religion*. DeKalb: Northern Illinois University Press.

McCullough, M. E., Bono, G., & Root, L. M. (2005). Religion and forgiveness. In R. F. Paloutzian & C. L. Park (Eds.), *Handbook of the psychology of religion and spirituality* (pp. 394–411). New York: Guilford Press.

McCullough, M. E., Emmons, R. A., & Tsang, J. (2002). The grateful disposition: A conceptual and empirical topography. *Journal of Personality and Social Psychology, 82*, 112–127.

McCullough, M. E., Kilpatrick, S. D., Emmons, R. A., & Larson, D. B. (2001). Is gratitude a moral affect? *Psychological Bulletin, 127*, 249–266.

McCullough, M. E., & Willoughby, B. L. B. (2009). Religion, self-regulation, and self-control: Associations, explanations, and implications. *Psychological Bulletin, 135*, 69–93.

McCullough, M. E., & Worthington, E. L., Jr. (1999). Religion and the forgiving personality. *Journal of Personality, 67*, 1142–1164.

McDermott, F., Stringer, C., Grun, R., Williams, C. T., Din, V., & Hawkesworth, C. (1996). New late Pleistocene uraniumthorium and ESR dates for the Singa hominid (Sudan). *Journal of Human Evolution, 31*, 507–516.

McDougall, I., Brown, F. H., & Fleagle, J. G. (2005). Stratigraphic placement and age of modern humans from Kibish, Ethiopia. *Nature, 433*, 733–736.

McGinn, C. (1991). *The problem of consciousness*. Oxford: Oxford University Press.

McGrath, A. (2005). *Dawkins' God*. London: Blackwell.

McGrath, A. (2007). *The Dawkins delusion*. London: SPCK.

McGrath, A., & McGrath, J. C. (2007). *The Dawkins delusion? Atheist fundamentalism and the denial of the divine*. London: IVP Books.

McLeod, P., & Jenkins, S. (1991). Timing accuracy and decision time in high speed ball games. *International Journal of Sports Psychology, 22*, 279–295.

McNeill, W. (1995). *Keeping together in time: Dance and drill in human history.* Cambridge, MA: Harvard University Press.

McPherron, S. (2000). Handaxes as a measure of the mental capabilities of early hominins. *Journal of Archaeological Science, 27*, 655–663.

McRae, C., Cherin, E., Yamazaki, G., Diem, G., Vo, A. H., et al. (2004). Effects of perceived treatment on quality of life and medical outcomes in a double-blind placebo surgery trial. *Archives of General Psychiatry, 61*, 412–420.

Melis, A. P., Hare, B., & Tomasello, M. (2007). Chimpanzees recruit the best collaborators. *Science, 311*, 1297–1300.

Mellars, P. (1973). The character of the Middle-Upper Paleolithic transition in southwestern France. In C. Renfrew (Ed.), *The explanation of cultural change* (pp. 255–276). London: Duckworth.

Mellars, P. (1996). *The Neanderthal legacy.* Princeton, NJ: Princeton University Press.

Mellars, P. (2006). Why did modern human populations disperse from Africa *ca.* 60,000 years ago? A new model. *Proceedings of the National Academy of Science, 103*, 9381–9386.

Meltzoff, A. N., & Moore, M. K. (1977). Imitation of facial and manual gestures by human neonates. *Science, 198*, 75–78.

Menzel, C. R. (1999). Unprompted recall and reporting of hidden objects by a chimpanzee (*Pan trogolodytes*) after extended delays. *Journal of Comparative Psychology, 113*, 426–434.

Merrill, R. M., Salazar, R. D., & Gardner, N. W. (2001). Relationship between family religiosity and drug use behavior among youth. *Social Behavior and Personality 29*, 347–357.

Milinski, M., & Rockenbach, B. (2007). Spying on others evolves. *Science, 317*, 464–465.

Milinski, M., Semmann, D., & Krambeck, H.-J. (2002). Reputation helps solve the tragedy of the commons. *Nature, 415*, 424–426.

Miller, F. G., & Kaptchuk, T. J. (2008). The power of context: Reconceptualizing the placebo effect. *Journal of the Royal Society of Medicine, 101*, 222–225.

Miller, K. R. (1999). *Finding Darwin's god.* New York: Cliff Street Books.

Miller, W. (1990). *Bloodtaking and peacemaking: Feud, law, and society in Saga Iceland.* Chicago: University of Chicago Press.

Milton, J., Solodkin, A., Hlustik, P., & Small, S. L. (2007). The mind of expert motor performance is cool and focused. *NeuroImage, 35*, 804–813.

Minkel, J. R. (2006). Offerings to a stone snake provide the earliest evidence of religion. *Scientific American* online: www.sciam.com/article.cfm?articleID=3FE89 A86-E7F2-99DF-366D045A5BF3EAB1 (accessed 5/21/07).

Mirsky, J. (1937). The Eskimo of Greenland. In M. Mead (Ed.), *Cooperation and competition among primitive peoples* (pp. 51–86). New York: McGraw-Hill.

Mitchell, J. P. (2008). Contributions of functional neuroimaging to the study of social cognition. *Current Directions in Psychological Science, 17*, 142–146.

Mithen, S. (1996). *A prehistory of the mind.* London: Thames & Hudson.

Mithen, S. (2003). *After the ice: A global human history.* Cambridge, MA: Harvard University Press.

Mithen, S. (2006). *The singing Neanderthals.* Cambridge, MA: Harvard University Press.

Moehlman, P. (1979). Jackal helpers and pup survival. *Nature, 277*, 382–383.

Monsma, S. V. (2007). Religion and philanthropic giving and volunteering: Building blocks for civic responsibility. *Interdisciplinary Journal of Research on Religion, 3*, 2–28.

Morgan, A. H. (1973). The heritability of hypnotic susceptibility in twins. *Journal of Abnormal and Social Psychology, 82*, 55–61.

Morrison, M. A., & Morrison, T. G. (2002). Development and validation of a scale measuring modern prejudice toward gay men and lesbian women. *Journal of Homosexuality, 43*, 15–27.

Morwood, M. J. (2002). *Visions of the past: The archaeology of Australian Aboriginal art*. Washington, DC: Smithsonian Institution Press.

Mulcahy, N. J., & Call, J. (2006). Apes save tools for future use. *Science, 312*, 1038–1040.

Mullet, E., Barros, J., Frongia, L., Usai, V., Neto, F., & Shafihi, S. R. (2003). Religious involvement and the forgiving personality. *Journal of Personality, 71*, 1–19.

Muraven, M., & Baumeister, R. F. (2000). Self-regulation and depletion of limited resources. Does self-control resemble a muscle? *Psychological Bulletin, 126*, 247–259.

Muraven, M., Baumeister, R. F., & Tice, D. M. (1999). Longitudinal improvement of self-regulation through practice: Building self-control strength through repeated exercise. *Journal of Social Psychology, 139*, 446–457.

Muraven, M., & Slessareva, E. (2003). Mechanism of self-control failure: Motivation and limited resources. *Personality and Social Psychology Bulletin, 29*, 894–906.

Murdock, G. P. (1980). *Theories of illness: A world survey*. Pittsburgh, PA: HRAF University of Pittsburgh Press.

Murphy, N., & Ellis, G. (1996). *On the moral nature of the universe*. Minneapolis: Fortress Press.

Myers, D. G. (2000). The funds, friends, and faith of happy people. *American Psychologist, 55*, 56–67.

Myowa, M. (1996). Imitation of facial gestures by an infant chimpanzee. *Primates, 37*, 207–213.

Myowa-Yamakoshi, M., Tomonaga, M., Tanaka, M., & Matsuzawa, T. (2004). Imitation in neonatal chimpanzees (*Pan troglodytes*). *Developmental Science, 7*, 437–442.

Nagy, E., & Molnar, P. (2004). *Homo imitans* or *Homo provocans*? The phenomenon of neonatal imitation. *Infant Behavior and Development, 27*, 57–63.

Naqshbandi, M., & Roberts, W. A. (2006). Anticipation of future events in squirrel monkeys (*Saimiri sciureus*) and rats (*Rattus norvegicus*): Tests of the Bischof-Kohler hypothesis. *Journal of Comparative Psychology, 120*, 345–357.

Nee, D. E., Berman, M. G., Moore, K. S., & Jonides, J. (2008). Neuroscientific evidence about the distinction between short-term and long-term memory. *Current Directions in Psychological Science, 17*, 102–106.

Nelson, R. (1993). Searching for the lost arrow: Physical and spiritual ecology in the hunter's world. In S. R. Kellert & E. O. Wilson (Eds.), *The biophilia hypothesis* (pp. 201–228). Washington, DC: Island Press.

Nemeroff, C., & Rozin, P. (1994). The contagion concept in adult thinking in the United States: Transmission of germ and interpersonal influence. *Ethos: Journal for the Society of Psychological Anthropology, 22,* 158–186.

Newberg, A. B. (2006). Religious and spiritual practices: A neurochemical perspective. In P. McNamara (Ed.), *Where God and science meet, Vol. 2* (pp. 15–31). Westport, CT: Praeger.

Newberg, A., Alavi, A., Baime, M., Pourdehnad, M., Santanna, J., & d'Aquili, E. (2001). The measurement of regional cerebral blood flow during the complex cognitive task of meditation: A preliminary SPECT study. *Psychiatry Research: Neuroimaging Section, 106,* 113–122.

Newberg, A. B., d'Aquili, E., & Rause, V. (2001). *Why God won't go away.* New York: Ballantine Books.

Newberg, A. B., & Lee, B. Y. (2006). The relationship between religion and health. In P. McNamara (Ed.), *Where God and science meet, Vol. 3* (pp. 35–65). Westport, CT: Praeger.

Newberg, A., Pourdehnad, M., Alavi, A., & d'Aquili, E. (2003). Cerebral blood flow during meditative prayer: Preliminary findings and methodological issues. *Perceptual Motor Skills, 97,* 625–630.

Nielsen, M. E. (2002). Religion's role in the terroristic attack of September 11, 2001. *North American Journal of Psychology, 3,* 377–383.

Nilsson, M. P. (1950). *The Minoan-Mycenaean religion and its survival in Greek religion.* New York: Biblo and Tannen.

Nisbett, R. E., & Miyamoto, Y. (2005). The influence of culture: Holistic versus analytic perception. *Trends in Cognitive Sciences, 9,* 467–473.

Nishida, T., Hasegawa, T., Hayaki, H., Takahata, Y., & Uehara, S. (1992). Meat-sharing as a coalitional strategy by an alpha male chimpanzee. In T. Nishida, W. C. McGrew, P. Marler, M. Pickford, & F. B. M. de Waal (Eds.), *Topics in primatology, vol. 1: Human origins* (pp. 159–174). Tokyo: University of Tokyo Press.

Noble, W., & Davidson, I. (1996). *Human evolution, language and mind.* Cambridge: Cambridge University Press.

Norenzayan, A., & Atran, S. (2002). Cognitive and emotional processes in the cultural transmission of natural and nonnatural beliefs. In M. Shaller & C. Crandall (Eds.), *The psychological foundations of culture* (pp. 149–169). Mahwah, NJ: Erlbaum.

Nowak, M. A., & Sigmund, K. (1998). Evolution of indirect reciprocity by image scoring. *Nature, 393,* 573–577.

Nunez, M., & Harris, P. L. (1998). Psychological and deontic concepts: Separate domains or intimate connections? *Mind and Language, 13,* 153–170.

Oatley, K. (1999). Why fiction may be twice as true as fact: Fiction as cognitive and emotional simulation. *Review of General Psychology, 3,* 101–117.

Oberg, K. (1973). *The social economy of the Tlinglit Indians.* Seattle: University of Washington Press.

Oldroyd, B. P., Smolenski, A. J., Cornuet, J.-M., & Corzier, R. H. (1994). Anarchy in the beehive. *Nature, 371,* 749.

Olsson, A., Ebert, J. P., Banaji, M. R., & Phelps, E. A. (2005). The role of social groups in the persistence of learned fear. *Science, 309,* 785–787.

Oman, D., & Reed, D. (1998). Religion and mortality among the community-dwelling elderly. *American Journal of Public Health, 88*, 1469–1475.

Oman, D., & Thoresen, C. E. (2003). Spiritual modeling: A key to spiritual and religious growth? *International Journal for the Psychology of Religion, 13*, 149–165.

Oman, D., & Thoresen, C. E. (2007). How does one learn to be spiritual? The neglected role of spiritual modeling in health. In T. G. Plante & C. E. Thoresen (Eds.), *Spirit, science, and health: How the spiritual mind fuels physical wellness* (pp. 39–54). Westport, CT: Praeger.

O'Neill, P., & Petrinovich, L. (1998). A preliminary cross cultural study of moral intuitions. *Evolution and Human Behavior, 19*, 349–367.

Orme-Johnson, D. W., & Herron, R. E. (1997). An innovative approach to reducing medical care utilization and expenditures. *American Journal of Managed Care, 3*, 135–144.

Ortega, S. T., Crutchfield, R. D., & Rushing, W. A. (1983). Race differences in elderly personal well-being. *Research on Aging, 5*, 101–118.

O'Shea, J., & Zvelebil, M. (1984). *Oleneostrovski mogilnik*: Reconstructing the social and economic organization of prehistoric foragers in northern Russia. *Journal of Anthropological Archaeology, 3*, 1–40.

Ostrom, E., Walker, J., & Gardner, R. (1992). Covenants with and without a sword: Self governance is possible. *American Political Science Review, 86*, 404–417.

Osvath, M., & Osvath, H. (2008). Chimpanzee (*Pan troglodytes*) and orangutan (*Pongo abelii*) forethought: Self-control and pre-experience in the face of future tool use. *Animal Cognition*, DOI 10.1007/s10071-008-0157-0.

Otto, R. (1923). *The idea of the holy*. Oxford: Oxford University Press.

Owens, D., & Hayden, B. (1997). Prehistoric rites of passage: A comparative study of transegalitarian hunter-gatherers. *Journal of Anthropological Archaeology, 16*, 121–161.

Owens, D. D., & Owens, M. J. (1984). Helping behavior in brown hyenas. *Nature, 308*, 843–845.

Oxman, T. E., Freeman, D. H., & Manheimer, E. D. (1995). Lack of social participation or religious strength and comfort as risk factors for death after cardiac surgery in the elderly. *Psychosomatic Medicine, 57*, 5–15.

Packer, C., Lewis, S., & Pusey, A. E. (1992). A comparative analysis of non-offspring nursing. *Animal Behavior, 43*, 265–281.

Paige-English, M. (1997). Germany vs. Scientology. Available at http://slate.msn.com/id/1045/ (accessed 6/29/05).

Palmer, J. (1979). A community mail survey of psychic experiences. *Journal of the American Society for Psychical Research, 73*, 221–251.

Paloma, M. M., & Gallup, G. H., Jr. (1991). *Varieties of prayer: A survey report*. Philadelphia: Trinity Press International.

Parfitt, S., & Roberts, M. (1999). Human modification of faunal remains. In M. B. Roberts & S. Parfitt (Eds.), *Boxgrove, A Middle Pleistocene hominid site at Eartham Quarry, Boxgrove, West Sussex* (pp. 395–415). London: English Heritage.

Pargament, K. I., Ensing, D. S., Falgout, K., Olsen, H., Reilly, B., Van Haitsma, K., & Warren, R. (1990). God help me: (I): Religious coping efforts as predictors of the outcomes to significant negative life events. *American Journal of Community Psychology, 18*, 793–824.

Pargament, K. I., Koenig, H. G., Tarakeshwar, N., & Hahn, J. (2001). Religious struggle as a predictor of mortality among medically ill elderly patients: A two-year longitudinal study. *Archives of Internal Medicine, 161*, 1881–1885.

Parish, S. M. (2004). The sacred mind: Newar cultural representations of mental life and the production of moral consciousness. In J. Corrigan (Ed.), *Religion and emotion* (pp. 149–188). Oxford: Oxford University Press.

Parrinder, G. (1976). *African traditional religion.* New York: Harper & Row.

Patterson, D. R., Burns, G. L., Everett, J. J., & Marvin, J. A. (1992). Hypnosis for the treatment of burn pain. *Journal of Counseling and Clinical Psychology, 60*, 713–717.

Pelegrin, J. (2005). Remarks about archaeological techniques and methods of knapping: Elements of a cognitive approach to stone knapping. In V. Roux & B. Bril (Eds.), *Stone knapping: The necessary conditions for uniquely hominin behaviour* (pp. 23–33). Cambridge: McDonald Institute.

Pepitone, A., & Saffioti, L. (1997). The selectivity of nonmaterial beliefs in interpreting life events. *European Journal of Social Psychology, 27*, 23–35.

Peterson, C., & Seligman, M. E. P. (2004). *Character strengths and virtues.* Oxford: Oxford University Press.

Petraglia, M., Korisettar, R., Boivin, N., Clarkson, C., Ditchfield, P., et al. (2007). Middle Paleolithic assemblages from the Indian subcontinent before and after the Toba super-eruption. *Science, 317*, 114–116.

Petrovic, P., Kalso, E., Peterson, K. M., & Ingvar, M. (2002). Placebo and opioid analgesia—imaging a shared neuronal network. *Science, 295*, 1737–1740.

Petrovich, O. (1997). Understanding of non-natural causality in children and adults: A case against artificialism. *Psyche and Geloof, 8*, 151–165.

Pettitt, G. (1946). *Primitive education in North America.* Berkeley: University of California Press.

Phelps, K. E., & Woolley, J. D. (1994). The form and function of young children's magical belief. *Developmental Psychology, 30*, 385–394.

Piaget, J. (1929). *The child's conception of the world.* New York: Harcourt Brace.

Piaget, J. (1932/1965). *The moral judgment of the child.* New York: Free Press.

Pika, S., Liebal, K., Call, J., & Tomasello, M. (2005). The gestural communication of apes. *Gesture, 5*, 41–56.

Platvoet, J. G. (1993). African traditional religions in the religious history of humankind. *Journal for the Study of Religion, 6*, 29–48.

Polkinghorne, J. C. (1996). *Faith of a physicist.* Minneapolis: Fortress Press.

Pollner, M. (1989). Divine relations, social relations, and well-being. *Journal of Health and Social Behavior, 30*, 92–104.

Poloma, M. M., & Gallup, G. H. Jr. (1991). *Varieties of prayer: A survey report.* Philadelphia, PA: Trinity Press International.

Potvin, R. H. (1985). *Seminarians in the eighties.* Washington, DC: National Catholic Education Association.

Poundstone, W. (1992). *Prisoner's dilemma: John von Neumann, game theory, and the puzzle of the bomb.* Oxford: Oxford University Press.

Povinelli, D. J. (2000). *Folk physics for apes.* New York: Oxford University Press.

Powell, J. H. (1914). "Hook-swinging" in India. A description of the ceremony, and an enquiry into its origin and significance. *Folklore, 25,* 147–197.

Power, C. (1998). Old wives' tales: The gossip hypothesis and the reliability of cheap signals. In J. R. Hurford, M. Studdert-Kennedy, & C. Knight (Eds.), *Approaches to the evolution of language: Social and cognitive bases* (pp. 111–129). Cambridge: Cambridge University Press.

Power, C., & Watts, I. (1996). Female strategies and collective behavior. The archeology of earliest Homo sapiens sapiens. In J. Steele and S. Shennan (Eds.), *The archeology of human ancestry. Power, sex and tradition* (pp. 306–330). London: Routledge.

Prager, D., & Telushkin, J. (1975). *Nine questions people ask about Judaism.* New York: Touchstone.

Pressman, P., Lyons, J. S., Larson, D. B., & Strain, J. J. (1990). Religious belief, depression, and ambulation status in elderly women with broken hips. *American Journal of Psychiatry, 147,* 758–759.

Price, D. D., Finniss, D. G., & Benedetti, F. (2008). A comprehensive review of the placebo effect: Recent advances and current thought. *Annual Review of Psychology, 59,* 565–590.

Price, D. D., Milling, L. S., Kirsch, I., Duff, A., Montgomery, G. H., et al. (1999). An analysis of factors that contribute to the magnitude of placebo analgesia in an experimental paradigm. *Pain, 83,* 147–156.

Price, T. D., & Brown, J. A. (1985). *Prehistoric hunter-gatherers: The emergence of cultural complexity.* Orlando, FL: Academic Press.

Prince, R. (1982). The endorphins: A review for psychological anthropologists. *Ethos, 10,* 299–302.

Provine, W. (1989). Evolution and the foundation of ethics. In S. Goldman (Ed.), *Science, technology, and social progress,* (pp. 253–267). Bethlehem, PA: Lehigh University Press.

Rabin, B. S. (2001). Understanding how stress affects the physical body. In H. G. Koenig & H. J. Cohen (Eds.), *The link between religion and health: Psychoneuroimmunology and the faith factor* (pp. 43–68). New York: Oxford University Press.

Radcliff-Brown, A. R. (1922). *The Andaman Islanders.* Cambridge: Cambridge University Press.

Radin, P. (1937). *Primitive religion.* New York: Viking.

Ramachandran, V. S., & Blakeslee, S. (1998). *Phantoms in the brain.* New York: Morrow.

Raman, L., & Winer, G. A. (2004). Evidence of more imminent justice responding in adults than children: A challenge to traditional developmental theories. *British Journal of Developmental Psychology, 22,* 255–274.

Rappaport, R. A. (1968). *Pigs for the ancestors.* New Haven, CT: Yale University Press.

Rappaport, R. A. (1999). *Ritual and religion and the making of humanity.* Cambridge: Cambridge University Press.

Rasmussen, K. (1929). *The intellectual culture of the Iglulik Eskimos.* Copenhagen: Gyldendalske.

Ratnieks, F. L. (1988). Reproductive harmony via mutual policing by workers in eusocial hymenoptera. *American Naturalist, 132*, 217–236.

Reader, S. M., & Laland, K. N. (2002). Social intelligence, innovation, and enhanced brain size in primates. *Proceedings of the National Academy of Sciences USA 99*, 4436–4441.

Reddy, V. (2008). *How infants know minds*. Cambridge, MA: Harvard University Press.

Rege, M., & Telle, K. (2004). The impact of social approval and framing on cooperation in public good situations. *Journal of Public Economics, 88*, 1625–1644.

Reichel-Dolmatoff, G. (1978). Drug-induced optical sensations and their relationship applied to art among some Columbian Indians. In M. Greenhalgh & V. Megaw (Eds.), *Art and society* (pp. 289–304). London: Duckworth.

Ressler, R. H. (1966). Inherited environmental influences on the operant behavior of mice. *Journal of Comparative and Physiological Psychology, 61*, 264–267.

Rice, P. C. (1982). Prehistoric Venuses: Symbols of motherhood or womanhood? *Journal of Anthropological Research, 37*, 402–414.

Richerson, P. J., & Boyd, R. (2001). The evolution of subjective commitment to groups: A tribal instincts hypothesis. In R. M. Nesse (Ed.), *Evolution and the capacity for commitment* (pp. 186–220). New York: Russell Sage Foundation.

Richerson, P. J., & Boyd, R. (2005). *Not by genes alone: How culture transformed human evolution*. Chicago: University of Chicago Press.

Richert, R. A., & Barrett, J. L. (2005). Do you see what I see? Young children's assumptions about God's perceptual abilities. *International Journal for the Psychology of Religion, 15*, 283–295.

Richert, R. A., & Harris, P. L. (2006). The ghost in my body: Children's developing concept of the soul. *Journal of Cognition and Culture, 6*, 409–427.

Richert, R. A., & Harris, P. L. (2008). Dualism revisited: Body *vs.* mind *vs.* soul. *Journal of Cognition and Culture, 8*, 99–115.

Richeson, J. A., Baird, A. A., Gordon, H. L., Heatherton, T. F., Wyland, C. L., Trawalter, S., & Shelton, J. N. (2003). An fMRI investigation of the impact of interracial contact on executive function. *Nature Neuroscience, 6*, 1323–1328.

Richman, B. (1987). Rhythm and melody in gelada vocal exchanges. *Primates, 28*, 199–223.

Ridley, M. (1996). *The origins of virtue*. New York: Viking.

Riel-Salvatore, J., & Clark, G. A. (2001). Grave markers: Middle and early Upper Paleolithic burials and the use of chronotypology in contemporary Paleolithic research. *Current Anthropology, 42*, 449–479.

Rigaud, J.-P., Simek, J. F., & Thierry, G. (1995). Mousterian fires from Gotte XVI (Dordogne, France). *Antiquity, 69*, 902–912.

Rinck, M., & Bower, G. H. (1995). Anaphora resolution and the focus of attention in situation models. *Journal of Memory and Language, 34*, 110–131.

Ringdal, G. I., Gotestam, K. G., Kaasa, S., Kvinnsland, S., & Ringdal, K. (1996). Prognostic factors and survival in a heterogeneous sample of cancer patients. *British Journal of Cancer, 73*, 1594–1599.

Roberts, R. C. (1997). Introduction: Christian theology? In R. C. Roberts & M. R. Talbot (Eds.), *Limning the psyche: Explorations in Christian psychology* (pp. 1–19). Grand Rapids, MI: Eerdmans.

Roby, A. C., & Kidd, E. (2008). The referential communication skills of children with imaginary companions. *Developmental Science, 11*, 531–540.

Roche, H. (2005). From simple flaking to shaping: Stone knapping evolution among early hominins. In V. Roux & B. Bril (Eds.), *Stone knapping: The necessary conditions for uniquely hominin behaviour* (pp. 35–48). Cambridge: McDonald Institute.

Roebroeks, W. (1984). The Middle Paleolithic site Maastricht-Belvedere (Southern Limburg, the Netherlands). *Helinium, 24*, 3–17.

Roes, F. L., & Raymond, M. (2003). Belief in moralizing gods. *Evolution and Human Behavior, 24*, 126–135.

Rohner, R. P. (1975). *They love me, they love me not*. New Haven, CT: HRAF Press.

Rokeach, M. (1973). *The nature of human values*. New York: Free Press.

Rolston, H. (1999). *Genes, Genesis, and God*. Cambridge: Cambridge University Press.

Rosen, B. C. (1950). Race, ethnicity, and the achievement syndrome. *American Sociological Review, 24*, 47–60.

Rosengren, K. S., & Hickling, A. K. (1994). Seeing is believing: Children's explanations of commonplace, magical, and extraordinary transformations. *Child Development, 65*, 1605–1626.

Ross, D. M., Menzler, S., & Zimmermann, E. (2008). Rapid facial mimicry in orangutan play. *Biology Letters, 4*, 27–30.

Ross, H. S., & Lollis, S. P. (1987). Communication within infant social games. *Developmental Psychology, 23*, 241–248.

Rossano, M. J. (2001). Artificial intelligence, religion, and community concern, *Zygon: Journal of Religion and Science, 36*, 57–75.

Rossano, M. J. (2003). Expertise and the evolution of consciousness. *Cognition, 89*, 207–236.

Rossano, M. J. (2006). The religious mind and the evolution of religion. *Review of General Psychology, 10*, 346–364.

Rossano, M. J. (2007a). Supernaturalizing social life: Religion and the evolution of human cooperation. *Human Nature, 18*, 272–294.

Rossano, M. J. (2007b). Religion on which the devout and skeptic can agree. *Zygon: Journal of Religion and Science, 42*, 301–315.

Rossano, M. J. (2007c). Did meditating make us human? *Cambridge Archaeological Journal, 17*, 47–58.

Rossano, M. J. (2008). The moral faculty: Does religion promote "moral expertise"? *International Journal for the Psychology of Religion, 18*, 169–194.

Rossano, M. J. (2009). Ritual behaviour and the origins of modern cognition. *Cambridge Archaeological Journal, 19*, 243–256.

Roth, A. E., Prasnikar, V., Okuno-Fujiwara, M., & Zamir, S. (1991). Bargaining and market behavior in Jerusalem, Ljubljana, Pittsburgh, and Tokyo: An experimental study. *American Economic Review, 81*, 1068–1095.

Roth, G. (2001). The evolution of consciousness. In G. Roth & M. F. Wullimann (Eds.), *Brain, evolution and cognition* (pp. 555–582). New York: Wiley.

Roux, V., & David, E. (2005). Planning abilities as a dynamic perceptual-motor skill: An actualist study of different levels of expertise involved in stone knapping.

In V. Roux & B. Bril (Eds.), *Stone knapping: The necessary conditions for uniquely hominin behaviour* (pp. 91–108). Cambridge: McDonald Institute.

Rouzaud, F., Soulier, M., & Lignereux, Y. (1996). LaGrotte de Bruniquel. *Spelunca, 60,* 28–34.

Rowatt, W. C., & Kirkpatrick, L. A. (2002). Dimensions of attachment to God and their relation to affect, religiosity, and personality constructs. *Journal for the Scientific Study of Religion, 41,* 637–651.

Rowatt, W. C., Ottenbreit, A., Nesselroade, K. P., & Cunningham, P. A. (2002). On being holier-than-thou or humbler-than-thee: A social psychological perspective on religiousness and humility. *Journal for the Scientific Study of Religion, 41,* 227–237.

Russell, B. (1961). *Religion and science.* New York: Oxford University Press.

Sabbagh, M. A. (2004). Understanding the orbitofrontal contributions to theory-of-mind reasoning: Implications for autism. *Brain and Cognition, 55,* 209–219.

Samorini, G. (2002). *Animals and psychedelics: The natural world and the instinct to alter consciousness.* Rochester, VT: Park Street.

Sandarupa, S. (1996). *Life and death in Toraja.* Ujung Pandang: Tiga Taurus Ujung Pandang.

Sanday, P. R. (1986). *Divine hunger.* Cambridge: Cambridge University Press.

Sanders, E. P. (1992). *Judaism: Practice and belief 63 BCE–66 CE.* London: SCM Press/ Trinity Press International.

Sanfey, A. G., Rilling, J. K., Aronson, J. A., Nystrom, L. E., & Cohen, J. D. (2003). The neural basis of economic decision-making in the ultimatum game. *Science, 300,* 1755–1758.

Sapolsky, R. M. (1993). Endocrinology alfresco: Psychoendocrine studies of wild baboons. *Recent Progress in Hormone Research, 48,* 437–468.

Saski, H., & Nagasaki, H. (1989). The mental distance: Its differences in educational circumstances. *Journal of Human Development, 25,* 1–10.

Sawada, M. (2001). Rethinking methods and concepts of anthropological studies of African pygmies' world view: The creator—god and the dead. *African Study Monographs, 27*(Suppl), 29–42.

Schele, L., & Freidel, D. (1990). *A forest of kings.* New York: Morrow.

Schick, K. D., & Toth, N. (1993). *Making silent stones speak.* New York: Simon & Schuster.

Schjoedt, U., Stødkilde-Jørgensen, H., Geertz, A. W., & Roepstorff, A. (2009). Highly religious participants recruit areas of social cognition in personal prayer. *Social Cognitive and Affective Neuroscience, 4,* 199–207.

Schwartz, B. L., & Evans, S. (2001). Episodic memory in primates. *American Journal of Primatology, 55,* 71–85.

Seyfarth, R. M., & Cheney, D. L. (1986). Vocal development in vervet monkeys. *Animal Behavior, 34,* 1640–1658.

Seiffge-Krenke, I. (1993). Close friendship and imaginary companions in adolescence. *New Directions for Child Development, 60,* 73–87.

Seiffge-Krenke, I. (1997). Imaginary companions in adolescence: Sign of a deficient or positive development. *Journal of Adolescence, 20,* 137–154.

Semaw, S., Renne, P., Harris, J. W. K., Feibel, C. S., Bernor, R. L., Fesseha, N., & Mowbray, K. (1997). 2.5-million-year-old stone tools from Gona, Ethiopia. *Nature, 385*, 333–336.

Sethi, R., & Somanathan, E. (1996). The evolution of social norms in common property resource use. *American Economic Review, 86*, 766–788.

Sethi, S., & Seligman, M. E. P. (1993). Optimism and fundamentalism. *Psychological Science, 4*, 256–259.

Shariff, A. F., & Norenzayan, A. (2007). God is watching you: Priming God concepts increases prosocial behavior in an anonymous economic game. *Psychological Science, 18*, 803–809.

Sharon, T. L., & Woolley, J. D. (2004). Do monsters dream? Children's understanding of the fantasy-reality distinction. *British Journal of Developmental Psychology, 22*, 293–310.

Sharpe, R. A. (2007). *Forgiveness: How religion endangers morality*. Exeter, UK: Imprint Academic.

Shea, J. J. (2006). The Middle Paleolithic of the Levant: Recursion and convergence. In E. Hovers & S. L. Kuhn (Eds.), *Transitions before the transition: Evolution and stability in the Middle Paleolithic and Middle Stone Age* (pp. 189–211). New York: Springer.

Shermer, M. (2005). The soul of science. *American Scientist, 93*, 101. Retrieved June 14, 2007. www.americanscientist.org/template/AssetDetail/assetid/40803?&print=yes.

Shimabukuro, S. M., Prater, M. A., Jenkins, A., & Edelen-Smith, P. (1999). The effects of self-monitoring of academic performance on students with learning disabilities and ADD/ADHD. *Education & Treatment of Children, 22*, 397–414.

Shor, R. (1998). The significance of religion in advancing a culturally sensitive approach towards child maltreatment. *Families in Society, 79*, 400–409.

Shulman, Y. D. (1993). *The chambers of the palace: Teachings of the Rabbi Nachman of Bratslav*. Northvale, NJ: Aronson.

Sibinga, N. E. S., & Goldstein, A. (1988). Opioid peptides and opioid receptors in cells of the immune system. *Annual Review of Immunology, 6*, 219–249.

Siegal, M. (1988). Children's knowledge of contagion and contamination as causes of illness. *Child Development, 59*, 1353–1359.

Siegel, J. M. (1990). Stressful life events and use of physician services among the elderly: The moderating effects of pet ownership. *Journal of Personality and Social Psychology, 58*, 1081–1086.

Sigerist, H. (1987). *A history of medicine*. 2 vols. Oxford: Oxford University Press.

Silberbauer, G. (1981). *Hunter and habitat in the central Kalahari Desert*. Cambridge: Cambridge University Press.

Silberman, I. (2005). Religion as a meaning system: Implications for the new millennium. *Journal of Social Issues, 61*, 641–663.

Silk, J. B. (2001). Grunts, girneys, and good intentions: The origins of strategic commitment in nonhuman primates. In R. M. Neese (Ed.), *Evolution and the capacity for commitment* (pp. 138–158). New York: Russell Sage Foundation.

Silk, J. B., Alberts, S. C., & Altmann, J. (2003). Social bonds of female baboons enhance infant survival. *Science, 302*, 1231–1234.

Simoons, F. J. (1970). Primary adult lactose intolerance and the dairying habit: A problem in biologic and cultural interrelations: II. A culture historical perspective. *American Journal of Digestive Diseases, 15*, 695–710.

Simpson, G. G. (1953). The Baldwin effect. *Evolution, 7*, 110–117.

Singer, D. G., & Singer, J. L. (1990). *The house of make-believe: Children's play and developing imagination.* Cambridge, MA: Harvard University Press.

Singer, R., & Wymer, J. J. (1982). *The Middle Stone Age at Klasies River mouth in South Africa.* Chicago: University of Chicago Press.

Skully, G. W. (1997). Murder by the state. *New York Times*, section 4, December 14, p. 7.

Slagter, H. A., Lutz, A., Greischar, L. L., Francis, A., Nieuwenhuls, D. S., Davis, J. M., & Davidson, R. J. (2007). Mental training after distribution of limited brain resources. *PLOS Biology, 5*, e138.

Sloan, R. P., & Bagiella, E. (2002). Claims about religious involvement and health outcomes. *Annals of Behavioral Medicine, 24*, 14–21.

Sloan, R. P., Bagiella, E., & Powell, T. (1999). Religion, spirituality, and medicine. *Lancet, 2*, 664–667.

Sloboda, J. A. (1991). Musical expertise. In K. A. Ericsson & J. A. Smith (Eds.), *Toward a general theory of expertise: Prospects and limits* (pp. 153–171). Cambridge: Cambridge University Press.

Smith, E. E., & Jonides, J. (1994). Working memory in humans: Neuropsychological evidence. In M. S. Gazzaniga (Ed.), *The cognitive neurosciences* (pp. 1009–1020). Cambridge, MA: MIT Press.

Smuts, B. B., & Watanabe, J. M. (1990). Social relationships and ritualized greetings in adult male baboons (*Papio cynocephalus anubis*). *International Journal of Primatology, 11*, 147–172.

Snyder, C. R., Sigmon, D. R., & Feldman, D. B. (2002). Hope for the sacred and vice versa: Positive goal-directed thinking and religion. *Psychological Inquiry, 13*, 234–238.

Sober, E., & Wilson, D. S. (1998). *Unto others: The evolution and psychology of unselfish behaviors.* Cambridge, MA: Harvard University Press.

Social Capital Survey (2001). Retrieved June 25, 2007, at www.cfsv.org/community-survey/results2.html.

Soffer, O. (1985). *The Upper Paleolithic of the central Russian plain.* Orlando, FL: Academic Press.

Soffer, O. (1989). Storage, sedentism, and Eurasian Palaeolithic record. *Antiquity, 63*, 719–732.

Soffer, O. (1994). Ancestral lifeways in Eurasia—the Middle and Upper Paleolithic records. In M. Nitecki & D. Nitecki (Eds.), *Origins of anatomically modern humans* (pp. 101–109). New York: Plenum.

Solomon, G. E. (2001). The development and history of psychoneuroimmunology. In H. G. Koenig & H. J. Cohen (Eds.), *The link between religion and health: Psychoneuroimmunology and the faith factor* (pp. 31–42). New York: Oxford University Press.

Soltis, J., Boyd, R., & Richerson, P. J. (1995). Can group-functional behaviors evolve by cultural group selection? An empirical test. *Current Anthropology, 36*, 473–494.

Sorensen, M. V., & Leonard, W. R. (2001). Neandertal energetics and foraging efficiency. *Journal of Human Evolution, 40*, 483–495.

Sosis, R. (2000). Religion and intragroup cooperation: Preliminary results of a comparative analysis of Utopian communities. *Cross-Cultural Research, 34*, 71–88.

Sosis, R. (2006). Religious behaviours, badges, and bans: Signaling theory and the evolution of religion. In P. McNamara (Ed.), *Where God and science meet, Vol. 1* (pp. 61–86). Bridgeport, CT: Praeger.

Sosis, R., & Bressler, E. (2003). Cooperation and commune longevity: A test of the costly signaling theory of religion. *Cross-Cultural Research, 37*, 211–239.

Sosis, R., & Ruffle, B. (2003). Religious ritual and cooperation: Testing for a relationship on Israeli religious and secular kibbutzim. *Current Anthropology, 44*, 713–722.

Southard, D., & Amos, B. (1996). Rhythmicity and preperformance ritual: Stabilizing a flexible system. *Research Quarterly for Exercise and Sport, 67*, 288–296.

Spiegel, D., Bloom, J. R., Kraemer, H. C., & Gottheil, E. (1989). Effect of psychosocial treatment on survival with metastatic breast cancer. *Lancet, 2*, 888–891.

Spielvogel, J. J. (1996). *Hitler and Nazi Germany: A history*. Upper Saddle River, NJ: Prentice-Hall.

Spilka, B., Addison, J., & Rosensohn, M. (1975). Parents, self, and God: A test of competing individual-religion relationships. *Review of Religious Research, 16*, 154–165.

Spilka, B., Hood, R. W., Hunsberger, B., & Gorsuch, R. (2003). *The psychology of religion: An empirical approach*. New York: Guilford Press.

Srejovic, D., & Babovic, L. (1983). *Umetnost lepenskog vira*. Belgrade: Izdavachi Zavod.

Srejovic, D., & Letica, Z. (1978). Vlasac: A mesolithic settlement in the iron gates. *Monographs of the Serbian Academy of Sciences and Arts, 62*. Belgrade: Department of Historical Sciences 5.

Stark, R. (1996). *The rise of Christianity*. Princeton, NJ: Princeton University Press.

Stark, R. (1999). Micro foundations of religion: A revised theory. *Sociological Theory, 17*, 264–289.

Stark, R., & Iannaccone, L. R. (1994). A supply side reinterpretation of the "secularization" of Europe. *Journal for the Scientific Study of Religion, 33*, 230–252.

Staudinger, U. M., & Baltes, P. B. (1996). Interactive minds: A facilitative setting for wisdom-related performance. *Journal of Personality and Social Psychology, 71*, 746–762.

Stearman, A. M. (1994). Only slaves climb trees: Revisiting the myth of the ecologically noble savage in Amazonia. *Human Nature, 5*, 339–357.

Stenger, V. J. (2007). *God: The failed hypothesis*. Amherst, NY: Prometheus Press.

Sterelny, K. (1996). The return of the group. *Philosophy of Science, 63*, 562–584.

Sterelny, K. (2003). *Thought in a hostile world: The evolution of human cognition*. London: Blackwell.

Stern, D. N. (2000). *The interpersonal world of the infant*. New York: Basic Books.

Sternberg, R. J., Grigorenko, E. L., & Ferrari, M. (2002). Fostering intellectual excellence through the development of expertise. In M. Ferrari (Ed.), *The pursuit of excellence through education* (pp. 57–84). Mahwah, NJ: Erlbaum.

Stiner, M. C. (1991). The faunal remains at Grotta Guattari: A taphonomic perspective. *Current Anthropology, 32*, 103–117.

Stolle, D. (2001). Clubs and congregations: The benefits of joining an association. In K. S. Cook (Ed.), *Trust in society* (pp. 202–244). New York: Russell Sage Foundation.

Stout, D. (2005). The social and cultural context of stone-knapping skill acquisition. In V. Roux & B. Bril (Eds.), *Stone knapping: The necessary conditions for uniquely hominin behaviour* (pp. 331–340). Cambridge: McDonald Institute.

Stout, D., & Chaminade, T. (2007). The evolutionary neuroscience of tool making. *Neuropsychologia, 45*, 1091–1100.

Stout, D., Toth, N., Schick, K., & Chaminade, T. (2008). Neural correlates of early stone age toolmaking: Technology, language and cognition in human evolution. *Philosophical Transactions of the Royal Society B, 363*, 1939–1949.

Strawbridge, W. J., Cohen, R. D., Shema, S. J., & Kaplan, G. A. (1997). Frequent attendance at religious services and mortality over 28 years. *American Journal of Public Health, 87*, 957–961.

Strawbridge, W. J., Shema, S. J., Cohen, R. D., & Kaplan, G. A. (2001). Religious attendance increases survival by improving and maintaining good health practices, mental health, and stable marriages. *Annals of Behavioral Medicine, 23*, 68–74.

Strickland, B. R., & Shaffer, S. (1971). I-E, I-E, and F. *Journal for the Scientific Study of Religion, 10*, 366–369.

Stringer, C. B. (1996). Current issues in modern human origins. In W. E. Meikel, F. C. Howell, & N. G. Jablonski (Eds.), *Contemporary issues in human evolution* (pp. 115–134). San Francisco: California Academy of Sciences.

Stringer, C., & Andrews, P. (2005). *The complete world of human evolution*. London: Thames & Hudson.

Stringer, C., & Gamble, C. (1993). *In search of the Neanderthals*. London: Thames & Hudson.

Stuss, D. T., Binns, M. A., Murphy, K. J., & Alexander, M. P. (2002). Dissociations within the anterior attentional system: Effects of task complexity and irrelevant information on reaction-time speed and accuracy. *Neuropsychology, 16*, 500–513.

Suddendorf, T. S., & Corballis, M. C. (1997). Mental time travel and the evolution of the human mind. *Genetic Social and General Psychology Monographs, 123*, 133–167.

Swezey, S., & Heizer, R. (1993). Ritual management of salmonid fish resources in California. In T. C. Blackburn & K. Anderson (Eds.), *Before the wilderness* (pp. 299–327). Menlo Park, CA: Ballena Press.

Taborin, Y. (1993). Shells of the French Aurignacian and Perigordian. In H. Knecht, A. Pike-Tay, & R. White (Eds.), *Before Lascaux: The complex record of the Early Upper Paleolithic* (pp. 211–229). Boca Raton, FL: CRC Press.

Targ, E., Schlitz, M., & Irwin, H. J. (2000). Psi-related experiences. In E. Cardena, S. J. Lynn, & S. Krippner (Eds.), *Varieties of anomalous experience: Examining the scientific evidence* (pp. 219–252). Washington, DC: American Psychological Association.

Taylor, M. (1999). *Imaginary companions and the children who create them*. New York: Oxford University Press.

Taylor, M., & Carlson, S. M. (1997). The relation between individual differences in fantasy and theory of mind. *Child Development, 68*, 436–455.

Taylor, M., Carlson, S. M., Maring, B. L., Gerow, L., & Charley, C. M. (2004). The characteristics and correlates of fantasy in school-age children: Imaginary companions, impersonations, and social understanding. *Developmental Psychology, 40*, 1173–1187.

Thompson, S. (1966). *Motif-index of folk literature*. Bloomington: Indiana University Press.

Tice, D. M. (1992). Self-concept change and self-presentation: The looking glass self is also a magnifying glass. *Journal of Personality and Social Psychology, 63*, 435–451.

Tillich, P. (1948). *The shaking of the foundation*. New York: Scribner.

Tolson, C. L., & Koenig, H. G. (2004). *The healing power of prayer: The surprising connection between prayer and your health*. New York: Baker Books.

Tomasello, M. (1988). The role of joint attentional processes in early language development. *Language Sciences, 10*, 69–88.

Tomasello, M., & Call, J. (1997). *Primate cognition*. New York: Oxford University Press.

Tomasello, M., Call, J., & Hare, B. (2003). Chimpanzees understand psychological states—the question is which ones and to what extent. *Trends in Cognitive Sciences, 7*, 153–156.

Tomasello, M., Carpenter, M., Call, J., Behne, T., & Moll, H. (2005). Understanding and sharing intentions: The origins of cultural cognition. *Behavioral and Brain Sciences, 28*, 675–735.

Toth, N. (1985). The Oldowan reassessed: A close look at early stone artifacts. *Journal of Archaeological Science, 12*, 101–120.

Toth, N., Schick, K. D., Savage-Rumbaugh, S., Sevcik, R. A., & Rumbaugh, D. M. (1993). Pan the toolmaker: Investigations into stone tool-making and tool-using capabilities of a bonobo (*Pan paniscus*). *Journal of Archaeological Science, 20*, 81–91.

Townsend, J. B. (1999). Shamanism. In S. D. Glazier (Ed.), *Anthropology of religion* (pp. 429–469). Westport, CT: Praeger.

Tremlin, T. (2006). *Minds and gods: The cognitive foundations of religion*. Oxford: Oxford University Press.

Trevarthen, C. (1979). Communication and cooperation in early infancy: A description of primary intersubjectivity. In M. Bullowa (Ed.), *Before speech* (pp. 321–347). Cambridge: Cambridge University Press.

Trevarthen, C., & Aitken, K. J. (1994). Brain development, infant communication and empathy disorders: Intrinsic factors in child mental health. *Development and Psychopathology, 6*, 599–635.

Trinkaus, E. (1983). *The Shanidar Neanderthals*. New York: Academic Press.

Trinkaus, E. (1995). Neandertal mortality patterns. *Journal of Archaeological Science, 22*, 121–142.

Tronick, E. Z. (2003). Things still to be done on the still-face effect. *Infancy, 4*, 475–482.

Tronick, E., Als, H., & Adamson, L. (1979). The structure of face-to-face communicative interactions. In M. Bullowa (Ed.), *Before speech* (pp. 349–370). Cambridge: Cambridge University Press.

Tronick, E., Als, H., Adamson, L., Wise, S., & Brazelton, T. B. (1978). The infant's response to entrapment between contradictory messages in face-to-face interaction. *Journal of the American Academy of Child and Adolescent Psychiatry, 17,* 1–13.

Trout, A. L., Lienemann, T. O., Reid, R., & Epstein, M. H. (2007). A review of non-medication interventions to improve academic performance of children and youth with ADHD. *Remedial and Special Education, 28,* 207–226.

Tsang, J., McCullough, M. E., & Hoyt, W. T. (2005). Psychometric and rationalization accounts of the religion-forgiveness discrepancy. *Journal of Social Issues, 61,* 785–805.

Tsao, G. Y., Friewald, W. A., Knutsen, T. A., Mandeville, J. B., & Tootell, R. B. (2003). Faces and objects in the macaque cerebral cortex. *Nature Neuroscience, 6,* 989–995.

Tulving, E. (1983). *Elements of episodic memory.* Oxford: Clarendon Press.

Turner, J. H. (2000). *On the origins of human emotions.* Stanford, CA: Stanford University Press.

Turner, L. M. (1879/1984). *Indians and Eskimos in the Quebec-Labrador Peninsula.* Quebec: Presses COMEDITEX.

Turner, V. W. (1969). *The ritual process: Structural and anti-structure.* Chicago: Aldine Publishing.

Tylor, E. B. (1871). *Primitive culture.* London: John Murray.

Uller, C. (2004). Disposition to recognize goals in infant chimpanzees. *Animal Cognition, 7,* 154–161.

Underhill, P. A., Passarino, G., Lin, A. A., Shen, P., Lahr, M. M., Foley, R. A., Oefner, P. J., & Cavalli-Sforza, L. L. (2001). The phylogeography of Y chromosome binary haplotypes and the origins of modern human populations. *Annals of Human Genetics, 65,* 43–62.

Vandiver, P., Soffer, O., Klima, B., & Svoboda, J. (1989). The origins of ceramic technology at Dolni Vsetonice, Czechoslovakia. *Science, 246,* 1004.

Vanhaeren, M., & d'Errico, F. (2005). Grave goods from the Saint-Germain-la-Rivière burial: Evidence for social inequality in the Upper Paleolithic. *Journal of Anthropological Archaeology, 24,* 117–134.

Vanhaeren, M., d'Errico, F., Stringer, C., James, S. L., Todd, J. A., & Mienis, H. K. (2006). Middle Paleolithic shell beads in Israel and Algeria. *Science, 312,* 1785–1788.

van Lawick-Goodall, J. (1968). The behavior of free-living chimpanzees in the Gombe stream reserve. *Animal Behavior Monographs, 1,* 161–311.

van Roosmalen, M. G. M., & Klein, L. L. (1988). The spider monkeys, genus *Ateles.* In R. Mittermeier, A. B. Rylands, A. F. Coimbra-Filho, & G. A. B. da Fonesca (Eds.), *Ecology and behavior of neotropic primates* (pp. 445–537). Washington, DC: World Wildlife Fund.

Vase, L., Riley, J. L., & Prince, D. D. (2002). A comparison of placebo effects in clinical analgesia trials versus studies of placebo analgesia. *Pain, 99,* 443–452.

Vase, L., Robinson, M. E., Verne, G. N., & Price, D. D. (2003). The contributions of suggestion, expectancy and desire to placebo effect in irritable bowel syndrome patients. *Pain, 105*, 17–25.

Vase, L., Robinson, M. E., Verne, G. N., & Price, D. D. (2005). Increased placebo analgesia over trials in irritable bowel syndrome (IBS) patients is associated with desire and expectation but not endogenous opiate mechanisms. *Pain, 115*, 338–347.

Velmans, M. (2000). *Understanding consciousness.* London: Routledge.

Ventis, W. L. (1995). The relationship between religion and mental health. *Journal of Social Issues, 51*, 33–48.

Vergote, A. (1969). *The religious man.* Dublin: Gill and Macmillan.

Vergote, A. & Tamayo, A. (1981). *The parental figures and the representation of God.* The Hague: Mouton.

Verne, G. N., Robinson, M. E., Vase, L., & Price, D. D. (2003). Reversal of visceral and cutaneous hyperanalgesia by local rectal anesthesia in irritable bowel (IBS) patients. *Pain, 105*, 223–230.

Verweij, J., Ester, E., & Nauru. R. (1997). Secularization is an economic and cultural phenomenon: A cross-national analysis. *Journal for the Scientific Study of Religion 36*, 309–324.

Virkler, M., & Virkler, P. (1986). *Dialogue with God.* Gainesville, FL: Bridge-Logos.

Vitebsky, P. (1993). *Dialogues with the dead: The discussion of mortality among the Sora of Eastern India.* Cambridge: Cambridge University Press.

Vitebsky, P. (2000). Shamanism. In G. Harvey (Ed.), *Indigenous religions* (pp. 55–67). London: Cassell.

Volgyesi, F. A. (1969). *Hypnosis of man and animals.* Baltimore: Williams and Williams.

Wachholtz, A. B., & Pargament, K. I. (2005). Is spirituality a critical ingredient of meditation? Comparing the effects of spiritual meditation, secular meditation, and relaxation on spiritual, psychological, cardiac, and pain outcomes. *Journal of Behavioral Medicine, 28*, 369–384.

Waddington, C. H. (1942). Canalization of development and the inheritance of acquired characteristics. *Nature, 150*, 563–565.

Waddington, C. H. (1975). *The evolution of an evolutionist.* Ithaca, NY: Cornell University Press.

Wadley, L. (2001). What is cultural modernity? A general view and a South African perspective from Rose Cottage Cave. *Cambridge Archaeological Journal, 11*, 201–221.

Wagner, M. W., & Ratzeburg, F. H. (1987). Hypnotic suggestibility and paranormal belief. *Psychological Reports, 60*, 1069–1070.

Wagner, T., Rilling, J. K., Smith, E. F., Sokolik, A., Casey, K. L., et al. (2004). Placebo-induced changes in fMRI in the anticipation and experience of pain. *Science, 303*, 116–127.

Walker, H. (1984). Extinctions in hominid evolution. In M. E. Nitecki (Ed.), *Extinctions* (pp. 119–152). Chicago: University of Chicago Press.

Walker, S. (1999). Culture, domain-specificity, and conceptual change: Natural kind and artifact concepts. *British Journal of Developmental Psychology, 17*, 203–219.

Walker, W. H. (2001). Ritual technology in an extranatural world. In M. B. Schiffer (Ed.), *Anthropological perspectives on technology* (pp. 87–106). Albuquerque: University of New Mexico Press.

Wallace, A. (1966). *Religion: An anthropological view*. New York: Random House.

Wallace, R. K., Benson, H., & Wilson, A. F. (1971). A wakeful hypometabolic physiological state. *American Journal of Physiology, 221*, 795–799.

Walters, J. R., & Seyfarth, R. M. (1987). Conflict and cooperation. In B. B. Smuts, D. L. Cheney, R. M. Seyfarth, R. W. Wrangham, & S. T. Struhsaker (Eds.), *Primate societies* (pp. 306–317). Chicago: University of Chicago Press.

Ward, K. (2000). *Religion and community*. Oxford: Clarendon.

Watson, R. I. (1973). Investigation into deindividuation using cross-cultural techniques. *Journal of Personality and Social Psychology, 25*, 342–345.

Watts, I. (2002). Ochre in the Middle Stone Age of southern Africa: Ritualized display or hide preservative? *South African Archaeological Bulletin, 57*, 15–30.

Wedekind, C., & Milinski, M. (2000). Cooperation through image scoring in humans. *Science, 288*, 850–852.

Weeden, J., Cohen, A. B., & Kenrick, D. T. (2008). Religious attendance as reproductive support. *Evolution and Human Behavior, 29*, 327–334.

Weidenreich, F. (1943). *The skull of Sinanthropus Pekinensis*. Pehpei, Chungking: Geological Survey of China.

Weinberg, R. S., & Gould, D. (2003). *Foundations of sport and exercise psychology*. Champaign, IL: Human Kinetics.

Weiss, R. S. (1974). The provisions of social relationships. In Z. Rubin (Ed.), *Doing unto others* (pp. 17–26). Englewood Cliffs, NJ: Prentice-Hall.

Weiss, R. S. (1986). Continuities and transformation in social relationships from childhood to adulthood. In W. W. Hartup & Z. Rubin (Eds.), *Relationships and development* (pp. 95–110). Hillsdale, NJ: Erlbaum.

West-Eberhard, M. J. (2003). *Developmental plasticity and evolution*. Oxford: Oxford University Press.

Westergaard, G. C., Liv, C., Haynie, M. K., & Suomi, S. J. (2000). A comparative study of aimed throwing by monkeys and humans. *Neuropsychologia, 38*, 1511–1517.

White, R. K. (1982). Rethinking the Middle/Upper Paleolithic transition. *Current Anthropology, 23*, 169–192.

White, R. (1985). *Upper Paleolithic land use in the Perigord*. Oxford: BAR.

White, R. (1993). Technological and social dimensions of "Aurignacian age" body ornaments across Europe. In H. Knecht, A. Pike-Tay, & R. White (Eds.), *Before Lascaux* (pp. 277–299). Boca Raton: CRC Press.

White, R. K. (2003). *Prehistoric art: The symbolic journey of humankind*. New York: Harry Abrams.

White, T. D. (1986). Cut marks on the Bodo Cranium: A case of prehistoric defleshing. *American Journal of Physical Anthropology, 69*, 503–509.

White, T. D., Asfaw, B., DeGusta, D., Tilbert, H., Richards, G. D., Suwa, G., & Howell, F. C. (2003). *Homo sapiens* from Middle Awash, Ethiopia. *Nature, 423*, 742–747.

Whitehead, A. N. (1925). *Science and the modern world*. New York: Free Press.

Whitehouse, H. (1995). *Inside the cult: Religious innovation and transmission in Papua New Guinea*. Oxford: Oxford University Press.

Whitehouse, H. (1996). Rites of terror: Emotion, metaphor and memory in Melanesian cults. *Journal of the Royal Anthropological Institute, 2*, 703–715.

Whitham, J. C., & Maestripieri, D. (2003). Primate rituals: The function of greetings between male guinea baboons. *Ethology, 109*, 847–859.

Wiech, K., Farias, M., Kahane, G., Shackel, N., Tiede, W., & Tracey, I. (2008). An fMRI study measuring analgesia enhanced by religion as a belief system. *Pain, 139*, 467–476.

Wiessner, P. (1982). Risk, reciprocity, and social influences on !Kung San economics. In E. Leacock & R. Lee (Eds.), *Politics and history in Band Societies* (pp. 61–84). Cambridge: Cambridge University Press.

Wilkinson, G. S. (1984). Reciprocal sharing in the vampire bat. *Nature, 308*, 181–184.

Williams, G. C. (1966). *Adaptation and natural selection: A critique of some current evolutionary thought*. Princeton, NJ: Princeton University Press.

Wilson, C., & Oswald, A. (2002). How does marriage affect physical and psychological health? A survey of the longitudinal evidence. www2.warwick.ac.uk/fac/soc/economics/staff/faculty/oswald/wilsonoswaldmarriage-jan2002.pdf

Wilson, D. S. (2002). *Darwin's cathedral: Evolution, religion and the nature of society*. Chicago: University of Chicago Press.

Wilson, S. C., & Barber, T. X. (1978). The creative imagination scale as a measure of hypnotic responsiveness: Applications to experimental and clinical hypnosis. *American Journal of Clinical Hypnosis, 20*, 235–249.

Wiltermuth, S. S., & Heath, C. (2009). Synchrony and cooperation. *Psychological Science, 20*, 1–5.

Winkelman, M. (1990). Shamans and other "magico-religious" healers: A cross-cultural study of their origins, nature, and social transformation. *Ethos, 18*, 308–352.

Winkelman, M. (1999). Altered states of consciousness and religious behaviour. In S. Glazier (Ed.), *Anthropology of religion* (pp. 393–428). Westport, CT: Greenwood Press.

Winkelman, M. (2002). Shamanism and cognitive evolution. *Cambridge Archaeological Journal, 12*, 71–101.

Winton, V. (2005). An investigation of knapping-skill development in the manufacture of Palaeolithic handaxes. In V. Roux & B. Bril (Eds.), *Stone knapping: The necessary conditions for uniquely hominin behaviour* (pp. 109–116). Cambridge: McDonald Institute.

Woodward, A. L. (1998). Infants selectively encode the goal object of an actor's reach. *Cognition, 69*, 1–34.

Woodward, M. R. (2000). Gifts for the sky people: Animal sacrifice, head hunting and power among the Naga of Burma and Assam. In G. Harvey (Ed.), *Indigenous religions* (pp. 219–229). London: Cassell.

Woolfendon, G. E., & FitzPatrick, J. W. (1984). *The Florida scrub jay: Demography of a cooperative breeding bird*. Princeton, NJ: Princeton University Press.

Woolley, J. D. (1995). Young children's understanding of fictional versus epistemic mental representations: Imagination and belief. *Child Development, 66*, 1011–1021.

Woolley, J. D. (2000). The development of beliefs about direct mental-physical cau-sality in imagination, magic, and religion. In K. S. Rosengren, C. N. Johnson, & P. L. Harris (Eds.), *Imagining the impossible: Magical, scientific, and religious think-ing in children* (pp. 99–129). Cambridge: Cambridge University Press.

Woolley, J. D., Browne, C. A., & Boerger, E. A. (2006). Constraints on children's judg-ments of magical causality. *Journal of Cognition and Development, 7*, 253–277.

Woolley, J. D., Phelps, K. E., Davis, D. L., & Mandell, D. J. (1999). Where theories of mind meet magic: The development of children's beliefs about wishing. *Child Development, 70*, 571–578.

Worl, R. (1999). Inupiat. In R. B. Lee & R. Daly (Eds.), *The Cambridge encyclopedia of hunters and gatherers* (pp. 61–65). Cambridge: Cambridge University Press.

World Values Survey (1997). Available at www.umich.edu/~newsinfo/Releases/1997/Dec97/r121097a.html (accessed 11/12/04).

Wreschner, E. E. (1980). Red ochre and human evolution: A case for discussion. *Current Anthropology, 21*, 631–644.

Wright, R. V. S. (1972). Imitative learning of a flaked-tool technology: The case of an orang-utan. *Mankind, 8*, 296–306.

Wulff, D. M. (1991). *Psychology of religion: Classic and contemporary views*. New York: John Wiley and Sons.

Wuthnow, R. (1994). *God and mammon in America*. New York: Free Press.

Wymer, J. (1982). *The Paleolithic age*. London: Croom Helm.

Wynn, T. (1981). The intelligence of Oldowan hominids. *Journal of Human Evolution, 10*, 529–541.

Wynn, T. (1996). The evolution of tools and symbolic behaviour. In A. J. Locke & C. R. Peters (Eds.), *Handbook of human symbolic evolution* (pp. 263–287). Oxford: Clarendon Press.

Wynn, T. (2002). Archaeology and cognitive evolution. *Behavioral and Brain Sciences, 25*, 389–402.

Wynn, T., & Coolidge, F. L. (2003). The role of working memory in the evolution of managed foraging. *Before Farming, 2*, 1–16.

Wynn, T., & Coolidge, F. L. (2004). The expert Neanderthal mind. *Journal of Human Evolution, 46*, 467–487.

Yamagishi, T. (1986). The provision of a sanctioning system as a public good. *Journal of Personality and Social Psychology, 51*, 110–116.

Yamagishi, T., & Yamagishi, M. (1994). Trust and commitment in the United States and Japan. *Motivation and Emotion, 18*, 129–166.

Ybarra, O., Burnstein, E., Winkielman, P., Keller, M. C., Manis, M., Chan, E., & Rod-riguez, J. (2008). Mental exercising through simple socializing: Social interac-tion promotes general cognitive functioning. *Personality and Social Psychology Bulletin, 34*, 248–259.

Young, F. (1965). *Initiation ceremonies*. New York: Bobbs-Merrill.

Zagzebski, L. T. (1996). *Virtues of the mind*. Cambridge: Cambridge University Press.

Zimmerman, B. J. (2002). Achieving academic excellence: A self-regulatory perspec-tive. In M. Ferrari (Ed.), *The pursuit of excellence through education* (pp. 85–112). Mahwah, NJ: Erlbaum.

Zinnbauer, B. J., & Pargament, K. I. (2005). Religiousness and spirituality. In R. F. Paloutzian & C. L. Park (Eds.), *Handbook of the psychology of religion and spirituality* (pp. 21–42). New York: Guilford Press.

Zwaan, R. A., & Radvansky, G. A. (1998). Situation models in language comprehension and memory. *Psychological Bulletin, 123*, 162–185.

Index